THE RIGHT TO HEALTH OF THE CHILD

THE RIGHT TO HEALTH OF THE CHILD

An analytical exploration of the international normative framework

Sarah Ida Spronk-van der Meer

intersentia

Cambridge – Antwerp – Portland

Intersentia Ltd
Sheraton House | Castle Park
Cambridge | CB3 0AX | United Kingdom
Tel.: +44 1223 370 170 | Email: mail@intersentia.co.uk

Distribution for the UK:
NBN International
Airport Business Centre, 10 Thornbury Road
Plymouth, PL6 7PP
United Kingdom
Tel: +44 1752 202 301 | Fax: +44 1752 202 331
Email: orders@nbninternational.com

Distribution for the USA and Canada:
International Specialized Book Services
920 NE 58th Ave Suite 300
Portland, OR 97213
USA
Tel.: +1 800 944 6190 (toll free)
Email: info@isbs.com

Distribution for Austria:
Neuer Wissenschaftlicher Verlag
Argentinierstraße 42/6
1040 Wien
Austria
Tel.: +43 1 535 61 03 24
Email: office@nwv.at

Distribution for other countries:
Intersentia Publishing nv
Groenstraat 31
2640 Mortsel
Belgium
Tel.: +32 3 680 15 50
Email: mail@intersentia.be

The Right to Health of the Child. An analytical exploration of the international normative framework
Sarah Ida Spronk-van der Meer

ISBN 978-1-78068-272-3
D/2014/7849/159
NUR 828

British Library Cataloguing in Publication Data. A catalogue record for this book is available from the British Library.

Dedicated to my family

"Our deepest fear is not that we are inadequate.
Our deepest fear is that we are powerful beyond measure.
It is our light, not our darkness that most frightens us.
We ask ourselves, who am I to be brilliant, gorgeous, talented, fabulous?
Actually, who are you not to be? You are a child of the light.
Your playing small does not serve the world.
There is nothing enlightened about shrinking
so that other people won't feel insecure around you.
We are all meant to shine, as children do.
We were born to make manifest the glory of light that is within us.
It's not just in some of us; it's in everyone.
And as we let our own light shine,
we unconsciously give other people permission to do the same.
As we are liberated from our own fear,
our presence automatically liberates others."

from *A Return to Love*, by Marianne Williamson

ACKNOWLEDGEMENTS

Children's rights are a relatively young area in the law practice. As a result, many areas in both the national and the international child and youth sector can be discerned wherein developments are strongly needed, such as the (legal) support for children suffering from maltreatment, refugee children, child soldiers, sick children, orphans and homeless children. Whereas many of these children are vulnerable, I find a great motivation in their resilience and in their creative optimism.

The right to participation of children is one of the main pillars of the United Nations Children's Rights Convention. Its aim is to give children an active role in all matters affecting them, such as decisions on medical treatments, family reunification and protection measures. I believe that the fulfillment of this right can help to strengthen the position of children and to develop their potential. My goal is to support children in developing their capacities, simultaneously learning from their experiences.

The conduct of this research was a challenge that required a lot of patience, persistence and passion. It would not have been possible without the support and inspiration of so many people around me. I whole-heartedly thank all of you for your continuous inspiration, critical reflections and various forms of support. Every page of this book is dedicated to one of you.

Several persons I want to thank in particular. First of all, I want to thank my supervisors professor Mariëlle Bruning and professor Jaap Doek, who both provided me with so many valuable insights and who continuously sharpened my mind. More importantly, their strong involvement with children's rights in both the Netherlands and abroad continuously inspired me to delve deeper into the interesting topic of the right to health of the child. Professor Bruning helped me to focus on one theme and to not loose myself in the many intriguing other topics of the children's rights domain. Professor Jaap Doek supported me in understanding the right to health of the child from an international perspective.

I also want to thank the respectable members of the PhD. Committee: Prof.mr.dr. K. Arts, Prof.mr. A.C. Hendriks, Prof.dr. R. Reis, Prof.dr. J.J. Sloth-Nielsen, and Prof. W. Vandenhole, for reviewing my manuscript and providing me with valued comments that have without doubt enriched this thesis.

Furthermore, I want to thank Toine van Oisterhout, who generously gave me the opportunity and freedom to conduct this research. Although the topic shifted from a focus on children and privacy to the right to health of the child, the undertaking of this long-term research project has been made possible by his initial support.

I also want to thank professor Simone Buitendijk, who inspired me to focus on studying the right to health of the child. Looking back, it was in a church in Leiden on the occasion of the 20th anniversary of the Convention on the Rights of the Child in 2009, that we discussed the negligence of the health of children in the public domain. We identified that it would constitute a perfect bridge between my interests in international children's rights ánd in health. I am very much inspired and motivated to further develop the concept of the right to health of the child and to help to gradually put it into practice.

Many thanks to my roommate Maria de Jong-de Kruijf, who provided me with so much 'English drop' that I literally had the biggest babies ever. Your daily humor and our deliberations on day-to-day children's rights issues ensured a sense of normality in the challenging and sometimes lonely process of doing a PhD research.

Many thanks also to the medical anthropological PhD group, who so well understood my connection with children and nurtured both my intellectual and physical needs (healthy soups!). It was a great pleasure to participate in the challenging discussions and to share experiences on research with and by children and adolescents.

Many more people supported and inspired me along the way, Mirjam Blaak, Martin Buyse, Alex-Geert Castermans, Bernardine Dohrn, Caroline Forder, Simone van 't Hof, Ursula Kilkelly, Ton Liefaard, Peter Rodrigues, my former colleagues at the University of Leiden and my current colleagues at the Ministry of Foreign Affairs, including my diplomatic class and the many people working for children's rights organizations, foundations and institutions: Defence for Children, UNICEF, Save the Children, IPPF, Terre des Hommes, Chlid Helpline International, the Child-to-Child Trust, Keki, Kinderrechtennu, Stichting Alexander and Stichting Kind en Ziekenhuis and NJCM. It is an enormous pleasure to work with so many people who are highly committed and engaged with children and improving their rights. I also want to thank Fred Lafeber from the Ministry of Health (now the World Health Organization) for taking me to the ministerial meeting in Lissabon in 2011 where the Guidelines on Child-Friendly Health Care of the Council of Europe were officially signed and where again – I met many committed pediatricians and advocates of children's rights, including the TAT Group. And most importantly, I thank the children and students who shared their experiences in health care with me in a private context.

In the course of this research, I very much enjoyed all the support and hours of laughter with my friends and family. The guest parents who took care of my little girls with so much attention, joy and creativity while I was working on this book also deserve a big thank you and a smile.

I especially and whole-heartedly want to thank my parents, brother, sister-in-law and family-in-law for their never-ending support, love and confidence that you gave to me. Not only in the conduct of this research, but in everything I do. Our discussions, practical support and weekends out in the (urban) jungle repeatedly gave me the inspiration and energy to continue with renewed enthusiasm.

Last but certainly not least, I want to thank Nicolaas and my two beautiful little girls Carmen and Zoë for being with me all the time. Having you all in my life is the biggest joy I could wish for. Nicolaas, you often wondered what on earth inspired me to engage in such a long-term research project. Notwithstanding, you have always stood by my side and your practical tips helped me to bring it to an end. Your unconditional love, care and never ending support enabled me to engage in this research project and to maintain a healthy balance in our own family life. Even more important, you are my living example of what it really means to give children a voice. Thank you very much. I love you!

Carmen, Zoë and the newly expected one, my love for you is far beyond every possible way of expression. Our literal symbiosis in the writing of this PhD research has inspired every single word of it. I am extremely happy and grateful to see you flourish and develop in vibrant health and I am looking forward to every future step that you're making.

CONTENTS

LIST OF ABBREVIATIONS

AAAQ	Availability, accessibility, acceptability, quality
ACHPR	African Charter on Human and People's Rights
ACRWC	African Charter on the Rights and Welfare of the Child
ACSD	Accelerated child survival and development program
ACWC	Asian Committee on the promotion and the protection of the rights of Women and Children
ADHD	Attention Deficit Hyperactivity Disorder
AIDS	Acquired immunodeficiency syndrome
AIHCR	Asian Intergovernmental Committee on Human Rights
ASEAN	Association of South East Asian Nations
AWBZ	Algemene Wet Bijzondere Ziektekosten
BC	Biomedical Convention
CCRA	Centre on Children's Rights Amsterdam
CEDAW	Convention on the Elimination of all forms of Racial Discrimination
CESCR	Committee on Economic, Social and Cultural Rights
CERD	Convention on the Elimination of all forms of Racial Discrimination
CFHI	The Child-Friendly Healthcare Initiative
CFREU	Charter of Fundamental Rights of the European Union
CoE	Council of Europe
CRED-PRO	Child Rights Education for Professionals
CRC	Convention on the Rights of the Child
CRC OP	Optional Protocol to the Convention on the Rights of the Child
DALY	Disability-adjusted life year
Doc.	Document
EACH	European Association for Children in Hospital
EC	European Community
ECHR	European Convention for the Protection of Human Rights and Fundamental freedoms
ECOSOC	UN Economic and Social Council
ECPAT	End Child Prostitution, Child Pornography and Trafficking of Children for Sexual Purposes
ECSR	European Committee on Social Rights
EctHR	European Court on Human Rights
ECHR	European Court on Human Rights
E.g.	Exempli gratia (for example)
ESC	European Social Charter

EU	European Union
EVRM	Europees Verdrag van de Rechten van de Mens
FGM	Female Genital Mutilation
GA	General Assembly
GC	General Comment
GC I-IV	Geneva Convention I-IV
GC AP	Geneva Convention Additional Protocol
GDP	Gross Domestic Product
GNI	Gross National Income
GOBI	Growth monitoring, oral rehydration, breastfeeding and immunization
GOBI-FFF	Growth monitoring, oral rehydration, breastfeeding and immunization – family planning, food supplies and female education.
HIV	Human immunodeficiency virus
HD	Human Development
HDI	Health Data Institute
ICC	International Criminal Court
ICCPR	International Covenant on Civil and Political Rights
ICESCR	International Covenant on Economic, Social and Cultural Rights
IHL	International Health Regulations
IICRD	International Institute on Child Rights and Development
ILO	International Labour Organization
IMCI	Integrated Management of Childhood Illnesses
IND	Immigratie- en Naturalisatiedienst
KNMG	Koninklijke Nederlandse Maatschappij ter bevordering van de Geneeskunst
LLM	Master of Laws
MRI	Magnetic resonance imaging
MSc	Master of Science
NCD	Non-communicable diseases
NGO	Non-governmental organization
NKFK	Nederlands Kenniscentrum voor Farmacotherapie bij kinderen
OAS	Organization of American States
OIC	Organization of Islamic Conference
OP	Optional Protocol
PDCO	The Paediatric Committee
PHC	Primary Health Care
PhD	Doctor of Philosophy
PSQ	Patient Satisfaction Questionnaire
QALY	Quality-adjusted life year
RAND	Research And Development
REC	Recommendation

RES	Resolution
SARS	Severe Acute Respiratory Syndrome
SRHR	Sexual and reproductive health rights
TFEU	Treaty on the Functioning of the European Union
UNHDI	United Nations Human Development Index
UDHR	Universal Declaration of Human Rights
UK	United Kingdom
UN	United Nations
UNHCHR	UN High Commissioner for Human Rights
UNICEF	United Nations Children's Fund
USA	United States of America
USSR	Union of Soviet Socialist Republics
VN	Verenigde Naties
WGBO	Wet op de geneeskundige behandelingsovereenkomst
WHA	World Health Assembly
WHO	World Health Organization
WMA	World Medical Association

I. INTRODUCTION

1.1. INTRODUCTION

Every woman giving birth to a child wishes her baby is born and raised in good health. This single factor, health, plays a crucial role in the viability of the newborn. It is a matter of daily concern and it has a major impact on the well-being of the individual and its opportunities to go to school, work, participate in family and community activities. The Preamble of the Constitution of the World Health Organization (WHO) specifically mentions that the healthy development of the child is of basic importance and that the ability to live harmoniously in a changing environment is essential to such development.[1] The WHO even considers health as our most basic and essential asset.[2] Similarly, Navi Pillay, the United Nations High Commissioner for Human Rights commented that the right to health is the foundation for all other human rights.[3]

Last but not least, the health condition of babies and young children lays down the fundaments of health in later life.[4] Article 24 of the Convention on the Rights of the Child (CRC) provides for the right of children to the highest attainable standard of health and to facilities for the treatment of illness and rehabilitation of health. Furthermore and in order to achieve the highest attainable standard of health, article 24 CRC provides that 'States Parties shall strive to ensure that no child is deprived of his or her right of access to such health care services'. However, unclear is what the right to the highest attainable standard of health of children entails, what obligations States and parents have to ensure this right to the highest attainable standard of health of children and how it can be enforced.

---

1 Preambule to the Constitution of the World Health Organization, as published in World Health Organization, *Basic documents*, 45th edition, Geneva, 2006. The WHO Constitution was signed in 1946 and entered into force on 7 April 1948.

2 WHO Factsheet No. 31 on the Right to health, Office of the United Nations High Commissioner for Human Rights, Geneva, June 2008.

3 4 March 2013, Report in preparation to the Day of General Discussion on Human Rights on the right of the child to the enjoyment of the highest attainable standard of health.

4 See also the Barker-hypothesis, which postulates that several common adult diseases may be related to impaired foetal growth or disrupted genes, caused by nutritional inadequacies or other environmental influences at particular stages of pregnancy. D.J. Barker, 'Fetal Origins of Coronary Heart Disease', *British Medical Journal* 1995, 311, p. 171–174.

The basic importance of children's health has been laid down and reassured in many international documents.[5, 6] During the 1990 World Summit for Children, a 10-point programme was adopted that focused on enhancing children's health, promoting prenatal care and lowering infant and child mortality.[7] This commitment was reaffirmed in the Report 'A World Fit for Children', which speaks of the need to ensure 'the best possible start in life' for children by 'making concerted efforts to fight infectious diseases, tackle major causes of malnutrition and nurture children in a safe environment that enables them to be physically healthy, mentally alert, emotionally secure, socially competent and able to learn'.[8] In the field of health, the Report established 25 priorities, which concomitantly lay down the fundaments for the Action Plan that is intended to 'break the intergenerational cycle of malnutrition and poor health'.[9]

Goal 4 of the Millennium Development Goals aims to reduce by two thirds the mortality rate among children under five by the year of 2015.[10] This goal, consisting of infant (0–1) and under-five (0–5) mortality rates, constitutes one of the most important indicators to assess the degree to which the right to health of children is prioritized within a country.[11] However, promising infant and under-five mortality rates in a country do not reveal the underlying disparities in health between different subgroups in that country.

Taking a look at the Concluding Observations of the Committee on the Rights of the Child for several countries of the last five years, it becomes clear that different groups of vulnerable children lack (sufficient) access to basic health care facilities and/or underlying determinants of health, such as safe drinking water,

---

5 See 'The World Declaration on the Protection, Survival and Development of Children' and 'The Plan of Action for Implementing the World Declaration on the Protection, Survival and Development of Children in the 1990s', adopted by the World Summit for Children, New York, 30 September 1990. In § 10, 'enhancement of children's health and nutrition is qualified as a first duty, because infant and child mortality are unacceptably high and readily preventable. In § 11 and 12, specific attention is demanded for ensuring care and protection for 'disabled children, girls and children in very difficult circumstances'. Furthermore, safe motherhood must be promoted in all possible ways, including family planning and birth spacing, § 14.

6 See the Report 'A World Fit for Children', adopted by the United Nations General Assembly Resolution A/RES/S-27/2, 11th October 2002. Available at: www.unicef.org/specialsession/docs_new/documents/A-RES-S27-2E.pdf.

7 Ibidem supra note 4, § 20.
Measures promulgated included the provision of clean drinking water, ensuring universal access to sanitation, eradicating hunger, malnutrition and famine, promotion of family planning, child spacing, safe motherhood and breastfeeding. In the concomitant Action Plan, focus is placed on preventing childhood diseases and strengthening primary health care and basic health care services in all countries.

8 Ibidem supra note 5, § 7, point 4.

9 Ibidem supra note 5, § 35–37.

10 See the UN Millennium Development Goals Report, New York, 2010, p. 26. Available at: www.un.org/millenniumgoals/pdf/MDG%20Report%202010%20En%20r15%20-low%20res%2020100615%20-.pdf.

11 A. Eide & W.B. Eide, *A Commentary on the UN CRC Article 24: The right to health*, Leiden: Martinus Nijhoff Publishers 2006, p. 17.

nutritious food, housing and health education.[12] Similar observations have been done by paediatricians in both high-income and low-income countries.[13, 14] Great differences have been observed in access to health care, including preventive medicine such as immunization between and within developed and developing countries, particularly impacting upon children in war zones and countries affected by sanctions.[15]

In high-income countries there are vulnerable groups of children who suffer from significant health problems and who have limited access to primary health care facilities, such as refugee children, children of minority groups and children who are confronted with domestic violence.[16, 17, 18, 19] For example, the infant mortality rate in the Netherlands in 2008 was 4/1000 and the under five mortality rate was 5/1000.[20] However, these excellent youth health indicators disguise the fact that many refugee children suffer from infectious diseases, diarrhoea, malaria and mental health problems, because they remain deprived of the basic necessities for good health.[21, 22, 23] Also within low-income countries, there are big differences between health indicators for different groups of children, reflecting the differences in political will, organizational capacity and dissemination of knowledge to ensure children's right to health.[24] General Comment 15 on the right of the child to the enjoyment of the highest attainable standard of health

---

12 See for example the Concluding Observations of the Committee on Argentina (2010), § 31 en § 58, Australia (2005), § 72 en § 88, Uganda (2005), § 242c, § 258, § 267, § 276, Lebanon (2006), § 409b, § 432, § 433–437, Bulgaria (2008), § 45–46, the Netherlands (2009) Doc. CRC/C/NLD/CO/3 27 March 2009, § 51–52.

13 T. Lindberg, 'The Child's Right to Health and Treatment', *Medicine, conflict and survival* 1999, Volume 15, p. 336. Published by Frank Cass, London.

14 D. Southall et al., 'The Child-Friendly Healthcare Initiative (CFHI): Healthcare Provision in Accordance With the UN Convention on the Rights of the Child', *Pediatrics* 2000, Vol. 106 No. 5 November 1, p. 1054 -1064.

15 Ibidem supra note 4.

16 A. Hjern & P. Bouvier, 'Migrant children – a challenge for European paediatricians', *Acta Paediatrica* 2004, Volume 93, pp. 1535–1539. Stockholm.

17 R. Romero-Ortuño, 'Access to health care for illegal immigrants in the EU: should we be concerned?' *European journal of Health Law* 2004, Volume 11, p. 245–272, Martinus-Nijhoff Publishers.

18 N. Davidson e.a., 'An issue of access: delivering equitable health care for newly arrived refugee children in Australia', *Paediatric Journal Child Health* 2004, Volume 40, p. 569.

19 F.S. Mendoza, 'The health of Latino children in the United States', *Critical health issues for children and youth* 1994, Volume 4, number 3.

20 UNICEF Statistics by country, At a glance: Netherlands. See website: www.unicef.org/infobycountry/netherlands_statistics.html.

21 'Medical care of underage refugees', *Nederlands Tijdschrift voor de Geneeskunde* 1999, July 24; Volume 143, Number 30, p. 1569–72.

22 K. Mink & J.P. Kleijburg, *Jaarbericht Kinderrechten 2008*, Voorburg/Amsterdam: Unicef Nederland and Defence for Children International Nederland 2008.

23 K.C. Braat, *Ik ben er wel, maar ze zien me niet*, Amsterdam: Defence for Children International Nederland 2004.

24 A. Eide & W.B. Eide, *A Commentary on the UN CRC Article 24: The right to health*, Leiden: Martinus Nijhoff Publishers 2006, p. 16.

establishes the right of children to opportunities to survive, grow and develop to their full potential as the basic presumption.[25]

1.2. PROBLEM STATEMENT AND RESEARCH QUESTIONS

Large numbers of children all over the world face significant health risks, such as infectious and chronic diseases, injuries and the consequences of natural disasters, protracted armed conflicts and poverty.[26] Every year, 4 million babies die within the first month of their life and almost 8 million children under the age of five die from preventable diseases such as malaria, pneumonia, measles and diarrhoea.[27]

These general statistics do not reveal the underlying inequalities in health between and within countries. For example, the under-five mortality ratio in 2008 ranged from 257/1000 in Afghanistan to 2/1000 in Liechtenstein.[28] Whereas developing countries face basic health risks such as infectious diseases, malnutrition and birth complications, developed countries predominantly face health problems such as cancer, asthma, diabetes, coronary and heart diseases, eating disorders, problems resulting from smoking, alcohol and drugs abuse and mental health problems.

One of the causes of the inequalities is that, in many countries, vulnerable groups of children have no or only limited access to adequate health care facilities,[29, 30, 31] consequently running larger health risks than other groups of children in the mainstream society. For example, refugee children in developed countries, especially the ones that have come from tropical areas and the ones who have resided in refugee camps, suffer from the basic health risks that usually occur in developing countries.[32]

---

25 CRC/C/GC/15, 17 April 2013, § 1. General Comment 15 on the right to the highest attainable standard of health of the child.

26 UNICEF report 'The State of the World's children 2010', Statistical Table on Basic Indicators.

27 Ibidem supra note 26.

28 Ibid, Statistical table on under-five mortality ratios. The under-five mortality ratio is defined as the probability of dying between birth and exactly five years of age, expressed per 1000 live births.

29 See for example the Concluding Observations of the Committee on Argentina (2010), § 31 en § 58, Australia (2006), § 72 en § 88, Uganda (2006), § 242c, § 258, § 267, § 276, Lebanon (2006), § 409b, § 432, § 433–437, Bulgaria (2008), § 45–46, the Netherlands (2009), § 51–52. Reports can be found through the website: www.unhcr.org/refworld/publisher,CRC,CONCOBSERVATIONS,ARG,4c32dae02,0.html.

30 Davidson et al., 'An issue of access: Delivering equitable health care for newly arrived refugee children in Australia', *Journal of Paediatry* 2004, 40, p. 569–575.

31 F.S. Mendoza, 'The Health of Latino Children in the United States', *Critical Health Issues for Children and Youth* 1994, 4 (3), p. 43–72.

32 A. Tjon, W.E. Ten & T.W. Schulpen, 'Medical care of underage refugees', *Nederlands Tijdschrift voor de Geneeskunde* 1999, 143 (30), p. 1569–72.

As a result of the financial hardship due to the current economic crisis, children face additional risks to deprivation of basic health care requirements. In the Netherlands for example, children are disproportionately represented in the poorest households, predominantly by being part of one-parent families.[33] This financial situation has impact on their (financial) access to health care, social insurances, healthy food, water and gas supply, access to information (e.g. through internet, newspapers and television) and other housing conditions.[34] Numerous studies come to similar conclusions that children living in poverty face larger health risks than their wealthier peers, such as higher infant and child mortality rates, lower birth weight, higher risks to suffer from neglect and abuse, general disabilities and severe chronic illnesses.[35] Generally speaking, the health related quality of life of children and youth is worse for those living in less advantaged socioeconomic conditions.[36]

The relevance of investigating the international right to health is also related to its international dimension. The highest attainable standard of health is not a right of which the implementation should be limited to the territory of the State.[37] Increasingly, discussion arises as to the external influence of the right to health.[38, 39, 40] This is exemplified by the increasing inclusion of international health arrangements in national health policies and the harmonisation of health policies across foreign and regional policies.[41] Similarly, Nolan and others argue

33 'Armoedesignalement 2010, Sociaal en Cultureel Planbureau/Centraal Bureau voor de Statistiek, Den Haag, december 2010'. In the Netherlands in 2009, 7% of the general population was categorized as a low-income household, whereas 10% of the minors was categorized as such.

34 Ibidem supra note 33.

35 B. Zuckerman & S. Parker, 'Preventive pediatrics: New models of providing needed health services', *Pediatrics* 1995, *95*(5), p. 758– 762.

36 A.E. Simon, K.S. Chan & C.B. Forrest, 'Assessment of children's quality of life in the United States with a multidimensional index', *Pediatrics* 2008, 121(1), e118– e126.

37 General Comment No. 14 (2000) The right to the highest attainable standard of health: 11/08/2000. E/C.12/2000/4. CESCR, § 38–42.

38 See for example: L. Oldring, 'Advancing a Human Rights Approach on the Global Health Agenda', in: A. Clapham & M. Robinson, *Realizing the Right to Health*, Swiss Human Rights Book Volume 3, 2009, Ruffer & Rub, p. 100–108.

39 See also: J.W. Owen & O. Roberts, 'Globalisation, health and foreign policy: emerging linkages and interests', *Global Health* 2005, Volume 1, Number 12. (Published online 2005 July 29, available at: www.ncbi.nlm.nih.gov/pmc/articles/PMC1188066/.).

40 H. Feldbaum, K. Lee & J. Michaud, 'Global health and foreign policy', *Epidemiologic reviews* 2010, Volume 32, Issue 1, p. 82–92.

41 See for example the Dutch policy document 'Responsibility for Freedom', April 2011, p. 10, specifically addressing the Dutch commitment to help to realize access to pre- and postnatal health care, sexual and reproductive health rights and family planning. Available at: www.rijksoverheid.nl/documenten-en-publicaties/rapporten/2011/04/05/notitie-verantwoordelijk-voor-vrijheid.html. For more information on health diplomacy see: www.who.int/trade/diplomacy/en/.

that extra-territorial obligations of States to realize children's right to health contain at least the duty to protect and respect the right to health.[42]

At least three central objectives are discerned in adopting a border-crossing approach to ensuring children's right to health: i) the combat of infectious diseases, ii) the construction of shared health policies and health indicators and iii) the provision of humanitarian aid in case of humanitarian crises. Another issue that impacts upon the right to health of children in other countries is the role of the private sector in realizing the right to health of children, such as the role of pharmaceutical companies in testing (new) medicines and ensuring availability and affordability to everyone.

With regard to the first point, recent upsurges of infectious diseases such as Ebola, SARS and MERS, avian influenza and the Mexican flu, demonstrate the epidemiological interrelatedness and its potential impact on the realisation of human rights, on public health and on trade within and between nations.[43, 44] Ensuring good health for people in other countries in the entire world is therefore an essential requirement for ensuring the right to health of people within states.

Secondly, the enormous numbers of people travelling over the world for business, immigration, refugee or tourism purposes, have increased global awareness of the impact of aid, trade, conflicts and travelling itself on health and living circumstances across different countries and regions of the world, resulting in moral, ethical, political and economic demands to further investigate and address health policies across the different countries in the world. The right to health is a logical first pretext to start developing and implementing such policies, given its widely accepted legal recognition in both the WHO Constitution and the ICESCR and the internationally oriented interpretation of the provisions incorporated therein, for example in the Concluding Observations of the ECOSOC Committee on the individual Country Reports submitted to it.[45] Some countries have even integrated a human rights approach in their foreign policy,[46] so that national governments do not only serve their national interests but also aim to advance the right to health (among other human rights) around the world. However, in order to effectively cooperate with other developing and donating countries, a common human rights framework for improving the public

42 A. Nolan, A.E. Yamin & B.M. Meier, Submission on the Content of a Future General Comment on the Right of the Child to the Enjoyment of the Highest Attainable Standard of Health (art. 24).

43 D.P. Fidler, & N. Drager, 'Health and foreign policy', *Bulletin of the World Health Organization* 2006, September, Issue 86, Number 9, p. 687. Available at: www.who.int/bulletin/volumes/84/9/06-035469.pdf.

44 In 2008, a WHO conference was organized in Geneva, addressing the issue of foreign policy and global health.

45 See Concluding Observations of the Committee on Economic, Social and Cultural Rights. Available at: www.ishr.ch/treaty-body-monitor/cescr.

46 Ibidem supra note 41.

health system is necessary.[47] Furthermore, it is required to develop shared and internationally applicable health indicators.[48]

NGOs and intergovernmental organizations such as the WHO, UNICEF and the World Bank are specifically addressed to contribute to the realization of the right to health. In the Concluding Observations on Country Reports of the Committee on the Rights of the Child, States are repeatedly stimulated to seek assistance from organizations such as UNICEF and the WHO to find ways to realize children's right to health.[49] Article 2 of the WHO Constitution makes the WHO responsible for playing a leading role in setting the health research agenda, norms and standards of global health policy, providing technical support to countries and monitoring and assessing health trends.[50] However, the process of priority setting by the World Health Organization does not seem to be guided by the right to health, nor have NGOs been systematically involved.[51]

Thirdly, in the case of sudden crisis situations, States have a strong obligation to provide emergency care to affected regions and populations, especially if local authorities have been affected and are therefore not able to promptly respond to the need of its population, as was for example the case in the aftermath of the Haitian earthquake in January 2010. An assessment of the relief provided after the tsunami in South-East Asia led to the division of responsibilities between different UN organizations and other international organizations involved in emergency relief.[52]

---

47 L. Oldring, 'Advancing a Human Rights Approach on the Global Health Agenda', in: A. Clapham & M. Robinson, *Realizing the Right to Health*, Swiss Human Rights Book Volume 3, 2009, Ruffer & Rub p. 104.

48 Kinney and Clark convincingly demonstrated that incorporation of the right to health in the national constitution does not relate to the actual commitment of states to realize this right. They even found that countries with the most ambitious provision ensuring the right to health were often to the highest degree violating or neglecting this right (e.g. Haïti previous to the 2010 earthquake). It may be assumed that a similar conclusion may be drawn with respect to the commitment to respond to international commitments, especially given the disputed justiciability of economic and social rights. See: E.D. Kinney & B.A. Clark, 'Provisions for Health and Health Care in the Constitutions of the Countries of the World', *Cornell International Law Journal* 2004, Volume 37, p. 287.

49 General Comment No. 14 (2000) The right to the highest attainable standard of health: 11/08/2000. E/C.12/2000/4. CESCR, § 63–65.

50 The WHO Department on Ethics, Trade, Human Rights and Health Law aims to integrate a human rights based approach to health. WHO Factsheet No.31 on the Right to Health, prepared by the Office of the United Nations High Commissioner for Human Rights, p. 29.

51 Submission of Nord-Sud XXI to the UN Committee on the Rights of the Child for the preparation of General Comment 14 to the CRC on the right to health: www2.ohchr.org/english/bodies/crc/callsubmissionsCRC_received.htm.

52 During a meeting with Mrs. A. Golaz at UNICEF Geneva, May 2012, I was informed that a division of tasks was made in responding to the consequences of natural disasters. For example, the WHO is responsible for the provision of health care, UNHCR and the International Organization on Migration are responsible for camp coordination and management, UNICEF and Save the Children take the lead on education and UNCHR and IFRC take the lead in ensuring shelter for affected people.

1.2.1. RESEARCH QUESTION

The scope of the right to the highest attainable standard of health has been subject to much debate, ranging from a narrow interpretation of a right to health as a right limited to health services to a broad interpretation incorporating other human rights such as the right to adequate nutrition, water, sanitation, housing, privacy and education.[53] In a variety of international legal documents,[54] the right to health is defined as 'the highest attainable standard of health in view of the available financial resources'. The right to health of the child is thus dependent upon the available resources. The approach taken in this research is predominantly legal. The additional value of a legal approach is that it sets objective standards for the right to health of the child instead of formulating subjective ambitions that can change easily. Such an approach is important, because many countries, especially in the current economic crisis situation, are faced with cutbacks in financial budgets on health expenditure. Therefore, the question is which aspects of the right to health of the child must be prioritized within these challenging circumstances. These priorities should ensure a minimum standard of health for all children that can not be derogated off. Furthermore, a legal approach creates the opportunity for legal remedies that help to improve children's health, although it must be noted that the justiciability of the right to health of children as a social rights disputed.

According to international law standards, the right to the highest attainable standard of health of children as laid down in article 24 CRC is insufficiently realized in both low-income and in high-income countries. As a result, large numbers of children suffer and even die from easily preventable diseases. Also, it has been established that poor health care access leads to higher rates of hospitalization for chronic diseases.[55]

A central problem in the realization of the right to health of the child is the interpretation of 'the highest attainable standard of health' of children. The vagueness of the concept of 'the highest attainable standard of health' makes it difficult to identify the elements of the right to health that must be prioritized for implementation in a country's health policy. Secondly, the realization of the right to the highest attainable standard of health is dependent upon the (limited) financial resources available. Thirdly, the realization of children's right to the highest attainable standard of health depends on both situational circumstances and individual characteristics such as the genetic predisposition and lifestyle of both the parents and the child. Unclear is therefore what elements of the right

[53] See General Comment of the Committee on Economic Social and Cultural Rights on the right to the highest attainable standard of health, U.N. Doc. E/C.12/2000/4, 11 August 2000, § 4.

[54] See for example the Preamble of the WHO Constitution, art. 12 of the International Covenant on Economic Social and Cultural Rights (ICESCR) and art. 24 of the UN Convention on the Rights of the Child.

[55] A.B. Bindman, 'Preventable hospitalizations and access to health care', *Journal of the American Medical Association* 1995; 274, Volume 4, p. 305–311.

to the highest attainable standard of health fall under the responsibility of the State and what the responsibilities are of medical professionals, the parents and the child itself. Fourthly, the qualification of the right to the highest attainable standard of health as a social human right means that there is on-going debate over its legal effect. Unclear is whether the right to health of the child can be enforced as an obligation of effort or as an obligation of result and what the scope is of this obligation. If so, how far does this obligation extend?

This research aims to identify the standards in international law for realizing the right to the highest attainable standard of health. Can we speak of progressive standards and if so, how can they be enforced?

The central questions that will be analysed in this thesis are:

(a) *what priorities derive from the concept of the highest attainable standard of health of the child, its definition and the interpretation of the key constituent elements on the basis of international human rights law?*
(b) *how should this concept be implemented in the light of the international human rights standards?*

Consequently, the following sub questions will be answered in the subsequent chapters:

I. What priorities relating to the right to the highest attainable standard of health of the child can be derived from the interpretations of this right found in the international children's right domain?

II. How are the priorities relating to the international children's rights domain with respect to the interpretation of the highest attainable standard of health of the child explained in the Concluding Observations of the CRC Committee on Country Reports for countries with different levels of development?

III. What priorities related to the right to the highest attainable standard of health of the child can be derived from the interpretation found in the international health and human rights law? What is the additional value of this body of law for the interpretation of the right to the highest attainable standard of health in the children's rights domain?

IV. What priorities relating to the right to the highest attainable standard of health of the child are found in the interpretation found in the human rights law in Europe?

V. How does the process of realization influence the interpretation of the highest attainable standard of health of the child and which actors are responsible in the process of implementation?

1.3. METHODOLOGY

1.3.1. THEORETICAL FRAMEWORK: THE CAPABILITY APPROACH

This research builds on the capability approach of Amartya Sen.[56] The focus of this approach is on people's capabilities, on their abilities to effectively do and become what lies within them. As such, the capability approach differs from philosophical theories that take people's happiness or basic needs as a starting point. It also differs from utilitarian theories that focus on the benefit to society that can be derived from developing individuals.

The capability approach focuses on the intrinsic (or innate) opportunities that people have. It assumes that people have the freedom to choose the capabilities that they wish to realize in order to live a life which they find valuable. Examples of capabilities are the capability to be healthy, the capability to be a successful athlete or the capability to become a medical doctor. As such, the capability approach takes into account the heterogeneity of people, as is exemplified in relation to the human physic by the different health needs of children based on their age, gender, health status, bodily weight, climate or social environment. For example, a very tall and sporty adolescent boy needs different quantities and types of nutrition than an infant girl to be healthy. According to Sen 'Human diversity is no secondary complication (to be ignored, or to be introduced 'later on'); it is a fundamental aspect of our interest in equality'.[57]

It is important to distinguish between capacities and capabilities. A capacity is the realized ability to perform a certain act, such as walking, talking, dancing or reproducing. It is clear that very young children have limited capacities, since they haven't had the time to (fully) develop yet. A capability, on the other hand, refers to the *potential* to develop. Young children do have the potential to develop a wide variety of functionings. In identifying potential capabilities that can be realized, debate is ongoing on the possible level of determination that should be achieved. Nussbaum, for example, has compiled a list of ten central human capabilities that can be achieved, including physical health. She uses her elaboration of the capability approach as a 'justification of the central constitutional principles

---

56 A.K. Sen, *Equality of What?* Stanford University: Tanner Lectures on Human Values 1979. A.K. Sen, *Commodities and Capabilities*, North-Holland 1985.

57 A.K. Sen, *Inequality Reexamined*, Oxford: Oxford University Press 1992, p. xi.

that citizens can demand from their governments'.[58] Sen, on the other hand, explicitly rejects the compilation of such a list, although he does introduce the notion of basic capabilities, capabilities that are necessary for physical survival.[59] Sen argues that an exhaustive list limits the opportunity to be open to the wide diversity of individual capabilities. As such, the adoption of an exhaustive list of capabilities would limit the possibilities to take into account all possible best interests of individual children.

In addition to the concept of capabilities, Sen introduces the concept of functionings. The distinction between capabilities and functionings is that capabilities are freedoms or *possible* achievements of people in the future, whereas functionings are *effectively realized* achievements. As phrased by Sen 'Functionings are the "beings and doings" of a person, whereas a person's capability is "the various combinations of functionings that a person can achieve.'[60] For example, children have the capability to be healthy. Related functionings could be 'birth weight', 'lung capacity', 'height', 'life expectancy' and 'child and mortality ration'. Robeyn describes the difference as 'Achieved functionings are (at least indirectly) measurable, whereas the person's capability would also include all the opportunities this person had but chose not to take.' Furthermore, functionings are measurable and comparable.

Freedom of choice is thus a central notion in the capability approach. Two children (e.g. twins) with exactly the same characteristics, may have exactly the same capabilities, but achieve completely different functionings, because they have or develop fundamentally different opinions upon what it means to lead a good life. Furthermore, the transformation of capabilities into (a set of) functionings, is influenced by individual (sex, intelligence, age, metabolism, physical condition, reading skills), social (power relations and social and religious norms, discriminatory practices and gender roles) and environmental (climate, infrastructure, availability of underlying determinants of health) conversion factors. Both by assuming different individual capabilities and by taking into account the different choices that individuals can make to achieve a set of functionings, the capability approach thus accounts for interpersonal variations. With a view to realizing the highest attainable standard of children's health, it is therefore essential to identify the capabilities of individual children, being dependent on their innate genetic predispositions, the circumstances in which they are brought up, including the support provided by their caretakers, the underlying determinants, such as quality of food, medicines or drinking water, that they have at their disposal and also the influence of the choices that they and

58 M. Nussbaum, 'Capabilities as fundamental entitlements: Sen and social justice', *Feminist Economics* 2003, 9(2/3), p. 33–59.

59 A.K. Sen, 'Capabilities, Lists, and Public Reason: Continuing the Conversation', *Feminist Economics* 2004, 10, no. 3, p. 77–80. (A frequently cited interview with Amartya (A.K.) Sen in which he elaborates on his rejection of a fixed list of capabilities).

60 A.K. Sen, *Inequality Reexamined*, Oxford: Oxford University Press 1992.

their parents make with regard to the capabilities that they wish to realize, the health choices that they make.

The capability approach of Amartya Sen has four fundamental elements:

I. Having the same amount and quality of resources, individuals can differ greatly in the functionings they wish and the functionings they are able to achieve. For example, a pregnant woman having a certain amount of food will realize other functionings (namely becoming a mother) than a woman who has that same amount of food not being pregnant. Therefore, an approach that only focuses on resources available to a person is insufficient because it does not take into account the agency of the person in transforming those resources.

II. People can take the circumstances in which they live for granted. For example, someone living with a chronic disease can state that he feels very healthy and thereby influence the overall perception of his quality of life. An approach that only takes people's subjective experience into account thus misses the evaluation of the objective circumstances in which people live.

III. Notwithstanding the functionings that people achieve, it makes a great difference whether those functionings were opted for or forced into. For example, someone who becomes very sick because he did not have access to vaccination has not opted for becoming sick. On the other hand, someone who refuses a vaccination has deliberately taken the risk to become sick. Therefore, both the resultant functionings and the freedom of choice must be taken into account.

IV. Reality is complicated and individuals have their own variable truths. Therefore, an open-mind is essential to integrating the many different choices made on the sets of functionings that people wish or are able to achieve.

1.3.2. RELATING THE CAPABILITY APPROACH TO THE HIGHEST ATTAINABLE STANDARD OF HEALTH

Sen's capability approach offers a lens through which normative frameworks, such as the international legal framework on children's right to health, can be assessed. As identified by Robeyn, 'The capability approach to well-being and development evaluates *policies* – or in the case of this research – according to their impact on people's capabilities.[61] It asks whether people are being healthy, and whether the resources necessary for this capability, such as clean water, access to medical doctors, protection from infections and diseases, and basic knowledge on health issues, are present.'

Translated to the field of children's health, the capability approach thus looks at the capability of children to be or to become healthy. It relates to the legal question of what is the highest attainable standard of health of children. The achievement of the highest attainable standard of health is necessarily dependent on the individual choices, characteristics and living circumstances of each child and its family and the choices they make. Subdivided into separate legal domains; the children's rights domain, other sources of international health and human rights and human rights in the European region, the international legal framework on children's right to health will be assessed for their impact on realizing the highest attainable standard of health of the child, i.e. the capability of the child to be healthy.

Applying the capability approach to the children's rights domain, offers a way to take into account both the child's present and the child's future needs and rights. Peleg has taken this approach with respect to the child's right to development. He argues that the approach taken by the Committee on the Rights of the Child primarily approaches children as 'human becomings' instead of 'human beings', thereby 'focusing on the child as a future adult, without respecting its present agency and voice'.[62]

The capability approach offers room to approach children as individual human beings in their own right and holding their own (children's) rights, because they are assumed to have the freedom to choose between the capabilities that they wish to realize. As such, they can exercise agency, shape their own life and take an active role in realizing their own right to health.[63] In that way, they have the freedom to express their unique individuality. According to Peleg, it is the duty bearers, being the primary caretakers and the government, that are to enable children to exercise their agency and capabilities.[64] Peleg contests the standpoint taken by critics that children lack the competency to self-determination, stating that 'debates on children's capabilities and capacities do not relate to children's ability to choose, but rather to the space that society, adults and the law give to children and the tolerance that they have towards presumed mistakes'.[65] This point is very important, since it is only by enabling children to express themselves and their opinions, for example with respect to medical consent, that their abilities to do

61 I. Robeyn, *The Capability Approach: a theoretical survey*, Journal of Human Development, Volume 6, Number 1, March 2005. Available at: www2.dse.unibo.it/ardeni/ESCA_2012/Robeyns.pdf.
62 N. Peleg, *Reconceptualising the Child's Right to Development: Children and the Capability Approach*, in: International Journal on Children's Rights, 2013, Volume 21, Issue, pp. 523–542.
63 Ibidem supra note 62, p. 527.
64 Ibidem supra note 62, p. 531.
65 Ibidem supra note 62, p. 533–534.

so become visible. I would even argue that taking children seriously in their own right and giving them the space, support and information necessary to make their own decisions concerning their health, contributes significantly to developing their abilities to choose between the capabilities that they wish to realize.

With respect to the linkage between human rights and capabilities, Sen claims that human rights law can establish the framework to impose obligations on states to provide for the capabilities necessary to achieve human development. At the same time, ensuring human rights can provide for a safe space to achieve the functionings that individuals opt for. With respect to realizing the rights of (vulnerable) children, a balance must therefore be struck between creating a safe space for children to flourish, while at the same time preserving the room to develop, make mistakes, fall and stand-up again.

Sen does not presume that capabilities, in terms of opportunities of people to be healthy, can only be corrected by the government. Indeed, it seems logical to assume that other actors, including children and their families themselves, but also private companies, non-governmental organizations, fellow citizens as well as life events and natural disasters, can have a significant impact or even play a central role in increasing the capability of children to be healthy and thus in increasing their opportunity to realize the right to health of the child. Therefore, the presumption underlying this research is that the responsibility to realize the highest attainable standard of health of the child is shared between the child itself, its parents, the government and other actors that influence upon the realization of the right to the highest attainable standard of health of the child.

1.3.3. RESEARCH METHODOLOGY

The research methodology will consist of a literature research of the relevant international legal documents, the *travaux préparatoires*, General Comments, the Concluding Observations of the Committee on the Rights of the Child on the Country Reports, UN documents, EU documents and relevant scientific literature. In the following paragraphs, the basic concepts of this study, namely the concept of health (paragraph 4), health as a right (paragraph 5), primary health care (paragraph 6), vulnerable children (paragraph 7) and responsible actors (paragraph 8) will be elaborated. This research covers the period between January 2010 and January 2014. Literature after this date has not been included. Given the focus of the capability approach on the unique development of individual children and the role of different actors in realizing the right to health of the child, three key elements are structurally taken into account in the analysis of the relevant legal documents. The identification of priorities of the right to health of the child is done on the basis of these elements. The elements are:

- Measures that relate to the role of children and parents themselves in ensuring the right to health of children.
- Measures that clarify the attribution of responsibilities to different actors involved in realizing the right to health of children.
- Measures required to ensure that children grow up in healthy circumstances, including access to necessary health services.

The research looks at the international legal framework on the right to health of the child. As an example of a regional interpretation of the right to health of the child, chapter 5 takes a closer look into the legal framework in Europe, since there have been considerable developments in interpreting the right to health of the child. Further research in other regions on the right to health of the child is highly relevant. However, it would be too extensive too include all regions in this research. Furthermore, although this research does not aim to clarify the applicable international legal framework on the right to health of the child for the Netherlands, it does use some examples of national laws and implementation measures of this country.

1.4. DEFINITION OF HEALTH

1.4.1. RELEVANCE OF A DEFINITION OF HEALTH

Defining the concept of health has been subject to debate across all cultures and throughout all periods of time, being a highly subjective experience.[66] Identifying the content of the concept of health for exploring the right to health of children has both theoretical and practical relevance.[67] Theoretically, it forms the basis for understanding the phenomena of health and disease and practically it influences people to determine what they should individually and socially do to advance health. A clear and acceptable definition of health is also necessary to allow for comparisons.[68] Furthermore, in understanding the right to health, the question of what health is, determines what steps are required to realize the right to health.

Ruger argued that in order to provide a workable operationalization of the right to health, a shared standard of health must be identified.[69] She refers to the Aristotelian capability view to argue that 'social justice and the right to

[66] B.C.A. Toebes, *The Right to Health as a Human Right in International Law*, Antwerp: Intersentia 1999, p. 20.

[67] L. Breslow, 'A Quantitative approach to the World Health Organization Definition of Health: Physical, Mental and Social Well-being', *International Journal of Epidemiology* 1972, Volume 1, Number 4, p. 349.

[68] J.P. Ruger, 'Toward a Theory of a Right to Health: Capability and Incompletely Theorized Agreements', *Yale Journal of Law & the Humanities* 2006, Volume 18, p. 312.

[69] J.P. Ruger, 'Toward a Theory of a Right to Health: Capability and Incompletely Theorized Agreements', *Yale Journal of Law & the Humanities* 2006, Volume 18, p. 279.

health require a universally shared norm of health to establish a framework for interpersonal health comparisons' and 'the prioritization of health dimensions when resources are scarce'. The central idea of the Aristotelian capability view as identified by Ruger, is that the right to health must be treated as an ethical demand and that this involves both legal instruments for enforcement as internalization by individuals, states and non-state actors of this public ethical norm in their daily functioning to enhance implementation and compliance with the right to health in international human rights policy and law. She argues that the progressive realization of the right to health is more likely to occur 'when individuals within a given society take ownership of the public moral norm as a guiding principle for their individual and collective efforts, as evidenced by their domestic social, political and economic activity'.[70] This will be more likely when they can identify with the moral norm on the basis of their own notion of health and duties and obligation to achieve that state of health. The difficult question now is what would be a workable definition of health throughout different countries and cultures in the world in order to further clarify the content and scope of the right to health.

1.4.2. IN SEARCH OF A DEFINITION OF HEALTH

Throughout European history, the concept of health has varied from physical to mental and even spiritual well-being. The ancient Greek notion, exemplified by a statement by Aristotle, focused on the physical well-being: 'In the case of the body, excellence is health in the form of making use of the body without illness...'[71] Hippocrates considered health as a harmonious mixture of the humours of the body; blood, phlegm, black bile and yellow bile deriving from four organs; the heart, brain, liver and spleen. Sickness, in his theory, was caused by any imbalance of the system and health could be restored by nature, special diets and special medicines.[72] It has also been noted by Sigerist that the concept of health was mainly 'aristocratic' in character, being directed only to a few individuals, rather than on improving the public health of many.[73]

During the earlier part of the Roman period, the physically oriented notion of health from the Greek changed to a balance between body and mind: 'ut sit mens sana in corpore sano'.[74] Parallel to the increasing familiarity with Greek

[70] J.P. Ruger, 'Toward a Theory of a Right to Health: Capability and Incompletely Theorized Agreements', *Yale Journal of Law & the Humanities* 2006, Volume 18, p. 278.

[71] Aristotle, On Rhetoric, New York/Oxford: Oxford University Press, 1991 (G.A. Kennedy Translation).

[72] J.S. Larson, 'Conceptualization of health', *Medical Care Research & Review* 1999, Issue 56, p. 124.

[73] H.E. Sigerist, *Medicine and Human Welfare*, New Haven/London: Yale University Press/ Oxford University Press 1941, p. 53–104.

[74] Your prayer must be for a sound mind in a sound body (Juvenal, Satires, x, 356).

philosophical ideas in the later Roman era, the concept changed again to a predominant physical approach.

During the Christian era, the physical orientation of the meaning of health was completely reversed to a more spiritual interpretation of health: 'It is the soul that counts. Everybody is sick without Christ. No diets nor exercise are needed, but baptism is the bath that gives health.'[75] The second difference with the classical definitions of health was that health was not intended for the lucky few, but for all. This was reflected by the increasing attention for collective hygiene.[76] These examples show that the clarification of the definition of health is determinative for the question what people, in particular children, need to achieve or maintain that level of health, and thus what entitlements they should have on the basis of their right to health.

To provide a further basis on which the right to health in an international context will be established, several examples of interpretations of health from different parts of the world will now be identified.

Across different cultures in the world, the modern definition of 'health' is broadly diversified, reflecting the core themes of the underlying cultures. For example, the Han people, numerically and politically dominant in China, define health as 'a harmonious relationship between humans and the cosmos and among humans'.[77] A healthy body is a body in which Qi, an energy flow that runs through the universe, and blood, vital essence, body fluid and nutrients are in careful balance. Any imbalance in this system results in illness. Another example of an understanding of health is found in the ancient Egyptian doctrine, wherein health (senb) is seen as 'the action that establishes harmony within duality'. The definition of healing in ancient Egyptian natural medicine is the establishment of harmony in this life and beyond, by developing the inner resources of the patient.[78] According to the Egyptian natural medicine, we must have good eating habits, a good exercise system for the nine bodies and a good system for conducting our emotions. If we manage to establish harmony between our nine bodies and between these systems, health will be ours for our lifetime ánd for eternity.[79] Other examples of health include the concept of health found in the Amazon base of Venezuela and Brazil, where the Yanomamo Indians believe that illnesses are caused by spirits, ghosts or ancestors and the interpretation of health

---

75 H.E. Sigerist, *Medicine and Human Welfare*, New Haven/London: Yale University Press/Oxford University Press 1941, p. 53–104.

76 H.E. Sigerist, *Medicine and Human Welfare*, New Haven/London: Yale University Press/Oxford University Press 1941, p. 53–104.

77 M. Singer & H. Baer, *Introducing medical anthropology*, Lanham: AltaMira Press 2007, p. 69.

78 In the Egyptian doctrine, our nine bodies consist of *Ren* (the sound body), *Eb* (the heart body), *Khat* (the physical body), *Sekhem* (the electromagnetic body), *Ka* (the desire body), *Kihibit* (the astral body), *Ba* (the soul body), *Saah* (the spiritual body) and *Khu* (the universal spirit of God within every atom). See www.siaacademy.com/html/Monthly.html.

79 Www.siaacademy.com/html/Monthly.html.

of the !Kung San of the Kalahari Desert in south-western Africa: the ability to sweat is regarded as good health since it is regarded as a life-giving substance.[80]

In the current western literature on health, the focus is on individual determinants of health. Health care is focused on subparts of the human body, the medical organizational system being subdivided into separate compartments, such as cardiology, gynaecology, dermatology, neurology and psychiatry. This approach is exemplified by the definition of health in the Oxford Dictionary: 'Soundness of body; that condition in which its functions are duly and efficiently discharged'. Both the physical and the functional aspect are predominant in this definition. Furthermore, the concept and measurement of health in the current western medical domain has generally focused on ill health.[81] Doctors approach patients from their pathology and medical textbooks bundling an enormous collection of diseases.[82] The presence of a disease in this interpretation can be identified through various bodily signs, such as a high or low temperature, blood pressure, or heart rate.[83] As such, it can be established by a professional such as a biomedical physician or another formally recognized medical practitioner. Applied to the broader context, public health is measured by determining infant and child mortality and morbidity. A population is said to be healthy when these rates are low.[84]

Over time and across cultures, the different concepts of health thus varied from an emphasis on physical, mental, social or spiritual health to a combination of these three approaches.[85] Another distinctive feature shifted between the more 'negative' description, such as 'the absence of disease or infirmity' to a more positive formulation, such as 'health is well-being' or 'health is the capacity to work and love'.[86] Over time, when the so-called 'positive idea of health' emerged, the holistic and positive definition of the WHO has been adopted as an international

80 M. Singer & H. Baer, *Introducing medical anthropology*, Plymouth: Altamira Press 2007, p. 69.

81 L. Breslow, 'A Quantitative Approach to the World Health Organization Definition of Health: Physical, Mental and Social Well-being', *International Journal of Epidemiology* 1972, Volume 1, No. 4, Oxford University Press, p. 1.

82 The insight that western medicine is heavily oriented towards a negative formulation of health was acquired from Richard Smith in his blog for the British Medical Journal, entitled 'The end of disease and the beginning of health', 8th July 2008. Available at: http://blogs.bmj.com/bmj/2008/07/08/richard-smith-the-end-of-disease-and-the-beginning-of-health/.

83 M. Singer & H. Baer, *Introducing medical anthropology*, Lanham: AltaMira Press 2007, p. 64–66.

84 L. Breslow, 'A Quantatative approach to the World Health Organization Definition of Health: Physical, Mental and Social Well-being', *International Journal of Epidemiology* 1972, Volume 1, Number 4, Oxford University Press, p. 347.

85 H.E. Sigerist, *Medicine and Human Welfare*, New Haven/London: Yale University Press/Oxford University Press 1941, p. 53–104.

86 This formula was cited by Erik Erikson, but it is not to be found in Freud's works, although the sentiment is sometimes implied. During his long engagement Freud stated that his own ambition in life was to have Martha as his wife and to be able to work (e.g. "Couldn't I for once have you and the work at the same time?" Freud-Martha Bernays 21 October 1885). Freud also referred to Eros and Ananke [Love and Necessity] as the foundations of society. In 'Civilization and Its Discontents' (1930) he wrote: "The communal life of human beings had, therefore, a

standard. The World Health Organization defines health as 'a state of complete physical, mental and social well-being, and not merely the absence of disease or infirmity'.[87] This means that the health concept is positively formulated, not dependent on the concepts of disease and illness. This is a remarkable approach to health, as we have seen that most modern doctors focus on diseases, not on health and thus apply a negatively formulated definition of health.

However, the holistic WHO definition of health has been heavily criticized. Whereas it was acknowledged that the widening of the concept of health was a major advance including the underlying determinants of health, the concept is said to be so broad that it has no operational value and that it 'ensures that hardly anybody is truly healthy'.[88] Huber righteously argued that due to highly sensitive modern diagnostic tools, it is fairly impossible to reach a state of complete health.[89] As a result of the far-reaching technological possibilities for genetic testing, blood tests and MRI scanning, it is even stated that health is an illusion, as there always is a (genetic) predisposition encountered for the existence of latent diseases.[90] The result is that the concept of health as adopted by the WHO has often been said to be too vague and not subject to scientific application.[91] Huber righteously points to the risk that the ever further reaching search for medical treatments significantly increases the risk of medicalization of society and people.[92] She eloquently poses that the WHO definition becomes counterproductive, because 'it minimizes the role of human capacity to cope with life's ever changing physical, social and emotional challenges'. One could even argue that the increased medicalization of society significantly reduces people's inclination to take responsibility for their own health and possibly also for the health of their children. However, the parallel development in which people have better access to health information runs against this development, because people are better able to question doctors

---

two-fold foundation: the compulsion to work, which was created by external necessity, and the power of love…". (S.E. XXI.101). See for more information: www.freud.org.uk/about/faq/.

87 Preamble to the Constitution of the World Health Organization as adopted by the International Health Conference, New York, 19–22 June 1946; signed on 22 July 1946 by the representatives of 61 States (Official Records of the World Health Organization, no. 2, p. 100) and entered into force on 7 April 1948.

88 R. Saracci, 'The world health organization needs to reconsider its definition of health', *British Medical Journal* 1997, Volume 314, Number 1409. Available at: www.bmj.com/content/314/7091/1409.

89 M. Huber e.a., 'How should we define health?', *British Medical Journal* 2011, Volume 343, number b4163. Available at: www.bmj.com/content/343/bmj.d4163.

90 This insight was acquired from Richard Smith in his blog for the British Medical Journal, entitled 'The end of disease and the beginning of health.' 8th July 2008. Available at: http://blogs.bmj.com/bmj/2008/07/08/richard-smith-the-end-of-disease-and-the-beginning-of-health/.

91 L. Breslow, 'A Quantitative approach to the World Health Organization Definition of Health: Physical, Mental and Social Well-being', *International Journal of Epidemiology* 1972, Volume 1, Number 4, Oxford University Press, p. 348.

92 M. Huber e.a., 'How should we define health?', *British Medical Journal* 2011, Volume 343, number b4163. Available at: www.bmj.com/content/343/bmj.d4163.

on the proposed treatments and stand up for their own and their children's right to the highest attainable standard of health.

A further elaboration of the concept of health was promoted at the Alma-Ata conference in 1978, wherein health was no longer seen as a technically complex medical matter, but as a daily concern which individuals can and must face themselves. It is thus much broader than the sporadic encounters with medical professionals.

Following from this the concept of primary health care was officially launched (see discussion in paragraph 5), aiming to reach the entire population.

Two contributors to the British Medical Journal have tried to overcome the problem of the limited practical value of the WHO definition and did an extensive search for further information on the concept. As this produced little information, an online invitation by the British Medical Journal was posted to revise the current definition, amounting to a vast amount of suggestions, ranging from, 'Health is the state of the organism when it functions optimally without evidence of disease' to 'Health is inner peace'.[93] Interesting is the question whether the increasing expectations of health due to changes in diagnostic abilities lead to a broader conceptualization of the right to health.

More recent work on the concept of health in the context of enforcing it as a right has been done by Ruger. The definition proposed by Ruger is the following:

> '(1) The state of the organism when it functions optimally without evidence of disease or abnormality. (2) A state of dynamic balance in which an individual's or a group's capacity to cope with all circumstances of living is at an optimum level. (3) A state characterized by anatomic, physiologic, and psychologic integrity, ability to perform personally valued family, work and community roles, ability to deal with physical, biologic, psychologic, and social stress; a feeling of well-being; and freedom from the risk of disease and untimely death.'[94]

Ruger claimed that this model is useful because it includes physical, mental and social aspects of humans.[95] It is also valued for including both potential as well as actual health status and because it respects the freedom of individuals to pursue their health capabilities through the health functions that are available to them.[96] The definition contains several elements worth noticing: the element of dynamicity is reflected in the second sentence by the phrase 'a state of dynamic balance'. As can be seen in the third sentence, this dynamic balance requires the ability to perform in societal roles and to deal with a variety of stress factors.

---

93 A.R. Jadad & L. O'Grady, 'How should health be defined?', *British Medical Journal* 2008, Volume 337, no. a2900. See also: www.bmj.com/content/337/bmj.a2900.full?rss=1.

94 J.P. Ruger, 'Toward a Theory of a Right to Health: Capability and Incompletely Theorized Agreements', *Yale Journal of Law & the Humanities* 2006, Volume 18, p. 316.

95 Ibidem supra note 94.

96 Ibidem supra note 94, p. 317.

By incorporation of this element it is acknowledged that health is not a static situation, but that it requires continuous effort and adjustment to ever changing circumstances to attain and to maintain a state of health. This state of health, as can be seen in sentence 1 and 2, should function 'at an optimum level'. Sentence one particularly refers to the functioning of the organism, whereas sentence 2 emphasizes (external) circumstances of living in assessing the potential optimal level of functioning. This element, 'optimal functioning' reflects the notion that the 'highest attainable level of health' may differ according to personal and situational circumstances (within and between different countries and populations). That same idea of a different standard of health is also found in the general definition of health of the WHO, which states that individuals have a right to '*the highest attainable standard*' of health, leaving space for differentiation between distinct living circumstances in prioritization and goal-setting. The question is what this variable concept of the highest attainable standard of health means for the enforcement of health as a right, as will be discussed in the following paragraph and beyond.[97]

Another element in Ruger's definition of health is the particular mentioning of 'the individuals and the groups capacity' to cope with differing circumstances. This accounts for the differing requirements for ensuring an individual's (right to) health and the requirements for developing public health policies. This notion gives room for discussing whether social determinants, such as the availability of clean water and the establishment of hygienic sanitary conditions should receive a higher prioritization than ensuring high-tech medical care for individuals. It has been acknowledged that social determinants have a greater impact on health than access to medical services.[98] On the other hand, it must be acknowledged that the illness of an individual may spread through the entire society through schools, work environments, clubs, religious institutions etcetera, thereby impacting upon the health of both the individual and large numbers of others.[99] More importantly, the rights of an individual should not in principle be subordinated to the rights of the majority.

Whereas the whole of Ruger's suggested definition of health seems to be more practical than the definition of the WHO, the phrase in the last sentence 'freedom from the risk of disease and untimely death' seems somewhat utopian again, as it is impossible to be completely free of the *risk* to disease or untimely death. (Unknown) risks are always present and can (and should) not be completely ruled

---

97 In Chapter 3 the different interpretations of children's right to health in countries with different levels of human development will be discussed on the basis of the Concluding Observations of the UN Committee on the Rights of the Child.

98 G. Sreenivasan, 'Opportunity is not the Key', in: B. Steinbock, A.D. Arras & A.J. London, *Ethical Issues in Modern Medicine*, New York: McGraw-Hill 2009, p. 235.

99 W.M. Sage, 'Solidarity: Unfashionable, But Still American', *Connecting American Values with Health Reform* 2009, The Hastings Centre, p. 10.

out. Such a definition would lead to a level of risk-aversion that does not seem desirable for a flourishing life.

Key elements in Ruger's definition of health match well with the recently introduced definition of health by Huber. Criticizing the static nature of the WHO definition of health 'a complete *state* of physical, mental and social well-being' as well as the inability to ever reach a state of *complete* state health, she introduces the definition that health is the 'ability to adapt and self-manage in the face of social, physical and emotional challenges'.[100] This definition takes adaptability of the human being to life's changing circumstances as well as resilience as a starting point.[101] Not only does this definition better take into account the continuously changing nature of people's living circumstances, but it also enhances opportunities for operationalization. The requirement to augment people's resilience requires the development of so-called 'health-literacy', people's capacities for engaging in healthy behaviour and for developing the capacities of individuals to take responsibility for their own health and the health of their children. Not only does this increase the overall capacity of people involved in realizing the highest attainable standard of health of children, but it also improves people's sense of self-reliance and well-being.[102] This focus on the freedom and responsibility of individuals to realize their own right to health and to make choices in favour of or against healthy behaviour (of their children) and thereby achieve certain functionings, is in line with Amartya Sen's capability approach. The implications of this new vision on health for the interpretation and realization of health as a right are discussed in the following section.

1.5. HEALTH AS A RIGHT

The acknowledgement of the State's co-responsibility to ensure health for its citizens goes back to old times, when ancient civilisations, including Egypt, India, Troy, the Roman Empire and the Inca society established water supply and drainage systems, aiming to prevent community infections.[103] The Greek philosopher Aristotle supports such ancient State practices with theory, by stating that the end that all political activity should strive for is human flourishing.[104] He recognizes that there are natural and social impediments to human flourishing. According to Ruger, 'this justifies health as a primary objective of health policy, having both an intrinsic and an instrumental value.'[105] Also, whereas the right

[100] Ibidem supra note 92 Huber.
[101] Ibidem supra note 92 Huber.
[102] Ibidem supra note 92 Huber.
[103] G. Rosen, *A History of Public Health*, Baltimore/London: The John Hopkins University Press 1993, p. 47, 55, 106, 111, 244.
[104] J.P. Ruger, 'Toward a Theory of a Right to Health: Capability and Incompletely Theorized Agreements', *Yale Journal of Law & the Humanities* 2006, Volume 18, p. 288.
[105] Ibidem supra note 104, p. 290.

to health may be qualified as a basic civil or political right, it may be an essential precondition for the realization of those rights.[106]

The modern development of health as a right was only instigated following the age of enlightenment and the establishment of universal human rights in the 18th century. In this period, the importance of health and its social effects were recognized, leading to the establishment of a 'medical police' in the larger cities of Europe and the United States, aimed at improving the public sanitation and hygiene.[107] One of its instigators, Johann Peter Frank, emphasized the link between poverty and health and called for the need to exchange health information on an international level in his 'Letter of Invitation to Scholars'.[108] More influential to the development of the right to health was the Industrial Revolution in the 19th century, creating unhealthy living and working conditions for large amounts of workers and their families.[109] In his 'Report on an Inquiry into the Sanitary Conditions of the Labouring Population of Great Britain', Chadwick promoted the need to guarantee health based on the utilitarian belief that a healthy working class benefits the entire society. This led to the passage of the Public Health Act in 1848, leading to the establishment of sewage systems, water supply and Medical Officers of Health.[110]

Other approaches included the need to protect health as a property right of the working man by Neumann,[111] as he claimed that this was the only right of those who have no other property than the labour they deliver. However, this foundation of health as a right does not provide for a strong entitlement for children, as they could not be qualified as formal workers yet, nor did they have the duty to provide for their families' living. Others saw health as a social and political value in its own right.[112]

Later in the 19th century, a series of International Sanitary Conferences were organized. The purpose of the conferences seemed to be the protection of Europe

---

106 See: F.I. Michelman, 'Forword: On Protecting the Poor Through the Fourteenth Amendment', *Harvard Law Review* 1969, Issue 7, p. 7. See also: A.E. Buchanan, 'The Right to a Decent Minimum of Health Care', *Philosophy and Public Affairs* 1984, Volume 13, no. 1, p. 61. [According to Rawls, certain social goods can be qualified as 'primary goods', meaning that virtually all individuals value them despite interpersonal differences in desires and life goals. Rawls concludes that at least some forms of health care seem to bear the earmarks of Rawlsian primary goods: they facilitate the effective pursuit of ends in general and may also enhance our ability to criticize and revise our conceptions of the good.'] found in: R. Korobkin, 'Determining health care rights behind a veil of ignorance', *University of Illinois Law Review* 1998, no. 3, p. 806.

107 A. de Swaan, *In Care of the State*, Oxford/Cambridge: Basil Blackwell/Polity Press 1988, p. 126.

108 Epistola Invitatoria ad Eruditos, 1776, Rosen 1993, p. 267.

109 C.F. Brockington, *Public Health in the Nineteenth Century*, London, England: Livingston 1965.

110 G. Rosen, *A History of Public Health*, Baltimore/London: The Johns Hopkins University Press 1993, p. 196.

111 S. Neumann, *Die öffentliche Gesundheitspflege und das Egeintum [Public Health Care and Property]*, Berlin: Adolf Riek 1847.

112 M. Susser, 'Ethical components in the definition of health', *International Journal of Health Services* 1974, volume 4, pp. 539–548.

against alien diseases, being a hindrance to international trade.[113] It was not until the 11th edition in 1907, that the Rome Agreement was signed to establish an international office of public health in Paris. This Office was linked to the League of Nations until the creation of the United Nations.[114]

Following the atrocities of World War II, the United Nations Charter in article 1 affirmed the dignity and worth of the human person as the cornerstone of human rights. In 1946, the Constitution of the World Health Organization was signed,[115] being the first international human rights document to formulate the individual's right to health, without distinction of race, religion, political belief, economic or social condition.[116] Particular mention is made of the basic importance of the healthy development of the child: the ability to live harmoniously in a changing total environment is essential to such development. The adopted definition of health reflects the notion that the right to health is broader than only the provision to ensure health care facilities, referring to the responsibility of the government to provide for adequate health ánd social measures.

This broad formulation of health as a human right was reaffirmed in 1948, when the United Nations adopted the Universal Declaration on Human Rights encompassing article 25, which reads: 'Everyone has the right to a standard of living adequate for the health and well-being of himself and his family, including food, clothing, housing and medical care and necessary social services, and the right to security in the event of unemployment, sickness, disability, widowhood, old age or other lack of livelihood in circumstances beyond his control.' The Committee on Economic Social and Cultural Rights elaborated upon this provision in article 12 of its International Covenant. This article is in line with the WHO Constitution, as it refers both to a right to health care as to a broader range of public health measures to ensure the underlying determinants of health (or 'healthy conditions') to be taken by States. It provides for key provisions to progressively realize the right to health, including the provision for the reduction of the stillbirth rate, infant mortality and the healthy development of the child (12-2-a) and the creation of conditions which assure to all medical services and medical attention in the event of sickness. The right to health as laid down in article 12 ICESCR (1966) was further elaborated upon in General Comment 14 of the Committee on Economic Social and Cultural Rights (2000). The distinctive features of this general right to health are further discussed in chapter 5. The right to health in international health law is used as a shorthand expression for a

---

113 H.D.C. Roscam Abbing, 'Recht op gezondheidszorg: een beschouwing over grenzen aan het stellen van grenzen (liber amicorum voor Prof. Dr. H.J.J. Leenen), in: J.K.M. Gevers & J.H. Hubben, *Grenzen aan de Zorg: Zorgen aan de Grens*, Alphen aan de Rijn: Samsom/ H.D. Tjeenk Willink 1990, p. 91. See also, WHO, *The First Ten Years of the World Health Organization*, 1958, pp. 1–15.

114 WHO, The First Ten Years of the World Health Organization, 1958, p. 22–24.

115 The WHO Constitution was signed during the International Health Conference in New York on 22 July 1946 and entered into force on 7 April 1948.

116 Preamble of the WHO Constitution (see also note 95).

broad range of entitlements, including health care and underlying determinants of health. Other terms used include the right to health care, the right to health protection or the right to health maintenance. Neither of these covers the range of entitlements as defined in the WHO Constitution, namely the right to health care and the right to have the underlying determinants of health fulfilled. However, it does not go so far as to implicate a right to be healthy because this can not be guaranteed solely by the efforts of States. Health also depends on individual (biological) characteristics and behaviour. Furthermore, the right to 'the highest attainable standard of health' depends on the available resources of a State.

It has been acknowledged that the indeterminacy of the right to health is a central point of weakness in realizing the right to health.[117] In the modern debate, several aspects have been central. In determining the contents of the right to health, the focus has shifted between solely ensuring medical services to also ensuring the underlying determinants of health. Furthermore, shifts have been made between a focus on the individual and a focus on a collectively oriented appeal. This shift in focus has been attributed to the distinctive influence of the clinical sector, focusing primarily on the health status of individuals. In addition, the influence of the public health sector played a part, focusing on the health of populations and the need to ensure conditions under which people can be healthy.[118] The third dimension analysed is that the formulation of the right to health has shifted between a negative formulation, such as 'health is the absence of disease' to a positive formulation of health, such as the holistic interpretation of health by the WHO.

In the newly introduced definition of health by Huber the focus shifts from an external orientation with regard to entitlements to health services and underlying determinants to an internal orientation, in which people's capacities to self-manage their health status and to adapt to changing circumstances become key to ensuring the right to the highest attainable standard of health. From this perspective, the obligations of the State in realizing the right to the highest attainable standard of health have to enable and stimulate people to take responsibility over their own health. In that way, they regain their opportunity to choose the different functionings they wish to realize. What this approach means for the way in which the right to the highest attainable standard of health of the child is realized is investigated in this research.

117 D.P. Fidler, 'Geographical morality' Revisited International Relations, International law and the controversy over placebo – controlled HIV Clinical trials', *Harvard International Law Journal* 2001, Volume 42, no. 2, Issue 299, p. 348.

118 J. Asher, *The right to health, A resource manual for NGOs*, London: Commonwealth Medical Trust 2004, p. 18.

1.6. FOCUS ON THE PROVISION OF PRIMARY HEALTH CARE

Article 24(2)(b) CRC demands priority for ensuring the provision of necessary medical assistance and health care to all children with an emphasis on the development of primary health care. Thus the question arises what is meant with the phrase primary health care and how it can contribute to realizing the highest attainable standard of health of the child.

The content of primary health care was elaborated in the 1978 Declaration of Alma Ata on Primary Health Care, during a conference that was sponsored by UNICEF and the WHO. The UN General Assembly endorsed the Declaration by resolution 34/43 of 19 November 1979.[119]

The declaration contains an elaborate definition of primary health care, characterized by several key elements. First of all, primary health care is essential health care that is universally accessible and affordable for all individuals in the community.[120] Stated is that it is the first level of contact for individuals and families with the national health system and that it constitutes a central function and main focus of the country's health system. It aims to bring health care as close as possible to where people live and work. Thereto, primary health care envisages small, but widely accessible institutions and should be distinguished from more complex types of health care such as hospitals.[121]

The role and functioning of primary health care in society is further elaborated as being dependent on and therefore reflective of the economic, social, cultural and political rights in a country. The Declaration of Alma-Ata underlines that relevant research results and public health experiences must be applied in primary health care. It states that the key issues in primary health care require an integrated approach by all sectors of society to ensure a basic level of nutritious food, water, sanitation, mother and child health care, immunization against the major infectious diseases, adequate treatment of the most common diseases and injuries and the provision of essential drugs. The propagated approaches to achieve these targets include (education on) the promotion, prevention, curation and rehabilitation of the main health problems in a country. Because the health system relies on a wide variety of properly trained health workers, including traditional practitioners, individuals and communities they must be educated to take a proactive, participative and self-reliant role in the planning, organization and control of primary health care.[122] This is deemed necessary to make the fullest use of all available resources, in addition to internal resources of the country and external resources from other countries. Last but not least, the Declaration

---

119 International Conference on Primary Health Care, Alma-Ata, USSR, 6–12 September 1978.

120 See § VI-VIII of the Declaration International Conference on Primary Health Care, Alma-Ata, USSR, 6–12 September 1978.

121 A. Eide & W.B. Eide, *A Commentary on the UN CRC Article 24: The Right to Health*, Leiden: Martinus Nijhoff Publishers 2006, p. 21.

122 Ibidem supra note 120.

states that priority must be given to those most in need. Given the significant vulnerability of young children and the particular mention made of children's health in the Declaration of Alma-Ata, this irrefutably includes children aged 0–5, who by nature of their age have a relatively high level of vulnerability in comparison to older children.

The Declaration of Alma-Ata was revolutionary in the approach to health care, as earlier health campaigns in the 20th century were exclusively targeted at the eradication of specific diseases, such as smallpox. Successful community based health programs in China and several other countries led to the new approach of health care, which was characterized by a holistic approach to health, including not only the prevention of specific diseases, but also the principles of equity, health promotion, community involvement, recognition of multiple determinants of health and intersectoral collaboration. The initial enthusiasm over this approach led to the incorporation of Primary Health Care principles in national health programs.[123] However, economic constraints in the 1980s impeded effective implementation.[124] More importantly, when actual efforts were made to involve local communities in health programs, this appeared to be a serious threat to the elites, (central) governments and also the medical elites, who had maintained a powerful control over the practice and knowledge of healing.[125] This combination of governmental bureaucracy and lack of will by the medical community to relinquish its autonomy in the medical sector placed great obstacles in achieving the targets of the Primary Health Care Approach.[126] Under the banner of the Primary Health Care approach, high-tech government-run medical initiatives were launched in remote areas, replacing the locally-based initiatives by communities. This has led to conclusions that the Primary Health Care approach failed, but also to conclusions that the approach was never actually tried.[127] Scarce examples of comprehensive health programs very much in line with the Alma-Ata principles, suggest that the PHC approach can be very successful if three basic conditions are present: 1) political will to meet citizens' basic needs, 2) active popular participation to realize this goal and 3) social and economic equity.[128]

Following the objections of several governments and medical professionals, the Primary Health Care approach was reduced to several key elements, described

---

123 D. Sanders & D. Werner, 'The Politics of Primary Health Care and Child Survival', *HealthWrights*, 1997, p. 19.

124 J. Walsh & K. Warren, 'Selective Primary Health Care: An interim Strategy for Disease Control in Developing Countries, *New England Journal of Medicine* 1979, 301, number 18, p. 967–974.

125 D. Sanders & D. Werner, 'The Politics of Primary Health Care and Child Survival', *HealthWrights*, 1997, p. 19.

126 D. Sanders & D. Werner, 'The Politics of Primary Health Care and Child Survival', *HealthWrights*, 1997, p. 20.

127 See for example: B. Wisner, *Power and Need in Africa*, Trenton, New Jersey: Africa World Press 1989, p. 53–86. See also: D. Werner, 'The Life and Death of Primary Health Care or The McDonaldization of Alma Ata', *HealthWrights*, 1997.

128 D. Sanders & D. Werner, 'The Politics of Primary Health Care and Child Survival', *HealthWrights*, 1997, p. 21.

as the Selective Primary Health Care approach. One of its presumptions was the targeting of high risk groups that were carefully selected. Community participation, social and economic equity and intersectoral collaboration were excluded on the basis of recommendations by international health experts and it was widely stated that the goal to realize 'a complete state of physical, mental and social well-being' was unrealistic.

Focus was again placed on immunization against a selection of childhood diseases and outreach activities were organized to provide for a minimum healthcare package for families.[129] In line with this Selective Primary Health Care approach, UNICEF launched the IMCI, the integrated management of childhood illnesses in 1990, encompassing growth monitoring, oral rehydration, breastfeeding and immunization (GOBI). This campaign was expanded to GOBI-FFF (Family Planning, Food supplies and Female education), though never received as enthusiastically as the narrower GOBI-program. Some countries even narrowed their health policy to 'the engines of the child survival revolution', namely immunization and/or oral rehydration.[130] In 2002, the ACSD, the accelerated child survival and development program, directed at decreasing the high rates of infant mortality in 11 countries, was initiated. Critics said that these programs avoided discussing political and social causes of poor health, keeping health interventions under medical control.

It has thus become clear that the actual content of the concept of 'Primary Health Care' is strongly influenced by policy decisions of national governments. Given the relatively scarce resources available for improving (children's) health, it should be recognized that allocation of resources to tertiary health care (hospitals and more specialized methods of health care) benefits only a small number of people, limiting the possibility to reach everyone, both in rural as in urban areas, coming from all different subsections of the society, by primary health care.[131] Article 24(2)(b) emphasizes the need to prioritize resource allocation to primary health care.[132] This implicates a major challenge to stimulate commitment amongst all parties involved to establish a widely accessible primary health care system. In analysing the health systems in different countries, it must be kept in mind that the way in which primary health care is made accessible strongly differs. For example in the Netherlands, primary health care, or 'first line health care' is characterized by a first encounter with the family doctor who decides whether a referral to a specialized doctor, such as a gynaecologist, a paediatrician or a psychiatrist is required.[133] In other countries, in which this system of gatekeeping does not exist,

129 Ibid supra note 128.

130 Ibid supra note 128.

131 C. Sepúlveda, 'The right to child health: the development of primary health servies in Chile and Thailand', *Innocenti Occasional Research Papers Child Rights Series*, number 7.

132 A. Eide & W.B. Eide, *A Commentary on the UN CRC Article 24: The right to health*, Leiden: Martinus Nijhoff Publishers 2006, p. 21.

133 For a discussion on the gatekeeping role of the family doctor in the Netherlands and several other developed countries, see B. Meyboom-de Jong, 'De huisarts als poortwachter', Arts en

the hospital is the first step in the health care process. This difference unavoidably has consequences for the ways in which the key elements of primary health care can be realized.

1.7. CHILDREN AND VULNERABILITY

1.7.1. DEFINITION OF THE CHILD

Article 1 of the Children's Rights Convention defines children as 'every human being below the age of 18 years, unless under the law applicable to the child, majority is attained earlier.' The age of majority is recognized in law as being the threshold for ending minority and entering into adulthood. The minor ceases to be legally considered as a child and therefore assumes to have control over its own actions and decisions, thereby terminating the legal control over and the responsibilities of the parents or legal guardian. The age of legal majority is legally fixed, but it may differ depending on the jurisdiction of a particular country or on a particular subtheme. For example, in some countries the age of majority is determined at 18 years, whereas the legal threshold for being allowed to consume alcoholic beverages is 21 and whereas the legal age for consent to medical decisions is determined at 12 or 16 years of age. The concept of minority does not necessarily correspond to the actual physical or mental maturity of an individual. Provisions that could lead to an earlier ending of childhood include marriage before the age of eighteen,[134] having a baby[135] or the passage of certain rituals,[136] depending on the country and region of the world. Deviations from the international standard for the age of adulthood include Iran (15 years),[137] Scotland (16 years),[138] Indonesia (15 for girls and 18 for boys)[139] and Japan (20 years).[140]

Remarkable is that the beginning of childhood is not mentioned in article 1 CRC, so that this must be determined by regional treaties or domestic legislation

samenleving in: *Nederlands Tijdschrift voor de Geneeskunde*, 31 December 1994, 138(53), pp. 2668–2673. In the Netherlands, 6 key functions of the family doctor are mentioned, including accessibility for all patients, continuity in diagnosis, treatment and care, the permanent relationship with the patient, involvement in the family and living circumstances of the patient, prevention, triage and epidemiology in patient population.

134 See for example article 1:233 of the Dutch Civil Law Code (art. 1:233 BW).

135 See for example article 1:253ha of the Dutch Civil Law Code (art. 1:253ha BW).

136 In Jewish traditions, the age of adulthood is reached at the age of Bar Mitzwah (usually 13 for Jewish boys), when they have to learn the Torah and other Jewish principles.

137 See world law direct: www.worldlawdirect.com/forum/law-wiki/27181-age-majority.html.

138 Age of Legal Capacity (Scotland) Act 1991, article 1.

139 See world law direct: www.worldlawdirect.com/forum/law-wiki/27181-age-majority.html.

140 The age(s) of adulthood, The Japan Times Online, Sunday, February 24th 2008. http://search.japantimes.co.jp/cgi-bin/ed20080224a1.html. See also, World Law Direct: www.worldlawdirect.com/forum/law-wiki/27181-age-majority.html.

of states.[141] A legal determination of minority ages does not appear in the European Convention on Human Rights nor in the International Covenant on Civil and Political Rights. Some individual states define the conception as the starting point of childhood,[142] thereby prohibiting abortion if not for saving the life of the mother.[143] Others set a specific moment during pregnancy, for example the moment of viability of the foetus as the legal standard or the date of birth.[144]

The European Court on Human Rights has considered the question whether individual children are entitled to benefit from a specific right only on a case-by-case basis.[145] The question on the beginning of life has been considered in the context of the right to life in article 2, paragraph 1 of the European Convention on Human Rights.[146] The determination of the beginning of childhood (or life) is essential in answering the question whether abortion is permitted or prohibited under the European Convention.[147] This determination also has implications for neonatal testing or the admittance of medical drugs to pregnant women. A limited number of cases have been considered by the European Court, addressing the question

141 For a discussion on the issues raised during the drafting process of the CRC see: Leblanc, *The Convention on the Rights of the Child: United Nations Law Making on Human Rights*, Lincoln: University of Nebraska Press, pp. 66–73. See also the declarations of France (UN Doc. CRC/C/11/Add.1, p. 112) and the UK (UN Doc CRC/C/3/Add.15, p. 11).

142 Examples include Poland, Malta, Chili, Nicaragua, Saudi-Arabia. See: Abortion Policies, a global review, United Nations,: www.un.org/esa/population/publications/abortion/profiles.htm.

143 For a discussion on balancing the right to life of the mother and the unborn baby see M. Cornock & H. Montgomery, 'Children's rights in and out of the womb', *International Journal on Children's Rights* 2011, Issue 19, pp. 3–19.

144 For example, in the Dutch Penal Law (article 82a Sr.) the legal term until which abortion is admitted is 24 weeks.

145 G. Van Bueren, *Child Rights in Europe*, Council of Europe Publishing 2007, p. 51.

146 See for example *Paton v. the United Kingdom*, ECHR, 3. See also *Vo v. France*, European Court on Human Rights, 8 July 2004. In *Vo v. France*, no violation of the right to life in article 2 ECHR was found in a case where a pregnant woman who had been mistaken with another woman had to undergo a therapeutic abortion as a result of the mistake. The rationale was that no unintended homicide had been committed, since the fetus was not considered as a human being yet.

147 Hogan, 'The right to life and the abortion question under the European Convention on Human Rights', in: Heffernan (ed.), *Human Rights: A European Perspective*, 1994, p. 104.

of the beginning of childhood and the protection of (unborn) life,[148, 149, 150, 151] concomitantly leading to the conclusion that the child is protected under the European Convention on Human Rights from birth. European states have the discriminative authority to extend this protection to the prenatal period, although possible health risks for the mother can justify an abortion.[152] In deciding upon this highly sensitive issue, State Parties are left a great margin of appreciation.[153]

From the side of the medical profession, voices have been raised that notwithstanding the legal definition of the beginning of life of the child, it is especially the first term of the pregnancy that is crucial in ensuring the right to health of the child once it is born, because this is the period in which the

148 In the case of Paton, No 8416/78 *Paton v. UK*, Dec 13.05.80, 19 DR, p. 244, 3 EHHR 408, the Commission considered that the right to life as laid down in article 2 ECHR can be interpreted in three ways: 1) article 2 ECHR applies after birth, 2) the unborn child is entitled to protection subject to limitations and 3) article 2 recognizes the right to life of the unborn child as absolute. This last interpretation was rejected, because the right to life of the fetus would be deemed of higher value than the right to life of the pregnant woman. No choice was made between the two remaining interpretations and the question whether the right to life of the child is enjoyed by the unborn child thus remains unresolved. See also Harris, O'Boyle & Warbrick, *Law of the European Convention on Human Rights*, Oxford University Press 2009, p. 53–55.

149 In the case *H v. Norway, No17004/90 hudoc (1992)* it was held that an abortion of a 14-week-old fetus can be lawful, if 'pregnancy, birth or care for the child may place the woman in a difficult situation of life'. However, the Commission did state that 'in certain circumstances' article 2 may protect the right to life of a fetus younger than 12 weeks. However, these circumstances were not specified. The case of *A.B.C. v. Ireland No 25579/05 (2010)* involved three pregnant women who all had different reasons for requiring an abortion; A) having a baby while other children had been placed under custody would hinder reunion, B) a single parent would suffer from stigma and humiliation and C) a woman who was recovering from cancer, so that the check-ups could damage the child. The ECHR decided that Irelands failure to implement the existing constitutional right to abortion when a woman`s life is at risk (case C), constituted a violation of the right to a private and family life under article 8 ECHR. All other claims were dismissed.

150 In the case of *Boso v. Italy, No 50490/99 hudoc (2002) DA* the Commission held that if an abortion is performed under Italian law within the first 12 weeks of the pregnancy because of the risk for woman's physical or mental health, was not a breach of article 2 ECHR.

151 In the case of *R.R. v. Poland, No 27617/04 (2004)*, a woman was not allowed prenatal diagnostic support nor an abortion, although defects had been seen on the echo. The ECHR judged that Poland had violated article 3 (degrading treatment) and 8 (private and family life) of the ECHR. In the case of *Tysiac v. Poland, No 5410/03 (2007)*, the ECHR concluded that Polish law, applied tot the applicant's case, did not contain any effective mechanism to determine whether the conditions for obtaining a lawful abortion were met. Therefore, Ms Tysiac had suffered severe distress about the possible negative consequences of her pregnancy for her health, namely detoriation of her sight. Therefore, the Court concluded that her right to a private life as laid down in article 8 ECHR had been breached.

152 Bueren, van, G., *'Child rights in Europe'*, Council of Europe Publishing, 2007, p. 57.

153 As is commented by Harris, O'Boyle & Warbrick, see supra note 100, p. 54, generally, 'the limitations upon any right to life that the unborn child may have are capable of covering most cases in which voluntary abortion is sought.' Also, they identified that 'The Court state that 'given the absence of a European legal, medical, ethical, or religious consensus as to when life begins, a margin of appreciation applies, even to the point where the Court doubted whether it was desirable or even possible as matters stand, to answer the abstract question whether the unborn child is a person for the purposes of article 2 CRC.' See p. 55.

fundamental structures of the future body are formed.[154, 155] Therefore, protecting the right to health of the child after birth, is intrinsically linked to the health behaviour of the mother during (the first term of) her pregnancy, and thus also to the balancing of her rights against the right to life of the foetus.

In addition to static age limits, article 5 CRC refers to 'the evolving capacities' of the child, recognizing the increasing independency of children. This concept also gives space for a flexible level of protection, participation and autonomy, depending on the capacities of the individual child, the context and type of decision.[156]

1.7.2. DEFINITION OF VULNERABILITY

In essence, children are both vulnerable and resilient. The CRC Preamble highlights the need for special consideration for children who live in exceptionally difficult conditions. Sen's capability approach, takes children's capability or their potential for development as a starting point. This paragraph investigates the conceptualization of vulnerability of children in the international children's rights domain. It does so to identify in the following chapters the priorities required ensuring that all children, including those characterized by a high level of vulnerability can thrive in the best possible circumstances.

The CRC emphasizes the need for special protection and care for children who are vulnerable and at risk. In achieving this, the role of the family is very important, with the support of the state (article 18 CRC). Deriving from the CRC, several groups of particularly vulnerable children can be discerned; orphaned children and children who are separated from their family (article 9 and 20), adopted children (article 21), refugee children (article 22), mentally or physically handicapped children (article 23), children in need of medical care (article 24), children placed out-of-home (article 25), children belonging to minorities, including ethnic, religious, indigenous minorities and girls (article 2 and 30), children who are confronted with drugs (article 33), children who are vulnerable to (sexual) exploitation, abuse, trafficking and hazardous labour (articles 33–36), children in armed conflict (article 38) and children in conflict with the law (article 40). Although no particular provision is found in the CRC on special measures required for infants and toddlers, interpretative tools, such as General

---

154 H.J.J. Leenen, 'Leven in wording, prenatale diagnostiek en behandeling van de foetus', in: H.J.J. Leenen & J.K.M. Gevers redacteuren, *Handboek Gezondheidsrecht. Deel 1: Rechten van Mensen in de Gezondheidszorg*, Houten: Bohn Stafleu Van Loghum 2000. p. 152–4.

155 In a case in the Netherlands, a 30-year-old pregnant women was put under custody because she was addicted to cocaine. Medical professionals pledged for a stricter application of the Convention of the Rights of the Child in order to protect the future life of the unborn baby. See: Hondius, Stikker, Wenink en Honig, 'Wet BOPZ toegepast bij vroege zwangerschap van verslaafde', *Nederlands Tijdschrift voor de Geneeskunde* 2012, 156, A3818.

156 S. Meuwese, *Handboek Internationaal Jeugdrecht*, Nijmegen: Ars Aequi Libri 2005, p. 70.

Comment 7 to the CRC on Implementing Child Rights in early Childhood, offer strong argumentation for providing special care for the health and well-being of the youngest.

Generally, vulnerability is associated with the potential realization of an adverse outcome.[157] Taking the capability approach as a starting point, it becomes clear that young children have limited opportunities for choosing between the different functionings they wish to realize due to their large dependence on others.

Landsdown makes a distinction between inherent vulnerability of the child, exemplified by factors such as age, physical weakness, immaturity and lack of knowledge and lack of experience, versus structural vulnerability, meaning a lack of economic and political power, access to money, opportunities to express feelings and have their rights taken seriously.[158] This distinction is useful for identifying what aspects of vulnerability can be addressed through policy and legislation and what aspects can only be accepted as a matter of fact. Landsdown claims that there is a tendency to rely heavily on 'the presumption of innocence and vulnerability of children' in developing law and policy. Drawing a parallel with the emancipation of women and the establishment of their rights, she poses that inherent vulnerability is used as an excuse for their structural vulnerability, but that in fact it is the structures in which children live that make them vulnerable to abuse, exploitation, neglect and disregard for their views in situations of poverty, discrimination, conflict or disaster. This means that children's vulnerability is only partially dependent on their vulnerability as being a child, and partially based on circumstances being subject to policy and legal developments. Therefore, Landsdown stated that the adoption of the CRC has been a major achievement in promoting a rights-based approach to addressing the needs of vulnerable groups of children. As such, it has created plural opportunities for children to stand up for their own rights. This does not only lead to an urgent call for attention for vulnerable children, but it provides them with a legal basis to claim their right to the provision of basic determinants of health and a life in dignity to change the circumstances in which they live and diminish the level of structural vulnerability.[159] Furthermore, it specifically acknowledges children's right to be involved in decisions affecting them as a basic principle, so that they or their legal representatives can make a claim to actually influence their structural vulnerability.

Other factors identified that may lead to inherent vulnerability include dependency on adults, (traumatic) experiences in the past, a lack of future perspectives, cultural differences, language, health and developmental

157 G. Landsdown, *Taking Part: Children's Participation in Decision Making*, p. 35.

158 Ibidem supra note 157.

159 The additional value of the third Optional Protocol on a communications procedure for children for making (individual) claims will be discussed in chapter 7.

problems.[160] Factors identified as leading to structural vulnerability include living with caretakers with serious problems like poverty, illness (HIV/AIDS or chronic diseases), disabilities, trauma, substance addiction or abusive habits, living on the street, being forced into an early marriage, being accused of witchcraft or displaying certain physical traits such as being an albino or being part of a twin. Structural vulnerability can be further divided into permanent and temporal vulnerability.[161] In this distinction, permanent vulnerability results from long-term living conditions, such as a general lack of infrastructure or legal protection, whereas temporal vulnerability is the result of sudden, mostly unforeseen events, such as natural disasters. Vulnerability of the second category requires measures and action plans of a different nature, focused on mitigating the harmful consequences of a particular event.

Helpful in assessing children's vulnerability is also the Best Interests of the Child Model.[162] This model provides for 14 preconditions for the healthy development of the child.[163] Absence of these preconditions may be indicative of vulnerability.

Landsdown asserts that the degree of vulnerability of children decreases rapidly as they grow and develop.[164] Skinner, Tsheko et al. even qualify children as vulnerable on the basis of their limited access to basic needs, such as education, health and social services.[165] This identification recognizes that children can be vulnerable on the basis of material, emotional or social deprivation in itself.

The concept of children's vulnerability with respect to their right to health has been constructed by a myriad of factors, including their increased susceptibility to violations of their right to health, as they, especially the youngest ones, are less able to physically and verbally protect themselves, and as they are less capable

160 C. van Os & S. de Jong, *'The Dutch Report on 'Enhancing Vulnerable Asylum Seekers Protection' 2010*, Defence for Children International-ECPAT The Netherlands, pp. 18–21.

161 Ibidem supra note 157.

162 M.E. Klaverboer & A.E. Zijlstra, *Het Belang van het Kind in het Vreemdelingenrecht, Kinderen uit Asielzoekersgezinnen. Ontwikkeling, Perspectief en Juridische Positie*, Rijksuniversiteit Groningen: 2008.

163 The preconditions are divided into four categories; (A) Present Family Conditions, (B) Past and Future Family Conditions, (C) Present Societal Conditions and (D) Past and Future Societal Conditions.
A.I. (physical care) includes (1) adequate physical care and (2) a safe physical direct environment.
A.II. (care and upbringing) includes (3) an affective atmosphere, (4) a supporting, flexible upbringing structure, (5) adequate examples by parents and (6) interest.
B. includes (7) continuity and stability in upbringing conditions and a future perspective.
C. includes (8) safe wider physical environment, (9) respect, (10) social network, (11) education, (12) contact with peers or friends, (13) adequate examples in society.
D. includes (14) stability in life circumstances and a future perspective.

164 G. Landsdown, *Taking Part: Children's Participation in Decision Making*, p. 36.

165 D. Skinner, N. Tsheko, S. Mtero-Munyati, M. Segwabe, P. Chibatamoto, S. Mfecane, B. Chandiwana, N. Nkomo, S. Tlou, *Definition of orphaned and vulnerable children*, Cape Town: HSRC Press 2004.

to benefit from available protection and provision mechanisms.[166] Also, it has been identified that young children are less likely to have the necessary skills to participate in the democratic decision-making process to ensure that their rights (to health) are being taken into consideration and that sufficient resources are allocated to ensure adequate access to health care facilities.[167] Violations of children's right to health have therefore been identified as a result of 'deeply-rooted systemic inequality'.[168] Furthermore, the Office of the High Commissioner on Human Rights has identified that both the short-term and the long-term physical and psychological effects on children of violations of their right to health will usually be more intrusive than they are on adults, as they are not fully developed yet.[169]

The deprivation of continuous health care is especially pressing for 'mobile children', children who do not live in the same place for a considerable period of time and who risk discontinuous health care or even a loss of access to health care resulting from their mobility. This is particularly the case for refugee and immigrant children,[170, 171] children living on the street,[172, 173, 174] children in conflict and crisis situations,[175] Roma children[176] and also for children confronted with domestic violence.[177] In this last subgroup, it has occurred that parents maltreating their children often move around the country to avoid facing the

166 A. Nolan, 'The child's right to health and the courts', in: *Global Health and Human Rights: Legal and Philosophical Perspectives*, edited by J. Harrington & M. Stuttaford, London: Routledge, p. 137.
167 Ibidem supra note 166, pp. 137–139.
168 Ibidem supra note 166, p. 138.
169 Office of the High Commissioner on Human Rights, 2001.
170 A. Hjern & P. Bouvier, 'Migrant children – a challenge for European peadiatricians', *Acta Paediatrica* 2004, Issue 95, pp. 1535–1539.
171 B. Gushulak & D. Macpherson, 'The basic principles of migration health: Population mobility and gaps in disease prevalence', in: *Emerging themes in Epidemiology*, May 2006, p. 3. Accessed through: www.biomedcentral.com/content/pdf/1742-7622-3-3.pdf.
172 K. Panter-Brick, 'Street children, human rights and public health: A Critique and Future Directions', *Annual Review of Anthropology* 2002, Vol. 31, pp. 147–171.
173 L. Nodjadjim & K. Wyss, 'Access to health care by street children in the urban context of N'Djamena, Chad.', *International workshop paper*, Geneva, Palais des Nations – 3–6 May 2000.
174 *Making Health Care Accessible to Street Children: The 'Hospital on Wheels' Project* (2000- 2006), published by SNEHA, 2008, p. 13. Accessible through www.snehamumbai.org/download/hospital_on_wheels_report.pdf.
175 UNICEF, news report, New York, 28 December 2004. Available at: www.unicef.org/emerg/disasterinasia/index_24659.html.
176 Rechel, Boika and Blackburn, Clare, 'Access to health care for Roma children in Central and Eastern Europe: findings from a qualitative study in Bulgaria', *International Journal for Equity in Health*, Volume 8 (Article 24), 2009.
177 Moving frequently is one of the family characteristics identified as a risk factor for child maltreatment: See for example: *KNMG-Meldcode en Stappenplan Artsen en Kindermishandeling*, Utrecht, September 2008, page 36. See also: W. Ghent, 'Family violence: guidelines for recognition and management', *Canadian Medical Association Journal* 1985, 1 March, Volume 132, pp. 541–553. See also: F. Buffing, & R. v.d. Zanden, 'Signalen en signaleren van kindermishandeling', in: H. Baartman, H. & A. Montfoort (Red.), *Kindermishandeling. Resultaten van multidisciplinair onderzoek*, Utrecht: Bruna 1992.

same professionals, such as medical practitioners, thereby prohibiting the opportunity to develop a reliable and coherent analysis of the health status of children and the health situation they are living in.[178] Examples have even been noted of families moving to other countries to avoid confronting youth protection measures in their country of origin.[179] Continuity in health care is important to enhance the development of a stronger knowledge base and even to prevent future hospitalizations.[180]

Practical obstacles for different groups of vulnerable children to have access to primary health care facilities may range from inappropriate resource allocation to organizational and sociocultural circumstances,[181] resulting in discrimination of certain groups of children from having access to primary health care facilities.

1.7.3. EMPOWERMENT

In the Convention on the Rights of the Child, two visions of the child are discerned; children as vulnerable creatures in need of protection and children as autonomous, self-reliant persons. The concept of the 'evolving capacities of the child' as laid down in article 5 CRC is the line along which the focus shifts from protection to participation. Whereas age does influence a child's evolving capacities, other criteria such as experience, level of comprehension and the availability of health information all contribute to the determination of the evolving capacities of the individual child. Furthermore, although children aged 0–12 are to a large extent dependent on adults for the realization of their right to health, they do have innate capabilities that can be realized in the course of their future lives. Health choices made by the parents during pregnancy and after the birth of the child, directly influence the future health choices of children and their opportunities to realize the highest attainable standard of health. Taking children's capabilities as a starting point, this research investigates how the right to the highest attainable standard of health of the child can be realized and what the role is of the different actors involved in the realization process.

The shift of the child as a vulnerable individual in need of protection to a self-reliant individual that can take increasing responsibility for its own health evokes the question what minimum requirements must be met to enable children to realize their right to health. What elements fall under the responsibility of the State, the parents, the child and other actors and what level of flexibility is

---

178 Ibididem supra note 177.

179 A Dutch Documentary of 'Netwerk' revealed that Dutch families flee to Belgium to avoid a confrontation with youth care.

180 L.J. Weiss & J. Bluestein, 'Faithful patients: the effect of long-term physician-patient relationships on the costs and use of health care by older Americans', *American Journal of Public Health* 1996, Issue 86, pp. 1742–1747.

181 A. Eide & W.B. Eide, *A Commentary on the UN CRC Article 24: The right to health*, Leiden: Martinus Nijhoff Publishers 2006, p. 19.

required to leave room for the specific requirements and characteristics of the individual child.

1.8. OUTLINE OF THE PHD STUDY

In this introductory chapter of the study, the problem statement, research questions and key concepts in the study have been elucidated. In the following part, I will analyse, what opportunities, lacunae, contradictions and overlaps exist between the different bodies of law that have reference to the right to the highest attainable standard of health of the child. Hereto, chapter 2 and 3 will concomitantly present the analysis of the interpretation of the right to the highest attainable standard of health of the child in the international children's rights domain. Chapter 2 will address the sub question 'What priorities in the interpretation of the right to the highest attainable standard of health of the child can be derived from the international children's rights domain (CRC)?' Chapter 3 will focus on the question 'How are the priorities deriving from the international children's rights domain with respect to the interpretation of the highest attainable standard of health of the child explained in the Concluding Observations of the CRC Committee on Country Reports for countries with different levels of development?'. Focus will be placed on the right of the child to have access to health as a way to achieve the highest attainable standard of health in a selection of the Concluding Observations of the CRC Committee on individual Country Reports. Chapter 4 will answer the questions 'What priorities in the interpretation of the right to the highest attainable standard of health of the child can be derived from international health and human rights law (WHO, ICESCR, UDHR)?' and 'What is the additional value of this body of law for the interpretation of the right to the highest attainable standard of health in the children's rights domain?' Hereto, the analysis of the Constitution of the World Health Organization, the International Covenant on Economic Social and Cultural Rights and General Comment 14 of the Committee on Economic, Social and Cultural Rights will be presented and compared to the highest attainable standard of health of the child in the international children's rights domain. Chapter 5 will answer the question 'What priorities in the interpretation of the right to the highest attainable standard of health of the child are found in human rights law in Europe?'. Chapter 6 will analyse who are the responsible actors for realizing the identified priorities of children's right to the highest attainable standard of health and how the process of realization influences the interpretation of the right to the highest attainable standard of health. In this part, the legal value of the right to health of children as a social human right is investigated. The question is answered 'How does the process of realization influence the interpretation of the highest attainable standard of health of the child and which actors are responsible in this process?

Finally, the central question will be answered in the concluding chapter 7 'What elements does the right to the highest attainable standard of health entail and how should this concept be further implemented in light of the international human rights standards?'

II. THE RIGHT TO HEALTH OF THE CHILD IN THE CHILDREN'S RIGHTS CONVENTION

2.1. INTRODUCTION

This chapter of the thesis seeks to investigate what priorities are set in relation to the right to the highest attainable standard of health of the child in the interpretation found in the international children's rights domain; the Convention on the Rights of the Child and the General Comments of the Committee on the Rights of the Child. Identified will be what the core elements of article 24 CRC are. The underlying presumption is that children have capabilities that can be best achieved when children are stimulated to engage in healthy behaviour from the very beginning. In looking at this question from the perspective of the international children's rights domain, investigated will be how the differential roles and legal responsibilities of parents, the State and medical professionals are balanced in realizing the core elements of children's right to the highest attainable standard of health. In that way the question will be answered how article 24 CRC can contribute to realizing the highest attainable standard of health of the child.

To answer the research questions, a historical overview of the development of the right to the highest attainable standard health in the CRC will be provided in paragraph 2, reflecting the initial priority setting of the right to the highest attainable standard of health of children during the drafting phase. Consequently paragraph 3 will present the key elements of article 24 CRC, paragraph 4 will discuss the relevance of other CRC articles for the right to health of children and paragraph 5 will describe the elaboration of the right to health of the child in the General Comments of the Committee on the Rights of the Child. The roles and responsibilities of the parents (or caretakers) and the State will be addressed throughout these paragraphs. Paragraph 6 will specifically focus on the translation of the core elements of article 24 CRC to medical ethics to elucidate the potential influence of the right to health of the child on the actual realisation of the right to the highest attainable standard of health of the child in the daily medical practice.

2.2. HISTORICAL DEVELOPMENT OF THE RIGHT TO HEALTH OF THE CHILD IN THE CRC

For centuries, little attention was paid to the rights of children as individual persons. Children were seen as little adults, their rights and needs being subordinate to the needs and values of their families. Not until the 18th century was particular attention paid to the special needs of children in the development of human rights treaties and only from the beginning of the 20th century several western countries did adopt legislation for the protection of children.[182]

In 1924, instigated by a sense of urgency after the First World War, the League of Nations adopted the Declaration of Geneva, wherein children's rights were described at an international level for the first time. The large numbers of children suffering from the Second World War gave a second impulse to this development, which was reflected by the passing of the Declaration on the Rights of the Child[183] in the General Assembly of the United Nations on 20 November 1959. Inspired by the International Year of the Child in 1979 the discussion was raised whether this Declaration should be transposed into a binding treaty.[184] The Convention on the Rights of the Child was consequently drafted between 1978 and 1989 and entered into force on the 2nd of September 1990.[185] The initiative to adopt a Convention on the Rights of the Child was taken by Poland at the thirty-fourth session of the UN Commission on Human Rights, in early 1978. All countries of the world have signed the CRC, but which has not yet been ratified yet by Somalia, the United States and South-Sudan, although the last one is in the process of ratification.

The child's right to health as such, first appeared in the 1959 Declaration, formulated as:

> 'The child shall enjoy the benefits of social security. He shall be entitled to grow and develop in health; to this end, special care and protection shall be provided both to him and to his mother, including adequate prenatal and postnatal care. The child shall have the right to adequate nutrition, housing, recreation and medical services.'

Provisions in international human rights law instruments, predominantly the WHO Constitution, article 25 of the Universal Declaration of Human Rights (UDHR), article 12 of the International Covenant on Economic Social and

182 J. Dane et al., *Honderd Jaar Kinderbescherming (Hundred Years of Child Protection in the Netherlands)*, Edition on the occasion of the 100th Anniversary of the Council of Child Protection and Child laws. (1905–2005), First edition 2006, p. 7.

183 UN Doc. A/RES/44/25, 20 November 1989.

184 S. Meuwese, *Handboek Internationaal Jeugdrecht*, Nijmegen: Ars Aequi Libri, 2005, p. 1–3.

185 UN Doc. E/CN.4/L.1366/Rev.1. This was 30 days after the 20th ratification of the CRC (see article 49-1 CRC).

Cultural Rights (ICESCR) and article 10 of the Protocol of San Salvador,[186] all contain specific references to the right of the (infant) child and her/his mother to health care. These general provisions have shaped the content of the right to health of the child in the CRC. The *Travaux Préparatoires* of the CRC show that article 12 ICESCR and the holistic vision on health as found in the 1978 Declaration of Alma-Ata have been especially influential.[187, 188] This holistic vision is reflected in the broad interpretation including both health services and underlying determinants of health.

The inclusion of the right of the child to health in the CRC was first discussed in the 1980 meeting of the Open-Ended Working Group.[189] The basic working text recognized 'the highest attainable standard of health care of the child for his physical, mental and moral development', as laid down in article 12 ICESCR. Recommendations derived from the Declaration of Alma-Ata (1978),[190] such as the holistic vision on primary health care, have also influenced the development of the provision on the right to the highest attainable standard of health of the child in the CRC. This resulted in a focus in the discussions on the accessibility of health systems for all children, pre- and postnatal care and the lowering of the mortality index of babies. Proposals in the Working Groups in the following years included the prevention of the use of drugs by children,[191] the development of preventive health care programmes for children[192] and the support of action programmes for the benefit of international cooperation.[193]

During the 1985 meeting of the Open-Ended Working Group, proposals on the interpretation of the right to health were submitted by Poland and Finland.[194] Discussion arose to replace the phrase 'the state parties recognize' by the term 'shall ensure' in article 24 sub 1 CRC to enhance the actual enforcement of the right to health, but it was decided to stay in line with article 12 ICESCR. Several issues were central in the debate, among which the introduction of the words 'free of charge' to the provision of medical assistance and health care by the

186 Additional Protocol to the American Convention on Human Rights in the Area of Economic, Social and Cultural Rights, OAS. Treaty Series, November 17, 1988.

187 See *Legislative History of the Convention on the Rights of the Child*, Volume II, United Nations, New York and Geneva, 2007, pp. 580–603.

188 See also S. Detrick (ed.), *The United Nations Convention on the Rights of the Child. A Guide to the 'Travaux Préparatoires*, Dordrecht/Boston/London, Martinus Nijhoff Publishers 1992, pp. 343–359.

189 *Legislative History of the Convention on the rights of the Child*, Volume II, United Nations, New York and Geneva, 2007, pp. 580–603. See particularly U.N. Doc. E/CN.4/1349, pp. 4–5.

190 The 1978 Declaration of Alma Ata was adopted during the UNICEF and WHO sponsored International Conference on Primary Health Care, Alma-Ata, USSR, 6–12 September 1978. The UN General Assembly endorsed the Declaration by resolution 34/43 of 19 November 1979.

191 Ibidem supra note 187. See particularly U.N. Doc. E/1982/12Add.1, C.

192 Ibidem supra note 187. See particularly U.N. Doc. E/CN.4/1983/62, Annex II. This proposal was submitted by Canada and has been partly incorporated in the final text of article 24 CRC.

193 Ibidem supra note 187. See particularly U.N. Doc. E/CN.4/1984/71, Annex II, p. 1. This proposal was submitted by Iran, but it was not considered.

194 Ibidem supra note 187. See particularly U.N. Doc. E/CN.4/1985/64, pp. 3–8.

Soviet Union. The USA suggested that the term 'whenever possible' should be added, but Bangladesh and Senegal stated that this would lead to a situation of uncertainty. The issue reflected the notion that no child should be deprived of access to health care for financial reasons. In the final draft of the CRC this last phrase 'for financial reasons' has been omitted, suggesting that no reason justifies any deprivation of health care of children.

Also discussed in the 1985 meeting of the Open-Ended Working Group was the topic of the provision of Primary Health Care, objected by the Netherlands, but defended by Senegal, claiming that it was necessary to take into account the special needs of developing countries. The final text of article 24-2-b CRC now reads: 'to ensure the provision of necessary medical assistance and health care to all children with emphasis on the development of primary health care.' Later topics discussed were the encouragement of infant feeding and breastfeeding[195] and the prevention of accidents.[196] The NGO Group proposed to include articles on the recognition of economic problems in realizing the right to the highest attainable standard of health of the child and to safeguard notions on breastfeeding and child health care deriving from Islamic law. An example of a provision on children's right to health in Islamic law is the right for children to be breastfed during their first two years.[197]

In the 1986 and 1987 meetings of the Open-Ended Working Group, the issue of 'traditional harmful practices' was central to the discussion.[198] The UK and the USA proposed to specifically refer to female genital mutilation (FGM), whereas Senegal emphasized the need for prudence in dealing with cultural values and the risk of forcing the practice of FGM into clandestinity. The decisive argument made by the representative of the International Movement for Fraternal Union Among Races and Peoples, held that no specific reference should be made to FGM, as other traditional practices, including preferential care for boys, can also be harmful to children.[199]

---

195 Ibidem supra note 187. The delegation of the USA included the subparagraph 'including information about appropriate methods of infant feeding', to which the NGO Ad Hoc Group on Drafting the Convention added the phrase 'to actively promote and protect breastfeeding', pp. 3–8.

196 Ibidem supra note 187. The representative of the UK proposed to replace the word 'safety' by the phrase 'prevention of accidents', pp. 3–8.

197 Rule of Islamic law as found in verse of Qur'an II: 233. This information was discussed in a lecture on children's rights in Islamic Law at the University of Leiden on the 18th of September 2009. See for more information about children's rights and the Islam 'Covenant on the Rights of the Child in the Islam' of the Organisation of the Islamic Conference. Doc. OIC/9-IGGE/HRI/2004/Rep.Final. www.oicun.org/uploads/files/convenion/Rights%20of%20the%20Child%20In%20Islam%20E.pdf.

198 Ibidem supra note 187. The proposal was made by the NGO Ad Hoc Group on Drafting the Convention, reading 'The States Parties to the present Convention shall seek to eradicate traditional practices harmful to the health of children and shall take all appropriate action including necessary legislative, administrative, social and educational measures to ensure that children are not subjected to such practices. U.N. Doc. E/CN.4/1987/25, pp. 8–10.

199 Ibidem supra note 187, pp. 8–10.

On the initiative of India, the 1988 meeting of the Open-Ended Working Group focused on low-cost measures and readily available technologies, such as oral rehydration and immunization against common childhood diseases.[200] Thereupon, paragraph 2(e) was enriched with the elements 'nutrition, including breastfeeding, hygiene and environmental sanitation', though it was acknowledged that these elements of the right to health were already guaranteed in other human rights instruments.

Before the adoption of the final draft of article 24 CRC by the 1989 meeting of the Open-Ended Working Group, several additional topics were touched upon.[201] Australia suggested adopting the notion that treatment of children of an experimental nature should be guided by ethical guidelines and rules. Portugal and subsequent speakers emphasized that medical or scientific experimentation should be necessary for the individual child undergoing it and not only for children as a general group. The Soviet Union added that the consent of both the child and his parents (or legal guardians) must be sought when seeking consent for medical experimentation. Canada differentiated this by suggesting that the consent of the child should only be sought where appropriate. Examples were given that consent may not be possible in case of emergencies or in instances where the consent of parents cannot be asked for religious or privacy reasons. Finally, it was decided not to include a provision on medical experimentation for fear of abusive interpretations.[202] The Australian delegation concluded that other articles of the Convention protect children against medical experimentation that is not in the best interests of the (individual) child, such as article 19 CRC on the right of the child to protection and article 33 on the right of the child to protection against drugs.

2.3. KEY ELEMENTS OF THE RIGHT TO HEALTH OF THE CHILD IN THE CRC

2.3.1. SUBSTANCE OF ARTICLE 24 CRC

The final text of the right of the child to health is laid down in article 24 CRC. The article both encompasses the legal entitlement to services for the prevention and treatment of disease and to basic conditions necessary to ensure a minimum level of survival. The basic provisions explicitly mentioned in article 24 CRC include the entitlement of all children to nutritious food and safe drinking water (sub 2-c) hygiene and sanitary facilities (sub 2-e) and take into account the

200 Ibidem supra note 187. A proposal for revision of article 12 bis was made by India, U.N. Doc. E/CN.4/1988/WG.1/WP.14.

201 Ibidem supra note 187, more particularly U.N. Doc. E/CN.4/1989/48, pp. 70–74.

202 B.C.A. Toebes, *The Right to Health as a Human Right in International Law*, Intersentia 1999, p. 58.

risks of environmental pollution (sub 2-c). With a focus on health care, several priorities are set, namely the reduction of infant and child mortality (sub 2-a), the provision of necessary medical assistance, preferably primary health care for all children (sub 2-b), pre- and postnatal health care for mothers and their babies (sub 2-d). To enable children and their families to take responsibility over their own health the right to health education for both children and adults on basic knowledge of child health and nutrition, the advantages of breastfeeding, hygiene, environmental sanitation (sub 2-e), preventive health care, family planning (sub 2-f) are incorporated. The international orientation of article 24 becomes eminent in the general provision on the abolishing of harmful traditional practices (sub 3) and also in sub 4, which specifically encourages State Parties to engage in international cooperation. Hereto, particular attention must be paid to the special needs of developing countries (sub 4).

Altogether, these provisions constitute the broadest provision on the right to health in international human rights law.[203] Several other articles in international law instruments do contain more elaborate elements on particular topics, such as the requirements for ensuring the right to health in the work environment,[204] the (sexual and reproductive) health rights of women[205] and the health rights of disabled persons[206] and these issues can be directly relevant for children. For example, the sexual and reproductive health rights of young women have a direct impact on children's survival, because it influences both the age at which women have their first baby, the spacing between subsequent births and the education received by the mother to take good care of her children. Nevertheless, the right to the highest attainable standard of health as formulated in the CRC still covers the widest range of prioritized health topics. Namely, supplementary to the health provisions in other international health and human rights treaties, the CRC incorporates provisions for the elimination of traditional harmful practices, the development of primary health care and the provision of rehabilitation services.[207] However, the phrase 'physical and mental health' as found in article 12 ICESCR, is not included in article 24 CRC. Other elements not included in article 24 CRC are the improvement of hygiene in the working environment and the prevention and treatment of infectious diseases and occupational diseases.[208]

---

203 S. Detrick, *A Commentary on the United Nations Convention on the Rights of the child*, The Hague: Kluwer Law International and Martinus Nijhoff Publishers 1999, p. 399.

204 Article 12 International Covenant on Economic, Social and Cultural Rights, entry into force 3 January 1976.

205 Article 12 Convention on the Elimination of Discrimination against Women, entry into force 3 September 1981.

206 Convention on the Rights or Persons with Disabilities, entry into force on 3 May 2008.

207 Ibidem supra note 185.

208 L. Ling, *Internationale regelgeving over de rechten van het kind, het VN-kinderrechtenverdrag vergeleken met andere mensenrechten documenten*, Amsterdam: Defence for Children International Afdeling Nederland 1993, p. 109.

Several elements of article 24 CRC leave room for further interpretation. First of all, sub 2a and 2d are strongly connected; in order to diminish infant and child mortality (2a), appropriate pre- and postnatal health care for mothers is essential (sub 2d). The health of the (unborn) child is to a large extent dependent on the health of the pregnant woman and the quality of her food when lactating.[209] Whereas sub 2a focuses on the mere survival of infants and children, sub 2d extends this obligation to ensuring access to all health care required, thus not only for the survival but also for the general health of the unborn and the new-born child. The provision in sub 2a, on the other hand, also aims to ensure the survival of children and not only infants and unborn babies. Both elements thus emphasize different aspects of children's right to health.

Article 24 sub 2e and 2f both focus on the prevention of health problems; sub 2e mentions the education and involvement of the society as a whole, in particular parents and children in ensuring children's health, whereas sub 2f focuses on the preventive health care in general and family oriented measures and education for the prevention of health problems. Ideally in my opinion, a more transparent distinction between the two articles would have been recommendable, for example by distinguishing between society oriented and family oriented measures. The target groups and types of prevention now offer a blurred distinction. However, the close and explicated link between the health of mothers and their children in sub 2d and the explicit mentioning of the need to educate adults on children's health in subs 2e and 2f points to the central role of parents in ensuring their children's right to health. Also, the application of the term parents gives room for broadening the link between children and maternal health to also including the involvement of fathers in the healthy upbringing of their children. This notion of shared responsibility of both parents for the healthy upbringing of their children is also found in article 5 CEDAW, which specifically stipulates that 'family education must include a proper understanding of maternity as a social function and the recognition of the common responsibility of men and women in the upbringing and development of their children, it being understood that the interest of the children is the primordial consideration in all cases'.

States recognize the right of the child to the enjoyment of 'the highest attainable standard of health' and 'States Parties shall strive to ensure that no child is deprived of his or her right of access to such health care services.' Both the term 'recognize' and the inclusion of the term 'to strive to' in sub 1 impose relatively weak legal obligations. However, sub 2 mentions that State Parties 'shall pursue full implementation' of children's right to health and that they 'shall take appropriate measures', being specified in the following subparagraphs. This second part allows for a stronger entitlement to the children's right to the highest

[209] See also the Barker-hypothesis, which postulates that several common adult diseases may be related to impaired foetal growth or disrupted genes, caused by nutritional inadequacies or other environmental influences at particular stages of pregnancy. D.J. Barker, 'Fetal Origins of Coronary Heart Disease', *British Medical Journal* 1995, 311, pp. 171–174.

attainable standard of health under the CRC and thus also to more serious efforts by the State to be in compliance.[210] Karsten qualifies this obligation of States as proactive and prescriptive.[211]

However detailed article 24 CRC may be, the provisions remain broad enough to be applied world-wide and thus remain to be interpreted through a variety of contexts and conditions, changeable over time. Historically, the right to health has been differentiated by region, in time, by type, by age-group (e.g. infants over adolescents) and by technical or organizational level (such as primary health care over high-tech curative health care).[212] Choices made in favour of one group, excluded others, raising legal, ethical and practical questions. Van Bueren[213] and Kasper[214] commented that article 24 CRC provides a framework for setting priorities in creating equitable health-policies.

Interpretation must be sought in other sources, such as the General Comments on the Committee on the Rights of the Child and its Concluding Observations on individual Country Reports.[215] The practice of the CESCR Committee on article 12 ICESCR and its General Comments is also considered as useful interpretation material on the basis of article 41 CRC, which stipulates that 'nothing in the CRC shall affect other provisions in international law that are more conducive to the realization of the rights of the child.[216] Further attention must be paid to the implications of the different concepts of health across different countries and cultures: locally accepted, community-based priorities on ensuring the right to the highest attainable standard of health of the child may be in conflict with the generally accepted priorities as set in the CRC.

More research on this interaction between the general CRC provisions and interpretations in local contexts is required, using both medical-anthropological insights and a more in-depth study of the CRC Country Reports. In order to obtain a better insight into the interaction between the general CRC provision on the right to health of the child and the interpretations, I will present the results

---

210 S.C. Bischoff, *The UN Convention on the Rights of the Child. A Comparative Study*, 2 March 1999, p. 197.

211 J. Kasper 'The Relevance of U.S. Ratification of the Convention on the Rights of the Child for Child Health: A Matter of Equity and Social Justice', *Child Welfare* 2010, No. 89, Volume 5, p. 30.

212 C. Sepulveda, 'The right to child health: the development of primary health services in Chile and Thailand', *UNICEF Innocenti Research Centre Occasional Paper Number 7*, April 1994 pp. 1–8.

213 G. van Bueren, *The international law on the rights of the child*. Dordrecht: Martinus Nijhoff Publishers/Save the Children 1995a, p. 300.

214 J. Kasper 'The Relevance of U.S. Ratification of the Convention on the Rights of the Child for Child Health: A Matter of Equity and Social Justice', *Child Welfare* 2010, No. 89, Volume 5, p. 32.

215 A. Eide & W.B. Eide, 'Article 24, The Right to Health', in: A. Alen, J. Van de Lanotte, E. Verhellen, F. Ang, E. Berghmans & M. Verheyde (eds), *A Commentary on the United Nations Convention on the Rights of the Child*, Leiden & Boston: Martinus Nijhoff Publishers 2006, p. 1.

216 Ibidem supra note 215.

of an in-depth study of the Concluding Observations of the Committee on the Rights of the Child on the CRC country reports in the next chapter.

2.3.2. PROVISIONS ON IMPLEMENTATION OF ARTICLE 24 CRC

Article 24 CRC obligates States Parties to 'progressively' (sub 4) achieve the 'highest attainable standard of health' (sub 1). Hereto, States have to take all appropriate measures 'to the maximum extent of their available resources.' These phrases imply a rather vague and flexible standard for assessing degrees of compliance, as the highest attainable standard of health varies among states and periods of time.[217] The notion of flexibility is also found in article 4 CRC, which says that 'States Parties shall undertake measures for the implementation of the economic, social and cultural rights in the CRC to the maximum extent of their available resources and, where necessary, within the framework of international cooperation'. Regarding the provision of 'available resources', attention has been drawn to warn that the phrase could be used as an excuse for less-than-adequate performance.[218] Given the differing basic health conditions in different countries, 'the highest attainable standard of health' implies a different starting point for 'achieving the right to health for different countries'; attainability will differ according to financial resources and situational challenges of a country. For example, after the 2005 tsunami in Southeast Asia, Indonesia could not be expected to meet the same infant mortality rate as the Netherlands or even neighbouring countries that had not been affected in that same year, as it had to deal with high casualties and limited resources.[219]

It has been commented that article 24 CRC is especially geared to the health requirements of developing countries, being focused on prevention and basic health requirements.[220] This seems to be true as most developed countries have high percentages of immunization coverage and special methods in place to ensure access to health care for poor families.[221] For example, the immunization coverage in the Netherlands for 2009 was at least 96% for the major childhood

217 V.A. Leary, 'The right to health in international human rights law', *Health and Human Rights* 1994, 1 (1), p. 33, stating that 'The phrase implies a reasonable, not an absolute standard.'

218 Ibidem supra note 212, p. 1.

219 Chapter 4 will elaborate on the basic principles of non-retrogression and progressive realization in international health law. When applied to the CRC body of law, this could lead to the obligation to demonstrate that all possible efforts to minimize the total number of casualties have been made, for example by allowing foreign NGOs to enter the country and to take all necessary measures to prevent further casualties due to an outbreak of infectious diseases, violence or malnutrition.

220 Ibidem supra note 213, p. 197.

221 Immunization summary, A statistical reference containing data through 2009 (The 2011 Edition), UNICEF and WHO, pp. xii–xvii.

diseases.[222] However, the available resources of a country do not fully explain the status of children's right to health in a country. Budget allocation to specific child health policy domains has an enormous effect on children's health indicators, so that countries with a relatively low GDP may perform better on child health indicators than countries with a higher GDP, if they allocated larger percentages to health care for children.[223] It appeared that there are great differences in per capita expenditure on health as a percentage of the total government expenditure, so that great differences are discerned between countries with similar levels of GDP in both infant and child mortality rates and immunization numbers.[224]

The phrase 'maximum available resources' in article 4 CRC also implies that progress must be made in realizing children's right to health when additional resources become available.[225] It has been acknowledged that resource allocation in itself can be discriminatory, for example when no budget is allocated to healthcare that meets the particular needs of the Roma populations in Europe or the indigenous populations in the Americas, practically excluding them from access to health care.[226] This is also reflected by the fact that health indicators can vary widely between different groups of children within a country and between countries with similar levels of GDP.

The questions thus arises how to determine what the highest attainable standard of health in a particular country should be and over what period of time the progress made should be measured, so that States can be held accountable for the progress they have made in achieving a better health status for children. One approach to measure the degree of compliance of countries as often used by UNICEF is to compare the performance on the realization of the right to the highest attainable standard of health of a child of a country (e.g. by assessing

---

222 Ibidem supra note 221, p. 123.

223 Cuba is the famous example of a country with a low level of human development and very good health indicators, even comparable to those of developed countries. Many econometric studies have shown that, if used efficiently, health expenditures can have significant effects on immunization coverage and child mortality. For example, the African Development Bank's Study of 47 African countries showed that a 10 percent increase in per capita public health expenditure results in a reduction of 21–25% in under-five and infant mortality rates. Other factors included efficiency and resource utilization, institutional capacity of implementing agencies, the extent of resource leakage and skills and attitudes of workers. See for example Anyanwu & Erhijakpor, *Health Expenditures and Health Outcomes in Africa*, Economic Research Working Paper Series, African Development Bank, Tunis, 2007. See also: E. Anderson & Hague, *The impact of investing in children: Assessing the cross-country econometric evidence*, Working Paper 280, Overseas Development Institute, London, 2007. This information is reproduced from the 'The African Report on Child Wellbeing 2011: Budgeting for Children', inferior note 54, p. 65.

224 Report prepared by an expert team of the African Child Policy Forum *The African Report on child Wellbeing 2011: Budgeting for Children*, Intersentia, 2010, Addis Abeba, pp. 64–65. For example in 2008, Rwanda spent 20.4%, Burundi 18.1% and Madagascar 17.3% of government revenue on health in comparison to 2.7% by Libya, 3.0% by Congo Brazzaville and 4.2% by Equatorial Guinea.

225 Ibidem supra note 212, p. 15.

226 Ibidem supra note 212, p. 12.

the under-five-mortality rate or the percentage of children under five years who are underweight) with countries with similar levels of per capita income.[227] This approach has been considered practicable for its simplicity, but it may also suffer from weak statistics of countries.[228] In order to measure progress over time, it would be necessary to compare the outcome of this method between subsequent years.[229] A complementary approach is to gain knowledge from historical and analytical analyses of particular country experiences over time.[230] Given the increasing documentation on the status of children's rights in the *Concluding Observations* of the Committee on the Country Reports of individual Member States to the CRC, this can be used as a starting point for such an approach. Such an analysis will be presented in chapter 3.

2.4. THE RIGHT TO HEALTH AND ITS RELATION TO OTHER CRC ARTICLES

The Committee on the Rights of the Child has reaffirmed repeatedly that the CRC is to be applied holistically, taking into account the principles of universality, indivisibility and interdependence of all human rights.[231] Four of the CRC's articles are explicitly recognized as the umbrella articles of the CRC, namely the right to non-discrimination (art. 2 CRC), the duty to promote the best interests of the child as a primary consideration in all actions affecting children (art. 3 CRC), the right to survival and development (art. 6 CRC) and the right to be listened to and taken seriously (art. 12 CRC). In addition to the four key principles in the CRC, the Committee on the Rights of the Child has acknowledged that the articles 6.2 (life and survival), 23 (disabled children), 24 (health and health services), 18.3 (role of parents), 26 (social security) and 27 (standard of living) CRC are all essential to ensuring children's right to health.

2.4.1. ARTICLE 2: THE RIGHT TO NON-DISCRIMINATION

The principle of non-discrimination in article 2 CRC is key to ensuring access to health care for children. Discrimination can be defined as 'any distinction, exclusion or restriction made on the basis of various grounds having the effect or purpose of impairing or nullifying the recognition, enjoyment or exercise

227 See the annual series of UNICEF reports entitled 'The Progress of Nations'.
228 Ibidem supra note 212, p. 2.
229 Ibidem supra note 212, p. 2.
230 Ibidem supra note 212, p. 2.
231 See for example General Comment No.7, page 2. U.N. Doc. CRC/C/GC/7/Rev.1 20 September 2006.

of human rights and fundamental freedoms'.[232] Article 2 of the Convention of the Rights of the Child stipulates that children's right to health must be ensured without distinction on the basis of race, colour, sex, language, religion, political conviction, national, ethnic or societal origin, level of wealth, handicap, birth and neither if based on the beliefs, opinions, residence permit or activities of the parents of the child. This is especially important for (new-born) infants, who are fully dependent on their mothers care. Other grounds of discrimination include health status or sexual orientation.[233] Special caution must be taken for preventing discrimination on the basis of two grounds at the same time, for example minor girls, minority children or children with an HIV/AIDS infection. Or refugee girls, disabled refugee children and more.

Groups of people that are traditionally marginalized, often bear a disproportionate share of health problems. Several forms of discrimination hinder the effective access of children to health facilities. Kasper has identified that article 2 on non-discrimination is leading in ensuring children's health.[234] She elaborates that the principle of non-discrimination means that States need to actively protect children against discrimination and that they have to refrain from policies with a discriminative effect.[235] The prohibition of discrimination thus means that States must make proactive efforts to treat (vulnerable) children and adolescents in a non-discriminatory manner. This may entail taking affirmative action to ensure equal access to health care for specific vulnerable groups, such as girls, migrant children, disabled children etc.[236] An elaboration of the measures propagated by the CRC Committee to realize the right to the highest attainable standard of health for several particular vulnerable groups is found in paragraph 5.

Discrimination, or differential treatment occurs 'de iure', when legislation inhibits children to have access to health care or 'de facto', when legislation ensures access, but when individual agents practice discrimination on their own initiative or under the social pressure of colleagues or supervisors or by unawareness of the rules among receptionists, for example in face-to-face contacts for admittance in a hospital.[237]

The provision on non-discrimination of children contains three key elements that must be met in order to establish a violation of the principle of non-

232 WHO Factsheet No. 31 on the Right to Health, prepared by the Office of the United Nations High Commissioner for Human Rights, p. 7.

233 See also the elaboration on discrimination of children infected with HIV/AIDS in General Comment 3 to the CRC. U.N. Doc. CRC/GC/2003/3, General Comment 3 on HIV/AIDS and the rights of the child, 17 March 2003.

234 Ibidem supra note 213, p. 27.

235 Ibidem supra note 213, p. 28.

236 WHO Factsheet No. 31 on the Right to Health, prepared by the Office of the United Nations High Commissioner for Human Rights, p. 14 and 15.

237 B. Abramson, 'Article 2 the right of non-discrimination', in the Series: *A Commentary on the United Nations Convention on the Rights of the Child*, Leiden/Boston: Martinus Nijhoff Publishers 2008, pp. 33 and 51.

discrimination: 1) a differential treatment on a *forbidden ground*, 2) which causes a *violation/injury*, 3) in protecting a *certain interest*.[238]

2.4.1.1. Forbidden ground for discrimination

The first element of the right to non-discrimination contains the phrase 'forbidden ground'. This phrase is integrated in the definition of non-discrimination as there is a distinction between justified and non-justified grounds for making distinctions between different people. Many (medical) situations occur in which differential treatments are justified, for example, a child with a broken leg requires a different treatment than a child needing a tonsil section or a child with leukaemia. The principle of non-discrimination is violated when distinction is made on any of the non-exhaustive forbidden grounds, such as age, race, gender, religion or political conviction, resulting in the unequal treatment between equal cases. Different medical conditions may thus justify different treatments. However, when two girls of different ethnic origin suffer from the same kind of lung infection, they are entitled to the same level and methods of health care on the basis of their right to non-discrimination.[239]

However, in providing for differential treatments, caution must be taken that the provision of adjusted health care does not become a source of discrimination in itself. For example, General Comment 9 provides that in order to ensure maximum inclusion of disabled children in society, the necessary medical services must be integrated into the regular public health system for all children to reduce the risk of discrimination.[240]

Also for other groups of vulnerable children, States are required to make proactive efforts to ensure that all children receive health care and that this does not constitute an (unintended) cause for discrimination of the specified groups. General Comment 6 contains a separate paragraph to ensure that unaccompanied and separated children outside their country of origin have the same level of access to health facilities as nationals do.[241] In order to realize this States must take into account the specific vulnerabilities of these children, such as separation from their families, the experience of (gender-based) violence, war, loss and trauma. These children may have lost their trust in others, in particular government authorities after experiencing torture or threats[242] in their country of origin or during their flight and they need special sensitivity and attention in their care and rehabilitation.[243] They are entitled to health care

238 Ibidem supra note 237, pp. 18–30.

239 E.g. A.W. Musschenga & E. Borst-Eilers, 'Prioriteiten in de gezondheidszorg. Rechtvaardig verdelen, maar hoe?', *Medisch Contact* 1987, no. 1, pp. 13–19.

240 U.N. Doc. CRC/C/GC/9, GC 9: The rights of children with disabilities, 27 February 2007, § 52.

241 U.N. Doc. CRC/GC/2005/5, General Comment 6 on the treatment of unaccompanied and separated children outside their country of origin, § 46–49.

242 Ibidem supra note 173.

243 Ibidem supra note 240, § 47.

in the immediate period after resettlement.[244] For indigenous groups of children, the CRC Committee has acknowledged in General Comment 11 that indigenous children in both developing and in developed countries often suffer poorer health than non-indigenous children due to inferior or inaccessible health services.[245] By remaining without birth registration, they have a higher risk of remaining invisible to health professionals,[246] there are disproportionately higher numbers of infant and child mortality rates, diseases, extreme poverty and malnutrition among indigenous children.[247] Furthermore, indigenous communities often live in areas targeted for their natural resources or areas that because of remoteness serve as a base for non-state armed groups or disputes with foreign States in the vicinity of borders.[248] These circumstances lead to significantly worse health indicators. Measures propagated by the CRC Committee to meet the health needs of these children are further specified in paragraph 5.

2.4.1.2. Violation of the right to health

The second element of the right to non-discrimination says that there must be a violation of the substantive right (in casu the right to the highest attainable standard of health), which means that the right to non-discrimination does not refer to positive instances of discrimination such as preferential treatment:[249] one can not make a complaint for receiving exceptionally qualitative care. However, if other patients are excluded from quality care, that practice may amount to a situation of negative discrimination of those who are excluded from the right to the highest attainable standard of health. For example, if some children in a sub-Saharan village receive anti-malaria treatment whereas others do not and thus run the risk of being infected, this may amount to a violation of the right to health of the discriminated children. The question is how this element must be explained in situations of scarcity, when only half of the total number of patients can be given adequate treatment, for example in developing countries with extreme levels of poverty and in cases of sudden emergencies with high numbers of victims. Questions like these on triage have been dealt with from philosophical perspectives, aiming to find decisive principles that can be applied to make just choices.[250] These perspectives include egalitarian (first in, first out), utilitarian (a doctor must be helped first in order to increase the medical capacity so that more

244 Ibidem supra note 173.
245 U.N. Doc. CRC/C/GC/11, General Comment 11: Indigenous children and their rights under the Convention, January 2009, § 49.
246 Ibidem supra note 245, § 41.
247 Ibidem supra note 245, § 34, 50.
248 Ibidem supra note 245, § 64. Therein, referral is made to UNICEF Innocenti Digest No. 11, *Ensuring the Rights of Indigenous Children*, 2004, p. 13.
249 Ibidem supra note 237, p. 23.
250 A. Richters, 'Arts en oorlog: ethische aspecten van triage', in: J. Bierens e.a., *Urgentiegeneeskunde en Triage*, Maarssen: Elsevier Gezondheidszorg 2004, pp. 55–70.

people can be cured in the longer term) or evaluative decision-making schemes (the most serious cases must be treated first).[251] These instances demonstrate the tension that is encountered in realizing social rights such as the right to health between the amount of children in need of health care and the resources available. Priority measures could include the raising of budget allocated to children's health or cost reduction by enacting legislation to set aside patents for very expensive medicines. Secondly, policy decisions need to be taken on prioritizing whether focus is placed on ensuring basic health care access for all children or ensuring more qualitative health care access for a limited number of children. In both instances, the right to health and the right to non-discrimination of children require that additional efforts must be made by States to raise the health standard achieved to a higher level, until all children reach the highest attainable standard of health.

2.4.1.3. Protection of a certain interest

With regard to the third element of discrimination, the protection of a certain interest, the distinction between direct and indirect discrimination is relevant. Direct discrimination is defined as 'treating one person less favorably than another person on the ground of race (sex, etc.)'. An example is when a certain group of inhabitants such as refugee children or indigenous children is legally completely deprived of adequate health care. Indirect discrimination occurs when an 'apparently neutral provision' puts 'members of one group at a disadvantage in comparison to others' that 'can not be justified'.[252] For example, when children are formally entitled to right to the highest attainable standard of health care, they may still be indirectly discriminated when they are not provided with sufficient resources to pay for the medical care. Another example of indirect discrimination with respect to the right to the highest attainable standard of health is when children are not registered at birth. Both types of discrimination are prohibited, as they limit children's enjoyment of the right to the highest attainable standard of health.

The duty of the State to prevent discrimination thus applies to overt discrimination, such as discriminatory legislation directed at the discriminated group itself and to covert discrimination, such as actual practices benefiting one (major) group while being discriminatory to others or when a neutral looking law appears to result in discriminatory practices.[253] In recognizing discriminatory legislation, it is important to realize that a discriminatory law often has a positively formulated objective, such as 'for the benefit of society', 'to maintain

251 See for a discussion on the impact of different principles A.W. Musschenga & E. Borst-Eilers, 'Prioriteiten in de gezondheidszorg. Rechtvaardig verdelen, maar hoe?', *Medisch Contact* 1987, p. 13.

252 Ibidem supra note 220, pp. 33 and 67.

253 Ibidem supra note 220, p. 50.

order' or 'to protect public health', whereas simultaneously the right to non-discrimination may be violated.[254] Webb has made a useful categorisation of the different forms of discrimination of children, being distinguished between direct (or overt)[255] and indirect (or covert) discrimination.[256] Given the strong specific focus on discrimination on children's health issues, the elaboration is particularly relevant for this research. An overview of the different forms of child-specific discrimination with respect to their right to health is provided in table 1.

Table 1. Modes of discrimination of children in health care (based on Webb[257])

Direct discrimination by:	Indirect discrimination:
1. *Exclusion* of children from adult spheres as a natural state of well-being (separateness of the child's world).	1. *Girls/women*: Low pay of single-mothers and poor maternity provisions resulting in inadequate resources for health care for children.
2. *Marginalisation:* as 'constructed otherness'. E.g. underrepresentation of children in funding for research and development, resulting in an inadequate evidence-base for paediatric practice.	2. *Parents:* No or little parental leave for child illness, inadequate or unaffordable childcare services and little attention of dual role of working parents, resulting in stress on care for (ill) children.
3. *Age-blindness*: Ignoring or denying differences in needs for children, for example in waiting areas or hospitals.	3. *Ethnic minorities:* Increased risk of growing up in poverty, having inadequate access to quality and culturally appropriate health care. Illiterate parents.
4. *Deficit model of childhood*: Perceiving children as immature/unfinished and therefore incapable of medical decision-making.	4. *Asylum seekers:* Ibidem number 3 and lack of health insurances, translation on and information on the health system, whereas many are traumatized.
5. *Victim blaming*: Blaming children for injuries or abuses instead of addressing the real underlying structural causes.	5. *Homeless families:* Ibidem number 3 and low compliance with health care treatments and suffering from stigmatization.
6. *Stereotyping*: Perceiving distressed and disadvantaged children as inherently bad, resulting in unbelief of reports of right violations.	6. *Disabled:* Children having difficulties in obtaining adequate access, being marginalized or overseen in public health policy because of their disability.
7. *Internalised discrimination*: Children seeing themselves as inferior, having nothing worth to listen to and thus not actively participating.	7. *Mentally and chronically ill carers:* Unsupported children take up caregiver roles or risk being neglected, abused or stigmatized by their carers.
8. *Exploitation:* Using children against their will for age-inappropriate activities, such as abuse, child labour or political goals.	8. *Poor families:* Risk of stigmatization and poor access to health care (insurances) and underlying determinants for children.

---

254 Ibidem supra note 220, p. 33 and 34.

255 E. Webb, 'An Exploration of the Discrimination-Rights Dynamic in Relation to Children', in: A. Invernizzi & J. Williams (eds), *The Human Rights of Children: From Visions to Implementation*', Ashgate 2011, pp. 287–306. Webb qualifies overt discrimination as 'childism', discrimination against children as children per se.

256 Ibidem supra note 255, pp. 287–306.

257 Ibidem supra note 255, pp. 287–306.

In the second paragraph of article 2, the element of prohibiting discrimination of children on the basis of their parent's characteristics is specific for the prohibition of discrimination in the Convention on the Rights of the Child. This means for example that when parents do not have an official residence permit and consequently do not have a health insurance, this should not impair the possibility of their children to have access to adequate health services. In the *travaux préparatoires* to the Convention on the Rights of the Child the proposal to refuse undocumented children to have access to health care was explicitly rejected.[258] Also, it means that children may never be punished for actions, beliefs or the status of their parents or guardians. This includes for example children who were born out of wedlock, whose parents are incarcerated, members of subversive political parties, social movements, religious sects or illegal organizations (article 2-2a).[259] This prohibition explicitly extends to State practices that try to punish or convince parents by harming their children (article 2-2b).

In order to address the different forms and consequences of discrimination, States may decide to take affirmative actions, special measures to remove barriers for children so that they can enjoy their right to the highest attainable standard of health. Non-discriminatory affirmative action can only be achieved when additional possibilities are created for groups of children, without reducing the opportunities of others.[260] Thus, when additional possibilities are created for refugee children to have access to health care, this may not reduce the possibilities of other (vulnerable) groups of society to have access to health services. Whereas this is a laudable obligation, it is difficult to realize in practice, because in many circumstances, not all children can be reached at the same time. Furthermore, conflicting rights and values can complicate this.[261] For example, when the right to health care and the right to freedom of religion are at odds when Jehovah witnesses do not want their child to receive a blood transfusion, when sex education at schools is opposed by religious parents or when cultural practices lead to discussion on potential harm to the child.[262] Also, discrimination may occur unintended when a certain interest is pursued having consequences for the enjoyment of the right of the child.

The obligation of the State to prevent and eliminate discrimination against children extends to (state) sectors that fall within their authority. It does not include all actions of individuals and other private actors who may discriminate against sick children. For example, when parents forbid their child to play with another child who has an infectious disease or whose parents are very ill, the State

---

258 *Legislative History of the Convention on the Rights of the Child*, Volume II, United Nations, New York and Geneva, 2007, pp. 580–603. See particularly U.N. Doc. E/CN.4/1349, pp. 4–5.

259 Ibidem supra note 237, p. 129.

260 Ibidem supra note 237, pp. 33 and 77.

261 Ibidem supra note 255, pp. 300–301.

262 Usual examples include female genital mutilation, cupping or sending a child to bed without food as a punishment.

is not expected to intervene in this practice, whereas it may constitute an act of discrimination towards the child. When this kind of behaviour is practiced on a large-scale by parents towards all children with a particular disease, the State may be required to establish a public campaign aiming to reduce this widespread practice of discrimination of (sick) children. However, it is difficult to determine where to draw the line between (overt or covert) discriminatory practices in which the State should intervene or where this falls within the responsibility of the private actor. More research is needed to determine when such practices by private actors lead to practices of widespread discrimination requiring a public response.

2.4.2. ARTICLE 3: THE BEST INTERESTS OF THE CHILD

The best interests of the child in article 3 of the CRC provide that the best interests of the child shall be a primary consideration in *all* measures concerning the child.[263] This implies that all children must be approached in the first place as being a child (of a certain age) and only in the second place as migrants, refugees, indigenous or ill children. In that respect, it may be argued that it is central in ensuring all individual children's rights. The downside of this principle is that it can be interpreted so broadly, that even prejudices and harmful traditional practices can be applied under the alibi of a legal instrument.[264] Different cultures also use different concepts of what the best interests of the child are, as becomes rather clear in the discussion of the issue on the circumcision of boys which is propagated by certain religions, whereas it is discouraged by others. The same is true for the performance of abortions in teenage girls. In the Netherlands it is seen by many as being in the best interests of both the baby as of the child mother, whereas under several religions and life considerations it is strongly opposed, notwithstanding social exclusion of children and their mothers who give birth out-of-wedlock. Actually, some of the most difficult cases in taking the best interests of the child into account have been identified in medical decision-making by Freeman.[265] In determining the influence of the best interests of the child in medical decisions, a large margin of appreciation must be assumed, being further divided in short-term and long-term considerations on the best interests of the child, which may be a source of conflict. Freeman has identified that 'current interests tend to be formulated in relation to experiential considerations,

263 G.C.A.M. Ruitenberg, *Het Internationaal Kinderrechtenverdrag in de Rechtspraak*, Amsterdam: SWP 2003, p. 61.

264 I. Thèry, 'The Interests of the Child and the Regulation of Post-Divorce Family' in: C. Smart & S. Sevenhuijsen, *Child Custody and the Politics of Gender*, 1989, London: Routledge, p. 82.

265 M. Freeman, *A Commentary on the United Nations Convention on the Rights of the Child, Article 3: The Best Interests of the Child*, Martinus Nijhoff Publishers 2007, p. 3.

whereas future-oriented interests focus on developmental considerations'.[266] For example, in operating upon a child to cure it from a disease the child may suffer from short-term consequences, such as pain, tiredness and immobility, but in the long term, it may protect the child against further deterioration or even death. The consideration of protecting children against fear of needles must be balanced against the potential benefits of vaccinations.

Article 3 sub 2 of the CRC is of particular importance for children's right to health, stating that State Parties have the obligation to ensure that 'institutions, services and facilities responsible for the care or protection of children shall conform with the standards established by competent authorities, particularly in the areas of safety and health, in the number and suitability of their staff, as well as competent supervision.' In the context of the health sector, the best interests of the child therefore imply that there must be a multi-disciplinary team available to treat children, ensuring not only a qualitative medical treatment, but also taking into consideration their psychological and social well-being and their opportunities to maintain a relatively normal life. This paragraph also implies that staff must be well trained and appropriately qualified, especially now that in recent years many examples have been revealed of children who were abused in the residences were they were formally taken care of.[267, 268] The timing and way in which a medical treatment is delivered must be balanced against the requirements of other important interests of a child, such as contacts with friends and family, development in school and social and psychological well-being. This holistic consideration of children's right to health reflects the interpretation of the role of the best interests of the child when explained as 'informed and constrained by the rights and other principles of the Children's Rights Convention', such as the right of children to play, the right to education and the right not to be separated from its family.[269] It leads to the conclusion that children's in realizing children's right to health, their best interests must be taken into account.

The best interests of the child must also be balanced against the right to participation of the child. It can be argued that when an anorexic child refuses food it is still in her best interest to provide her with artificial feeding. However, on the basis of the child's right to participation, it could be argued that children's views must be taken seriously and acted upon. The question of protection versus autonomy of children is at stake here. In this context, an interesting comment has been made by Fortin, noting that 'there are respectable jurisprudential arguments for maintaining that children's rights do not prevent interventions to stop children making short-term choices, thereby protecting their potential

266 Ibidem supra note 265, p. 3.
267 Ibidem supra note 265, p. 72.
268 U.N. Doc.E/CN.4/1989/48, § 144.
269 Ibidem supra note 265.

for long-term autonomy'.[270] This idea can also be applied for the medical sector, for example in deciding upon the extent of children's participation in their own treatment.[271]

Problems in the interpretation of children's best interests in particular situations may arise when the best interests of the child may be in conflict with the best interests of the (juvenile) mother (for example during pregnancy or childbirth[272]) or when the best interests of one group of children conflict with those of other children.[273] Freeman gives a clear example of two conjoined twins, of whom the stronger one would benefit from separation, whereas this would cause her sisters death.[274] The judges decided that the weaker twin did not have a quality of life while being conjoined and that it was in her best interests to at least momentarily experience bodily autonomy.[275] Another dilemma occurs when a teenage mother suffers from pregnancy complications that endanger her life. Whose interests should prevail then? Those of the juvenile mother or those of the baby yet to be born? For groups of children, related questions have been identified in allocating limited budgets to either a neonatal unit or to enforcing health care for school going children or adolescents.[276]

The best interests of the child must be considered in its social context. This is also the reason why the cultural and religious values of the community in which a child is raised play an important role in the interpretation of the best interests of the child. As elaborated in chapter 1, concepts and notions of health are strongly diverse between and within different communities. This will certainly influence the interpretation of what is in the best interest of the child. FGM is the most debated example, but other examples include different visions on vaccinations by certain religious communities, blood transfusions by Jehovah witnesses and western, symptom based medical treatments versus more holistic approaches such as acupuncture and reiki.

270 J. Fortin, 'Children's rights: are the courts taking them more seriously', *King's College Law Journal* 2004, Volume 15, p. 270.

271 Some state that professionals tend to believe that children pay more attention to short-term than to long-term consequences, for example fear of pain when receiving immunization. However, this standpoint seems to be a bit too simplistic, especially for children who undergone many medical treatments and are well aware of their medical situation.

272 U.N. Doc./E/CN.4/1989/48, § 121, reproduced in Freeman, M., *A Commentary on the United Nations Convention on the Rights of the Child, Article 3: The Best Interests of the Child*, Martinus Nijhoff Publishers, 2007, p. 61.

273 Ibidem supra note 265, p. 63.

274 Ibidem supra note 265, p. 62.

275 Case Re A.: Two judges (the trial judge and Robert Walker L.J. in the Court of Appeal) considered that the best interests of achieving bodily integrity outweighed the poor quality of life while conjoined, while giving the chance of life to the twin who would be capable of surviving. Available at: www.ncbi.nlm.nih.gov/pubmed/15069933.

276 Ibidem supra note 265, p. 64.

2.4.3. ARTICLE 6: THE RIGHT TO LIFE, SURVIVAL AND DEVELOPMENT

The right to life and development particularly envisages the obligation of states to reduce infant and child mortality and to increase life expectancy.[277] As such, it relates to the obligation in article 24-1 CRC. The basis of this article was laid down in 1948 in article 3 of the Universal Declaration on Human Rights, stating that 'Everyone has the right to life, liberty and security of person'[278] and it was further elaborated in article 6 of the International Covenant on Civil and Political Rights (the ICCPR), as 'Every human being has the inherent right to life and no one shall be arbitrarily deprived of his life.' In the International Covenant on Civil and Political Rights the first outline of the protection of children's right to life as laid down in article 6 of the ICCPR could be discerned in paragraph 5, specifying that any 'sentence to death shall not be imposed for crimes committed by persons under the age of 18 nor shall it be carried out on pregnant women', thereby also protecting the life of the unborn child. A more explicit prohibition of the death penalty is found in article 37. Article 6 of the Convention on the Rights of the Child does not speak of the relevance of sentences to death. However, its protection extends beyond the protection of life itself by not only recognizing 'that every child has the inherent right to life', but also that 'States Parties shall ensure to the maximum extent possible the survival and development of the child'. In explicating the child's right to development, the link between children's right to life and children's right to health becomes evident, as children with health problems often experience stagnation or setbacks in development concomitantly. Riedel even states that 'without an effective guarantee of the right to life, all other rights would be meaningless'.[279] Others memorize that the right to life has amounted to ius cogens and that it can not even be derived from in times of emergency.[280] The relation between the right to life and the right to health is also reflected in the regularly published child mortality rates. Good health (care) is required to prevent high rates of children's diseases and consequent high child mortality rates. The right to (emergency) health care, including care for women in labour, must be fulfilled in order to meet the requirements of the right to life. Without adequate perinatal care both the (unborn) child and the mother run

---

277 E. Riedel, 'The Right to Life and the Right to Health, in particular the obligation to reduce child mortality', in: A. Invernizzi & J. Williams (eds.), *The Human Rights of Children: From Visions to Implementation*, Ashgate, 2011, pp. 351–369.

278 Universal Declaration of Human Rights, General Assembly resolution 217A (III), U.N. Doc A/810 at 71 (1948). The UDHR was adopted with 48 votes in favour, none against and 8 abstentions (Belorussia, Czechoslovakia, Poland, Ukraine, USSR, Yugoslavia, Saudi-Arabia and South Africa).

279 Ibidem supra note 277.

280 M.J. Bossuyt, *Guide to the Travaux Préparatoires of the ICCPR*, Dordrecht: Martinus Nijhoff 1987, p. 121. See also Riedel, supra note 260.

increased risks of infections and other birth complications resulting in higher infant and maternal mortality rates.

The right to life, survival and development of the child also requires that children have access to continuous care throughout the different phases of their life and that the services provided should be adapted to changing circumstances, such as the child's age and living environment, cutbacks in budgeting and changes in environmental circumstances such as increased industrialization, armed conflicts and natural disasters. These adaptations are necessary to ensure the survival and development of children in all different phases of their lives.

The relevance of the right to life for children's right to health is also eminent in the discussion on the necessity to immunize children against the major childhood diseases and in the tolerance of high levels of malnutrition among groups of children, leading to serious growth disturbances and possibly even to death. When certain religious groups refuse to immunize their children against possibly lethal diseases, such a choice may be in conflict with children's right to health ánd development, because children run the increased risk of contracting seriously debilitating diseases. The counterargument to this standpoint is that the right to life only protects against actual infringements of children's health and life and not against potential risks to such infringements. However, this standpoint does not match with the focus in article 24 CRC on the prevention of health problems and on the important role of parents on ensuring their children's right to health.

Several issues related to the right to life of the child are particularly controversial, such as the rights of the unborn child to protection against (selective) abortions, the protection of (unborn) children against HIV/AIDS infections[281] and the protection of children against harmful traditional practices, such as preferential feeding and girl infanticide.[282] Also, modern reproductive technologies evoke discussions as to the extent to which life can be artificially created and how this affects the health of (unborn) children. For example, much is still unknown on the long-term safety of reproductive technologies.[283] Growing

281 Sexual education to prevent different modes of HIV/AIDS transmission, such as through sexual intercourse and mother-to-child transmission may be objected for religious or cultural reasons.

282 High rates of abortions and (selective) infant and child mortality rates have led to numerous questions of both the Committee on the Rights of the Child as of the CESCR. For example, the CRC Committee questioned the Netherlands on the relatively high number of abortions of children with congenital defects in 2009, U.N. Doc. CRC/C/NLD/CO/3, 27 March 2009, § 31. India was questioned on the practices of sex selective abortions and infanticide of girls, India, U.N. Doc. CRC/C/15/Add.115, 23 February 2000, § 49. See also the Concluding Observations of the CESCR on India, U.N. Doc. E/C.12/IND/CO/5, 16 May 2008, § 73–79.

283 E. Blyth, 'To be or not to be? A critical appraisal of the welfare of children conceived through new reproductive technologies', *International Journal of Children's Rights* 2008, Issue 16, pp. 505–522.

evidence on the increased incidence and concomitant risks[284] of artificially conceived twins and on the increased risk of congenital malformations is counterbalanced by the question whether 'bringing children into the world can ever be regarded as contrary to their interests'.[285] This may be the case for children who are conceived as 'saviour siblings'; brothers or sisters who are conceived to donate stem cells or bone marrow to their seriously ill sibling or children who are deliberately selected for their gender, for example when a hereditary disease is linked exclusively to the Y or X chromosome (e.g. haemophilia, Duchenne Muscular Dystrophy). Although some claim that, 'it may always be in the best interests of the child to be born, save for exceptionally rare instances, when the child would be exposed to a life that is not worth living',[286] a contrary proposition asserts that 'children should not be knowingly or intentionally be brought into the world unless they will not be affected negatively in any foreseeable way'.[287] This has even been drawn so far as to prohibit the conception of saviour siblings, siblings in one-parent families, parents of similar sex and post-menopausal mothers, possibly leading to instances of discrimination when such parents have a deep wish to have children.

These types of conception are all characterized by a potential discrepancy between the rights to life and health of the child and the rights of the parents to reproductive autonomy and possibly also the rights to life and health of siblings. This discrepancy is also at stake with regard to the rights of the unborn child when a pregnant woman considers a (selective) abortion or when she decides upon undergoing a natural delivery or an alternative medical operation for the baby to be born.[288] The right to life of the unborn child must further be balanced against the rights to life and to health of the pregnant woman, for example when the pregnancy poses serious threats to the life or health of the mother.

As long as the child is in the womb, it is part of the mother's bodily integrity. The crucial difference for the protection of the unborn child is then dependent upon its capacity to be born alive. In practice, this distinction is difficult, because 'what may be seen as a heroic fight for life in one setting may be classified as a hopeless case in another'.[289] Also, there are instances in which babies were kept alive against all expectations whereas others unexpectedly gave up.

---

284 Risks include health implications for both the children and the mothers, including increased perinatal and maternal death rates and neurological, respiratory and gastrointestinal problems. Economic, social and psychological challenges for the families and increasing pressures on neonatal, health and social services may also be augmented. Ibidem supra note 283, p. 508.

285 Ibidem supra note 283, p. 506.

286 J. Harris, *On cloning: thinking in action*, London: Routledge 2004. See also: J. Savulescu, 'Deaf lesbians, 'designer disability', and the future of medicine', *British Medical Journal* 2002, Issue 325, pp. 771–773.

287 Ibidem supra note 283, p. 515.

288 M. Cornock & H. Montgomery, 'Children's rights in and out of the womb', *The International Journal of Children's Rights* 2011, Issue 19, pp. 3–19.

289 Ibidem supra note 288, p. 15.

Fundamental in deciding upon such highly sensitive questions is the quality of life of the child when it survives. Again, the question is at stake, whether it is ever in conflict with a child's best interests to save its life. Quality of life refers to the conditions in which children live. It is an important concept for children with chronic or terminal diseases and it plays a central role in decisions on the continuation of medical treatments and the start of palliative care. According to the WHO, palliative care can be defined as 'The active total care of the child's body, mind and spirit, and also involving the support given to the family'.[290] Palliative care is intended to provide relief from pain and other distressing symptoms; it affirms life and regards dying as a normal process; it intends neither to hasten or postpone death; it integrates the psychological and spiritual aspects of patient care; offers a support system to help patients live as actively as possible until death and to help the family cope during the patients illness and in their own bereavement; it will enhance quality of life, and may also positively influence the course of illness'.[291] With respect to children, it has been established that 'palliative care requires a multidisciplinary approach, including the family and making use of community resources.'[292]

In my opinion, in deciding upon these highly sensitive issues, children's resilience and capacity to recover should be the basic premise, although at some point, the continuance of medical treatment may become more painful than letting go of life. The decision of where this point lies should be left to individual discretion of the child and its parents. Support from medical practitioners, friends, family, religious and spiritual coaches should be family-sensitive and respectful of the choices made in the intimate family context.

2.4.4. ARTICLE 12: THE RIGHT OF THE CHILD TO BE HEARD

Children's right to participation is laid down in article 12 CRC. Dr Hart has defined the concept of participation as 'The process of sharing decisions which affect one's life and the life of the community in which one lives'.[293] This definition implies active involvement that can be effectuated in decision-making. Others even argue that participation of children can transform practices that exclude

---

[290] Www.who.int/cancer/palliative/definition/en/.

[291] Ibidem supra note 288.

[292] Ibidem supra note 288.

[293] R. Hart, *Children's participation: From tokenism to citizenship*, Florence: UNICEF International Child Development Centre: 1992. See also: R. Hart, *Children's participation, the theory and practice of involving young citizens in community development and environmental care*, London: Earthscan Publications Ltd. 1997.

them.[294] On the other hand, whereas a focus on autonomy[295] is central in bioethics as a whole, the opposite sometimes seems to be the case for children in the health care sector.[296] Contrary to children's increasing capacities, it is often assumed that children do not have sufficient knowledge or insight to make well-founded medical decisions. However, this question can also be posed to adults.

Article 12 CRC has three elements which can be considered as the basis for child participation, although the actual word 'participation' is not explicitly mentioned in the provision. These elements are: the right to 'express views freely', 'the right to be given due weight to these views in accordance with the age and maturity of the child' and 'the right to be heard in official proceedings'. These elements are both relevant for individual children as for groups of children.[297] The concept of participation is described in General Comment 12 of the Committee on the Rights of the Child as 'an ongoing process, including information sharing and dialogue between children and adults based on mutual respect, and in which children can learn how their views and those of adults are taken into account to shape the outcome of such processes.'[298] As the concept of participation refers to a range of different practices, a distinction has been made between the private or personal domain of participation, such as the household or family and the social or public domain, such as the school, the community and government.[299]

The element of expressing views freely means that children should not be pressured or manipulated in expressing their opinions.[300] Specifically for the health sector, children must be given the opportunity of confidential counselling, for example by speaking to the health professional and/or to the parent in private, so that they will feel free and secure to express themselves.[301] It may also require adults to accept choices of the child that they do not support, for example when a terminally ill child wishes to terminate a medical treatment against the will of the parents or doctor. Lastly, it may even require affirmative action to enable children with very rare diseases to express themselves or to enable particularly vulnerable or discriminated children to express themselves without having to

---

294 C. Dedding, *Delen in macht en onmacht, Kinderparticipatie in de (alledaagse) diabeteszorg*, Academisch proefschrift, verdedigd op 30 september 2009 aan de Universiteit van Amsterdam, p. 31. Available at: http://dare.uva.nl/document/146511.

295 See paragraph 6 for a further discussion on the relation between the right to participation of children and the principle of autonomy in bioethics.

296 L.F. Ross, 'Health Care Decision Making by Children. Is it in their best interest?' in: *Children, Medicine and the Law*, Hastings Center Report, November-December 1997, p. 487.

297 U.N. Doc. CRC/C/GC/12, 20 July 2009, General Comment 12 on The right of the child to be heard, § 28, § 9 and 72.

298 Ibidem supra note 297, § 3.

299 S. Moses, 'Children and participation in South Africa: An overview', *The International Journal on Children's Rights* 2008, Issue 16, pp. 327–328.

300 Ibidem supra note 297, § 22.

301 Ibidem supra note 297, § 101. Elaborated is that the right to receive confidential counseling is distinct from the right to give medical consent and that it therefore applies to children of all ages.

fear repercussions from the government or other groups in society.[302] Articles 16, 28 and 29 CRC further elaborate that education must ensure that children develop the ability to seek and understand information to participate meaningful in medical decisions and health care in general by seeking access to the kind of health care that they wish to enjoy. Children's right to participation thus also requires the fulfilment of their right to information, as they can not participate meaningfully if they do not have all relevant information.

The second element means that the views of the child are given due weight according to the age and maturity of the child. According to article 5 CRC and General Comment 12, the evolving capacities of the child must be taken into account in the exercise of the right to participation. Children's capacities differ according to their age, level of development and comprehension and also according to children's experiences. In the healthcare sector, it has been acknowledged that children undergoing long-term treatments develop and mature throughout the process, so that their wishes and expectations of the healthcare provided will also change and develop.[303, 304] Bluebond-Langner demonstrated that experiences of children were crucial in establishing maturity among children; children of 4–5 years old having experiences with medical treatments appeared to better understand their medical situation and prognoses than intelligent children of 9 years old without such experiences.[305] This is proof of the central importance of experience of children on specific topics or in specific contexts for establishing their competency to make choices in their own health care.[306] This finding also implies that age limits for determining children's legal ability to be involved in medical decisions, as laid down in Dutch health legislation for example,[307, 308] may not

---

302 Ibidem supra note 297.

303 U. Kilkely & M. Donnelly, *The Child's Right to be heard in the Healthcare Setting: perspectives of children, parents and health professionals*, The National Children's Strategy Research Series, October, 2006, p. 3.

304 See also *Children's consent to surgery*, Open University Press, Buckingham, 1993, pp. 154–163.

305 M. Bluebond-Langner, *The private worlds of dying children*', Princeton, New Jersey: Princeton University Press 1978.

306 D. Mannaerts, 'Minderjarigen en participatie in de gezondheidszorg', *Rechten van minderjarigen in de gezondheidszorg* 2004, Kinderrechtencoalitie Vlaanderen vzw, 1e jaargang, nr. 2, pp. 23–37.

307 In the Netherlands, on the basis of article 7:465-1, 7: 450-2 and 7:447 WGBO a distinction is made between children between 0–12 years old, 12–16 years old and children older than 16. The first category has the right to be informed about their medical situation, possible decisions and consequences, but parents are primarily responsible. For children in the second category, parents and children have a joint responsibility and for children in the last category, children are responsible to decide for themselves. For more information on exceptions on this scheme, most predominantly in the case of 'common medical treatments for children between 12–16 years', highly controversial decisions and decisions to protect children under the age of 16 against irresponsible decisions of their parents see: V.E.T. Dörenberg, *Kind en Stoornis, Een systematisch onderzoek naar de rechtspositie van minderjarigen in de kinder- en jeugdpsychiatrie*, Den Haag: Boom Juridische Uitgevers 2010, pp. 76–81.

308 See also supra note 297, § 102.

always reflect the actual capacity of children to decide upon their treatment.[309, 310] Giving due weight further implies that when a child communicates pain or sorrow, action should be undertaken to support the child or provide medicines, health care or other necessary actions and to provide feedback on those actions taken in response to comments made by the child.

The third element is that children have the right to be heard in official proceedings affecting the child. In my opinion, this should include the involvement of children in procedures of disciplinary law against medical practitioners who have violated the right to health of the child or of other rights in the provision of health care to children, such as inclusion of children in medical decision-processes, informed consent for participation in clinical research and the shaping and organization of children's health care. Also, in order to further improve and realize children's participation in healthcare, children must be fully informed and given the opportunity to give and receive feedback on the way their views were taken into consideration in the medical process, for example when the child makes a complaint against a medical treatment it has undergone. To ensure that children can participate meaningfully in the health care processes that affect them, they must be provided with clear and accessible information on their right to participation and the way in which it is effectuated.[311] Furthermore, standards and indicators must be developed to assess the participation of children in health care.[312] Last but not least, article 12 must be understood to mean that the child also has the right not to exercise his right to participation.[313]

Participation can be effectuated directly or through a representative.[314] However, precaution must be taken to ensure that children can genuinely participate. Several levels of participation have been discerned, ranging from manipulation and tokenism, in which children's participation is mentioned but

309 This dilemma was also discussed during the preparation of the Dutch legislation on age limits. See *Kamerstukken II* 1989/91, 21 561, no. 6, p. 49 (MvA). Criticism included that strict age limits would not take into account the capacity of the minor child to oversee the extent of its medical treatment, notwithstanding its age. See Brands & Brands-Bottema 1991 vs. Hermans 1990, p. 95–96 [reproduced in Dörenberg], p. 81. However, it was eventually decided to stick to the strict age limits. Somewhat contradictorily, the Dutch government elaborated in the same document that if a severely sick patient of 11 years old consciously refuses certain treatments, he can not be forced to undergo that treatment. See document above, p. 58 and *Kamerstukken II* 1991/92, 21 561, no. 11, p. 31.

310 Ibidem supra note 289. Mannaerts explains that using age limits to determine children's competency in medical decision making leads to both under inclusion of competent children and over inclusion of incompetent children (and adults).

311 Ibidem supra note 297, § 103 and 134.

312 Ibidem supra note 297, § 104.

313 Ibidem supra note 297, § 16.

314 Ibidem supra note 297, § 35–37.

not really effectuated, to participatory processes in which children initiate and develop programs in cooperation with adults.[315, 316]

2.4.5. THE DILEMMA BETWEEN PROTECTION AND CHILDREN'S AUTONOMY

In the realization of children's right to be heard in health care the dilemma of weighing the importance of children's protection against their right to participation or individual autonomy arises. Children undergoing medical treatment have a fourfold vulnerability for being dependent in their position as a minor *vis-à-vis* adults, for being dependent on highly informed medical professionals for being ill, for being sick and suffering from lack of energy and lastly because treatments affect both their short and long-term health prospects. However, their dependency is an argument in itself to give explicit room for their right to be heard. Children in health care must be empowered to have a say in their own medical treatment, so that children will not only be protected against 'wrong' choices or choices based on incomplete information, but also against harm deriving from neglecting their personal wishes.[317] Especially when highly intrusive medical treatments are considered, it is important that vulnerable children can freely and safely express their views and fears independently of the persons they are dependent on: confidential counsellors should be available for these children and actively provide assistance when children are confronted with (serious) medical decisions.[318, 319]

---

315 See for a further elaboration of this concept the 'The Ladder of Children's Participation by Hart', supra note 264. Eight different levels of (non-)participation are discerned: 1. manipulation; 2. decoration; 3. tokenism; 4. assigned but informed; 5. consulted and informed; 6. adult-initiated, shared decisions with children; 7. child-initiated and directed; 8. child-initiated, shared decisions with adults.

316 See also Shier, identifying 5 levels of participation, namely 1. children are listened to; 2. children are facilitated in expressing their views; 3. children's views are taken into account; 4. children are involved in decision-making processes; 5. children share power and responsibility for decision-making.
An overview of different typologies of children's participation is found in: N. Thomas, 'Towards a theory of children's participation', *International Journal on Children's Rights* 2007, Issue 15, p. 199.

317 Ibidem supra note 306. Mannaerts discusses that children's involvement in their own medical treatment may be shaped as informed consent (legally binding) or assent (approval, though not legally binding).

318 In a study conducted in the European Union among more than 2000 children from various countries, it was found that out of the top 10 recommendations of children on their involvement in health care, 4 concerned the importance of communication; 49.1% being able to understand the doctor; 47.3% being heard; 44.6% having the opportunity to ask questions and 44.1% explanation and preparation to treatment. 'The views and experiences of children and young people in Council of Europe Member States', 2011, Dr. U. Kilkelly, University of Cork.

319 Other research has indicated that children's experiences improved with their age, that speaking to nurses was more favourable than speaking to doctors and that children in specialist hospitals reported a much better preparation for medical procedures than children

Other arguments in favour of participation include findings that participation of children in decision-making processes promotes their protection, enhances their skills, autonomy competences and self-esteem.[320] Last but not least, children's involvement in medical decisions has been found to increase the understanding of their diseases and medical treatment and thereby also their adherence to the treatment.[321] On the other hand, it is also argued that children require a safe period in which they can develop without jeopardizing their future life chances and without being burdened with the responsibility to make difficult decisions.[322]

To justify violating children's short-term autonomy, the need to protect their long-term autonomy and chances in life is put forward.[323] Children's legally enshrined incapacity to act proves that focus is structurally placed on their need for protection. The consequence is that children have a heavier burden of proof than adults to show that they are competent.[324] This is especially problematic when (seriously) ill children suffer from tiredness, weakness, pain and a lack of focus and clear communication skills, especially when adults are convinced of the necessity to opt for a particular choice.

A second argument against children's participation concerns questions on children's competency and lack of life experience to fully oversee the consequences of any medical treatment. If factors such as age, maturity and experience in the medical sector concomitantly influence a child's perception of the medical treatment required, how can the individual competency of the child be determined? Appelbaum and Grisso discern four elements that are central in assessing children's competency,[325, 326] namely:

---

in general hospitals. Kilkelly, U. and Donnelly, M., 'Participation in Healthcare: The views and experiences of children and young people', in: *International Journal on children's rights*, Issue 19, 2011, pp. 107–125.

320 G. Landsdown, *Promoting Children's Participation in Democratic Decision-Making*, Florence: UNICEF Innocenti Research Centre 2001.

321 Ibidem supra note 320 Landsdown. For a discussion of the importance of developing autonomy of children in healthcare see also Dodds, S., 'Choice and control in feminist bioethics' in: C. Mackenzie & and N. Stoljar (eds.), *Relational Autonomy: Feminist Perspectives on Autonomy, Agency and the Social Self*, New York: Oxford University Press 2000, p. 229. Reproduced in M. Donnelly & U. Kilkelly, 'Child-friendly healthcare: delivering on the right to be heard', *The Medical Law Review* 2011, 19 (1), pp. 27–54.

322 L. Friedman Ross, 'Health Care Decision Making by Children. Is it in their best interest?' in: *Hastings Center Report* 1997, Vol. 27, No. 6, pp. 41–45.

323 P. Baines, 'Medical ethics for children: applying the four principles to paediatrics', *Journal of Medical Ethics* 2008, Issue 34, p. 142.

324 Ibidem supra note 306 Mannaerts pp. 23–37. Adults on the other hand, have greater difficulty in demonstrating that they are incompetent.

325 Appelbaum & Grisso, 'Assessing patient's capacities to consent to treatment', *New England Journal of Medicine* 1988, vol. 319, no. 25, pp. 1635–1638.

326 Similar (less elaborate) analyses have been made by Buchanan & Brock, 'Deciding for others: the ethics of surrogate decision making', *Cambridge University Press* 1989, and Mannaerts, supra note 280. Central in these analyses are the capacity to make and communicate rational choices.

- the capacity to communicate choices;
- the capacity to understand relevant information;
- the capacity to evaluate the information in the context of their own situation;
- the capacity to weigh possible advantages and risks of the different options available.

Central in the analyses of elements of competency are the capacity to make and communicate rational choices. Although these elements provide a structure for determining children's competency for participation in healthcare, the question remains who is capable of assessing the child's competency. Mannaerts convincingly argues that in practice, the establishment of children's competency is often motivated by their willingness to follow a doctor's advice.[327] Incompetency is assumed, if children refuse to follow the advice. This means that the pre-existing ideas and values of the medical professional are replacing the actual assessment of children's competency to take medical decisions and thus that children are not truly given the opportunity to participate in their own healthcare. Therefore, in assessing children's competency for participating in health care, a distinction has to be made between their competency on the one hand and the willingness of adults to respect and accept children's choices in the second place. As mentioned before, realizing children's right to the highest attainable standard of health may require the acceptance of choices that are not supported by the parents or medical sector. Therefore, truly respecting children's right to participation in health care requires an independent and unprejudiced assessment of competency by an independent counsellor or health advocate for children.

A third argument critical of participation of children in their health care is that children's autonomy must be balanced against the autonomy of the parents to give direction to the child during its development. In several researches, it was suggested that parental opposition to their children's participation could pose a considerable barrier to effective participation.[328] Some nervous parents transmitted their fears to their children.[329] Others were reluctant to communicate serious diagnoses fully to their children.[330] Others found that some children welcomed their parents' role in buffering threatening information.[331] Also, if

---

327 Ibidem supra note 289 Mannaerts, pp. 4–5.

328 M. Donnelly & U. Kilkelly, 'Child-friendly healthcare: delivering on the right to be heard', *The Medical Law Review* 2011, 19 (1), pp. 27–54.

329 Ibidem supra note 328.

330 E. Kübler-Ross, *On Children and death, how children and their parents can and do cope with death*, Touchstone, Simon & Schuster 1997. On the other hand, Young et al found that some children relied upon their parents to manage the communication and welcomed their parents' role in buffering potentially threatening information. B. Young and others, 'Managing communication with young people who have a potentially life threatening chronic illness: qualitative study of patients and parents', *British Medical Journal* 2003, p. 305. A study was conducted involving 13 families: 19 parents and 13 patients aged 8–17. All patients suffered from cancer or a brain tumour.

331 Ibidem supra note 330.

parents face their child's choice to terminate a potentially life-saving medical treatment, they have a strong personal interest in the decision made. Given the questions on competency and lack of life experience of children to decide upon these issues, parents' hesitance to let the child decide on its own is understandable. Therefore, it would be both practically and legally unjust for medical practitioners to simply override parents' objections to their child's participation when they want to provide the child with information on their medical condition. Proper communication to both parents and children is essential in ensuring participation of children that is compliant with the best interests of the child. This is especially important given the insights that in a triad relationship between doctors, children and their parents, there is a tendency for the development of coalitions between two parties.[332] Therefore the role of the medical professional in responding to parents' or children's involvement in health care is crucial.

2.4.6. ARTICLES 5 & 18: THE ROLE OF THE PARENTS IN ENSURING THEIR CHILDREN'S HEALTH

On the basis of article 18 CRC, parents (or legal guardians) have the primary responsibility for the development and upbringing of their children. The role of parents in ensuring children's right to health can hardly be overestimated, especially for children in their early childhood, as they are fully dependent on the care and attention of their parents or caretakers. However, Freeman establishes that there are inconsistencies in the terminology on parents' responsibilities in upbringing their children versus those of the State and the extended family and local community.[333] Terms such as 'parents', 'legal guardians', 'persons taking care of the child', 'others responsible for the child' and 'family environment' have been used inconsistently in the Convention on the Rights of the Child. This lack of clarity requires further work to establish who can be addressed when children require access to health care.

In the relation between children and their parents, children are seen as the right holders and parents as the duty-bearers. Parents have the primary responsibility to provide the child with healthy food and a safe and healthy environment. They also have a crucial role in deciding whether children are going to see a medical doctor. Parents are the first to decide whether health care is necessary for their children.[334] Already during pregnancy and delivery they

332 Gabe and others, 'It takes three to tango: a framework for understanding patient partnership in paediatric clinics', *Social Science Medicine* 2004, Issue, 59, pp. 1071 and 1074. See also M. Donnelly & U. Kilkelly, supra note 310.

333 Ibidem supra note 265, p. 65. See articles 3-2, 5, 7-1, 9, 10, 14-2, 18, 19, 20-3, 26-2, 27, 29-2 and 40-2.

334 K.L. Hanson, 'Is insurance for children enough? The link between parents' and children's health care use revisited', *Inquiry* (a journal of medical care organization, provision and financing) 1998, Volume 35, Issue 3, pp. 294–302.

decide whether and when a medical professional is contacted.[335] The nutrition and health behaviour of the future mother is crucial in ensuring the healthy development of the foetus. When the child is born, the parents usually decide whether the child is breastfed, whether it receives healthy food and what choices are made with respect to the medical (non-)treatment of children. Even when excellent health facilities are available for children, negligent or over-burdened parents may postpone the decision to take their child to a doctor (see also the discussion on General Comment 13 in paragraph 5). For example, in a family with many (young) children in need of supervision, a single-parent may have great difficulties in reaching a doctor when the clinic is far away or when the family does not have a proper health insurance. On the other hand, situations in which parents make their children go to medical doctors more often than is beneficial to them also exist, as is the case with the Munchhausen by-proxy-syndrome, possibly resulting in unnecessary medical treatments and physical harm.[336] Others refuse to immunize their children against the common childhood diseases.[337] Whereas the particular role of mothers in ensuring their children's health is emphasized in article 24-1d and in article 12 of the Convention on the Elimination of All forms of Discrimination against Women on the basis of the intrinsic physical relationship during and after the pregnancy period, there is less attention for the influence of the daily health behaviour of both mothers and fathers on the health of their children.

In addition to the consequences of parents' decisions on their children's health, they also play a very important role in stimulating healthy behaviour of their children by daily providing examples of healthy behaviour and ensuring safety and good sanitary conditions in the living environment. The daily examples of parents' healthy behaviour, such as consumption patterns, sleep, amount and intensity of exercise and relaxation, sun-bathing, hygiene, smoking, alcohol and drug use, violent behaviour, work-related stress and time spent together with the family are important indicators in predicting their children's (future) health

---

335 'De vrijheid en waardigheid van de zwangere vrouw en het ongeboren kind. Een gezondheidsrechtelijk dilemma' in: *Grondrechten in de gezondheidszorg*, Liber Amicorum voor prof. Mr. J.K.M.Gevers, onder redactie van A.C. Hendriks et al., Houten: Uitgeverij Bohn Stafleu van Loghum 2010, p. 6.

336 See for more information on this classified form of child maltreatment for example Medlineplus encyclopedia, available at: www.nlm.nih.gov/medlineplus/ency/article/001555.htm.

337 D.S. Diekema, 'Responding to Parental Refusals of Immunization of Children', *Pediatrics* 2005, Volume 115, Number 5, May, p. 1428–1431. Available at: http://aappolicy.aappublications.org/cgi/reprint/pediatrics;115/5/1428.pdf.

behaviour.[338, 339, 340, 341, 342, 343] Especially for boys, the health behaviour of their fathers is a direct example for their own future health behaviour. These examples show that health is a living reality: notwithstanding the normative rules that parents like to abide by, their daily health behaviour of both mothers and fathers is crucial in guiding their children towards a healthy future.

The important role of parents in ensuring children's right to the highest attainable standard of health is reflected in the dominant role attributed to parents under article 24-2 e and f CRC in the prevention of health problems. Therein, explicated is that all segments of the society, *in particular parents and children*, must be 'informed, have access to education and be supported in the use of basic knowledge of child health and nutrition, the advantages of breastfeeding, hygiene, environmental sanitation and the prevention of accidents'. In sub f, it is propagated that preventive health care, guidance for parents and family planning education and services must be developed. As is made clear from the focus on basic health knowledge on child health, the empowerment of both parent and children through the provisions of health education is an essential building block in realizing children's right to the highest attainable standard of health. In doing so, parents are in a direct position to promote, support and enhance their children's health.

Based on the interdependence of the CRC articles, measures for health protection must be specifically tailored for different age groups, such as infants, small children and adolescent youth, taking into account the evolving capacities of the child (art. 5 CRC). Article 5 CRC also mentions the role of parents in providing for appropriate direction and guidance in the exercise of children's rights. In accordance with this provision, parents have to continuously adjust the ways in which they guide and direct their children as required by their continuous growth and development.

The role of parents as a possible barrier to realizing the right to the highest attainable standard of health of the child is especially relevant to children in early childhood, as they are entirely dependent on the care of their parents. For

338 S.T. Borra and others, 'Developing health messages: Qualitative studies with children, parents, and teachers help identify communications opportunities for healthy lifestyles and the prevention of obesity', *Journal of the America Dietetic Association* 2003, Volume 103, Issue 6, June, pp. 721–728.

339 S.J.H. Biddle, 'Health-enhancing physical activity and sedentary behavior in children and adolescents', *Journal of Sports Sciences 2004*, Volume 22, Issue 8, pp. 679–701.

340 R.L. Repetti and others, 'Risky Families: Family Social Environments and the Mental and Physical Health of Offspring', *Psychological Bulletin* 2002, Volume 128, Number 2, pp. 330–366.

341 M. Okada and others, 'Influence of parents' oral health behaviour on oral health status of their school children: an exploratory study employing a causal modelling technique', *International Journal of Paediatric Dentistry* 2002, volume 12, number 2, March, pp. 101–108.

342 C.L. Perry, 'Parent involvement with children's health promotion: the Minnesota Home Team', *American Journal of Public Health* 1988, Volume 78, Issue 9, pp. 1156–1160.

343 S. Golombok, *Parenting, what really counts?*, London: Routledge 2000.

example, when a baby has high fever, it is up to the parents or primary caretaker to assess whether and with what urgency it is necessary to contact a doctor.

In the implementation guide on General Comment 7 on the rights of children in early childhood provided by UNICEF and the Bernard van Leer Foundation,[344] the implementation of child rights in early childhood is directly linked to the rights of families, being divided in several subsequent steps. The first step in realizing children's right to health is the necessary support and advice to the pregnant mother, ensuring healthy behaviour during pregnancy (nutritious food, no smoking, alcohol and drug consumption, stress etc.). The second step entails the conduct of childbirth, highly impacting upon the possible development of health problems resulting from birth complications and also upon the building of a loving mother-child relationship from the very beginning of a child's life. The third step underlines the importance of family-centred care, particularly when children need neonatal or intensive care and the provision of information and support to young parents on breastfeeding, vaccination programs, healthy nutrition and other preventive health measures. Last but not least, the well-functioning of child-friendly health facilities during the entire childhood is required.

Whereas parents (article 5 CRC) and at a certain age children themselves have the primary responsibility to ensure adequate conditions of living, the State has to provide additional assistance and support with regard to nutrition, clothing and housing and the State is also responsible for the establishment of preventive, curative and rehabilitative health care policies, institutions and measures.[345] Furthermore, whereas parents are not directly bound by international human rights treaties, States Parties are required to adopt national legislation and measures to ensure the fulfilment of the provisions of the human rights treaties they are party to. The legal relation between parents and States has as such been beautifully interpreted as 'parents have a wide, but not unlimited margin of appreciation *vis-à-vis* the State concerning the ways to implement their responsibility towards the child.'[346]

A common avenue for States to fulfil its *secondary* responsibility to ensure children's right to health is by providing adequate health and social insurances and taking other measures to ensure an adequate standard of living. Furthermore, several examples can be given in which the State may take over the role of parents in taking care of the child, for example when disputing parents do not give permission for a medical treatment or when overanxious or attention seeking parents try to have their children examined more often or more vigorously then

344 'A Guide to General Comment 7: Implementing Child Rights in Early Childhood', produced by Bernard van Leer Foundation and UNICEF, 2006, p. 75.

345 Ibidem supra note 215, p. 6.

346 A. Eide, 'Article 27: The Right to an Adequate Standard of Living', in Series: *A CRC Commentary on the United Nations Convention on the Rights of the Child*, Leiden: Martinus Nijhoff Publishers 2006, § 50.

is beneficial for them. In cases of child maltreatment, the State may need to step in the place of the parents or in more extreme cases even protect the child against the parents. However, conflicts may arise when parents and doctors disagree over the need to perform a potentially life-saving treatment on a child. It has been established that patients and their family often face a big challenge in refusing medical treatments not being in line with the usual practice in highly organized and technical medical institutions. It is important to ensure that both children and their parents are given the opportunity to express their views in medical decision-making and that these views are seriously considered. It would be highly counterproductive and ethically wrong if States take over the responsibility for children if parents do not act in accordance with standard medical practices. As laid down in article 18 CRC, parents have the primary responsibility over their children and only in exceptional circumstances should this be replaced by the State.

In summary, under article 24 CRC, parents (or other caretakers) have the primary responsibility to ensure the right to health of their children, whereas States must ensure the necessary health infrastructure to enable parents to take this responsibility. Only in exceptional circumstances; when parents neglect or abuse their children, when children do not have parents or when parents are incapable of taking good care of their children (for example when they are severely ill or severely and acutely injured) may the State (temporarily) take over this parental role for the children. Well-established legislation and criteria must be in place to avoid any instances of arbitrary decisions.

2.4.7. ARTICLES 26 & 27: SOCIAL SECURITY AND AN ADEQUATE STANDARD OF LIVING

The role of the family in ensuring the right to the highest attainable standard of health of the child is central to the implementation of articles 26 and 27 of the Children's Rights Convention. Articles 26 and 27 CRC ensure that the child benefits from social security, including social insurance and to an adequate standard of living for the child's physical, mental, spiritual, moral and social development. Social security plays a crucial part in ensuring children's right to have (financial) access to health.[347] Therefore, this right it is categorized in the Reporting Guidelines in the cluster on basic health and welfare.[348] As such, it has been mainly applied in an instrumental way, being required to fulfil other rights

347 Research Report by UNICEF, Defence for Children and Pharos, 'Undocumented children and access to hospital health care', June 2010.

348 UN Office of the High Commissioner for Human Rights, *Manual on Human Rights Reporting Under Six Major International Human Rights Instruments*, 1997, HR/PUB/91/1 (Rev.1), p. 406. available at: www.unhcr.org/refworld/docid/428085252.html.

in the CRC, such as the right to health.[349] The Committee has even insisted that an adequate social security system particularly has to improve access to health care and health insurance for children.[350] If possible, a social security system should lead to a reduction of the costs of health care or even establish free access to health services for children.[351]

Delineation of the two rights in article 26 and 27 is sometimes difficult, but it has been suggested that the right to social security as laid down in article 26 CRC can be the avenue for guaranteeing the right to an adequate standard of living in article 27 CRC.[352] Furthermore, when read in conjunction with other human rights provisions on social security, article 26 constitutes a more concrete protection in practice than the more vague phrasing of 'the adequate standard of living'.[353, 354, 355]

Article 26 CRC elaborates that children have the right to *benefit from* social security.[356] Whereas the definition entails a result obligation, namely that the child should actually benefit from the social security granted to his family or legal guardian, this does not directly imply that the child has the right to have a social insurance in its own right. The question then is what this provision means for children without families or other responsible caretakers, for children whose parents are not or not sufficiently insured or for children whose parents or other caretakers are not aware or who do not make an appeal on the social security necessary for the medical treatment of their children. In these situations, children may not be able to (indirectly) benefit from their parents' or caretakers' social insurance.

Paragraph 2 of article 26 CRC gives more insight in these more complicated situations, by stating that the application can be made *by or on behalf* of the child. This phrasing indicates that the child does also have a right to social security when his parents or legal representatives do not apply for him or when they use

---

349 U.N. Doc. CRC/GC/2003/3, General Comment 3 on HIV/AIDS and the rights of the child, 17 March 2003, § 6.

350 U.N. Doc. CRC/C/15/Add.174, 2002, § 54d; CRC Committee Concluding Observations on Malawi. See also: W. Vandenhole, 'The right to benefit from social security', in the Series: *A Commentary on the United Nations Convention on the Rights of the Child*, Leiden: Martinus Nijhoff Publishers 2007, p. 41.

351 U.N. Doc. CRC/C/15/Add.171, 2002, § 52c; CRC Committee Concluding Observations on Gabon. See also Vandenhole, p. 41.

352 Ibidem supra note 350 Vandenhole, p. 1.

353 See for example article 25(1) of the UDHR 1948, referring to an adequate standard of living for 'himself and his family' ánd to the right to social security in case of sickness or disability (amongst others).

354 See also article 3 CERD, guaranteeing the enjoyment of social security, notably in the enjoyment of the right to public health, medical care and social security. Article 10(2) CERD offers special protection for pregnant and lactating mothers.

355 The 1952 ILO Social Security Convention Number 102 covers nine predominant social risks, among which health care, sickness benefit, family benefit, maternity benefit, invalidity benefit and survivor's benefit.

356 Ibidem supra note 202, p. 461. See also *Travaux préparatoires* U.N. Doc. E/CN.4/1984/71, 1984, § 81.

it for other purposes than the maintenance of the child. It may even imply that children do have the right to apply for social security. This also derives from the request of the CRC Committee to States in its General Reporting Guidelines to specify in what circumstances 'children are allowed to apply for social security measures either directly or through a representative'.[357] The Dutch reservation to article 26 that children do not have an independent entitlement to social security indicates that a possible interpretation of article 26 does entail such an independent entitlement for children.[358]

For vulnerable groups of children, especially those without parents, such as street children, internally displaced children, refugee and asylum-seeking children, an adequate social security system could be very beneficial in providing access to health care and in cases even in preventing them from becoming extremely vulnerable.[359] The CRC Committee refers to this idea in General Comment 9 on children with disabilities.[360] It elaborates that it vulnerable children should be informed about the existence of such a system of social security and of the way in which they can apply for benefits. Furthermore, the way in which such information is provided plays a crucial role in the actual efforts that people make to get health care. It has been found in the Netherlands, that even when financial compensation for health care is available for undocumented health care seekers, the way in which bills are handled and communicated by service desks and health care professionals may constitute a significant barrier to seeking adequate health care.[361] This could lead to a situation wherein social security for having access to primary health care is available, though not being used. Therefore, States are recommended to ensure that the system of social security is transparent and that it is clear for families and their children how they can apply for social security benefits.[362]

When article 26 CRC is read in conjunction with article 4 CRC it appears that children's right to benefit from social security must be achieved progressively. In progressively developing this system, the need for cost-sharing between all different beneficiaries is highlighted, aiming to ensure that all disadvantaged population groups are included. The CRC Committee has highlighted (the risk of) exclusion of female-headed households,[363] non-working parents,[364] children

---

357 U.N. Doc. CRC/C/58/Rev.1, 2005, § 100.

358 Ibidem supra note 350, Vandenhole, p. 14.

359 Ibidem supra note 350, Vandenhole, p. 13.

360 U.N. Doc. CRC/C/GC/9, GC 9: The rights of children with disabilities, 27 February 2007, § 20.

361 S.E. Duijs, 'Het recht op zorg én de plicht om te betalen', Dokters van de Wereld, July 2010.

362 U.N. Doc. CRC/C/15/Add.192, 2002, § 40b, CRC Committee Concluding Observations on Moldova. See also supra note 350, Vandenhole, p. 39.

363 U.N. Doc. CRC/C/TTO/CO/2, 2006, § 57–58; CRC Committee Concluding Observations on Trinadad and Tobago. See also supra note 350, Vandenhole, p. 31.

364 U.N. Doc. CRC/C/15/Add.217, 2003, § 59; CRC Committee Concluding Observations on Pakistan and U.N. Doc. CRC/C/MEX/CO/3, 2006, § 54; CRC Committee Concluding Observations on Mexico. See also supra note 350, Vandenhole, p. 31.

with temporary residence permits[365] amongst others and aims to achieve universal social security coverage of all children and their families.[366] Measures to enlarge the amount of children reached by social security systems are therefore encouraged.[367] All possible discrimination grounds for having access to social security must be eliminated.[368] This is explicitly stated for children residing on the territory of a State without having a (permanent) residence permit, suggesting that this is also the case for illegally residing children.[369]

Article 27 CRC recognizes the child's right to an adequate standard of living to ensure the child's full and harmonious development, including at the physical, mental, spiritual, moral and social levels.[370] It elaborates on article 6 CRC, confirming the child's right to survival and development. The standard of living must be ensured by healthy nutrition, adequate clothing and housing. Here again, the primary responsibility for providing for such a standard of living is attributed to the parents, who have a common responsibility to take care of their children (article 18 CRC). However, the responsibility of parents for the upbringing of their children is required 'within the limits of their abilities and financial capacities'. This phrasing leads to a situation in which the realization of children's right to health is dependent upon their parents, whereas the living conditions differ enormously between and within countries to an extent that is not always within the reach of parents or caretakers. Even good-willing parents may have limited (financial) means, resources and sufficient time available to ensure an adequate standard of living for (all of) their children.

Furthermore, the type and quality of care provided is dependent on the composition of the family in which a child lives, such as a single-parent family, a family with many children or even child-headed households.[371] Therefore, to ensure a certain minimum level of living, States have the duty to provide assistance to parents in addition to the primary role of parents themselves; on the basis of article 18 paragraph 2, States Parties have the duty 'to render appropriate assistance to parents and legal guardians in the performance of their child-rearing responsibilities and shall ensure the development of institutions, facilities and services for the care of children'.

The involvement of both parents and the State leads to the question where the demarcation line lies; under article 27 CRC States have the duty to intervene, but at the same time they must respect the rights of parents in raising their own

365 U.N. Doc. CRC/C/ 15/Add.268, 2005, § 64, CRC Committee Concluding Observations on Australia, Ibidem supra note 350, Vandenhole, p. 31.

366 Ibidem supra note 350, Vandenhole, p. 31.

367 U.N. Doc. CRC/C/15/Add.172, 2002, § 55; CRC Committee Concluding Observations on Mozambique, Ibidem supra note 350, Vandenhole, p. 32.

368 Ibidem supra note 350, Vandenhole, p. 32.

369 U.N. Doc. CRC/C/15/Add.167, 2001, § 53; CRC Committee Concluding Observations on Uzbekistan. Ibidem supra note 350, Vandenhole, p. 34.

370 Ibidem supra note 202, p. 462.

371 Ibidem supra note 346 Eide, § 11 and 12.

children. In the CRC Commentary on article 27 it is elaborated that children can make a claim in first instance upon their parents for ensuring an adequate standard of living and in the second place on the State.[372] Parents are primarily responsible for the daily care of their children: nurturing and dressing them, taking them to school, to bed, to the doctor or the dentist. Families are defined by the CRC as 'a family refers to a variety of arrangements that can provide young children's care, nurturance and development, including nuclear family, extended family and other traditional and modern community-based arrangements', provided these are consistent with children's rights and best interests.'[373] Important in such arrangements, is that there should be no distinction between biological children and other, adopted or foster children.[374] It must also be acknowledged that reality is much more complex than the ideal type family of two parents living together with their children.[375] There exist great variations in family arrangements in rural or urban environments and the role of the family is changing towards different compositions.

It is important to acknowledge (article 18-1) that the primary responsibility of parents to care for their children must be shared between both the father and the mother.[376] All parents or caretakers involved, including adoptive parents, separated parents and foster parents, have the same responsibilities as the natural parents (article 21 CRC). This also requires that children are legally recognized by both of their parents and that they receive a birth certificate that will guarantee access to maintenance by the parents and receive primary health care for the child.[377] Illegitimacy should not be a barrier to receive such access, not when children are born outside a marriage, outside the borders of their country of origin or conceived in a one-night stand or with single, marginalized women.[378]

The obligations of the State in ensuring an adequate standard of life for children can be divided into the obligation to *respect* the primary responsibility of the parents to raise their children, the obligation to *protect* the rights of the child if the parents neglect it or do not sufficiently fulfil their responsibility and thirdly, the obligation to fulfil the child's right to an adequate standard of living – especially if the parents don't or when the child does not have parents.[379]

The obligation to fulfil can be achieved directly or indirectly through the support of parents by subsidizing or providing (cost free) youth health care institutions, water and sewage systems, emergency care, housing and nutrition, if so required, accessible social insurances and by adopting legislation to ensure

---

372 Ibidem supra note 346 Eide, §. 5.
373 U.N. Doc./CRC/GC2005/7, 2005, CRC Committee General Comment No.7: Implementing child rights in early childhood, § 15.
374 Ibidem supra note 346 Eide, § 55.
375 Ibidem supra note 346 Eide, § 68.
376 See also article 5 of the CEDAW.
377 Ibidem supra note 346 Eide, § 92–94.
378 Ibidem supra note 346 Eide, § 94.
379 Ibidem supra note 346 Eide, §. 6 and 7.

universal access for all children, including those marginalized and belonging to social minorities. In principle, parents are responsible for ensuring their children's right to have a standard of living and the State must ensure the required infrastructure to enable parents to fulfil this right. States are furthermore responsible to address the large scale consequences of societal problems, affecting children's right to health and standards of living on a large scale such as corruption, natural disasters and situations of violence.

The scope of the right to an adequate standard of living is phrased in article 27 CRC (2 and 3) mentioning 'the conditions of living necessary for the child's development' and 'the provision of support programs particularly with regard to nutrition, clothing and housing'. No particular mention is made of health care. However, in explanations of the separate elements of the right to an adequate standard of living by the CESCR, reference was made to its connection to the right to health.[380] For example with regard to the right to *adequate* housing, it is elaborated that houses must not be built on polluted sites or in proximity to pollution sources that threaten the health of the inhabitants. More importantly in relation to the realization of the right to the highest attainable standard of health of the child is the specification that housing must be in a location that allows for access to health care facilities.[381]

Another link between the right to an adequate standard of living and the right to health is found in the provision of breastfeeding. Nutritious food must be economically and physically accessible and culturally appropriate. This allows for the adoption of national guidelines and policies to adjust the work environment for lactating women. Another example is the duty of the State to assist parents to reconcile their responsibilities as parents and as employees,[382] because many parents are dependent on their daily work to be able to provide their children with an adequate standard of living.

2.4.8. PARTIAL CONCLUSION

The CRC provision on children's right to health has a clear focus on prevention of health problems and on ensuring basic health care for all children. Key elements are the prevention of infant and child mortality by providing for the underlying determinants of health and necessary health care, including emergency care, perinatal care and preferably also including primary health care for all and for ensuring coverage of all children by immunization programs. On the basis of articles 6 and 24 CRC the health services must be continuous and adapted to the changing circumstances in which children live. Also, starting from the concept of

380 U.N. Doc. E/1992/23, 1994, CESCR Committee, General comment No. 4: The right to adequate housing, § 41.

381 Ibidem supra note 380, § 8d and f.

382 Ibidem supra note 346 Eide, § 79.

children's evolving capacities in article 5 CRC, services must be responsive to the changing needs of children. Therefore, four levels of priority have been identified in the organization of health care for young children:

1. Provision of health care and information to the mother during pregnancy.
2. Obstetric health care around the birth of the child.
3. Neonatal health care for the mother and the child immediately after birth.
4. Quality health care during childhood.

In order to realize these key elements, measures must be taken to prevent children from being excluded from the health services and from the underlying determinants of health being provided. Secondly, in shaping the way in which health services are organized, the best interests of the child as a child in its own social context must be leading and not only the interests of the child as a sick person. This means that the right to the highest attainable standard of health not only encompasses the provision of health services, but it also requires to take into account children's needs in other aspects of their daily life, such as the continuation of school and leisure activities, contacts with family and friends and support for both the child and its family members in dealing with the consequences of a diagnosis for the daily life and future perspectives of the child. To meet the needs of the individual child, it is required to involve both children and their parents in the identification of the child's particular needs in healthcare and in other areas of life.

To enable the child and its parents to be involved in the selection of medical treatments, quality and age-adjusted health information must be provided. This includes information on medical decision making at the individual level and the provision of preventive health information to all parents and children. While the provision of health information is required, it is also required to maintain confidentiality and provide for confidential counselling for children of all ages. The CRC Committee has underlined that the obligation to inform and involve people in children's health must also be realized *vis-à-vis* very young children, because they are considered as rights holders from the very beginning of their lives. Stimulating children to become involved in their own health care from the very beginning gradually enhances their capacities to take ownership of their own health during the rest of their lives. Simply listening to children is not sufficient. Feedback must be given on what has been done with their input. Although adapted to the level of comprehension of the child, adults must respect children's views and communicate with children as equal partners. It is important to realize that disagreement with children does not justify the setting aside of their views. It may even be required to accept children's views that are highly contested.

The next paragraph will further investigate the elaboration and implications of the right to the highest attainable standard of health of the child and the respective role of parents and the State in ensuring this by the Committee on the

Rights of the Child as found in the relevant General Comments. The last paragraph will then discuss the implications of this legal framework for the work of medical professionals by taking the medical ethical framework as a point of reference for integrating the right to health of the child in the daily medical practice.

2.5. INTERPRETATION OF THE CHILD'S RIGHT TO HEALTH IN THE GENERAL COMMENTS

The UN Committee on the Rights of the Child regularly issues General Comments (GC) in which an interpretation is given of the content of children's rights provisions. Specifically related to the right to health are GC no. 3 on 'HIV/AIDS and the right of the child'[383] and GC no. 4 on 'adolescent health'[384] and GC 15 on the right of the child to enjoy the highest attainable standard of health.[385] Other GC's contain passages referring to the right of the child to health in a particular context. For example, GC no. 10 contains a very brief reference to the right of juveniles to be examined by a physician on admission to an institution and to receive adequate medical care from the regular community health services during their stay in the institution.[386] Also, GC no. 13 indicates that the right of the child to be free from all forms of violence is necessary to achieve good physical and mental health.[387] In the following, further insight will be provided in the elaboration of the right to the highest attainable standard of health in the General Comments of the Committee on the Rights of the Child. Particular attention is paid to the right to health of children in their early childhood.

2.5.1. GENERAL COMMENT 3: HIV/AIDS AND THE RIGHTS OF THE CHILD

GC no. 3 on the prevention of HIV/AIDS draws attention to the fact that children are extremely vulnerable to infection. The majority of infections occur among adolescents and young people (15–24). Also, because of a lack of information on the prevention of AIDS among women, their children become unknowingly

[383] U.N. Doc. CRC/GC/2003/3, General Comment 3 on HIV/AIDS and the rights of the child, 17 March 2003.

[384] U.N. Doc. CRC/GC/2003/4, General Comment 4 on Adolescent health and development in the context of the Convention on the Rights of the Child, 1 July 2003.

[385] U.N. Doc. CRC/C/GC/2013/15, General Comment 15 on the Right of the Child to the Highest Attainable Standard of Health, 17 April 2013.

[386] U.N. Doc. CRC/C/GC/10, General Comment 10 on Children's rights in juvenile justice, 25 April 2007, § 89, p. 23.

[387] U.N. Doc. CRC/C/GC/13, General Comment 13 on the right of the child to be free from all forms of violence, 18 April 2011.

infected with HIV/AIDS, resulting in an increase in infant and child mortality ratios.

The Committee on the Rights of the Child has identified a large number of rights relevant to the prevention and treatment of HIV/AIDS among children and youth. Central to this is art. 24 CRC, but the Committee has stressed that the HIV/AIDS epidemic is more than a health problem. Other relevant CRC articles provide for further protection of children's health, including art. 9 (right not to be separated from parents), art. 16 (right to privacy), art. 17, 24-f and 28 (right to information and education, particularly on sexual health and family planning), art. 23 (rights of disabled children), art. 26 and 27 (right to an adequate standard of living and the right to social security, including health insurance) and art. 19 and 32–37 (right to protection against violence, abuse, abduction and sale, inhuman and degrading treatment). These provisions are particularly relevant in the context of the right to non-discrimination, as children infected with HIV/AIDS often suffer from stigmatization and a lack of access to health care. Several groups are mentioned to be particularly vulnerable to discrimination such as minority children, disabled children, orphaned children, children living on the street, children abusing drugs and children suffering from sexual exploitation.

The Committee sets several related priorities in the combatting of the HIV/AIDS epidemic, among which the access to age appropriate, child friendly information is considered essential to prevention, testing, counselling, treatment and care. The Committee stresses the importance of an open dialogue in families, schools and in the community to stimulate a positive and healthy attitude towards sexuality. These priorities correspond to article 24 CRC, particularly elaborating on sub 2a on the reduction of infant mortality, 2b on the right to access for children to health services. Sub 2d on pre- and postnatal health care and sub 3 on the importance of breastfeeding are reflected in an elaboration of the need for and the particular guidelines for breastfeeding in the case of an HIV infection of the mother and the prevention of mother-to-child-transmission.

In general, GC no. 3 on the prevention of HIV/AIDS among children aims to strengthen the understanding and promote the realization of all children's rights in the context of HIV/AIDS by promoting child-oriented laws, policies and programs.[388]

2.5.2. GENERAL COMMENT 4: ADOLESCENT HEALTH AND DEVELOPMENT

General Comment 4 elaborates upon a large number of health topics particularly relevant for adolescents.[389] This General Comment is partly relevant for infants

388 Ibidem supra note 382, § 4.

389 Ibidem supra note 383, § 12, 23, 24.

and children as it addresses the prevention of teenage pregnancies and the need to support teenage mothers and their babies.

Much attention is drawn to the need to respect the views of the child and involve adolescents in their own health and development. Hereto, an elaboration is provided on the right to informed consent, privacy and confidentiality in the healthcare setting.[390] In addition, adolescents must be given access to adequate information for health and development and participate meaningfully in society. It is stated that school programs must be targeted at the development of the child's fullest potential, that they should be given the skills to take good care of themselves, for example by cooking healthy meals, paying attention to hygiene, coping with stress and educating them about sexual and reproductive health to prevent sexually transmitted diseases and early pregnancies. No marketing activities are deemed allowed to promote unhealthy lifestyles.[391]

Another important issue in General Comment 4 is the necessity to prevent violence to prevent health problems among adolescents. For example, it is stated that adolescents must be taught how to make decisions in a non-violent manner, that they should be involved in the development of programmes and measures to protect them against violence, abuse, neglect and exploitation and that adolescents must be raised in a safe and supportive environment and be given the opportunity to discuss (health) problems openly. Specific violence-related problems that must be targeted are violence in the family, interpersonal violence among peers, participation in gangs, the participation of child soldiers in armed conflicts, violence targeted at orphans and disabled children, harmful traditional practices and honour killings. Measures to be taken to prevent violence impacting on adolescents' health include the restriction of access to (light) weapons and to alcohol and drugs.

Several guidelines are given for the provision of health services for adolescents: qualitative services must be available, accessible and acceptable to vulnerable groups such as physically and mentally disabled children, homeless children, sexually exploited children, children with mental health problems, minority and indigenous children and former child soldiers.[392] For this last group, particular rehabilitation and reintegration services must be established.

In order to improve the health status of adolescents, a multi-sectorial approach is propagated, wherein linkages and partnerships are established between all relevant actors, including practitioners in public health and traditional health practices, pharmaceuticals, special organizations for vulnerable groups and international (UN) agencies and international NGOs.[393]

The empowerment of adolescents by providing with necessary health information is important for the prevention of health problems resulting from

[390] Ibidem supra note 383, § 26–33.
[391] Ibidem supra note 383, § 17 & 25.
[392] Ibidem supra note 383, § 34–38.
[393] Ibidem supra note 383, § 43.

sexually transmitted diseases, mental health problems, alcohol and drugs, injuries and violence. Educating adolescents about their sexual and reproductive health rights (SRHR) benefits young children, because it increases the age at which girls first become pregnant. This increases the chance that girls finish their education and obtain good jobs so that they can provide their children with quality care and food. Secondly, education on SRHR benefits young children because it influences the spacing between subsequent births. This in its turn influences the value of the care and nutrition given to the children.[394]

2.5.3. GENERAL COMMENT 7: CHILDREN'S RIGHTS IN EARLY CHILDHOOD

General Comment 7 particularly aims to contribute to the realization of children's rights in early childhood and 'to encourage recognition of young children as social actors from the beginning of life, with particular interests, capacities and vulnerabilities, and of requirements for protection, guidance and support in the exercise of their rights'.[395] In an elaboration of the right to life (art. 6 CRC), State Parties are urged to improve perinatal care for mothers and babies, reduce infant and child mortality, and create conditions that promote the well-being of young children.[396] Mention is made of the role of malnutrition and preventable diseases and the interaction between physical health and psychosocial wellbeing. Here again, the holistic approach to the enforcement of the right to health integrates the right to health and the right to adequate nutrition and a healthy and safe environment (art. 24-2c and 29 CRC). Explicit referral is made to the duty to empower young children to adopt a healthy and disease-preventing lifestyle. The notion to empower children to play an active role in their development has been further developed in General Comment 12 on the right to participation of the child.

The right to non-discrimination as elaborated in General Comment 7 assures that no child is refused access to health care (art. 24-2b). Explicit mention is made of disabled children, children infected with HIV/AIDS and girls, regularly suffering from selective abortion, infanticide, inadequate feeding in infancy and female genital mutilation. Vulnerable groups of children need extra attention to ensure their right to health, as they are more prone to health risks such as

394 For a further discussion on the advantages and disadvantages of birth spacing see for example the Report of a WHO Technical Consultation on Birth Spacing, Geneva, Switzerland, 13–15 June 2005, available at: www.who.int/maternal_child_adolescent/documents/birth_spacing.pdf.

395 U.N. Doc. CRC/C/GC/7/Rev.1, General Comment 7 on Child rights in early childhood, 20 September 2006, § 2.

396 Ibidem supra note 395, § 2.

malnutrition, infectious disease, injuries, abuse and neglect, substance abuse and unhealthy working conditions.

Among the comprehensive programs for young children is the provision to ensure health care.[397] The highest attainable standard of health care must be ensured by States Parties in order to reduce infant mortality (art. 24-2a). This duty ranges from the provision of adequate drinking water, nutrition and sanitation to immunization campaigns, medical services and a stress-free environment. Education about healthy behaviour for both adults and children is also mentioned, including child-centred health education programmes. Finally, attention is drawn to the need for prevention of HIV/AIDS and early diagnosis, effective treatment and alternative forms of support for infected and orphaned children.

With respect to young children's capacities to engage in meaningful participation, the CRC Committee acknowledges in General Comment 7 that 'young children's agency – as a participant in family, community and society – is frequently overlooked or rejected as inappropriate on the grounds of age and immaturity.' They often suffer from social ideas that they first need training and socialization before they can make and communicate choices. Therefore, the Committee emphasizes that article 12 applies to younger children as much as it does to older children and that they are 'acutely sensitive to their surroundings and very rapidly acquire understanding of the people, places and routines in their lives, along with awareness of their own unique identity. They make choices and communicate their feelings, ideas and wishes in numerous ways, long before they are able to communicate through the conventions of spoken or written language.' Therefore, the CRC Committee underlines that the right to be heard of the child is implemented from the very earliest stage and that it must be fully integrated in the child's daily life, including in early childhood health.[398]

Parents play a crucial role in the realization of the rights of young children. Especially babies and toddlers are highly dependent on the good care of their parents or caretakers. However, they are not passive recipients of care and guidance, but they actively seek care, nurturance and direction and soon after their birth they recognize their parents. In this way, close relationships develop between children and their parents.[399] In responding to their children's needs, parents must continuously adapt to the changing needs of their children. This should be seen as a positive and enabling process, in which parents are encouraged to provide guidance in a child-centred way. In that way, they are best able to enhance children's capacities to take increasing responsibilities for their own health. To enhance young children's opportunities to express themselves, parents and professionals must be stimulated to adopt a child-centred attitude, to listen patiently to children and respect their views and use creativity in 'adapting

[397] Ibidem supra note 395, § 24.
[398] Ibidem supra note 395, § 14b.
[399] Ibidem supra note 395, § 16.

their expectations to the interests, levels of understanding and preferred ways of communication of young children'.[400]

2.5.4. GENERAL COMMENT 9: THE RIGHTS OF CHILDREN WITH DISABILITIES

The Committee has stressed that disabled children have the right to an adequate standard of living, including adequate food, clothing and housing, and to the continuous improvement of their living conditions.[401] Adequate allocation of budgetary resources is recommended as well as ensuring that children with disabilities have access to social protection.[402] Herein, health is mentioned as a particular focus area to ensure maximum inclusion of children in society,[403] further mentioning that care and assistance must be designed to ensure effective access to health services for disabled children. This means that special services are often required, whereas these necessary medical services must be integrated into the regular public health system for all children to reduce the risk of discrimination.[404]

In allocating the available financial means, the ultimate responsibility of the State to ensure the (physical) access of disabled children to health services is emphasized given the current developments of decentralization and privatization wherein private parties tend to take over or neglect this responsibility.[405] In meeting this responsibility, States are encouraged to cooperate with international organizations such as UNICEF, the WHO and NGOs to ensure that they operate in full compliance with the convention.

Central in the approach to improve knowledge, skills and capabilities on the prevention and treatment of disabilities, is the recommendation to exchange information between countries.[406] This can help to attain early identification of disabilities and enhance a community-supported approach to support families, as well as the systematic training of (medical) professionals working with children. Information must also be dispatched to the children and their families themselves, so that they are aware of causes, management and prognoses of their disabilities.[407] The knowledge will also help to make informed medical decisions. Dependent on the type of disability, means of communication must therefore be adapted, for example by using Braille materials for blind children. Given the fact that disabled children often have multiple health issues, it is recommended to

400 Ibidem supra note 395, § 14c.
401 U.N. Doc. CRC/C/GC/9, GC 9: The rights of children with disabilities, 27 February 2007, § 3.
402 Ibidem supra note 401, § 20.
403 Ibidem supra note 401, § 11.
404 Ibidem supra note 401, § 52.
405 Ibidem supra note 401, § 59.
406 Ibidem supra note 401, § 22.
407 Ibidem supra note 401, § 37.

address the health issues in a team approach of professionals, such as neurologists, psychologists, psychiatrists, orthopaedic surgeons and physiotherapists.[408]

The identified causes of disabilities are multiple and prevention must therefore be targeted through different methods, including the prevention of inherited diseases due to consanguineous marriages, appropriate preconception testing, universal immunization campaigns to prevent communicable diseases causing disabilities, poor nutrition (e.g. blindness is caused by a Vitamin A deficiency), adequate assistance during delivery and the prevention of road accidents by traffic laws and guidelines on wearing safety belts.[409] Education and support of pregnant women will be targeted to prevent disabilities such as the foetal alcohol syndrome due to alcohol or drug abuse. Policies to prevent dumping of hazardous materials and other means of polluting the environment, such as the prevention of radiation accidents must also be in placed. Last but not least, the attention for prevention is drawn to the harmful effects of armed conflicts resulting from the massive spread of small arms and landmines.[410] The Committee recommends that laws and policies must be put in place to continue to locate and dismantle landmines, to keep children away from hazardous areas and to ensure access of affected children to rehabilitative health services.

With regard to the access of disabled children to health care, several aspects are predominant. In the first place, mention is made that disabled children are more vulnerable to non-registration at birth.[411] This increases the risk that they become invisible to government officials and thereby are excluded from access to health services. Other barriers to effective access identified result from discrimination (disabilities are sometimes viewed upon as a bad omen), inaccessibility due to a lack of suitable information, necessary (extra) finances and physical access to health facilities. The requirement of physical access encompasses the need to ensure adequate means of transportation so that disabled children can actually reach health institutions.[412] Recommended is therefore that health programs must be comprehensive and include early detection of disabilities, early intervention and rehabilitation measures (the provision of physical aids such as free of cost limb prostheses, mobility devices, hearing and visual aids).[413] Early detection and intervention require high awareness among parents, teachers and health personnel and an easy access of these services.[414]

---

[408] Ibidem supra note 401, § 58.
[409] Ibidem supra note 401, § 53–54.
[410] Ibidem supra note 401, § 55.
[411] Ibidem supra note 401, § 35.
[412] Ibidem supra note 401, § 39.
[413] Ibidem supra note 401, § 51.
[414] Ibidem supra note 401, § 56.

2.5.5. GENERAL COMMENT 11: INDIGENOUS CHILDREN AND THEIR RIGHTS UNDER THE CONVENTION

Given the previously identified vulnerability of indigenous groups of children (see § 4), State Parties are urged to apply specific measures to ensure that indigenous children have access to culturally appropriate health services.[415] Central in this General Comment is the urge for respect for culturally sensitive and community based health services in the language of the indigenous children.[416] Particular attention is required to ensure access to health services for indigenous peoples who reside in rural and remote areas or in areas of armed conflict or who are migrant workers, refugees or displaced and for the culturally sensitive needs of disabled indigenous children.[417] Therefore, the Committee advocates that in the provision of health care, preference must be given to health care workers and medical staff from the indigenous community, as they could function as a bridge between traditional medicine and conventional medical services.[418] They should receive the necessary means and special training to fulfil this role in a way that is mindful of their culture and traditions.[419] This could also be effective in combating harmful traditional practices, furthermore supported by the implementation of laws and programs to change attitudes and address gender roles that contribute to these practices.[420] To achieve these targets, States are stimulated to allocate additional financial and human resources to implement economic, social and cultural rights and where necessary seek help from the international community.[421]

2.5.6. GENERAL COMMENT 12: THE RIGHT OF THE CHILD TO BE HEARD

The right of the child to be heard has been elaborated specifically for application in the health care sector.[422] It applies both to individual health decisions and to children's involvement in the development of health policy and services. This extents to the determination of the services needed, how and where they are best provided, the identification of discriminatory barriers to and attitudes of

415 Ibidem supra note 245, § 25.
416 Ibidem supra note 245, § 51.
417 Idem, supra note 245.
418 Ibidem supra note 245, § 52.
419 In this context, the Committee recalls article 25(2) of the ILO Convention No. 169 and articles 24 and 31 of the United Nations Declaration on the Rights of Indigenous Peoples on the right of indigenous peoples to their traditional medicines, A/RES/61/295, Articles 24, 31.
420 Ibidem supra note 245, § 7.
421 Ibidem supra note 245, § 34.
422 U.N. Doc. CRC/C/GC/12 on the Rights of the Child to be heard, 20 July 2009, § 98–104.

professionals to have access to health care and the elaboration of ways to best involve children of different ages.[423]

In order to be able to engage in meaningful ways of participation, children must be provided with understandable information (art. 17 CRC) about proposed treatments, their (side-)effects and outcome in a manner consistent with their evolving capacities (art. 5 CRC). In fulfilling the right to information the Committee on the Rights of the Child states that States must ensure confidentiality. This right to confidential information and counselling applies to all children, irrespective of their age and maturity. It must therefore be distinguished from the right to informed consent, which usually has a certain age threshold beyond which children have the right to independent consent or refusal to any medical treatment without the approval of their parents and without an assessment of their capacities.

Often the criticism is made that the capacities of very young children are too limited to engage in meaningful participation. However, the CRC Committee has explicitly rejected this standpoint in its considerations on the right of children in their early childhood to be heard in all matters and procedures affecting them. The basis of its argumentation is that children should be approached as rights-holders from the very beginning of their lives and that 'young children should be recognized as active members of families, communities and societies, with their own concerns, interests and points of view'.[424]

The CRC Committee considers that 'States parties should presume that a child has the capacity to form her or his own views and recognize that she or he has the right to express them', even 'if the child is not yet able to verbally express itself'.[425]

While the CRC Committee discourages States to introduce age limits in its national legislation, it explains the concept of children's evolving capacities as an obligation for States to 'assess the capacity of the child to form an autonomous opinion to the greatest extent possible'.[426] Particularly, this requires the 'recognition of, and respect for, non-verbal forms of communication including play, body language, facial expressions, and drawing and painting, through which very young children demonstrate understanding, choices and preferences.[427]

The CRC Committee furthermore considers that children don't need to have a comprehensive understanding of all aspects of the matter affecting them; they only need to have 'sufficient understanding to be capable of appropriately forming her or his own views on the matter'.[428] States Parties are under the obligation to ensure that children have the required modes of communication at their disposal

---

423 Ibidem supra note 422, § 104.
424 Ibidem supra note 422, § 21.
425 Ibidem supra note 422, § 20–21.
426 Ibidem supra note 422, § 20.
427 Ibidem supra note 422, § 21.
428 Ibidem supra note 422, § 21.

to express their views and that all measures need to be in place to protect children from manipulation or pressure or in expressing their views and that they should not be interviewed too often.[429] The CRC Committee particularly warns for the potentially negative consequences of inconsiderate practices in (not) hearing young children, especially on sensitive issues.[430]

Simply listening to children is not sufficient.[431] Their views must be seriously considered and feedback must be given on the ways in which children's views were weighed.[432] This must be done by a case-by-case examination, because different levels of information, experience, levels of support and social and cultural expectations all influence the capacities of children to form its own views.[433]

In principle, in assessing children's evolving capacities, States Parties shall also respect the responsibilities, rights and duties of parents, legal guardians, or members of the extended family or community to give direction and guidance to the child in her or his exercise of its rights'. In this way, the lack of knowledge or experience of the child is compensated by the guiding of its parents or caretakers.[434] Whereas children should be approached as rights holders from the very beginning, their responsibilities increase as they grow older and mature.

2.5.7. GENERAL COMMENT 13: THE RIGHT OF THE CHILD TO FREEDOM OF ALL FORMS OF VIOLENCE

General Comment 13 focuses on the protection of children against all forms of violence.[435] The Committee has considered that the extent and intensity of violence against children is alarming, violence being defined as 'all forms of physical and mental violence, injury or abuse, neglect or negligent treatment, maltreatment or exploitation, including abuse' as phrased in article 19-1 CRC and in conformity with the terminology as used in the 2006 UN Study on Violence against Children.[436] Whereas the Committee recognizes that families have the greatest potential to protect children,[437] it is acknowledged that the majority of violence takes place in the context of (extended) families so that intervention and support may therefore be required when children become victims of domestic violence or when violence is imposed upon families as a whole. Furthermore, the

---

429 Ibidem supra note 422, § 21.
430 Ibidem supra note 422, § 21.
431 Ibidem supra note 422, § 28.
432 Ibidem supra note 422, § 45.
433 Ibidem supra note 422, § 29.
434 Ibidem supra note 422, § 84.
435 U.N. Doc. CRC/C/GC/13 on Article 19: The right of the child to freedom from all forms of violence, 17 February 2011.
436 Ibidem supra note 435, § 3 and U.N. Doc. A/61/299, Report of the independent expert for the United Nations study on violence against children, 29 August 2006.
437 Ibidem supra note 435, § 65d.

public health sector is identified as having a significant role to play in the primary prevention of violence ánd in providing for recovery and social reintegration services.[438] The 2006 UN Study on Violence against Children comes to a similar recommendation to provide for recovery and social reintegration services in calling for accessible, child-sensitive and universal health and social services, including pre-hospital and emergency care for children and their families.[439]

The impact of violence on children's (right to) health is elaborated in General Comment 13. In the first place, securing well-being, health and development of the child is identified as the ultimate goal of child care and protection.[440] From this central premise, both the short and the long-term health consequences of violence on children's survival and development, as protected under article 27-1 CRC, are specified, including fatal injury and non-fatal injury, possibly leading to disabilities, physical health problems such as failure to thrive, lung, heart and liver problems, sexually transmitted diseases, mental health problems and health-risk behaviours.[441] In the explanation of the Committee on the Rights of the Child on the different forms of child maltreatment, several aspects relate to the impact of violence on children's health. For example, the Committee elaborates that neglect includes the failure to meet children's physical and psychological needs, such as basic necessities like food, water, clothing and essential medical care and failure to obtain medical and birth registration necessary to have access to health services.[442] It is further exemplified that physical violence, including corporal punishment and harmful traditional practices may lead to fatal or non-fatal injuries, possibly leading to lifelong physical and psychological harm, requiring medical care and recovery.[443] This is particularly true for forced sterilisations (often inflicted upon disabled children), deliberate infliction of disabilities for the purpose of exploitation by begging on the streets, violence in the guise of treatment (electroconvulsive therapy to control children's behaviour), female genital mutilations, amputations, burning, scarring, binding and branding, force-feeding, virginity testing, exorcism of children accused of witchcraft, uvulectomy and teeth extractions.[444] Self-harm, including eating disorders and substance abuse, automutilation and suicidal thoughts, attempts and suicides also result in violations of children's right to health.[445] Failure to protect children against the different kinds of violence, including a lack of supervision, is qualified as neglect.[446] On the societal level, both direct and indirect costs are identified,

---

438 Ibidem supra note 435, § 2 and § 38.

439 A/61/299, Report of the independent expert for the United Nations study on violence against children, 29 August 2006, p. 26.

440 Ibidem supra note 435, § 17 and 52.

441 Ibidem supra note 435, § 14.

442 Ibidem supra note 435, § 19.

443 Ibidem supra note 435, § 24.

444 Ibidem supra note 435, § 21–27.

445 Ibidem supra note 435, § 26.

446 Ibidem supra note 435, § 19.

including the costs of necessary medical care, social services and alternative care and social problems resulting from disabilities.

While the range of possible violations impacting upon children's right to health is broad and diverse, it is important to identify who can be held responsible for protecting children against violence and who is responsible for providing the necessary medical care to recover. General Comment 13 provides several indications to answering this question by elaborating on the concept of caregivers as defined in article 19 CRC, being responsible for the safety, health, development and well-being of the child.[447] Such caregivers include the biological, foster or adoptive parents, the legal guardians of the child, extended family members, community members, school and early childhood personnel, child caregivers employed by parents, institutional and health care personnel, in short all persons caring for the child for a shorter or longer period. The settings where these caregivers are primarily expected to watch over the child include places where children reside permanently or temporarily, medical, rehabilitative and care centres and refugee camps for children who are displaced by conflict or natural disasters.[448]

The recommended measures to ensure the protection of children against violence and the recovery after suffering from it, include general measures such as budget allocation, social welfare programmes to support children and caregivers, academic teaching on children's rights, research programmes and the identification and prevention of hindered access for vulnerable groups of children to health services.[449] Specifically related to health, recommendations are made to implement public health policies, improving access to health and ensure registration of children to ensure access to health and social services.[450] The recommendations extend to the provision of pre- and postnatal services, home visitation programmes, strengthening the link between mental health services for adults, substance abuse treatments and child protection services and[451] the provision of medical, mental health and social services for children who have experienced violence and the establishment of help lines particularly aimed at offering public health and social support.[452]

When coming to measures to protect children's health and well-being at the level of individual children, the Committee on the Rights of the Child gives a very extensive enumeration of all groups of children who are particularly vulnerable to suffer from violence. It is acknowledged that babies and young children are most vulnerable due to their immaturity and complete dependency on adults.[453]

447 Ibidem supra note 435, § 31.
448 Ibidem supra note 435, § 32.
449 Ibidem supra note 435, § 38–40.
450 Ibidem supra note 435, § 40–43.
451 Ibidem supra note 435, § 43.
452 Ibidem supra note 435, § 45 and 48.
453 Ibidem supra note 435, § 65f.

Among the many other groups of vulnerable children, mention is made of children who are separated from their biological families, children living on the street, physically disabled children, children with congenital, acquired or chronic illnesses, malnourished children and children who are hospitalized without adequate supervision.[454]

All in all, General Comment 13 on the protection of children against violence pays extensive attention to the harmful effects of violence on children's health and the recommended measures to prevent these effects. A central role in protecting children is attributed to the primary caregivers, being responsible to take care of the child in both private and professional environments.

2.5.8. THE NEWLY ADOPTED GENERAL COMMENT 15 ON CHILDREN'S RIGHT TO HEALTH

In December 2011, the UN Committee on the Rights of the Child issued a call for submissions on the interpretation of children's right to health in preparation of the forthcoming General Comment on the right of the child to the enjoyment of the highest attainable standard of health. From all over the world, academics, NGOs, other interest groups and ombudspersons submitted contributions focussing on either the general principles underpinning the right of the child to the enjoyment of the highest attainable standard of health or zooming into a particular subtheme relating to this right.[455]

In March 2013, the UN Committee on the Rights of the Child issued General Comment 15 on the right of the child to the enjoyment of the highest attainable standard of health. This General Comment elucidates the interpretation by the Committee of the normative content of article 24 CRC, the resulting obligations of State Parties and the responsibilities of non-state parties and it provides for a framework for implementation and accountability for any intervention identified, political commitment and sufficient allocation of resources are deemed essential.[456]

---

454 Ibidem supra note 435, § 65g.

455 The 36 resulting submissions were published online: www2.ohchr.org/english/bodies/crc/callsubmissionsCRC_received.htm. Particular subtopics included in the submitted contributions deal with reproductive and sexual health rights of children, the health rights of lesbian, gay, bisexual, transgender and intersex children, disabled children, children born with drug addicted parents, parents who denied their pregnancy, children in need of palliative care, children in detention, children in out-of-home care, children without parental guidance or children as caretakers, children with mental health problems, children in hospitals, children participating in medical research, and children in rural areas.

456 U.N. Doc. CRC/C/GC/15 on the right of the child to the enjoyment of the highest attainable standard of health, 14th March 2013, § 2–4.

2.5.8.1. *Holistic approach to health*

In interpreting the right to the highest attainable standard of health, the Committee deliberately emphasizes the need to take a holistic approach to realizing the right to the highest attainable standard of health. General Comment 15 stipulates that children not only have a right to timely and appropriate prevention, health promotion, curative, rehabilitative and palliative health care but also that children have 'the right to opportunities to survive, grow and develop to their full potential and to live in conditions that enable them to attain the highest attainable standard of health'.[457] Healthy living conditions are thus deemed essential for the enjoyment of the highest attainable standard of health of the child.[458] The approach taken in the General Comment is deliberately generic in order to be applicable to a wide variety of health problems, contexts and countries.[459]

The requirement to approach the right to health of the child holistically also follows from the identification of the broad range of stakeholders that should or can contribute to the realization of the right to the highest attainable standard of health of the child.[460] It is not only children, parents, medical professionals and policy makers who can contribute, but in fact any participant in society whose activities directly or indirectly influence the realization of the right of the child. A further investigation into ways in which all potential stakeholders can contribute to the realization of the right to health of the child will be conducted in chapter 6 on the realization of the right to health of the child.

2.5.8.2. *Active involvement of all stakeholders*

In several instances, the need to involve all stakeholders in the different stages of the realization process of the right to the highest attainable standard of health of the child is highlighted. For example, in the organization of primary health care, health services must be organized around people's needs and expectations, collaborative models of policy dialogue must be sought and stakeholder participation must be increased in the demand and appropriate use of services.[461] In order to empower young women to combat instances of gender discrimination such as female infanticide and preferential feeding their (political) participation is deemed necessary.[462] Most specifically, the central role of parents and other caregivers must be better recognized, for example in acknowledging the relation between the realization of the right to health of the mother and decreasing

---

[457] Ibidem supra note 456.
[458] Ibidem supra note 456, § 2, 5, 13, 17, 18, 43–50.
[459] Ibidem supra note 456, § 3.
[460] Ibidem supra note 456, § 3, 76–85.
[461] Ibidem supra note 456, § 4, 15, 19.
[462] Ibidem supra note 456, § 9.

rates of perinatal mortality and in improving breastfeeding practices.[463] It is acknowledged that the socialisation process and thus the health behaviour of children is heavily influenced by the parents and parents are considered to be an important source for early diagnosis and primary care in small children.[464] Therefore, participatory consultations must be held separately with parents and children in order to learn about children's health problems, developmental needs and expectations to improve the design of health programmes and interventions.[465] The involvement of parents and other caregivers is also highlighted in preventing health problems.[466]

All participatory initiatives must take into account the age and evolving capacities of the children involved. Thereto, understanding of the life course is essential. Special consideration must be given to involving vulnerable children in the realization of the right to health of the child, because they often have the fewest opportunities to exercise their autonomy.[467] The particular involvement of children in realizing their own right to health is highlighted by stating that children must be enabled to claim their own right to health and in the acknowledgement that children have the right to control one's own health and body with increasing maturity.[468] General Comment 15 elaborates very precisely several issues in which children's views must be sought:[469]

- What services are needed?
- How and where are these services best provided?
- What barriers do children encounter in accessing or using these services?
- How do children assess the quality of the services available to them?
- How do children assess the attitudes of health professionals?
- How can children's capacities be strengthened to take increasing responsibility for their own health and development?
- How can children be more effectively involved in the provision of services as health educators?

In order to enable all stakeholders to participate meaningfully in decisions on their own health and on the provision of medical services, health education is essential. Article 24.2 (e) CRC and its elaboration in General Comment 15 establish that States must ensure an environment in which parents and children are encouraged to pursue health-seeking behaviour. Schools can play a constructive role in stimulating children and their families to healthy behaviour

463 Ibidem supra note 456, § 6, 15, 18, 67.
464 Ibidem supra note 456, § 67.
465 Ibidem supra note 456, § 19, 32.
466 Ibidem supra note 456, § 67.
467 Ibidem supra note 456, § 21.
468 Ibidem supra note 456, § 6, 24.
469 Ibidem supra note 456, § 19.

by providing healthy food, health education, establishing school gardens and training teachers to stimulate healthy behaviour in their pupils.[470] This can be beneficial both in developing countries where the provision of (healthy) food can be a strong motivational factor for parents to send their children to school, but also in developed countries where the availability of healthy food in school canteens and the restrictions on marketing of unhealthy products are essential in reducing the alarming incidence of obesity among children.[471] Topics in health education should inter alia include healthy eating and promotion of physical activity, sports, recreation, accident and injury prevention, sanitation, hand washing and other personal hygienic practices and the dangers of alcohol, tobacco and drugs.[472]

Not only schools, but also private businesses and mass and social media have a role to play in stimulating healthy behaviour among children and adolescents. Mass and social media can play a role in this by exclusively promoting healthy lifestyles, providing free advertising spaces for health promotion, respecting privacy and confidentiality of children and providing access to health information.[473]

2.5.8.3. Primary health care

In line with article 24.1 and 24.2(b) CRC the provision of primary health care is prioritized as the main route to follow to achieve the right of the child to the enjoyment of the highest attainable standard of health.[474] As an absolute minimum, the facilities provided for the treatment of illness and the rehabilitation of health should include prevention, promotion, treatment, rehabilitation and palliative care.[475] The health care system also has a role in reporting violence and injustice.[476]

Whereas the Committee acknowledges that the exact configuration of health services varies per country, a few elements are qualified as essential, namely a robust financing system, a well-trained and adequately paid workforce, reliable information, well-maintained facilities and logistics systems to deliver quality medicines and technologies and strong leadership and governance.[477] Very specifically, special reference is made to the usefulness of 'The essential interventions, commodities and guidelines on reproductive, maternal, newborn and child health' for establishing a system of primary health care that meets the

470 Ibidem supra note 456, § 46.
471 Ibidem supra note 456, § 47.
472 Ibidem supra note 456, § 59.
473 Ibidem supra note 456, § 84.
474 Ibidem supra note 456, § 4.
475 Ibidem supra note 456, § 25.
476 Ibidem supra note 456, § 25.
477 Ibidem supra note 456, § 27, 36.

minimum requirements deriving from the right to health of the child.[478] Secondly, States have the obligation to make available all essential medicines for children as specified on the WHO Model Lists for Essential Medicines – Children. This list consists of a core and a complementary part, which respectively specify i) the list of efficacious, safe and cost effective medicines that are minimally required for a basic health care system and ii) the list of medicines for priority diseases that require specialized diagnosis, monitoring, treatment or training of professionals.[479]

The involvement of stakeholders in the provision of primary health care facilities is also required in the organization of primary health care, because the primary health care provided must be matched with community-based efforts, such as immunization programs, nutritional interventions, efforts to prevent health problems and injuries resulting from violence and traffic and provision of community-based health information.[480] This can be optimized by undertaking an in-depth analysis of priority health problems, where appropriate with children and their families.[481]

Universal access to primary health care should be achieved *inter alia* by setting up facilities in close proximity to children and families, for example by collaboration with or in close proximity to schools and by deploying mobile health clinics and health kits.[482] Mobile health clinics can be useful in areas where no permanent services are available due to a lack of resources (e.g. India), remoteness and low population density (e.g. Australia) or in emergency situations (Haiti after the earthquake).[483] General Comment 15 establishes that the private sector could play a role in making such mobile arrangements available so that all children can gain access to health services.[484]

Whereas States have a responsibility to establish a comprehensive primary health care system for all children as an absolute minimum, secondary and tertiary systems should be provided to the largest extent possible, including functional systems of referral.[485] Dependent on the age of the child, the care provided should adopt a i) baby-friendly, ii) child-friendly or iii) adolescent-friendly approaches, that are aimed at minimizing fear and suffering of children and their families.[486]

---

478 Ibidem supra note 456, § 37 and The essential interventions, commodities and guidelines on reproductive, maternal, newborn and child health, available at: www.who.int/pmnch/topics/part_publications/essentialinterventions14_12_2011low.pdf.

479 Ibidem supra note 456, § 37, 38 and WHO Model Lists for Essential Medicines – Children, 3rd list, March 2011, available at: http://whqlibdoc.who.int/hq/2011/a95054_eng.pdf.

480 Ibidem supra note 456, § 26, 35.

481 Ibidem supra note 456, § 32.

482 Ibidem supra note 456, § 36.

483 Ibidem supra note 456, § 40.

484 Ibidem supra note 456, § 41,42.

485 Ibidem supra note 456, § 24,28.

486 Ibidem supra note 456, § 53.

2.5.8.4. *Reduction of infant and child mortality*

General Comment further elaborates the requirements to reduce infant and child mortality as laid down in article 24.2(a). The Committee acknowledges that infant and child health is strongly related to maternal health. Therefore, timely and quality health care is required to prevent intergenerational transmission of health problems.[487] General Comment 15 specifies the interventions that should be made to address the main health problems leading to infant and child mortality, including the provision of essential care before, during and after delivery, safe abortion services, the provision of sexual and reproductive health information and services and social protection such as universal coverage and paid parental leave to ensure access for mothers and children to essential health care. The Committee furthermore provides for a non-exhaustive list that qualifies the health issues that must be addressed within the continuum of care of reproductive, maternal, newborn and child health: stillbirths, preterm birth complications, birth asphyxia, low-birth weight, mother-to-child transmission of HIV/AIDS and other sexually transmitted diseases, neonatal infections, pneumonia, diarrhoea, measles, under- and malnutrition, malaria, the prevention of accidents and violence.[488] Prevention of health problems is extensively elaborated and addresses not only communicable and non-communicable diseases, but also the prevention of health problems by combatting substance abuse and ensuring product and environmental safety.[489]

2.5.9. CONCLUDING OBSERVATIONS ON THE GENERAL COMMENTS

On the basis of the analysis in the preceding sections, we make the following concluding observations on the General Comments.

The achievement of the highest attainable standard of health must be realized for all children without discrimination. The General Comments emphasize that all groups of children must have access to age-adjusted, disability adjusted and culturally appropriate health services without discrimination. Several groups of children have been identified for being particularly vulnerable to violations of their right to health, including babies and very young children. It is acknowledged that vulnerable groups of children are more prone to health risks such as malnutrition, infectious diseases, injuries, (substance) abuse and neglect. Particular problems of discrimination in realizing the right to health of the child are identified when children are vulnerable in plural aspects. Measures required have to take into account the different aspects of all vulnerabilities present. These

[487] Ibidem supra note 456, § 53.
[488] Ibidem supra note 456, § 33, 34, 53.
[489] Ibidem supra note 456, § 62–66.

examples underline that ensuring children's right to health requires measures beyond the limited environment of the health care sector. This requirement similarly follows from the need to ensure and enforce existing community-based health programs for children. Although different groups of vulnerable children require special attention in receiving health care, this care must be integrated in the general health care system to prevent stigmatization and discrimination as a result of the special attention they receive. Furthermore, multi-sectorial health approaches are required that can respond to the differential needs of children. This should include mental health facilities and possibly also home visitations.

The achievement of the highest attainable standard of health must be realized from the basis, which is the prevention of health problems and empowerment of young children and their parents. Prevention starts with combating malnutrition and easily preventable diseases. Secondly, prevention can be achieved by early detection and early intervention. This in its turn requires awareness of health risks among all people involved in the care of a child. The third way to prevent health problems must therefore be achieved by providing child-centred health education to young children, adolescents, pregnant women, parents and other caretakers and medical professionals. Additional efforts are required to enhance open communication about sensitive health topics. Through the provision of health education young children are stimulated in their direct environment to adopt healthy lifestyles from the very beginning of their lives. Fourthly, a safe and healthy environment adds to the prevention of health problems resulting from injuries, violence or poisoning with hazardous materials.

The role of families is central to the achievement of the right to the highest attainable standard of health by young children. Children are highly sensitive to their surroundings and imitate large parts of the (health) behaviour witnessed in their direct environment. Therefore, parents must be aware of their own health behaviour. In providing guidance they must continuously adapt to the changing health needs of their children and positively stimulate children to take increasing responsibility for their own health. This requires the adaptation of modes of communication to the preferred ways of communication of children and to their level of comprehension. The capacities of very young children are complemented by the guidance of their parents. This involvement of parents can contribute to better meeting the needs of children in the health sector by helping to identify what health services are required, how they should be provided, what discriminatory barriers and attitudes they encounter and how children can best be involved in their own health care.

The ambivalent role of the (extended) family in the prevention and infliction of violence is highlighted. It is acknowledged that violence impacts heavily on the health of children of all ages, either directly through the infliction of physical harm or indirectly through the destruction of medical facilities and the disruption of social structures including families, schools and infrastructure for the distribution of food, water and medicines.[490] Armed conflicts play a complicating role in realizing the right to the highest attainable standard of health of children in remote areas and war zones. The health sector has an important role in identifying and treating health problems resulting from violence in the private or in the public sector.

The recently adopted General Comment 15 on the right of the child to enjoy the highest attainable standard of health offers a valuable and concise elaboration of the Committee's interpretation of the right to health of the child. It concretizes the different aspects of the right to health to the operational level. With a focus on the provision of primary health care it specifies the levels of health care that must be provided for as a minimum, namely, prevention, promotion, treatment, rehabilitation and palliative care. In doing so, priority must be given to the establishment of services for the continuum of care to ensure good maternal, new born and child health. Useful tools are furthermore suggested to determine the key interventions that must be taken, the minimum essential medicines that must be provided for and the most pressing health problems that must be addressed. Last but not least, General Comment 15 refers extensively to the need to involve all stakeholders to the greatest extent possible in the interpretation of the right to the highest attainable standard of health of the child and the prioritization of measures that must be taken to achieve that level of health for all children.

2.6. THE BASIC PRINCIPLES OF MEDICAL ETHICS FROM A CHILDREN'S RIGHTS PERSPECTIVE

The articles of the CRC constitute a useful legal basis for analysing the application of medical ethical principles in children's health care.[491, 492] Goldhagen and Mercer have developed a model that translates the principles of children's rights, social justice and health equity into children's health outcomes.[493] This is useful, because many medical professionals are not used to working with children's rights concepts. Therefore, the potential contribution of a rights-based approach to children's health often remains confined to the legal sector. Translation to the medical practice is crucial for implementation.

Whereas attention is righteously paid to the social determinants on health outcomes instead of narrowly focusing on medical care for children as a way to

490 See for example General Comment 4 on adolescent health and General Comment 6 on the treatment of unaccompanied and separated children outside their country of origin.

491 S. Nixon & L. Forman, 'Exploring synergies between human rights and public health ethics: a whole greater than the sum of its parts', *British Medical Journal on International Health and Human Rights 2008*, Volume 8, Issue 2.

492 Goldhagen & Mercer, 'Child Health Equity: From Theory to Reality', in: A. Invernizzi, *The Human Rights of Children*, p. 313.

493 Ibidem supra note 492.

realize children's rights to health, the overall approach is rather untransparent.[494,495] However, the component of health-equity ethics in which the four basic principles of the CRC[496] are related to the core principles in medical ethics (see Table 1 below[497]) is useful for answering the question how the principles of the CRC that are relevant for ensuring children's right to health can be translated to medical ethical principles, being the more common normative framework for medical professionals.

Table 1. Relating the core principles of child rights and medical ethics

Children's rights principles	Ethics principles
Non-discrimination (art. 2 CRC)	Justice
The best interests of the child (art. 3 CRC)	Beneficence
Survival and development (art. 6 CRC)	Non-maleficence
Listened to and taken seriously (art. 12 CRC)	Autonomy

The four core principles of medical ethics have a strong focus on the individual and the self-determination of the subject. The principle of autonomy refers to the inherent dignity of the individual and of human life in itself. Although autonomy is related to children's right to participation, the two concepts are not identical. Children's autonomy entails that children can act completely independently from others. Children's right to participation on the other hand, means that children are involved to a certain extent, depending on the opportunity they are given to participate and to the weight that is attributed to their opinions.[498] However, they are not granted the full responsibility to take (medical) decisions completely autonomously.[499] Baines elaborates that 'Children do not develop the abilities

494 Several sets of principles are combined; I. Child rights principles are defined as 'establishing the prerequisites for the health and well-being of children'; II. Social justice principles as 'providing insight and instructing how to allocate and distribute finite resources to ensure non-discrimination (art. 2 CRC), the best interests of the child (art. 3 CRC) and survival (art. 6 CRC)'; III. 'Health-equity ethics uses the CRC articles to establish an expanded set of ethical principles as a lens through which to view and analyse the world of children and the decisions that impact upon them'.

495 Where the heading states that four themes of the CRC are translated to the core ethics principles, 5 themes are addressed, namely economic, social, cultural, protective and civil and political rights. Examples like these create confusion in reading the article.

496 Www.unicef.org/crc/files/Guiding_Principles.pdf.

497 Ibidem supra note 492, p. 311.

498 M. Donnelly & U. Kilkelly, 'Child-friendly healthcare: delivering on the right to be heard', *The Medical Law Review* 2011, 19(1), pp. 27–54.

499 Donnelly and Kilkelly argue that two common aspects of participation and autonomous decision-making by children are the requirement of accessible information and the placing of the child at the heart of the decision-making process. However, as shown by the elaboration of the participation ladder by Hart and also the distinction made by Shier of different levels of children's participation, there are different levels of participation possible, that do not all place the child central. I would rather argue that truly placing the child central at the heart of the process is an essential condition for establishing their right to participation.

to act autonomously overnight.'[500] Therefore, the concept of children's right to participation with its varying degrees of involvement according to both the best interests (art. 3 CRC) and the evolving capacities of the child (art. 5 CRC), offers a very practical tool for medical practitioners to apply the principle of autonomy to children in the health care practice.

Following from the autonomy principle is the doctrine of informed consent, meaning that the subject has to receive sufficient and appropriate information to be able to give consent for a medical treatment. The amount of information that is actually provided, however, is determined by the parents or medical practitioners. As elaborated in paragraph 4 of this chapter, the role of the medical practitioner is crucial in shaping the degree of participation of the child that is achieved, especially when parents are objecting.

The principles of beneficence and non-maleficence are often viewed as different sides of the same coin, but there is a fundamental difference. Non-maleficence means doing no harm, which does not necessarily require action to be taken. Beneficence on the other hand, means that medical professionals have to make active efforts to do good to their patients. This can not be achieved by 'not taking action'. It would seem logical to relate the concept of non-maleficence to the right to protection of children and the principle of beneficence to the right to health. However, within the legal domain, protective rights also require proactive efforts to prevent children from being harmed, such as reporting mechanisms on situations of violence that are coupled with help-oriented services in the field of public health.[501] A legal translation of the principle of non-maleficence thus seems to lead to a broader scope than the strictly medical interpretation.

The last principle, justice, means that persons with equal characteristics must be treated equally and that health resources must be allocated equitably. The concept of equity, as further discussed in chapter 4 is central to this notion. Limiting access to health care on discriminative grounds is thus not in line with the justice principle.

With respect to the realization of children's right to health, several other CRC articles are also relevant for the interpretation and implementation of article 24 CRC.[502, 503] Therefore, translation of these provisions to the domain of medical ethics will be useful as well for realizing children's right to health. On the basis

500 P. Baines, 'Medical ethics for children: applying the four principles to paediatrics', *Journal of Medical Ethics* 2008, Issue 34, p. 142.

501 With respect to the protection of children against violence, see for example General Comment 13 of the Committee on the Rights of the Child, U.N. Doc. CRC/C/GC/13, 17 February 2011, § 36–51 for an enumeration of all appropriate protective measures. § 36 specifically emphasizes the proactive character of the protective measures enumerated.

502 See for example the explicitly enumerated articles in the Treaty-specific guidelines regarding the form and content of periodic reports to be submitted by States parties under article 44, paragraph 1(4) of the Convention on the rights of the Child, § 18–21. [art. 6.2, 18.3, 23, 26 and 27].

503 See also the article mentioned in the Implementation Handbook for the Convention on the Rights of the Child, prepared for UNICEF by Rachel Hodgkin and Peter Newell, fully revised

of the articles identified as being relevant for ensuring children's right to health, in Table 2 an attempt is made to relate those articles to the common principles in medical ethics. The principles in italics are not mentioned in the treaty-specific guidelines, nor in the Implementation Handbook for the Convention on the Rights of the Child, but given the relevance of birth registration for having access to health care and the widespread discrimination of refugee children from having access to health care, are deemed relevant for this overview.[504]

Table 2. Relating the health related principles of child rights with medical ethics

Children's rights principles relevant to children's right to health care	**Ethics principles**
The role of the parents in children's health: i. The role of the parents/legal guardians to provide direction and guidance (art. 5 CRC) ii. The right not to be separated from the parents (art. 9 CRC) iii. Parents have dual responsibility for the upbringing and development of the child. (art. 18 CRC) iv. Children of working parents must have access to child-care services (art. 18 CRC)	Autonomy Non-maleficence Autonomy Justice
The right to privacy (art. 16 CRC)	Autonomy, confidentiality
The right to information (art. 12, 13 and 17 CRC)	Autonomy (informed consent)
The right to protection (art. 19 and 20 CRC)	Autonomy and non-maleficence
The right to special care for disabled children (art. 23 CRC)	Autonomy, justice, beneficence.
The right to health (art. 24 CRC)	Autonomy, beneficence, justice, non-maleficence.
The right to periodic review of treatment (art. 25 CRC)	Non-maleficence and beneficence.
The right to social security (art. 26 CRC)	Justice
The right to an adequate standard of living (art. 27 CRC)	Justice
The right to (health) education (art. 28 and 29 CRC)	Autonomy
The right to protection from exploitation, child labour, drugs, sexual abuse and trafficking (art. 32–36 CRC)	Non-maleficence
The right to physical and psychological recovery and social reintegration of child victims (art. 39 CRC)	Beneficence
The right to birth registration and identity (art. 7 and 8 CRC)	*Autonomy*
The right to protection and humanitarian assistance for refugee children (art. 22 CRC)	*Justice, beneficence, non-maleficence*

The previous translation of the articles of the CRC for the children's health domain can help to further specify the application of the core medical ethical principles in the child's health care domain. Translating the CRC articles to the medical domain gives rise to a broader interpretation of the medical ethical principles than the strict medical context, including the relevance and necessity of ensuring

third edition, September 2007, p. XI-XXI. Available at: www.unicef.org/publications/files/Implementation_Handbook_for_the_Convention_on_the_Rights_of_the_Child.pdf.

504 The relevance of birth registration for the right to health of the child is found in General Comment 15 to the CRC. This relevance will be further addressed in chapter 3 below.

socioeconomic determinants and a rights-based treatment of minor patients. Secondly, it provides a useful tool for further developing child-friendly working methods in the health care setting on the basis of an integrated approach based on both medical ethical and children's rights principles. The translation of children's rights to practical guidelines for medical professionals can further operationalize their implementation and realization.[505, 506] Therefore, children's rights should be included in the education of all medical professionals working with children. This obviously includes paediatricians, gynaecologists and family practitioners, but it also extents to professionals who only occasionally encounter children in their daily work, such as radiologists, haematologists and others.

2.7. CONCLUSION

2.7.1. PRIORITIES IN INTERPRETING THE RIGHT TO THE HEALTH OF THE CHILD

Given the scarcity of resources, prioritization in ensuring children's right to health is necessary. This need is even more pressing in times of financial crisis and public debates over continuously rising health costs. This chapter has analysed what the key elements are of article 24 in interpreting the concept of the highest attainable standard of health of the child.

The priorities found in article 24 CRC, all contribute to children's survival in the first place (art. 24 sub 2a-2d), namely the reduction of infant and child mortality rates and secondly to leading a healthy life (art. 24 sub 2e-f). The achievement of the highest attainable standard of health must be realized from the basis, namely prevention of health problems, provision of basic health services and empowerment of young children and their parents to adopt healthy lifestyles.

505 Some progressive medical societies, especially in Anglo-Saxon countries, have established guidelines for guiding pediatricians in child-appropriate health care. These guidelines should be analyzed for their compliance with the Children's Rights Charter. See for example *Good Medical Practice in Paediatrics and Child Health: Duties and Responsibilities of Paediatricians* by the Royal College of Paediatrics and Child Health, London, 2002. See also the Child Friendly Health Care Initiative (www.cfhiuk.org), a Manual for health workers by Sue Nichelson and Andrew Clarke. The Manual is said to translate the CRC articles into simple CFH 'Standards' that are applicable to everyday healthcare practices. Available at: www.cfhiuk.org/publications/cfhi_manual/cfhi_manual.pdf.

506 An article on the implementation of the Child-Friendly Healthcare Initiative (CFHI) provided 12 standards for providing healthcare in accordance with the Convention on the Rights of the Child. The intention was expressed to implement the standards in six pilot countries in cooperation with the Department of Child and Adolescent Health and Development of the World Health Organization and UNICEF. Southall, D. P. (2000). 'The child-friendly health care initiative (CFHI): Health care provision in accordance with the United Nations Convention on the Rights of the Child', in: *Pediatrics*, 106(5), pp. 1054–1064.

Prevention must be achieved through the provision of underlying determinants of health, implementation of high coverage vaccination campaigns, combating malnutrition and easily preventable diseases, early detection and intervention of diseases and ensuring a healthy environment. Through the provision of child-centred and child-sensitive health education, children, parents and other caretakers are stimulated to adopt healthy lifestyles and take increasing responsibility for their own and their child's health.

In the provision of health care to children, the focus lies on basic health care. These services must be continuous and responsive to the changing circumstances in which children live and to the different developmental stages of children. Four different levels have been identified at which age-specific health care services should be provided:

1. Provision of health care and information to the mother during pregnancy.
2. Obstetric health care around the birth of the child.
3. Neonatal health care for the mother and the child immediately after birth.
4. Quality health care during childhood.

In the second place, health services must be responsive to the needs of different groups of (vulnerable) children and children from various sociocultural backgrounds. The right to the highest attainable standard of health entails that in providing for these health services, special attention must be given to include all groups of vulnerable children in the health care system by providing for age-adjusted, culturally and disability appropriate basic health services and information. Multisectoral health teams, home visits and mobile health clinics can contribute to integrating the particular needs of (vulnerable) children, including infants and very young children in the realization process of the right to the highest attainable standard of health.

An important avenue for identifying the best interests of the child is by involving both children and their parents in the different phases of the health care process. Furthermore, the right to the highest attainable standard of health requires that children's opinions on the impact of their health situation on other aspects of their daily life must be sought. Where young children have limited capacities to communicate their particular health needs, parents have a complementary responsibility in providing for guidance and communicating their children's needs. However, this must be done from the perspective of children as rights holders. Therefore, to the largest extent possible, children must be informed from the very beginning and in an age-appropriate way about their health status, options for treatment and prognosis. If necessary, this requires the application of creative and child-specific modes of communication. Involving children in their own health care from the very beginning gradually enhances their capacities to take ownership of their own health.

2.7.2. RESPONSIBLE ACTORS

With regard to the responsibility to ensure the right to the highest attainable standard of health of the child, the provisions related to health constitute a dual responsibility between individual children and their parents on the one hand and States Parties on the other. The State has the overall responsibility to ensure the provision of non-discriminatory, accessible and acceptable health care facilities, the underlying determinants of health and the provision and implementation of legislation and national programs to ensure adequate health facilities and personnel. This responsibility includes the provision of affordable and accessible insurances for all children and protection of children against practices of overt and covert forms of discrimination in acquiring access to health care. The role of the State in ensuring children's right to health further focuses on enabling individuals and their families to take their primary responsibility to ensure their own health through the provision of health information. This requires the training of all medical professionals working with children in children's rights and in communicating with children.

Parents have the primary responsibility to ensure daily care and guidance to their children, thereby supporting them to develop in a healthy manner. The right to the highest attainable standard of health of very young children is directly related to the health of their families. Parents' role in ensuring their children's health contains several elements, related to their biological connection, behaviour of the mother during pregnancy and around the birth of the child as well as the health behaviour of both parents, the guidance given to the child on healthy behaviour. Central in the realization of the right to the highest attainable standard of health of the child is the need to continuously adapt to the changing circumstances in which children live and to take into account the evolving capacities of the developing child. Although young children are rights holders on their own, the capacities of very young children are complemented by the guidance of their parents. In providing guidance, parents must positively stimulate children to take increasing responsibility for their own health. This requires the adaptation of modes of communication to the preferred ways of communication of children and to their level of comprehension.

The primary responsibility for financing both the actual health care as the basic necessities in life lays with the parents. However, as specified in article 27, the responsibility of parents to take care of their children is limited to the abilities and financial capacities of the parents. This specification leaves room for a broad margin of appreciation to determine when the State should intervene. Special consideration must be given to children and families in difficult circumstances such as orphaned children, refugees or families without a residence permit, children of indigenous and minority groups, child headed households, single parent families and parents who are unemployed or who otherwise have limited means for ensuring the right to the highest attainable health of their child.

A problem remaining in the determination of the responsible actors is that whereas the CRC provisions hold parents primarily responsible, it is the State that is directly bound by the Convention. This incoherence results in uncertainty over the legal enforceability of the provision to hold parents accountable for ensuring their children's right to health. The same is true for several other groups of actors that are discerned in the newly adopted General Comment 15 on the right of the child to the enjoyment of the highest attainable standard of health, that have capacity and resulting responsibility to contribute to the implementation of the right of the child to the highest attainable standard of health. More research into this aspect will be conducted in chapter 6 on realizing the right to the highest attainable standard of health of the child.

Medical professionals can play a valuable role in enabling children to be involved in medical decisions on their individual treatment and on the organization of health services. They can also contribute to streamlining the communication with and between parents and their children and guiding parents in ways to stimulate their children to adopt healthy lifestyles. Thereto, all medical professionals encountering children in their daily work or just occasionally, must be educated about children's rights in health and trained in communicating with children and families in the health care sector. Since the role of families in ensuring children's right to health can be both enabling and harming to the realization of the right to health of the child, the health sector has an important role in identifying and treating health problems resulting from violence in the private sector. The same is true for health problems resulting from public health problems, such as obesity or alcohol and drug abuse, from (structural) violence and in humanitarian situations. In order to increase awareness and professionalism of best practices in different countries, both states and medical professionals must share information with professionals in other, less developed countries.

III. CHILDREN'S RIGHT TO HEALTH IN THE RECOMMENDATIONS OF THE COMMITTEE ON THE RIGHTS OF THE CHILD IN THE CONCLUDING OBSERVATIONS ON THE COUNTRY REPORTS

3.1. INTRODUCTION

Interpreting the concept of the 'highest attainable standard of health of the child encompasses the question what basic necessities of health children are entitled to. Article 24 of the UN CRC and the General Comments of the Committee on the Rights of the Child concomitantly lay down the fundaments of children's right to health in the children's rights domain. In this body of law, it has been identified that the highest attainable standard of health (article 24-1 CRC) must be achieved to the maximum extent of available resources (article 4 CRC). Several priorities are set, aiming to ensure the survival of (new-born) children, the prevention of disease, access to primary health care for all children and basic knowledge on children's health and nutrition.[507] Based on article 44 CRC and the priorities set in article 24 CRC, State Parties have to regularly report to the Committee on the progress made in ensuring children's right to health. The Committee on the Rights of the Child (further the CRC Committee), is thereby in the position to assess the degrees of implementation of countries in ensuring children's right to health, among other rights, over time.

One approach to measure compliance of countries is to compare the performance on child health indicators between countries with a similar level of per capita income, for example by comparing the under-five-mortality rate between countries or the percentage of children under five years who are underweight. This approach is often applied by UNICEF in the annual series

[507] See Convention on the Rights of the Child, Adopted and opened for signature, ratification and accession by General Assembly resolution 44/25 of 20 November 1989 entry into force 2 September 1990, in accordance with article 49.

of UNICEF reports entitled 'The Progress of Nations'.[508] Another approach is to gain knowledge from historical and analytical[509] reports on the status of children's right to health. This second approach is followed in this analysis of the Concluding Observations of the CRC Committee on the Country Reports submitted to it. The reason for this approach is that the Concluding Observations contain a wealth of information about the interpretation of children's rights by the CRC Committee, including the right to highest attainable standard of health of the child. This information is not quantitative and therefore of additional value for the annual UNICEF series, containing predominantly statistical data.

In order to gain further insight into the Committee's interpretation of the right to the highest attainable standard of health of the child, this contribution analyses the Concluding Observations of the CRC Committee. Primarily, the possible existence of systematically recurring recommendations is identified and secondly, it is investigated whether according to the CRC Committee the different levels of human development in countries lead to different standards of health right measures.

The Concluding Observations are used as a starting point for answering the questions how the right to the highest attainable standard of health of the child as laid down in the CRC domain is explained for four groups of countries selected on the basis of their size and level of human development and whether these standards lead to a similar or different system of prioritization of health measures, reflecting the notion of article 4 CRC that States must progressively achieve the highest attainable standard of health in line with the maximum extent of available resources. It is assumed that countries with different levels of human development are in different phases of ensuring children's right to health. It is further assumed that this is reflected in the Concluding Observations of the CRC Committee with regard to the right to health of the child.

The UN Human Development Index is used to categorize countries in one of four levels of development. This index was initially developed by Amartya Sen and Mahbub ul Haq and it is considered as one of the most influential capability metrics used. Although it does not fully reflect the complete range of opportunities of the capability approach, it does show how capability related information such as longevity and literacy can be used to supplement strictly economic methods of measurement.[510] As such, it creates room for the use of non-economic indicators for the assessment of well-being in a country. Since children's rights are intended

---

[508] See for example the 2010 Edition: Progress for Children, Achieving the MDGs with equity, Number 9, September 2010, UNICEF. Accessed through: www.unicef.ca/portal/Secure/Community/502/WCM/Reports/Progress%20for%20Children.pdf.

[509] Different types of analytical reports can be taken as a starting point. However, countries compared must be assessed on the basis of similar types of reports (e.g. NGO reports, legal reports). The advantage of taking the Concluding Observations of the CRC Committee as a starting point is that reports are available on almost all countries of the world.

[510] Sen's Capability Approach. Internet encyclopeadia of Philosophy. Available at: www.iep.utm.edu/sen-cap/.

to primarily improve the quality of life of children and not to increase the gross domestic product of a country, this index is better suited for the comparison of recommended measures for the realization of the right to the highest attainable standard of health between countries with different levels of development.

After describing the reporting procedure of the Committee on the Rights of the Child with respect to the right to health in paragraph 2, the methodology for analysing the Concluding Observations on the Country Reports will be explained in paragraph 3, followed by the results and a discussion of these results in paragraphs 4; an explanation of the right to have access to health care as interpreted by the Committee, 5; systematically recurring recommendations on the right to have access to health and 6; different standards for the implementation of the right to the highest attainable standard of health for country groups with different levels of human development. Paragraph 7 concludes by translating the results to practical recommendations to the Committee on the Rights of the Child.

3.2. THE REPORTING PROCEDURE ON BASIC HEALTH AND WELFARE IN THE COUNTRY REPORTS

Article 44-1a CRC obliges all member States to the CRC to submit regular reports to the Committee on the Rights of the Child on the implementation of its provisions. Initially, submission must be done two years after ratification of the CRC. Thereafter, a report must be submitted every five years. These reports are consequently commented upon by the CRC Committee in its Concluding Observations on the Country Reports.

Since 2003 and in accordance with article 43 of the Convention on the Rights of the Child the CRC Committee consists of 18 independent experts chosen by the member States to the Convention on the Rights of the child for a term of four years.[511] In order to achieve a structured reporting process, a set of guidelines has been developed and adjusted by the CRC Committee,[512] in which information on relevant legislative, judicial, administrative and other information, including statistical data[513] and indicators, is requested in the

511 Website of the Office of the United Nations High Commissioner for Human Rights.

512 See UN Doc. CRC/C/5 of 30 October 1991 for the original version and the revised versions in UN Doc. CRC/C/58 Rev. 1 of 3 June 2005 and the latest version UN Doc. CRC/C/58 Rev. 2 of 23 November 2010. The latest Set of Reporting Guidelines replaces the previous one. See UN Doc. CRC/C/58 Rev. 2, § 5.

513 With regard to the thematic cluster on health and well-being of children, disaggregated statistical data are required regarding a) rates of infant and under-five mortality, b) the proportion of children with low birth weight, c) the proportion of children being moderate and severe underweight, stunting and wasting, d) rate of child mortality due to suicide, e) % of households with access to safe drinking water and hygienic sanitation, f) % of 1-year olds

reports to provide the Committee with a good basis for analysis. The latest set of UN guidelines takes into account the requirements of reporting on the Optional Protocols to the Convention[514] and the General Comments adopted by the UN Committee on the Rights of the Child[515] and the harmonized guidelines on reporting to international human rights treaty bodies.[516] Subsequent reports must contain updated information and special references to previous periodic reports, including explanations on insufficient levels of implementation and measures taken to overcome challenges encountered.

Information on children's rights in countries is required on the categories 'factors and difficulties encountered', 'progress achieved', 'implementation priorities' and 'specific goals'. The guidelines group the different CRC articles according to content, such as (a) general measures of implementation of children's rights, (f) basic health and welfare and (h) special protection measures. Included in the cluster on general measures of implementation must be information on the efforts to bring domestic legislation into conformity with the Convention on the Rights of the Child and to adopt, implement and evaluate a comprehensive national action plan, information on the responsible government authorities for particular themes (such as health care) and the budget allocated to, for example, (primary) health care services and health personnel.[517]

With regard to the protection and provision of health services for children, the CRC Committee specifically demands States to provide an overview of the measures taken to realize articles 6.2 (survival and development), 23 (disabled children), 24 (health and health services), 18.3 (the role of parents), 26 (social security and the availability of child care services and facilities) and 27 (standard of living and measures to ensure quality nutrition, clothing and housing to ensure the healthy development of the child) CRC.[518] Furthermore, information must be included on the States' efforts to address the most prevalent health challenges, including communicable and non-communicable diseases, the promotion of physical and mental health and well-being of children and to address the promotion of a healthy lifestyle of adolescents and the measures taken to prohibit

---

fully immunized, g) rates and main causes of maternal mortality, h) proportion of pregnant women with access to pre- and postnatal health care, i) the proportion of children born in hospital, j) proportion of personnel trained in hospital care and delivery and k) proportion of mothers giving exclusive breastfeeding. Other data required under this thematic cluster refer to disabled children, adolescent health, child victims of drug and substance abuse and children incarcerated with their parents.

514 U.N. Doc. A/RES/54/263, 25 May 2000, entry into force 12 February 2002: Optional Protocol I to the Convention on the Rights of the Child on the involvement of children in armed conflict and Optional Protocol II to the Convention on the Rights of the Child on the sale of children, child prostitution and child pornography.

515 General Comment 3 on HIV/AIDS, General Comment 4 on Adolescent Health and General Comment 9 on Children with Disabilities are specifically referred to in the 2010 Reporting Guidelines to be included in the Country Reports.

516 U.N. Doc. HRI/GEN/2/Rev.6, 3 June 2009.

517 Ibidem supra note 512, § 18–21.

518 Ibidem supra note 516, § 34–36.

and eliminate harmful traditional practices and to prevent children from abusing drugs.[519]

This list of themes that must be included in the report reflects the broad scope of article 24 CRC to both health, health care and prevention of health problems for children and their parents. By working on thematic clusters of articles, such as the cluster on basic health and welfare, the comprehensive nature of the Convention is taken into consideration.[520] A holistic approach is applied by addressing governmental budget allocations (art. 4 CRC) in the context of the best interests of the child (art. 3 CRC) in the medical sector (art. 24 CRC).[521]

In addition to the actual implementation of the rights in the CRC, States are also requested to specify the nature and extent of their cooperation with governmental and non-governmental organizations.[522] Prior to consideration of a State's report, the CRC Committee holds a pre-sessional working group with non-governmental stakeholders, such as NGOs, UN bodies, youth organizations and other relevant organizations.[523] During this session, a list of prioritized issues is compiled for the country involved, which will be discussed during the following constructive dialogue between representatives of the State and the CRC Committee in the presence of relevant UN agencies. The CRC Committee collaborates intensively with other United Nations agencies and bodies on the implementation of the CRC as far as that falls within their particular mandates. As a final step in this evaluative process, the CRC Committee will give suggestions and recommendations in the Concluding Observations on the Country Reports at the end of the reporting process. As a follow-up, the State is expected in its subsequent report to provide detailed information on the measures taken and implemented to meet the recommendations of the CRC Committee, as well as the provision of information on new developments in the implementation of children's rights in the country.

In the Manual on Human Rights Reporting, it is elaborated that the CRC Committee emphasizes the need for detailed information on the relevant legal texts and statistical information on the status of children's rights that is disaggregated by sex, age, ethnic or national background and rural or urban environment.[524] This information is needed to allow for the consideration of individual rights for

---

519 U.N. Doc. HRI/GEN/2/Rev.6.

520 U.N. Office of the High Commissioner for Human Rights, *Manual on Human Rights Reporting Under Six Major International Human Rights Instruments*, 1997, HR/PUB/91/1 (Rev.1), p. 408. available at: www.unhcr.org/refworld/docid/428085252.html [accessed 23 February 2011].

521 J.E. Doek, 'Children and their right to enjoy health: A brief report on the monitoring activities of the Committee on the Rights of the Child.', *Health and Human Rights* 2001, 5 (2), p. 156.

522 Ibidem supra note 5, § 19-j.

523 Overview of the working methods of the Committee on the Rights of the Child. Found on the website of the Office of the United Nations High Commissioner for Human Rights: www2.ohchr.org/english/bodies/crc/workingmethods.htm.

524 UN Office of the High Commissioner for Human Rights, *Manual on Human Rights Reporting Under Six Major International Human Rights Instruments*, 1997, HR/PUB/91/1 (Rev.1), p. 406. available at: www.unhcr.org/refworld/docid/428085252.html.

different groups of children.[525] It is further acknowledged that the continuing reporting process is intended to ensure the continuous attention of States to improving the respect and implementation of children's rights, as it creates the possibility to evaluate the progress in implementation of children's rights over time, thus instigating the actual realization of children's rights over time.[526]

The thematic cluster on basic health and welfare in the Concluding Observations of the CRC Committee provides additional insight into the interpretation of the right to the highest attainable standard of health by the CRC Committee.[527] The principle of non-discrimination in article 2 CRC has been identified as central in ensuring access to health services for all groups of children.[528] Reports must therefore specify the existing network of health services and health personnel and the distribution of health facilities over urban and rural areas and the actual access of health services to the most vulnerable and disadvantaged groups of children.[529] Furthermore, within the thematic cluster on basic health and welfare three main areas have been prioritized: 1) the reduction of infant and child mortality and the provision of medical assistance and health care, 2) support for pregnant women and 3) the prevention of health problems, such as diseases and malnutrition, by providing families with information on healthy behaviour and survival competencies. Much attention in the area of prevention is paid to the prevention of AIDS. It is remarkable that several topics related to the prevention of health problems are categorized in the first area and not in the third; the necessity to provide information about existing programs of universal immunization, about the level of implementation of vaccination programs, and on the balance between curative and preventive health programs. It seems to be more logical to place them in the third category being focused on prevention. Other, separate topics that must be reported upon include the impact of environmental problems on children's health, the abolishment of harmful traditional practices and international cooperation in realizing the highest attainable standard of children's right to health through the support of UN agencies and other relevant organizations or in the framework of bilateral cooperation.[530]

In addition to the treaty-specific guidelines to report to the CRC Committee, the Implementation Handbook for the Convention on the Rights of the Child 'provides a detailed reference for the implementation of law, policy and practice to

525 Manual, p. 406.
526 Manual, p. 504.
527 Manual, pp. 454–462.
528 Manual, pp. 454–462.
529 Manual, p. 458.
530 Manual, p. 460.

promote and protect children's rights'.[531, 532] In addition to the articles enumerated in the treaty-specific guidelines on reporting (6.2, 18.3, 23, 24, 26 and 27) the UNICEF Implementation Handbook also qualifies the general principles of the CRC (articles 2, 3, 6 and 12) and articles 5 (parental guidance), 17 (right to information), 19 (protection from all forms of violence), 25 (right to periodic review of treatment), 28 and 29 (right to education and its aims), 32–36 (protection from various forms of exploitation) and 39 (recovery and reintegration for child victims) of particular relevance for interpreting article 24 CRC. Whereas not official, the implementation checklist is intended as a basis from which more detailed and sensitive checklists can be developed for national or local use, providing a framework to collect all relevant information for reporting.[533] Whereas the Checklists provide a clear overview and a practical basis for reporting, the additional value depends on the amount of pages attributed to each subtheme in the Country Reports, on the choices made by the governmental department responsible for reporting and taking into account the indivisibility and interdependence of the different rights in the Convention on the Rights of the Child.

The inclusion of article 18–3 CRC in the cluster on health and well-being indicates that the family has a central role to play in ensuring children's health and development. It furthermore underlines that the States Parties have to provide assistance to parents in fulfilling their responsibilities in the upbringing of their children as specified in article 18. Thirdly, it appears from the Manual that there is concern for the conciliation of the role of parents as educators of their children and the role of parents as employees.[534] The importance of the role of families in ensuring the right to the highest attainable standard of health of the child also appears from the phrasing in other articles. For example, article 26 specifies that children have the right to *benefit from* social security.[535] The phrasing implies that children have a right to social security that is derogative to derived from their family's right. Article 27 CRC recognizes the child's right to an adequate standard of living to ensure the child's full and harmonious development, including at the physical, mental, spiritual, moral and social levels.[536] It is identified in the Manual

531 Implementation Handbook for the Convention on the Rights of the Child, prepared for UNICEF by Rachel Hodgkin and Peter Newell, fully revised third edition, September 2007, pp. XI-XXI. www.unicef.org/publications/files/Implementation_Handbook_for_the_Convention_on_the_Rights_of_the_Child.pdf.

532 Each chapter discusses a separate CRC article in view of the collected interpretations of the CRC Committee in its General Comments and Concluding Observations on the Country Reports and in relation to other key UN treaties and policy documents. Each chapter is furthermore concluded with a non-official implementation checklist, being divided in general measures of implementation and specific issues in implementing article 24 CRC (and other articles).

533 Ibidem supra note 531, p. XIX.

534 Manual, p. 454.

535 Manual, p. 461.

536 Manual, p. 462.

on Human Rights Reporting that article 27 CRC specifically embodies the holistic nature of the CRC.[537] Here again, the primary responsibility for providing for such a standard of living is attributed to the parents, who have a common responsibility to take care of their children on the basis of article 18 CRC. In addition to this primary role of parents, the State has the duty to provide assistance to the parents to ensure the core elements of an adequate standard of living for the child. Thus, ensuring the right to the highest attainable standard of health of the child is a shared responsibility between parents and the State. For children without a family, the State's responsibility goes even further, namely to ensuring a safe and healthy place to live for children and be cared for appropriately.

3.3. RESEARCH METHOD

In order to gain insight into the CRC Committee's interpretation of the right to the highest attainable standard of health of the child, a study into the Committee's Concluding Observations on the Country Reports of 35 countries was conducted. A selection of 35 countries was made, based on country area, population size, human development indicators and geographical spread. Based on the United Nations Human Development Index for 2010,[538] four categories of countries were formed of 8 countries each; I. Very High Human Development, II. High Human Development, III. Medium Human Development and IV. Low Human Development. The Human Development Indices as established by the United Nations are based on the following indicators: life expectancy at birth, mean years of schooling, expected years of schooling and gross national income (GNI) per capita (PPP 2008 $). Attributed to these four categories of human development were the countries that were ranked highest on population size in 2010[539] and with a maximum of three countries per continent. To all categories, one small country (less than 10 million inhabitants) in a post-conflict situation was attributed, so that the groups remained comparable, while taking into account another range of countries that would otherwise remain completely out of sight.[540]

Countries were excluded when no Concluding Observations of the CRC Committee or data on human development indicators were available, as was the case for the United States of America, Afghanistan, Iraq and North-Korea (HDI). Of the countries analysed, all available Concluding Observations on the Country Reports, approximately 2–4 reports per country, were taken into consideration for the interpretations of and recommendations on the right to the highest attainable standard of health of the child in that particular country.

---

537 Manual, p. 462.

538 United Nations Human Development Index: http://hdr.undp.org/en/statistics/.

539 World Atlas: www.worldatlas.com/aatlas/populations/ctypopls.htm.

540 Notwithstanding relatively high levels of human development in countries, the existence of armed conflicts seriously affects the performance on the implementation of children's rights.

In Table 1, an overview is provided of the selected countries per category. Remarkably absent in the selection is the USA (ranked 3 on population size and 4 on developmental level), as this country has not ratified the CRC. Therefore, no Concluding Observations of the CRC Committee were available. It is also remarkable to see that the first category contains no African or Southern-American countries. The reason for this is that no countries in these continents were qualified as very high developed under the United Nations Human Development Indices. On the other hand, no European, North-American and very few Asian and Southern-American countries were qualified as low developed, being reflected in the high proportion of African countries in that category. The Netherlands, Lebanon and Cuba were separately considered, as they could not be included in the selection on the basis of the selection criteria, though there was another interest in researching these countries: the Netherlands is the homeland of the author, Lebanon is interesting given its mixed population on the basis of socio-economic, cultural and religious indicators and Cuba is particularly interesting as it is ranked medium on the general list of developmental levels, though general health indicators (e.g. life expectancy at birth) are comparable to those in countries qualified as showing very high human development.[541] The health indicators in Cuba are thus remarkably high compared to those of countries with similar level of human development.

Table 1. Selection of countries by population size per category of human development (HD) in 2010

I. Very High HD	II. High HD	III. Medium HD	IV. Low HD
10. Japan (11)	5. Brazil (73)	1. China (89)	7. Bangladesh (129)
14. Germany (10)	9. Russia (65)	2. India (119)	8. Nigeria (42)
20. France (14)	11. Mexico (56)	4. Indonesia (108)	19. DR Congo (68)
22. United Kingdom (26)	17. Iran (70)	16. Egypt (101)	24. Myanmar (32)
26. South Korea (12)	18. Turkey (83)	25. South Africa (110)	33. Sudan (54)
36. Canada (8)	29. Colombia (79)	56. Sri Lanka (91)	37. Uganda (43)
52. Australia (2)	35. Algeria (84)	66. Guatemala (16)	82. Haiti (45)
95. Israel (15)	123. Bosnia (68)	125. Moldova (99)	126. Liberia (62)

[541] See United Nations Human Development Index: http://hdr.undp.org/en/countries/profiles/CUB.html.

Table 2. Additional selection of countries based on an ad hoc variety of characteristics

I. Very High HD	II. High HD	III. Medium HD	IV. Low HD
60. The Netherlands (7)	Lebanon (n.a.)	74. Cuba (n.a.)	

Legenda for tables 1 and 2:
a. The numbers before the country names refer to the ranking on population size for the year 2010.
b. The numbers behind the country names refer to developmental level as found in the ranking of the UN Human Development Indices for 2010.

The Concluding Observations on the Country Reports were particularly analysed for recommendations relating to children's right to the highest attainable standard of health. Focus was placed on measures to ensure primary health care, as this level of health care should be present as a very minimum standard in countries with all different levels of human development (article 24-b CRC). Also, a General Comment further elaborating the right to health of the child had not been issued yet.[542] Primarily, the data were analyzed for the possible existence of systematically recurring recommendations in the Concluding Observations of the Country Reports related to children's access to primary health care. From this information, the question was answered how the standard of children's right to the highest attainable standard of health as laid down in article 24-b CRC is explained by the Committee on the Rights of the Child as evidenced by the Concluding Observations of the selected Country Reports. In doing so, focus was placed on recommendations related to the right to the highest attainable standard of health of children under 5, as this indicator constitutes one of the most important indicators to assess the degree to which the right to health of children is prioritized within a country.[543] This selection resulted in a limited consideration of the paragraphs on adolescent health, namely only as far issues were relevant for the realization of the right to the highest attainable standard of health of young children's health, as is the case with teenage pregnancies and mother-to-child transmission of HIV/AIDS.

We also investigated whether the different levels of human development lead to different standards of health right measures on the basis of article 24 CRC. Given the questions identified, the results were grouped in the following categories, elaborated in the following paragraphs:

542 In December 2011, a call for submissions was issued by the International Federation of Health and Human Rights Organisations to prepare for a General Comment on children's right to the highest attainable standard of health. Submissions were subsequently published at www2.ohchr.org/english/bodies/crc/callsubmissionsCRC_received.htm. On 17 April 2013, General Comment no. 15 on the right of the child to enjoy the highest attainable standard of health was adopted.

543 A. Eide & W.B. Eide, *A Commentary on the UN CRC Article 24: The right to health*, Leiden: Martinus Nijhoff Publishers 2006, p. 17.

I. Explanation of the right of the child to have access to health in the Concluding Observations of the CRC Committee on the Country Reports (paragraph 4).
II. Systematically recurring recommendations in the Concluding Observations related to children's right to the highest attainable standard of health (paragraph 5).
III. Different standards for the implementation of children's right to health for country groups with different levels of human development (paragraph 6).

3.4. RESULTS I: EXPLANATION OF CHILDREN'S RIGHT TO HAVE ACCESS TO HEALTH CARE IN THE CONCLUDING OBSERVATIONS OF THE CRC COMMITTEE

3.4.1. ACCESS AS A PREREQUISITE FOR REALIZING THE HIGHEST ATTAINABLE STANDARD OF HEALTH

The Concluding Observations of the CRC Committee contain recommendations to ensure children's right to health in different paragraphs of the Reports. It must be noted that the Recommendations of the Committee are non-binding, although the almost universal ratification of the UN Convention on the Rights of the Child and the systematic prioritization of the right to health of the child in both the Concluding Observations of the Committee on the Rights of the Child and the regional treaties[544] seem to lead to the existence of an *opinio iuris* that all children should at least be provided with a basic level of health care.[545]

In the first place, the paragraph on general principles, emphasizing children's right to non-discrimination as laid down in article 2 CRC, systematically mentions the right of all groups of children to have access to adequate and appropriate health care facilities as an example of basic services that must be ensured in implementing the CRC. The right to non-discrimination in having access to health care is further elaborated in the Concluding Observations by consequently emphasizing that particular attention must be paid to the most vulnerable groups in ensuring access to health care.

Earlier Concluding Observations on the Country Reports (1993–1997) do not mention the particular importance of guaranteeing the rights of vulnerable groups of children. In later Reports, extensive enumerations are found of

544 See the European Social Charter, the African Charter on the Rights and Welfare of the Child, the American Convention on Human Rights, the Asian Human Rights Charter and the Covenant on the Right of the Child in Islam and the Declaration of Rabat.

545 See for a more elaborate discussion on the universality of children's rights also: K. Arts, '21 Jaar VN-Verdrag voor de Rechten van het Kind: Een volwassen bijdrage aan kinderrechten in de wereld?', *Internationale Spectator* 2011, year 65, no. 6, June, p. 337.

vulnerable groups of children. In those later Reports, not only the thematic cluster on health and well-being, but also separate paragraphs on the 'protection of children' contain recommendations to ensure an adequate standard of living (nutrition, clothing and housing) ánd adequate access to health and education for vulnerable groups of children, such as street children, (former) child soldiers, refugee children and children in residential institutions.[546] Whereas the central idea is that all children have the right to have access to adequate and appropriate health care, there is a relatively strong focus on ensuring access to health care for vulnerable groups of children. However, this does not mean that only vulnerable children should receive adequate health-care. In order to ensure the right to have access to adequate health care for all children, particular measures are needed for vulnerable groups of children. What these measures should be is not extensively elaborated in the Concluding Observations. Still, several indications can be discerned. These will be discussed in section 5.

3.4.2. ACCESS TO HEALTH CARE FOR VULNERABLE CHILDREN

Whereas all Concluding Observations contain the recommendation that adequate access to health care facilities for all vulnerable groups of children must be ensured, the identified groups of children differ per country. Ennew observed that the Committee does not seem to have a systematic and consistent data collection, as is exemplified by the missing of a defined terminology for different groups of vulnerable children at all.[547] This finding is also found in the Concluding Observations on the Country Report on the UK mention is made of the particular needs of children living in poverty, Gypsy and Roma Travellers, refugee children living in detention centres, migrant and asylum-seeking children and gay/lesbian children.[548] Australia is urged to pay particular attention to take measures to ensure the access to adequate health facilities for homeless children, children in foster care, children living in remote and rural areas, indigenous children (Aboriginals and Torres Strait Islanders), minority children (Arabs and Muslims), asylum-seeking children and children with temporary visas.[549] For Canada it is acknowledged that the relatively high standard of health is not shared by all

[546] See for example the Concluding Observations on Canada, CRC/C/15/Add.215, 27 October 2003, § 53 and on the United Kingdom, CRC/C/15/Add.188, 9 October 2002, § 49 and 50.

[547] J. Ennew, 'Has Research Improved the Human Rights of Children? Or have the Information Needs of the CRC Improved Data about Children?' in: A. Invernizzi, *The Human Rights of Children*, p. 143. Ennew investigated 20 Country Reports from the period 1992–1993 and 7 Country Reports submitted in 2010.

[548] See for example the Concluding Observations on Canada, CRC/C/15/Add.215, 27 October 2003, § 53; United Kingdom, CRC/C/15/Add.188, 9 October 2002, § 15.

[549] Concluding Observations on Australia, CRC/C/15/Add.268, 20 October 2005, § 49, 63, 72 and 88.

children; indigenous children and rural children often remain (partially) deprived of basic services.[550] Other vulnerable groups of children identified in Canada include street children, disabled children,[551] children in juvenile institutions, abused children, indigenous children and refugee and asylum-seeking children. In the Concluding Observations regarding Israel, only Palestinian children are particularly identified as having problems in having access to adequate health facilities.[552] Particular problems for Palestinian children in having access are related to the permanent conflict situation in which they live, resulting in road closures, curfews, mobility restrictions, destruction of infrastructure, delay of medical convoys and shortages of medical supplies, malnutrition and high prices of foods.[553] It can be assumed however, that Palestinian children are not the only group of children in Israel requiring specific attention in having access to health care. Other vulnerable groups of children that are not explicitly mentioned by the Committee include refugee children,[554] children from minority groups such as the children in the unrecognized Bedouin villages of the Negev desert in Southern Israel,[555, 556] orphaned children, children living in rural, border or conflict affected areas,[557] disabled children and more. Presumably, the fact that the Concluding Observations depend on the information provided by the governments and NGOs involved, while being considered through the lens of the Committee's members, may lead to the (partial) exclusion of children who are not brought under the attention of the Committee. For example in the Netherlands,

550 Concluding Observations on Canada, CRC/C/15/Add.215, 27 October 2003, § 34.

551 Ennew notes that the Committee on the Rights of the Child puts a strong focus on the need for protection as a way to prevent disabilities in children, thereby ignoring the fact that disabilities are principally caused by congenital conditions or accidental injuries.

552 U.N. Doc. CRC/C/15/Add.195, Concluding Observations of the Committee on the Rights of the Child on Israel, 9 October 2002, § 44 and 45.

553 U.N. Doc. CRC/C/15/Add.195, Concluding Observations of the Committee on the Rights of the Child on Israel, 9 October 2002, § 44.

554 In 2010, there were an estimated 1500 refugees in Israel.

555 The Report 'The Bare Minimum Health Services in the Unrecognized villages in the Negev' by the NGO Physicians for Human Rights – Israel, 7 July 2009 demonstrates that there are significant differences in available health services and personnel for Muslim and Jewish communities. Other barriers include the limited office hours and the lack of roads and public transportation, the lack of electricity for refrigerating the medical supplies, running water and sewage disposal and the language barrier between Hebrew speaking doctors and predominantly Arab speaking patients, especially affecting the health care to mothers and children. Children living in the 11 unrecognized villages have extremely high levels of illness and death. For more information see www.phr.org.il/default.asp?PageID=130&ItemID=407.

556 The NGO Physicians for Human Rights – Israel, 27 April 2011 published a report on the limited access for Israeli Bedouin women. The infant mortality rate in Muslim Bedouin villages is 11.2 per 1000 births compared to 2.7 per 1000 births in Jewish communities. For more information see www.phr.org.il/default.asp?PageID=134&ItemID=973.

557 Between January and November 2010, 294 out of 3546 application by children for medical assistance were delayed and 11 denied. For more information see: CAAC Bulletin composed by UNICEF in collaboration with a wide range of other international organizations, Children Affected by Armed Conflict, Israel and the occupied Palestinian territory, 2010 Annual Review, p. 7.

it is important to consider that the joint report of NGOs in the Netherlands (the Child Rights Collective – het Kinderrechtencollectief) does not report on problems in the implementation of children's right to health. The predominant issues that are brought to the attention of the Committee on the Rights of the Child traditionally focus on a limited number of themes: child maltreatment and protection, protection against child trafficking and sexual abuse, juvenile justice, refugee children, children living in poverty, targeting children in development aid, participation of children, children's rights to play and education in children's rights.[558] Not either in the yearly report on children's rights mention is made of the implementation of children's right to health in the Netherlands.[559] However, the lack of reporting by the Dutch NGO Coalition on Children's Rights is not completely reflected to in the Concluding Observations of the Committee on the Rights of the Child on the Netherlands, because the information provided by the Dutch government on children's health is quite extensive.[560] However, when countries do not provide complete and reliable information on the implementation of children's right to health, it is more difficult for the Committee to make a complete report, especially in countries where NGOs are not allowed to work truly independently. The opportunity for NGOs to work independently from a State's supervision or even interference- both with respect to their funding as to the determination of agenda setting- is an essential requirement in achieving evidence-based evaluations. In addition, if available in a country, independent monitoring of governmental activities, as well as organizations and institutions working with children such as day-care, schools, child care and health care institutions and youth prisons by the National Child Ombudsperson constitute an important channel through which children's rights can be monitored.[561]

In order to achieve adequate access to health care, the Committee elaborates that existing legislation may need to be adapted when it excludes certain groups

---

558 Report: Children's rights in the Netherlands, The third periodic report of the Dutch NGO Coalition for Children's Rights on the Implementation of the Convention on the Rights of the Child; Jantje Beton, The Foundation for Children's Welfare Stamps Netherlands, UNICEF Netherlands, Save the Children Netherlands, Plan Netherlands, National Youth Council, National Association for Child and Youth Legal Advice Centres, Defence for Children International Netherlands, Netherlands Youth Institute (advice member), July 2008.

559 Jaarbericht Kinderrechten, Voorburg/Leiden 1 May 2011, see p. 6 for contents. www.ecpat.nl/images/20/1452.pdf.

560 See the Concluding Observations on the Netherlands, U.N. Doc. CRC/C/15/Add.114, 26 October 1999, § 18–20; U.N. Doc. CRC/C/15/Add.227, 26 February 2004, § 8, 33, 34, 43, 45, 47, 53; U.N. Doc. CRC/C/NLD/CO/3, 27 March 2009, § 23, 31, 48b, 50–52, 59, 60, 70.
Recommendations are made by the Committee on the provision of breastfeeding, the protection against female genital mutilation, access to medical advice and treatment without parental consent, the practice of euthanasia and the termination of life of newborn infants, infant and child mortality rates, access to basic services for unaccompanied asylum seeking children, for disabled children, universal vaccination, training for health personnel and the duty to report cases of child abuse for medical professionals.

561 See the link www.crin.org/enoc/members/index.asp for an overview of the Child Ombudspersons in Europe that are members of the European Network of Ombudspersons for Children.

of children from having adequate access to health care, as is the case for Roma children in Bosnia.[562] Furthermore, adequate access to health care implies having de facto access.[563] This notion is highlighted in the Concluding Observations on the Country Report of the Netherlands, wherein it is stated that the Report focuses too much on legislation, policies and programmes and too little on the actual enjoyment of rights.[564] Also, it elaborates that affirmative action may be required to ensure access for discriminated groups of children,[565] and that appropriate measures must be taken to ensure access to health care for migrant children, even if they do not have a residence permit.

Other causes for limits to access that have been identified by the Committee include physical barriers for disabled children, non-registration of refugee children, minority children and others, a lack of money for medical insurances to pay for medical care and hindered access to humanitarian convoys in cases of armed conflicts.[566] Access to health services may also be hampered as a result of climatic circumstances and even natural disasters. For example, health services in remote areas in Myanmar are especially inaccessible during the rainy season, resulting in big differences in the availability of health services between rural and urban areas and consequently in higher mortality rates in those areas due to inadequate access to health services.[567]

Whereas the general principle of non-discrimination of children in having adequate access to health facilities is structurally emphasized in the Concluding Observations, little information is found in the Concluding Observations on the practical barriers to provide children with access to health care, notwithstanding the fact that the Committee requires individual countries to specify the practical measures taken to realize children's rights in addition to the legislative and policy measures in place. This lack of specific, practical information in the Country Reports on the particular (barriers to) implementation of children's right to health makes that many reports seem to be more identical than can be expected on the basis of the actual situation of countries. For example, identical paragraphs are included in the Concluding Observations on the Country Reports of the Netherlands (1999, § 9 and 14), Iran (2005, § 21), Lebanon (2002, § 20), Bosnia (2005, § 24) and Columbia (2000, § 31), countries of different sizes, with different levels of development, highly divergent cultures and geographic characteristics. Whereas it must be said that the Recommendations of the

562 Bosnia, U.N. Doc. CRC/C/15/Add.260, 21 September 2005, § 47.

563 China, U.N. Doc., CRC/C/15/Add.56, 7 June 1996, § 2.

564 See U.N. Doc. CRC/C/15/Add.114, Concluding Observations of the Committee on the Rights of the Child on the Netherlands, 26 October 1999, § 2.

565 U.N. Doc. CRC/C/15/Add.227, 26 February 2004, § 30 and U.N. Doc. CRC/C/NLD/CO/3, 27 March 2009, § 27, both on the Netherlands.

566 See for example the Concluding Observations on Bosnia U.N. Doc. CRC/C/15/Add.260, 21 September 2005, § 26; Colombia U.N. Doc. CRC/C/COL/CO/3, 8 June 2006, § 95c; Lebanon U.N. Doc. CRC/C/LBN/CO/3, 8 June 2006, § 27.

567 Myanmar, CRC/C/15/Add.237, 30 June 2004, § 52.

Committee become more elaborate over time, especially since 2000, it is still required that Recommendations of the Committee on the Rights of the Child are further concretized and that more time bound and measurable targets are set for countries to achieve.

Partial conclusion: In all countries there are vulnerable groups of children in need of particular attention to ensure their right to have access to health care services. However, the specific groups identified differ per country, region and in some instances per period of the year. The problems identified lay both in the legislative and in the practical domain, so that ensuring children's right to have access to basic health care requires approaches on different organizational and technical levels. Countering legislative and practical instances of discrimination are key to ensuring adequate access to health care for all groups of children.

3.5. RESULTS II: SYSTEMATICALLY RECURRING RECOMMENDATIONS ON THE RIGHT OF THE CHILD TO THE HIGHEST ATTAINABLE STANDARD OF HEALTH IN THE CONCLUDING OBSERVATIONS

Several recommendations were made by the Committee in the Concluding Observations for countries of all different human development levels. A few recommendations were only found in separate categories of countries. These recommendations are discussed in paragraphs 5.5 to 5.8.

3.5.1. LACK OF DATA IN DEVELOPING AND DEVELOPED COUNTRIES

From the analysis of the Country Reports, it appears that the Committee systematically recommends that the States' Parties should 'strengthen and centralize the mechanism to compile and analyze systematically disaggregated data on all children under 18, with special emphasis on the most vulnerable groups'.[568] In line with the requirements laid down in the guidelines on reporting to the

[568] See the Country Reports on Lebanon, CRC/C/LBN/CO/3, 8 June 2006, § 20; China, U.N. Doc. CRC/C/CHN/CO/2, 24 November 2005, § 22; Egypt U.N. Doc. CRC/C/15/Add.145, 21 February 2001, § 16; South-Africa, U.N. Doc. CRC/C/15/Add.122, 22 February 2000, § 14; Sri Lanka, U.N. Doc. CRC/C/15/Add.207, 2 July 2003, § 18c; Guatemala U.N. Doc. CRC/C/15/ Add.154, 9 July 2001, § 16; Moldova, U.N. Doc. CRC/C/MDA/CO/3, 20 February 2009, § 19 and 20; CRC/C/SDN/CO/3-4, § 20; Uganda, U.N. Doc. CRC/C/15/Add.80, 21 October 1997, § 22.

Committee on the Rights of the Child, all Concluding Observations investigated contain paragraphs on the need to ensure systematic and disaggregated data collection on all areas covered by the Convention. Also in the discussions of the Committee itself on several particularly sensitive topics it was acknowledged that 'A common characteristic of the many recommendations formulated at the end of the discussion was the need for more collection, dissemination, awareness campaigns and access to information'.[569] In order to stimulate this practice, the Committee adopted General Comment 5, specifying the information required and the way in which this information should be gathered: sufficient and reliable data, disaggregated data, data over the whole period of childhood ánd all areas covered by the Convention, national coordination of data collection and national distribution of the States' Reports.[570] Following the identification of the need to enhance a system of disaggregated data collection, the Committee recommended that the collection of (health) data and indicators must be used as a basis to effectively formulate and evaluate policies and programmes for the implementation and monitoring of the Convention, including children's right to health.[571] The disaggregation will be helpful in mapping the gaps in the realization of the right to health for vulnerable groups of children. It is interesting to see that in some Concluding Observations, the recommendation was made to broaden the data collection to 'other areas than health and education, as was the case in Guatemala.[572] This suggests that these themes were considered to be priorities in implementing children's rights in that country. Whereas information must be disaggregated, health must not be the only theme covered in the report. The holistic nature of the CRC requires an integrated approach of children's well-being.

An example of an initiative helpful to the Committee in presenting well-founded recommendations to the States is given by the former chair of CRC Committee Doek 'the establishment of an office to gather information on children with disabilities into the monitoring activities of the Committee'.[573] The necessity to gather information taking into account the particular characteristics of different groups of vulnerable children is supported by Kasper in her statement that 'applying the tenets of the CRC requires disaggregation of national data by age, gender, rural or urban living environment and ethnic background, so that at-risk groups can be identified and equitable policies developed'.[574] However,

569 J.E. Doek, 'Children and their right to enjoy health: A brief report on the monitoring activities of the Committee on the Rights of the Child.', *Health and Human Rights* 2001, 5 (2), p. 158.

570 U.N. Doc. CRC/GC/2003/5, 27 November 2003, General Comment 5 on General measures of implementation of the Convention on the Rights of the Child, § 48–50.

571 Ibidem supra note 570.

572 Guatemala U.N. Doc. CRC/C/15/Add.154, 9 July 2001, § 16 and 17.

573 J.E. Doek, 'Children and their right to enjoy health: A brief report on the monitoring activities of the Committee on the Rights of the Child.', *Health and Human Rights* 2001, 5(2), p. 159.

574 J. Kasper, 'The Relevance of U.S. Ratification of the Convention on the Rights of the Child for Child Health: A Matter of Equity and Social Justice', *Child Welfare* 2010, no. 89, Volume 5,

Ennew observes that the majority of data in the Country Reports is quantitative and often not even child-centred,[575] thereby systematically neglecting the additional value of qualitative data, including the highly valuable insights that can be derived from actually talking to children and have them participate in the reporting process.[576]

Also in the developed countries, it has been identified by the Committee that a lack of information on the health status of all vulnerable groups of children such as children in minority groups, asylum seeking children, indigenous children and children with an illegal status, prohibited the full assessment of their health status by the Committee.[577] This lack of data on particular groups of children may reflect the low prioritization of their health care needs in comparison to other groups of children, both in countries with high as in countries with low levels of development. Children's vulnerability as a group that is hardly able to participate in public debate and decision-making, presumably limits the budget allocated to realizing their right to health.[578] This effect is even stronger for children that are vulnerable in several respects.

3.5.2. BUDGET ALLOCATION FOR THE IMPLEMENTATION OF ECONOMIC, SOCIAL AND CULTURAL RIGHTS

Without any exception, all the investigated Concluding Observations of the Committee contain recommendations to ensure sufficient budget allocation to ensure equal access to basic services for all (vulnerable) groups of children in all areas and regions of a country.[579] Quite remarkably, children's right to health (and children's right to education) is systematically emphasized as a priority

---

p. 27.

575 Ennew observes that in childhood data, the unit of analysis is often the family. Whereas the family unmistakenly plays a central role in ensuring (access to) health care for the child, data should also be available of the child as a person in its own right. See the earlier discussion of the role of the parents.

576 Ennew observes that little progress has been made in the use of data between 1992 and 2010. Her criticisms are relevant, though considerable expansion in the amount of has been noted. Further disaggregation and involvement of children in data compiling will be required. J. Ennew, 'Has Research Improved the Human Rights of Children? Or have the Information Needs of the CRC Improved Data about Children?', in: A. Invernizzi, *The Human Rights of Children*, p. 143, 145, 148 and 151.

577 See the Country Reports on Japan, CRC/C/15/Add.231, 26 February 2004, § 16; Australia, CRC/C/15/Add.268, 20 October 2005, § 70; United Kingdom, CRC/C/15/Add.188, 9 October 2002, § 18; Bosnia, CRC/C/15/Add.260 21 September 2005, § 19.

578 A. Nolan, 'The child's right to health and the courts', in: *Global health and human rights*, p. 138.

579 Nigeria, U.N. Doc., CRC/C/15/Add.61, 30 October 1996, § 10.

area for allocating sufficient resources.[580] This is elaborated in the Concluding Observations of the Committee, wherein emphasis is placed on the fact that all children, notwithstanding their age, gender, physical or mental condition, ethnicity, nationality, residence, minority, indigenous background or illegal status should have access to basic health services. To ensure the right to health, the available budget must be equally distributed over the different regions and (vulnerable) groups of children in a country.[581] Hereto, countries must develop and implement a coherent and comprehensive national plan at all levels: national, regional, federal, local and involving all vulnerable groups of children. Even in developed countries with existing health infrastructure 'a coordinated approach across all governmental departments to address the inequalities in access to health services[582]' or adequate measures 'to address prevailing disparities in living standards and in the quality of services of the different Länder (regions in Germany)[583]' is highlighted. To be able to evaluate the practical implementation of this right, the consequences of processes of decentralization of health care systems must be analysed.[584]

In the Concluding Observations it is not only mentioned that budget allocation should be prioritized to ensure equal access to health for all groups of children, it is also emphasized that budget must be allocated to the maximum extent of available resources. This means that the total country budget may need to be revised to allocate sufficient resources to the implementation of children's right to health. For example, in the Concluding Observations on the Country Reports of Sudan it is specified that more budget should be allocated to ensuring basic services, including health and less on military expenditure.[585] Also, in the time that Russia decided to reduce its military expenditure, the Committee on the Rights consequently advised to allocate the extra budget to the realization of children's rights, including the right of all children to access to basic health care services.[586] In the Concluding Observations on Cuba, on the other hand, it appears that even though the level of human development is relatively low, health

580 Democratic People's Republic of Korea, U.N. Doc. CRC/C/15/Add.239, 1 July 2004, § 18; Sudan, CRC/C/15/Add.10, 18 October 1993, § 27a; DRC, U.N. Doc. CRC/C/15/Add.153, 9 July 2001, § 12 and 13; Nigeria, U.N. Doc., CRC/C/15/Add.61, 30 October 1996, § 10.

581 Iran, U.N. Doc. CRC/C/15/Add.123, 28 June 2000, § 14; Russia, CRC/C/15/Add.110, 10 November 1999, § 12, 14, 17 and 22; Brazil, U.N. Doc. CRC/C/15/Add.241, 3 November 2004, § 22; Egypt, U.N. Doc. CRC/C/15/Add.145, 21 February 2001, § 32 and 40; South-Africa, U.N. Doc. CRC/C/15/Add.122, 22 February 2000, § 15; India, U.N. Doc. CRC/C/15/Add.228, 26 February 2004, § 5; Indonesia, U.N. Doc. CRC/C/15/Add.223, 28 February 2004, § 55 and 57a; Sri Lanka, U.N. Doc. CRC/C/15/Add.207, 3 July 2003, § 18a; Moldova, U.N. Doc. CRC/C/MDA/CO/3, 20 February 2009, § 18.

582 See for example U.N. Doc. CRC/C/GBR/CO/4., 20 October 2008, Concluding Observations of the Committee on the Rights of the Child on the United Kingdom, § 55.

583 See for example U.N. Doc. CRC/C/GBR/CO/4., 27 November 1995, Concluding Observations of the Committee on the Rights of the Child on the Germany, § 18.

584 Russia, U.N. Doc. CRC/C/RUS/CO/3, 23 November 2005, § 9 and 10a.

585 Sudan, CRC/C/SDN/CO/3-4, 22 October 2010, § 17 and 18.

586 Russia, U.N. Doc. CRC/C/15/Add.4, 18 February 1993, § 4.

indicators (such as low infant or child mortality rates and high percentages of immunizations) can be excellent if sufficient budget is allocated to health care.[587] This poses a clear example that adjusting the allocation of (limited) resources within a country can be beneficial to ensuring children's right to health.

Budget allocation is also relevant in the context of the processes of decentralization and privatization. It is explicitly stated by the Committee, that high costs in private medical institutions should not lead to the exclusion of groups of children and their families unable to pay for their medical treatments.[588] The removal of health care costs as a barrier to acquiring access to health for children is also at stake in the combat of corruption in having access to social services.[589] This is particularly troublesome for countries of medium and low levels of human development, wherein salaries are often insufficient to provide for an adequate standard of living, raising the vulnerability of people to fall for corruption.

In later reports (later than 2007), the Committee has provided several indications of ways to achieve sufficient allocation of resources for the establishment of quality health infrastructure for all groups of children. In the first place, specific budget lines must be defined for children in disadvantaged groups so that birth registration, IMCI (integrated management of childhood illnesses), nutrition interventions and early childhood care can be prioritized.[590] These strategic budget lines must be based on the child's rights approach and include a comprehensive assessment of children's needs.[591] The budget lines can consequently be used to assess and improve investments and prevent disparities based on gender, ethnicity, socioeconomic conditions or geographical location. Hereto, a tracking system of the budget allocated must be established to identify the differential impact on different groups of children.[592] With respect to budget allocated to international cooperation, it has been explicitly established that this must be guaranteed in times of economic crises or emergency situations.[593]

In the second place, the Committee recommends to thoroughly investigate existing social safety programmes for children, to identify incidences of inequality and discrimination, proposes remedies and to pay close attention to the possible short and long-term effects of the existing social safety programs on children's access to health care. In establishing the selection criteria for beneficiaries of social safety programmes, discriminatory provisions must be avoided. For example, if

---

587 Cuba, U.N. Doc. CRC/C/15/Add.72, 18 June 1997, § 3.

588 Lebanon, U.N. Doc. CRC/C/15/Add.169, 21 March 2002, § 42.

589 Bangladesh, U.N. Doc. CRC/C/BGD/CO/4, 26 June 2009 § 22 and 23.

590 Bangladesh, U.N. Doc. CRC/C/BGD/CO/4, 26 June 2009 § 21d and e.

591 Canada U.N. Doc. CRC/C/CAN/CO/3–4, 27 September 2012, § 16–17, Liberia U.N. Doc. CRC/C/LBR/CO/2–4, 18 September, § 16b-d, Egypte U.N. Doc. CRC/C/EGY/CO/3–4, 6 June 2011, § 20a-b.

592 Liberia U.N. Doc. CRC/C/LBR/CO/2–4, 18 September, § 16d.

593 Algeria, U.N. Doc. CRC/C/DZA/CO/3–4, 19 September 2006, § 20; Canada U.N. Doc. CRC/C/CAN/CO/3–4, 27 September 2012, § 18–19.

birth registration is ensured for refugee children, this must be guaranteed for all different groups of children and not only to a particular subgroup.[594]

3.5.3. TRAINING ON CHILDREN'S RIGHTS FOR PROFESSIONALS IN THE HEALTH SECTOR

The Committee elaborates that in order to achieve a truly integrated children's rights approach in ensuring children's health, systematic education and training programs on children's rights must be undertaken for professional health personnel.[595] In countries with a low level of human development, training is often completely absent.[596] This education will need to emphasize the need for non-discriminatory and culturally appropriate health facilities. Furthermore, the training should address both the general principles of the CRC for implementation in the health care sector as guidelines for health professionals to identify, report and manage cases of child abuse.[597] In the third place it is established that even if training on children's rights has previously been provided, additional training is required under changing circumstances, shifts of power, after a certain period of time and for specific subgroups such as disabled children.[598] Training for health professionals on the principles of the CRC must therefore be systematic and ongoing[599] and in order to be understandable for professionals in all regions, the training must be done in all existing languages in a country.[600] Last but not least, training must not only be directed at children, parents and health professionals in the youth sector, but also at traditional community leaders involved[601] and at birth attendants and midwives.[602] Training on the principles of the CRC and on the specific implications of the right to health of the child is relevant for traditional healers

594 Bangladesh, U.N. Doc. CRC/C/BGD/CO/4, 26 June 2009 § 71, 72, 78 and 79b.

595 See for example: U.N. Doc. CRC/C/15/Add.268, Concluding Observations of the Committee on the Rights of the Child on Australia, 20 October 2005; U.N. Doc. CRC/C/15/Add.241, Brazil, 3 November 2004, § 25 and 26; United Kingdom, U.N. Doc. CRC/C/15/Add.34, 15 January 1995, § 26; U.N. Doc. CRC/C/15/Add.195, 9 October 2002, Israel, § 23; Sudan, CRC/C/15/Add.10, 18 October 1993, § 23b; DRC, U.N. Doc. CRC/C/COD/CO/2, 10 February 2009, § 23, 48e and 51e.

596 Sudan, U.N. Doc. CRC/C/15/Add.10, 18 October 1993, § 10.

597 See for example the Concluding Observations of the Committee on the Rights of the Child on the United Kingdom U.N. Doc. CRC/C/GBR/CO/4., 20 October 2008, § 51; Israel, U.N. Doc. CRC/C/15/Add.195, 9 October 2002, § 39e; Egypt, U.N. Doc. CRC/C/15/Add.145, 21 February 2001, § 38.

598 Algeria U.N. Doc. CRC/C/15/Add.76, 18 June 1997, § 31 and U.N. Doc. CRC/C/15/Add.269, 12 October 2005, § 161e; Federal Republic of Yugoslavia, U.N. Doc. CRC/C/15/Add.49 13 February 1996, § 25; Moldova, U.N. Doc. CRC/C/MDA/CO/3, 20 February 2009, § 51f.

599 India, U.N. Doc. CRC/C/15/Add.115, 23 February 2000, § 23.

600 China, U.N. Doc. CRC/C/CHN/CO/2, 24 November 2005, § 25c.

601 South-Africa U.N. CRC/C/15/Add.122, 22 February 2000, § 16.

602 Guatemala, U.N. Doc. CRC/C/15/Add.58, 7 June 1996, § 22; Haiti, U.N. Doc. CRC/C/15/Add.202, 18 March 2003, § 45d.

and traditional midwives, because they have an important role in ensuring and allowing adequate access for children of all (minority) groups, in preventing FGM, early marriages and other harmful traditional practices directed at children, including child maltreatment and in reporting violations of children's right to have access to adequate health care facilities.

The necessity to educate politicians, health professionals and civil society about the rights enshrined in the CRC in order to integrate its tenets in concrete policies, budget priorities, child advocacy, new approaches to children's health care and assessing future health outcome, is also promoted from the side of paediatricians.[603, 604] Goldhagen establishes that the evolving concept of childhood and the incorporation of a broad notion of health, including economic and social dimensions of health care, should lead to a redefinition of the roles and responsibilities of paediatricians so that youth health care can become truly rights-based.[605, 606] Ideally, this should lead to the adoption of health care practices that involve children in decisions about pain relief, medical treatments and privacy and also to the establishment of a proactive responsibility of *all* health professionals and other professionals involved with children's health and well-being to make a case for all those children who do not have access to adequate health care. In my opinion, advocating for and explicit incorporation of all identified groups of vulnerable children in the daily medical practice should be interpreted as a duty to care of every health professional working with children, realizing access for all groups of children.

In order to respond to the identified need for child rights education for professionals, the international initiative of CRED-PRO, Child Rights Education for Professionals, supported by both the CRC Committee and the Office of the High Commissioner on Human Rights has been developed to provide for systematic children's rights training for professionals aiming to facilitate the actual implementation of children's rights.[607] It is acknowledged that the implementation of a rights-based approach in health care for children requires a radical shift in the attitude and role of medical health professionals.[608] This Boulton

603 J. Kasper, 'The Relevance of U.S. Ratification of the Convention on the Rights of the Child for Child Health: A Matter of Equity and Social Justice', *Child Welfare* 2010, Number 89, Volume 5, p. 32.

604 J. Goldhagen, 'Children's rights and the United Nations Convention on the Rights of the Child', *Pediatrics* 2003, 112-(3), pp. 742–745.

605 Ibidem supra note 603.

606 A similar standpoint is promoted in another article by Goldhagen and Mercer, stating that 'Child health professionals will need to move beyond their limited roles as clinicians to conceptualise themselves as child advocates functioning in the advocacy domains of practice, community and systems development and public policy formulation.' See: Goldhagen & Mercer, 'Child Health Equity: From Theory to Reality', in: A. Invernizzi, *The Human Rights of Children*, p. 322.

607 G. Landsdown, C. Heykoop & S. Hart, *CRED-PRO Child Rights Curriculum for Health Professionals*, International Institute for Child Rights and Development 2008, p. 4.

608 Ibidem supra note 607.

Initiative was established in partnership with the University of British Columbia Department of Pediatrics, the British Columbia Children's Hospital and the International Institute on Child Rights and Development (IICRD) resulting in the Child Rights Education for Professionals initiative (CRED-PRO). It brought together key partners in child health to set up a strategy to achieve realization of children's rights in health care practices. In this initiative, potential opportunities were identified for the incorporation of a child rights framework in the medical curriculum[609] providing for general recommendations and elucidating practical guidelines for achieving a child rights based approach in clinical practice.

The recommendations from the Boulton initiative are practically oriented, including the integration of child rights education in the existing training programs for medical students, so that children's rights-based health care is portrayed as an integral part of existing clinical medicine.[610] For example, it was found that some aspects of a child rights based approach, such as themes as refusal, informed consent, confidentiality and professional relationships with children can be integrated in the discussion of case studies of children presented with acute or chronic illnesses, requiring medico-legal, ethical and emotional considerations. In the second place, it is recommended to identify and build on synergies with other academic programs, as different academic fields compete for space in the curriculum. Particular electives can be offered to students on themes such as safe motherhood, child maltreatment, budget allocation to child health programs and communication with children and their families.[611] A third recommendation as formulated in the conclusions of the Boulton initiative is the incorporation of child rights based working skills in the general competency frameworks of (future) doctors.

The Boulton initiative also provides for practical building blocks to evaluate medical curricula for the existence of a child (and human) rights based approach. For example, curricular elements proposed include modules on the effects of violence on children, being differentiated between domestic violence and gross health and human rights violations (e.g. torture, rape and trauma as often found in conflict situations).[612, 613] The results of the Boulton initiative seem to provide

---

609 The specializations paediatrics, psychiatry and emergency medicine were taken as a starting point.

610 G. Landsdown, C. Heykoop & S. Hart, *CRED-PRO Child Rights Curriculum for Health Professionals*, International Institute for Child Rights and Development 2008, p. 26.

611 The International Federation of Medical Student Associations is a good example of a platform in which medical students have access to newsletters, conferences, additional trainings, medical projects, international exchange projects and internships. For example, the project 'Teddy Bear Hospital' aims to reduce fear for doctors among young children by 'curing' upon their teddy bears and dolls.

612 U.N. Doc. CRC/C/GC/13, 17 February 201, General Comment No. 13 of the Committee on the rights of the Child on Article 19: The right of the child to freedom from all forms of violence.

613 Modules include methods to recognize the different kinds of violence inflicted upon children, risk factors, possible reactions of health professionals, (local) legislation for the protection of children and the professional duty of care to address identified problems. Other basic

a useful specification of the general recommendations of the Committee on the Rights of the Child to provide training to health professionals to establish a children's rights based approach in children's health care. It will be interesting to evaluate the results of this initiative after implementation in different countries and social contexts. The requirements of children's right to health may then increasingly be realized in the daily health care for children.

3.5.4. BIRTH REGISTRATION AS A PREREQUISITE FOR SOCIAL SECURITY AND ACCESS TO HEALTH CARE

Birth registration is required to be accepted for social insurance policies and to be admitted to health care facilities. Without birth registration, children remain invisible to the authorities responsible for ensuring access to health care services, so that they can not be included in general prevention strategies, check-ups and vaccination programs. Therefore, birth registration is an essential prerequisite in ensuring children's access to health.

It is concluded from the Concluding Observations of the CRC Committee on the selected Country Reports, that the CRC Committee strongly recommends that all children receive a birth certificate immediately after birth and that this registration should be free of charge.[614] In situations in which (large amounts of) children have not been registered, the Committee provides several solutions to address the problem of unregistered children not having access to health care facilities. In the first place, if not yet existing, legislation must be adapted to ensure that all groups of children in all regions of a country can be registered as soon as possible after birth, including refugee children having a temporarily residence permit.[615]

In the second place, the provision of health insurances to children should not be dependent on the employment of parents.[616] Neither should it be dependent

---

modules proposed address the assessment of the normal development of the child (gross and fine motor development, language development and personal, social and adaptive skills), while acknowledging the uniqueness of each child, history taking (relationship between the child and its parents, observation and study), communicating about medical interventions and participation in scientific trials, the potential of advocacy of paediatricians for children encountered whose rights are violated and ethical questions such as informed consent, autonomy and paternalism, confidentiality, euthanasia and the treatment of children with special needs.

614 See for example Germany U.N. Doc. CRC/C/GBR/CO/Add.226, 26 February 2004, § 54e and 55e; Guatemala, U.N. Doc. CRC/C/15/Add.154, 9 July 2001, § 29; Mexico CRC/C/MEX/CO/3, 8 June 2006, § 32; Sudan 2010, CRC/C/SDN/CO/3-4, 22 October 2010, § 38; DRC. U.N. Doc. CRC/C/COD/CO/2, 10 February 2009, § 36.

615 Indonesia, CRC/C/15/Add.223, 18 February 2004, § 39; Bangladesh, U.N. Doc. CRC/C/15/Add.221, 27 October 2003, § 67.

616 Lebanon, U.N. Doc. CRC/C/15/Add.169, 21 March 2002, § 43b. China, U.N. Doc., CRC/C/15/Add.56, 7 June 1996, § 16.

on the issuing of visa or residence permits.[617] The Committee urges that even if children do not have official documentation, they should be allowed access to social services, such as health care.[618]

Thirdly, to ensure that de facto discrimination in the issuance of birth certificates does not occur, awareness-raising campaigns may need to be conducted and existing registration systems may need to be reviewed. Because special emphasis must be placed on reaching children in all rural and remote areas of a country, the Committee urges that innovative and accessible methods must be used to ensure birth registration for all children.[619] For example, birth registration could be achieved by deploying mobile birth registration units[620] and by allowing older children to be registered.[621] Also, manual birth registration systems could be replaced by national electronic systems.[622]

3.5.4.1. Recommendations for countries categories in groups II-IV

In the Concluding Observations on countries with lower levels of human development than category I several additional recommendations have been identified. These recommendations generally reflect the more limited budgets to ensure children's rights and an adequate standard of living in general in these countries.

3.5.5. STANDARD OF LIVING

In the Concluding Observations on countries in group II-IV of human development, the Committee has expressed its concern over the standard of living of (groups of) children affecting their health status and also their access to health care.[623] In the Low Human Development countries, child poverty and inequality pose serious problems, exacerbated by rapid urbanization, resulting in increasing numbers of children living in slums and substandard housing.[624] In countries with a high or medium level of human development, a poor standard of living is predominantly identified in particular groups of children or children living in particular areas or circumstances. In Mexico for example, children in

617 Colombia, U.N. Doc. CRC/C/COL/CO/3, 8 June 2006, § 67 and 69.

618 Bangladesh, U.N. Doc. CRC/C/BGD/CO/4, 26 June 2009, § 41.

619 Mexico CRC/C/MEX/CO/3, 8 June 2006, § 32.

620 South-Africa U.N. CRC/C/15/Add.122, 22 February 2000, § 20; India, U.N. Doc. CRC/C/15/Add.115, 23 February 2000, § 37; India, U.N. Doc. CRC/C/15/Add.228, 26 February 2004, § 39; Iran, U.N. Doc. CRC/C/15/Add.254, 31 March 2005, § 38; Nigeria, U.N. Doc. CRC/C/15/Add.257, 13 April 2005, § 36 and 37.

621 China, U.N. Doc. CRC/C/CHN/CO/2, 24 November 2005, § 43.

622 Bangladesh, U.N. Doc. CRC/C/BGD/CO/4, 26 June 2009 § 40 and 41.

623 Colombia, U.N. Doc. CRC/C/15/Add.30, 15 February 1995, § 11; U.N. Doc. CRC/C/COL/CO/3, 8 June 2006, § 66.

624 Bangladesh, U.N. Doc. CRC/C/BGD/CO/4, 26 June 2009 § 71.

juvenile institutions are identified as suffering from very low standards of living, including limited or no access to health care facilities and personal counselling. In other countries there are great disparities in standards of living of children between different regions of the country. In Algeria for example, there is concern about the living conditions of refugee children from the Western Sahara.[625] As a result of the low standards of living, there is limited access to health care facilities which is of great concern to the Committee. Therefore, the Committee recommends that countries guarantee the right to an adequate standard of living for all children.[626]

In countries with low levels of human development, the extremely poor living conditions of children and their families impede the holistic development of children.[627] This is especially true for conflict affected areas, where economic and social conditions are extremely poor and access to health care services is seriously hampered.[628] The need to ensure the basic necessities of living is therefore of paramount importance to ensure children's health and well-being.[629] Integrated in the thematic cluster on health and well-being of the Concluding Observations on countries with medium and low human development levels, the need to combat malnutrition and to ensure safe drinking water and sanitation for all children is prioritized, in combination with issues directly related to health such as the reduction of infant, child and maternal mortality rates and the prevention and curation of childhood illnesses.[630]

The scale of the problems of low developed countries makes it difficult to prioritize approaches to improve standards of living. Both an increase in human and financial resources, for example with support of the international community, is required and a revised allocation of the available resources, for example from military expenditure to the provision of social services.[631]

625 Algeria, U.N. Doc. CRC/C/15/Add.269, 12 October 2005, § 79.

626 China, U.N. Doc. CRC/C/15/Add.115, 23 February 2000, § 7,8,52 and 54.

627 Sudan, CRC/C/SDN/CO/3-4, 22 October 2010, § 60; Uganda, U.N. Doc. CRC/C/15/Add.80, 21 October 1997, § 5.

628 DRC, U.N. Doc. CRC/C/15/Add.153, 9 July 2001, § 6, 7 and 48.

629 DRC, U.N. Doc. CRC/C/15/Add.153, 9 July 2001, § 58 and 59.

630 India, U.N. Doc. CRC/C/15/Add.228, 26 February 2004, § 53; Indonesia, U.N. Doc. CRC/C/15/Add.223, 28 February 2004, § 57b; South-Africa U.N. CRC/C/15/Add.122, 22 February 2000, § 29; Sri Lanka, U.N. Doc. CRC/C/15/Add.207, 2 July 2003, § 38 and 39b; DRC, U.N. Doc. CRC/C/COD/CO/2, 10 February 2009, § 63, 64 and 67.

631 See for a more extensive elaboration of the role of international cooperation in implementing social children's rights: M. Wabwile, 'Implementing the Social and Economic Rights of Children in Developing Countries: The Place of International Assistance and Cooperation', *International Journal of Children's Rights* 2010, Volume 18, pp. 355-385. See also: W Vandenhole, 'Economic, Social and Cultural rights in the CRC: Is there a legal obligation to cooperate internationally for development?', *International Journal of Children's Rights* 2009, Volume 17, pp. 23-63.

3.5.6. PRIMARY HEALTH CARE INFRASTRUCTURE

In the Concluding Observations on countries with lower levels of human development (category II-IV), the importance of establishing primary health care facilities is systematically highlighted.[632] In the Concluding Observations on the Democratic Republic of the Congo, the improvement of health services is even mentioned as one of the top three priorities in improving children's living conditions.[633] Health services in very poor countries (category IV), especially in remote and rural areas, often remain insufficient due to a lack of adequate financial and human resources.[634] Therefore, health services and medical supplies must be distributed equally between and within regions.[635] It is stimulated to provide free health care for children under six and pregnant and lactating women and to adopt the UNICEF strategy to Integrated Management of Childhood Illnesses (IMCI).[636] Such a system is intended to benefit the nutritional status of children, the sanitary situation, to develop the skills of parents to prevent injuries and stimulate healthy behaviour for their children by ensuring universal access to maternal and child health-care services.[637]

In some instances, countries are recommended to reform the existing health sector to ensure access to quality primary health care for all children instead of excellent health care for a few and absent health care for the mass.[638] Suggested is that this could be done by decentralization of the healthcare system or by using mobile clinics or by establishing clinics in schools.[639] Also, the CRC Committee identifies that insufficient numbers of qualified health or traditional workers may result in limited access to adequate health facilities.[640] To ensure sufficient numbers of adequate health workers, sufficient budget must be allocated,

---

632 Egypt, U.N. Doc. CRC/C/15/Add.145, 21 February 2001, § 42; South Africa, U.N. Doc. CRC/C/15/Add.122, 22 February 2000, § 29; India, U.N. Doc. CRC/C/15/Add.115, 23 February 2000, § 48; Russia, U.N. Doc. CRC/C/RUS/CO/3, 23 February 2005, § 52; Sri Lanka, U.N. Doc. CRC/C/15/Add.207, 2 July 2003, § 39a; Sudan, CRC/C/SDN/CO/3–4, 22 October 2010, § 50a and 53a; DRC, U.N. Doc. CRC/C/15/Add.153, 9 July 2001, § 48 and 49.

633 DRC, U.N. Doc. CRC/C/15/Add.153, 9 July 2001, § 3.

634 South-Africa, U.N. Doc. CRC/C/15/Add.122, 22 February 2000, § 29; DRC, U.N. Doc. CRC/C/COD/CO/2, 10 February 2009, § 53a, d-f; Haïti, U.N. Doc. CRC/C/15/Add.202, 18 March 2003, § 45b; Liberia, U.N. Doc. CRC/C/15/Add.236, 1 July 2004, § 46 and 47.

635 Nigeria 1997, U.N. Doc. CRC/C/15/Add.61, 30 October 1996, § 41.

636 South-Africa, U.N. Doc. CRC/C/15/Add.122, 22 February 2000, § 29; India CRC/C/15/Add.115, 23 February 2000, § 49; Haiti, U.N. Doc. CRC/C/15/Add.202, 18 March 2003, § 44 and 45c; Nigeria, U.N. Doc. CRC/C/15/Add.257, 13 April 2005, § 48 and 49.

637 Federal Republic of Yugoslavia, U.N. Doc. CRC/C/15/Add.49 13 February 1996, § 36; Guatemala, U.N. Doc. CRC/C/15/Add.154, 9 July 2001, § 40 and 41.

638 Lebanon, U.N. Doc. CRC/C/LBN/CO/3, 8 June 2006, § 53; Colombia CRC/C/COL/CO/3, 8 June 2006, § 67a and 69a; Guatemala, U.N. Doc. CRC/C/15/Add.154, 9 July 2001, § 40 and 41.

639 Sudan, CRC/C/SDN/CO/3–4, 22 October 2010, § 50c; Guatemala, U.N. Doc. CRC/C/15/Add.154, 9 July 2001, § 40 and 41; Sudan, CRC/C/15/Add.10, 18 October 1993, § 12.

640 India, U.N. Doc. CRC/C/15/Add.115, 23 February 2000, § 48; India, U.N. Doc. CRC/C/15/Add.228, 26 February 2004, § 52 and 53; Sudan, CRC/C/SDN/CO/3–4, 22 October 2010, § 44 and 50b.

including for salaries for child health-care professionals.[641] In conflict situations, access should primarily be ensured by allowing national and international humanitarian missions.[642]

The CRC Committee elaborates in the Concluding Observations on countries of medium and low human development level that particular attention is required to ensure access to primary health care facilities for vulnerable groups of children,[643] including street children,[644] displaced and refugee children,[645] former child soldiers[646] disabled children,[647] children living in rural and remote areas[648] and children of minority and ethnic groups[649] and children in alternative care.[650] These vulnerable groups of children are often completely neglected, lacking access to all basic services and requirements for an adequate standard of living. Access to basic health care is prioritized as one of the minimal requirements that must be ensured for these children.

3.5.7. CHILDREN AFFECTED BY ARMED CONFLICT

Whereas there are no Concluding Observations available (nor Country Reports submitted) on countries in the midst of very harsh armed conflicts, such as Afghanistan and Iraq, it is acknowledged that armed conflicts have devastating effects on the access of children to health facilities. The CRC Committee emphasizes the need to ensure access to health care facilities for children in armed conflicts and for children affected by armed conflicts in the Concluding Observations of countries in (post-) conflict situations.[651]

---

641 Moldova 2002; § 33 and 34.

642 India, U.N. Doc. CRC/C/15/Add.228, 26 February 2004, § 71c; Sudan, CRC/C/15/Add.10, 18 October 1993, § 60f.

643 Moldova 2002; § 33 and 34; Uganda 1997, § 14; Haïti, U.N. Doc. CRC/C/15/Add.202, 18 March 2003, § 13, 25, 26.

644 India 2000, § 54, 55, and 62; India 2004, § 77b; Guatemala 2001, § 55; Moldova 2002, § 48a; Moldova 2009, § 67a and 73i; Sudan 2002, § 67; Sudan 2010, § 81f; DRC, U.N. Doc. CRC/C/15/Add.153, 9 July 2001, § 71. Interestingly, no reference is made of the need to ensure access to health care for street children in the Committee's Observations on Indonesia.

645 Sri Lanka, U.N. Doc., CRC/C/15/Add.40, 21 June 1995, § 20, 24 and 38; Sudan, CRC/C/SDN/CO/3-4, 22 October 2010, § 71a; DRC 2001, § 62; DRC 2009, § 76; Uganda 1997, § 21 and 37; Liberia, U.N. Doc. CRC/C/15/Add.236, 1 July 2004, § 60.

646 DRC, U.N. Doc. CRC/C/COD/CO/2, 10 February 2009, § 72–75.

647 India 2000, § 46 and 47; India 2004, § 56, Indonesia 2004, § 53; Moldova 2009, § 51a; Sudan 1993, § 45; DRC 2001, § 51; Haïti, U.N. Doc. CRC/C/15/Add.202, 18 March 2003, § 51b.

648 Guatemala 2001, § 40 and 41.

649 Indonesia 2004, § 90; Guatemala 2001, § 40 and 41; Moldova 2002, § 49 (Roma children); Bangladesh, U.N. Doc. CRC/C/15/Add.221, 27 October 2003, § 79.

650 DRC, U.N. Doc. CRC/C/15/Add.153, 9 July 2001, § 45.

651 Israel, U.N. Doc. CRC/C/15/Add.195, 9 October 2002; § 45. Bosnia, U.N. Doc. CRC/C/15/Add.260, 21 September 2005, § 5 and 17 and 43-g; Lebanon, U.N. Doc. CRC/C/15/Add.169, 21 March 2002, § 50; Sri Lanka, U.N. Doc. CRC/C/15/Add.40, 21 June 1995, § 20, 24 and 38; Colombia, U.N. Doc. CRC/C/COL/CO/3, 8 June 2006, § 94; Sudan, U.N. Doc. CRC/C/SDN/

It is acknowledged that specific challenges are identified in ensuring access to primary health care for children in conflict affected areas.[652] In Liberia for example, overwhelming challenges have been identified to rebuild the destroyed infrastructures and basic social services and to replace the vast majority of doctors, nurses and physician assistants that have left the country.[653] Also in Colombia, primary health care infrastructure has been strongly reduced by the devastating consequences of the ongoing civil war.[654]

Access to health care in conflict affected areas is directly hampered by the dangers of entering the conflict zones.[655] Medical professionals flee the conflict zones and humanitarian workers are denied access to patients of conflicting parties. In Sudan, humanitarian workers were directly attacked.[656] Conflicting parties deliberately block vital supplies of foods and medicines. The Committee therefore strongly urges conflicting parties to maintain the humanitarian principle of distinction between combatants and civilians and to admit humanitarian convoys to civilians of all parties, to refugees and internally displaced people under all circumstances.[657] This must particularly be guaranteed for discriminated groups of children affected by the conflict, such as (former) child soldiers,[658] refugee children,[659] street children, orphaned children[660] and minority children, as denial of humanitarian assistance increases the vulnerability of these groups of children.[661]

The Committee expresses its concern that conflict situations impact upon the availability of birth registration, thereby indirectly hampering access to health care services.[662] Last but not least, the Committee identifies that whereas conflicts increase the amount of children with mental health problems and disabilities, access to appropriate health care services is significantly reduced.[663]

Several of the most recent conflict situations have not been covered yet in Country Reports and Concluding Observations, such as the hostilities in Ivory Coast, Libya, Yemen, Syria and other Arab countries that are currently

---

CO/3-4, 22 October 2010, § 50, 53a and 71a; DRC, U.N. Doc. CRC/C/COD/CO/2, 10 February 2009, § 53, 67, 72–76; Liberia, U.N. Doc. CRC/C/15/Add.236, 1 July 2004, § 60.

652 Sri Lanka, U.N. Doc. CRC/C/15/Add.207, 2 July 2003, § 39a; India, U.N. Doc. CRC/C/15/Add.228, 26 February 2004, § 57a; Sudan, CRC/C/15/Add.10, 18 October 1993, § 9.

653 Liberia, U.N. Doc. CRC/C/15/Add.236, 1 July 2004, § 5 and 46.

654 Colombia, U.N. Doc. CRC/C/15/Add.137, 16 October 2000, § 10.

655 Sri Lanka, U.N. Doc. CRC/C/ 15/Add.40, 21 June 1995, § 24.

656 Sudan, U.N. Doc. Sudan, CRC/C/SDN/CO/3-4, 22 October 2010, § 72 and 76.

657 Colombia, U.N. Doc. CRC/C/COL/CO/3, 8 June 2006, § 79c and 94.

658 Sri Lanka, U.N. Doc. CRC/C/ 15/Add.40, 21 June 1995, § 12; Lebanon, U.N. Doc. CRC/C/LBN/CO/3, 8 June 2006, § 69 and 70.

659 Lebanon, U.N. Doc. CRC/C/LBN/CO/3, 8 June 2006, § 27; Iran, U.N. Doc. CRC/C/15/Add.254, 31 March 2005, § 62 and 63; Colombia, U.N. Doc. CRC/C/COL/CO/3, 8 June 2006, § 79c, 80 and 81.

660 Sri Lanka, U.N. Doc. CRC/C/ 15/Add.40, 21 June 1995, § 24.

661 Colombia, U.N. Doc. CRC/C/COL/CO/3, 8 June 2006, § 79c.

662 Colombia, U.N. Doc. CRC/C/COL/CO/3, 8 June 2006, § 94.

663 Liberia, U.N. Doc. CRC/C/15/Add.236, 1 July 2004, § 44 and 45b.

occurring.[664] It is to be expected that these situations have serious detrimental effects on the access of children to adequate health care services. In Libya for example, international media have reported indifferent targeting of any moving civilians, humanitarian convoys, hospitals and other facilities necessary to ensure adequate health care for all, including children.[665]

3.5.8. EMERGING THEMES

Since 2000, several new issues related to health have been addressed in the Concluding Observations. Among these, obesity is a problem that is identified predominantly in countries with high human development levels.[666] Also, increased attention for mental health problems is recognized in countries of all levels of development.

In the most recent Concluding Observations on Country Reports several topics related to the health of infants and young children have been integrated. In the first place, the importance of providing for baby-friendly hospitals is highlighted, including the stimulation of breastfeeding from the moment of birth of the child.[667] Repeatedly, the CRC Committee expresses its concern over low or decreasing numbers of children who are exclusively breastfed during the first six months of their lives.[668] Therefore, States are recommended to adopt and implement legislation, so that mothers have maternity leave and opportunities at work to continue breastfeeding their children for at least six months.[669] Measures required to stimulate mothers to breastfeed their children, include the implementation of awareness raising campaigns on the benefits of breastfeeding and further include the implementation of the International Code of Marketing

---

664 The developments in the course of the 'Arab Spring; a revolutionary wave of demonstrations and protests that has been taking place in the Middle East and North Africa since 18 December 2010'.

665 Integrated Regional Information Networks (IRIN), *Libyan Arab Jamahiriya: Aid workers call for access to the vulnerable*, 29 March 2011, available at: www.unhcr.org/refworld/docid/4d9572a8c.html [accessed 6 April 2011].
'Libya: 1 million children at risk' Wednesday 2 March 2011, Message by Save the Children UK, www.savethechildren.org.uk/en/libya-crisis.htm, 'Libya crisis' Call for help from the NGO Save the Children UK, www.savethechildren.org.uk/en/libya-crisis.htm, 'Children of the Libyan revolution', http://nos.nl/video/223510-de-kinderen-van-de-libische-revolutie.html; 'FLEEING LIBYA: HUNDREDS OF CHILDREN CAUGHT IN ITALY'S MIGRANT CRISIS' http://getstopic.com/fleeing-libya-hundreds-of-children-caught-in-italys-migrant-crisis-172186.html.

666 Mexico, U.N. Doc. CRC/C/MEX/CO/3, 8 June 2006, § 49 ; China, U.N. Doc. CRC/C/CHN/CO/2, 24 November 2005, § 62. Canada U.N. Doc. CRC/C/CAN/CO/3-4, 27 September 2012, § 63.

667 Egypt, U.N. Doc. CRC/C/EGY/CO/3-4, 6 June 2010, § 63c; Bosnia, U.N. Doc. CRC/C/BIH/CO/2-4, 19 September 2012, § 54.

668 Bosnia, U.N. Doc. CRC/C/BIH/CO/2-4, 19 September 2012, § 54d-e.

669 Canada U.N. Doc. CRC/C/CAN/CO/3-4, 27 September 2012, § 61.

of Breast-milk Substitute.[670] This Code is an excellent example of the recognition of the impact the business sector has and can have on the realization or violation of the highest attainable standard of children's right to health. Therefore, the CRC Committee demands States to adopt a legislative framework to hold private companies responsible for violations of children's rights both within and outside the country, such as marketing unhealthy foods or using child labourers in the production process.[671] Therefore, the CRC Committee recommends that business plans must be disclosed and that child rights impact assessments must be done before trade agreements can be concluded.[672] Lastly, remedies must be done in case of violation of children's rights by the business sector.[673]

Closely related to the health of young children is the provision of sexual and reproductive health rights training and services to adolescents. Such training and services not only benefit their own health, but they also impact upon the health of their (future) children, because it helps inter alia to prevent teenage pregnancies, unsafe abortions and mother-to-child transmissions of HIV/AIDS.[674]

Increasingly addressed is also the impact of environmental health and natural disasters on children's health.[675] To prevent the harmful effects of environmental pollution, it is recommended to facilitate the implementation of sustainable development programs.[676] The role of the business sector in refraining from activities that have detrimental effects to the environment in which children live is at stake here. Also, the impact of natural disasters on children's living circumstances is considered. In the past few years, the highly devastating tsunamis in Indonesia (2005) and Japan (2011), the floods in Pakistan (2010), the cyclones Nargis in Burma (2008) and Katrina in the US (2005) and the earthquake in Haiti (2010) have completely destroyed existing health infrastructure, posing enormous challenges to the countries affected to rebuild houses, roads and medical facilities.

---

670 Egypt, U.N. Doc. CRC/C/EGY/CO/3-4, 6 June 2010, § 63d;, U.N. Doc. CRC/C/BIH/CO/2-4, 19 September 2012, § 55d; Cuba U.N. Doc. CRC/C/CUB/CO/2, 8 June 2010, § 47; Myanmar U.N. Doc. CRC/C/MMR/CO/3-4, 19 January 2011, § 63f.

671 Liberia U.N. Doc. CRC/C/LBR/CO/2-4, 18 September 2012, § 29b;, U.N. Doc. CRC/C/BIH/CO/2-4, 19 September 2012, § 28; Canada U.N. Doc. CRC/C/CAN/CO/3-4, 27 September 2012, § 29a and 63-64; Myanmar U.N. Doc. CRC/C/MMR/CO/3-4, 19 January 2011, § 21-22 and 85.

672 Liberia U.N. Doc. CRC/C/LBR/CO/2-4, 18 September 2012, § 29b; Turkey, U.N. Doc. CRC/C/TUR/CO/2-3, 15 June 2012, § 23.

673 Turkey, U.N. Doc. CRC/C/TUR/CO/2-3, 15 June 2012, § 23d.

674 Liberia U.N. Doc. CRC/C/LBR/CO/2-4, 18 September 2012, § 59, 64, 65, 66, 68; Myanmar U.N. Doc. CRC/C/MMR/CO/3-4, 19 January 2011, § 66-68; Algeria U.N. Doc. CRC/C/DZA/CO/3-4, 19 June 2012, § 33 and 60; Egypt U.N. Doc. CRC/C/EGY/CO/3-4, 6 June 2010, § 64-65; Cuba U.N. Doc. CRC/C/CUB/CO/2, 8 June 2010, § 45.

675 Bangladesh, U.N. Doc. CRC/C/15/Add.221, 27 October 2003, § 7; Colombia, U.N. Doc. CRC/C/COL/CO/3, 8 June 2006, § 72 and 73; India, U.N. Doc. CRC/C/15/Add.115, 23 February 2000, § 8;.

676 South-Africa, U.N. Doc. CRC/C/15/Add.122, 22 February 2000, § 30. Bosnia, U.N. Doc. CRC/C/BIH/CO/2-4, 19 September 2012, § 56.

Last but not least, the Committee has commented upon narrow interpretations of the CRC, as found in certain legalistic or Islamic interpretations[677] and interpretations based on customary law and local traditional practices, discriminating between children of different groups in providing access to health care. These interpretations are found in countries with different levels of development.

3.6. RESULTS III: DIFFERENT STANDARDS FOR THE IMPLEMENTATION OF CHILDREN'S RIGHT TO HEALTH FOR COUNTRIES WITH DIFFERENT LEVELS OF HUMAN DEVELOPMENT?

3.6.1. IMPLEMENTATION OF THE RIGHT TO HEALTH OF THE CHILD IN DIFFERENT CIRCUMSTANCES AND REGIONS

From the analysis of the Concluding Observations on the Country Reports, several more or less 'universal' recommendations have been identified that are applicable in countries with different levels of human development. However, explanations on the particular ways to implement these recommendations for different countries, contexts and in different groups of people are rather casuistic. In many Concluding Observations, there is little explanation at all to be found. For example, it is elaborated that the establishment of primary health care infrastructure needs to be adapted to the specific requirements of local circumstances, such as mountainous areas, areas with much water, high or very low population density and conflict affected areas. The way in which this diversified infrastructure of primary health care should be established is not specified, neither are guidelines or possible solutions provided to identify the responsible organization or (non-) governmental institution for establishing the necessary health care facilities. The consequence is that the Concluding Observations of the CRC Committee remain a relatively weak instrument in guiding the implementation of children's rights in individual countries, especially when neither the government nor the medical professionals take ownership of the responsibility for the right to health of children, also resulting from unawareness of children's rights. Secondly, recommendation for countries as diverse as the Netherlands and Colombia are identical, which does underline the rather universal approach to countries and

677 South-Africa, U.N. Doc. CRC/C/15/Add.122, 22 February 2000, § 41; Iran, U.N. Doc. CRC/C/15/Add.123, 28 June 2000, § 2 and 6; Egypt, U.N. Doc. CRC/C/ 15/Add.145, 21 February 2001, § 6; India, U.N. Doc. CRC/C/15/Add.115, 23 February 2000, § 9 and 31.

places with highly diversified characteristics. Both aspects of the Concluding Observations may lead to a situation in which children remain fully or completely deprived of health care or in which no minimum standards are developed according to which the available health care must be organized, for example to treat children well and protect them against over-hospitalization[678] or practices of abuse in medical institutions. This lacunae are all the more remarkable, as the implementation checklist for article 24 CRC in the UNICEF Implementation Handbook for the Convention on the Rights of the Child starts with enumerating the need to identify and coordinate the responsible departments and agencies at all levels of government (particular relevance is attributed to the departments of health, welfare, education, planning and environment) in the first and the need to identify relevant non-governmental organizations and civil society partners in the second bullet.[679] Even when countries have not fulfilled their duty to identify the responsible governmental departments, the CRC Committee is in the position to suggest organizational structures, given its broader insight in the organization of health care systems in countries with different levels of development.

The recommendations of the Committee in its Concluding Observations should therefore be further translated to be relevant for specific circumstances and regions, both on the organizational level of establishing an infrastructure of primary health care facilities, as on the more practical level of guideline elaboration for the provision of health care for children and in a clear attribution of responsibilities to all actors involved, including medical professionals and policymakers. Lastly, measurable and timebound targets help to concretize and put into perspective the findings in different countries, which also allows for a more accurate assessment of progress achieved over time in the realization of the right to the highest attainable standard of health.

3.6.2. ACCESS TO HEALTH CARE FOR CHILDREN IN DEVELOPING AND DEVELOPED COUNTRIES

A second difference between the interpretation of children's right to health that can be discerned from the Concluding Observations are the prioritized (vulnerable)

[678] L. Shields e.a. 'A review of the literature from developed and developing countries relating to the effects of hospitalization on children and parents', *International Council of Nurses* 2001, Number 48, p. 30.
In this literature review on the effects of hospitalization on children it was found that several factors were found to have adverse effects on the emotional trauma suffered by children when admitted to hospital: a hospital stay longer than 2 weeks; painful or traumatic illnesses or injuries; inadequate preparation for admissions; previous adverse experiences; non-presence of the parents or a high level of anxiety of the parents; and lack of training of the pediatric staff.

[679] Implementation Handbook for the Convention on the Rights of the Child, prepared for UNICEF by Rachel Hodgkin and Peter Newell, fully revised third edition, September 2007, p. 376.

groups of children that are identified as being in greatest need to receive adequate health care. In countries with (very) high levels of development, attention is primarily drawn to ensuring access to health care for certain excluded groups of children, because the majority of the children are provided with adequate health care. In countries with lower levels of human development, however, attention is similarly drawn to particularly vulnerable groups of children, but it is also recognized that all children suffer from a lack of access to adequate health care services and that the establishment of adequate primary health care infrastructure must be prioritized for all children in that country. Therefore, the benchmark from which progress is measured differs for countries with lower and countries with higher levels of human development. Any progress made to improve access of (groups of) children to health care in countries with lower levels of development, can be considered as a step forward in the realization of children's right to have access to health. In countries with (very) high development levels, it can be assumed that progress made to ensure access to health care services, must at least include all groups of children.

On the basis of the provision in article 24 CRC that countries must progressively realize the highest attainable standard of health for all children, it is required that the realization of the right to health of the child gradually increases. Because access to health facilities can actually be reached, *all* children in countries with (very) high levels of human development are entitled to adequate health care. Although the minimum core content of the right to health includes the element to have access to primary health care, this is not always an achievable first step for countries with low levels of development. Therefore, it can be concluded that the highest attainable standard of health to be reached by countries, as laid down in article 24 CRC, varies according to the level of human development of countries: countries with (very) high levels of development must ensure children's right to health as an obligation of immediate result. Countries with medium or low levels of human development must show considerable improvement in ensuring access to health care for at least part of the population, for example by providing for mobile health clinics that visit areas without permanent health clinics on a regular basis. In this way, it is prevented that certain groups of children are prioritized in receiving health care, whereas other groups do not have access at all.

The human development level of countries is not the only factor determining the realization of the right to the highest attainable standard of health of the child. As identified in the recommendations on budget allocation, the percentage of the gross domestic product that is allocated to the establishment of adequate health infrastructure has a significant influence on the opportunity of children to have adequate access to health care services. Therefore, all countries should allocate *the maximum extent of available* resources to implement children's right to health, notwithstanding their level of development. Several suggestions can be made to determine the percentage of the Gross Domestic Product that should be allocated to the realisation of the right to health of the child. In the first place, the budget allocated should at least reflect the percentage of children in a population: for countries with relatively many children, such as Iran, Brazil or India,[680] the budget allocated to children's health care should be adjusted comparatively. Furthermore, an assessment of the health needs of children could provide further insight in the required resources for specific subgroups or the combat of highly prevalent diseases so that the allocated budget can be adjusted in line with the findings of that assessment. Attention must be paid to the fact that the allocated budget is spread equally over the different groups of children, so that all children will actually benefit from it. A way in which this can be achieved is by giving priority to ensuring access to primary health care for all children over costly individual treatments for just a few children. This suggestion is supported by findings of a study from Brazil on the influence of right-to-health litigation on the realisation of the right to health: it appeared that access to this type of litigation was easier accessible for more privileged members of society, resulting in worsening health inequities, as the more privileged gained access to better health care, whereas less budget remained available for the worst off.[681]

3.6.3. PRIORITIES SET FOR DEVELOPING AND FOR DEVELOPED COUNTRIES

In the third place, there seems to be a discrepancy between a child rights based approach in developed and in developing countries. For developing countries, recommendations on the provision of health care usually focus on the most elementary level of health care, including prevention, immunization, perinatal health care, health education and the basic underlying determinants of health. These are also the elements that are most extensively elaborated in article 24 of the Convention on the Rights of the Child. In developed countries, on the other hand, important discussions concerning the right to health of the child predominantly evolve around issues such as access to age-appropriate information for children, refusal to autonomy and refusal of medical treatment, informed consent, participation in research etc. Whereas children formally have a wide range of information and participation rights, these rights predominantly come into play when basic health care needs have been met. However, this second category of issues related to children's right to health is hardly reflected in the Concluding Observations on the Country Reports. For example, for the Netherlands, mention is made of the practice of euthanasia, without giving detailed comments on its

[680] See the website www.indexmundi.com/ for 2011 demographics profiles of countries in the world. The percentage of children between the age of 0–14 is 26.2% in Brazil, 29.7% in India and 24.1% in Iran as compared to 13.8% in Italy, 17% in the Netherlands, 17.3% in the United Kingdom, 20.1% in the United States and 17.6% in China.

[681] O. Luiz Motta Ferraz, 'The right to health in the courts of Brazil: worsening health inequities?', *Health and Human Rights* 2009, Volume 11, no. 2, pp. 33–45.

connection to children's right to health. Recent regional developments with respect to the requirements of 'child-friendly' health care have not been covered at all.[682] Therefore, it may be concluded from the analysis of the Concluding Observations that the Committee on the Rights of the Child –quite logically- prioritizes the access to adequate health care services over the participation rights of (groups of) children as long as universal access has not been achieved for all children. This position, however, does not fully take into account the actual situation that countries are responsible for *gradually improving* the level of health care and the health status of children within their country borders. For this reason, further elaboration of the progressive steps required by developed states is necessary, specifying whether priority must be given to enhancing the more elaborated health rights of children within the country borders of the developed states or to increasing the budget allocated to international development. Given the emphasis of the Committee on ensuring access to primary health care for all children in conjunction with the provisions in article 4 and article 24-4 CRC, explicitly promoting international cooperation for the realization of economic, social and cultural rights, this would be a laudable step forward in the realization of children's right to health.[683]

3.7. CONCLUSION AND RECOMMENDATIONS

In this chapter, the Concluding Observations of the CRC Committee have been used as a starting point for answering the question how the right to the highest attainable standard of health of the child as laid down in article 24 of the Convention on the Rights of the Child is interpreted by the CRC Committee for four groups of countries selected on the basis of their size and gross domestic product (GDP) and in what way these standards lead to different systems of prioritization of health measures.

3.7.1. IDENTIFIED PRIORITIES IN INTERPRETING THE RIGHT TO THE HIGHEST ATTAINABLE STANDARD OF HEALTH

It is remarkable that for all countries, even within those with extremely low levels of development, the element of ensuring access to necessary health, including maternal and new born health and to underlying determinants of

---

682 See for example the guidelines adopted by the Council of Europe on child-friendly health care, Lisbon, 21 September 2011.

683 See for a similar statement also Arts, K., '21 Jaar VN-Verdrag voor de Rechten van het Kind: Een volwassen bijdrage aan kinderrechten in de wereld?' in: *Internationale Spectator*, year 65, number 6, June 2011, p. 337.

health is structurally mentioned as a priority area for improving children's living conditions. The particular realization of this right is dependent upon the level of development of countries and on cultural values in interpreting this right. From the Concluding Observations of the CRC Committee on the Rights of the Child, although relatively general, several priority measures have been distinguished to ensure children's right to health. These include both direct and indirect measures.

Several recommendations are directed at all countries, namely the necessity to eliminate all forms of discrimination hampering access for all (vulnerable) groups of children to health care, the duty to ensure access to social security in order to be able to pay for health care, the provision of birth registration and residence permits to ensure visibility of all children and admittance to health facilities, the requirement of disaggregated data collection and specific allocation of available budgets to making health care facilities available and accessible and the need for establishing training for health professionals. Whereas these recommendations are rather general, the specific elaboration differs between different countries. For example in developing countries, training for health professionals must include basic knowledge on child health, the recognition of the most prevalent diseases, healthy nutrition and healthy behaviour. In addition, training on the integration of child-rights in health must be provided. In developed countries, training of doctors on basic health care has generally been achieved. The focus therefore shifts to the further elaboration of principles of participation, respect for the views and autonomy of the child and the provision of child-friendly health care in daily medical practices.

In the recommendations specifically oriented towards countries with lower levels of development, it is acknowledged that the right to health of children is seriously violated by inadequate standards of living and a deficient or even completely absent system of primary health care infrastructure. Therefore, it is recommended in situations of extreme scarcity and in even more problematic situations of violent conflicts to establish mobile health clinics to be able to reach all children, even in the most inadmissible and remote areas.

Another striking difference between countries with (very) high levels of development and countries with medium to low levels of development is the different groups of children that are most specifically identified to be in greatest need of provided with adequate access to health care. Whereas all children are entitled to the right to the highest attainable standard of health in article 24 CRC, much explicit attention is paid in the Concluding Observations to the most vulnerable groups of children. For more developed countries, this implies that most attention is paid to several particular groups of children, such as refugee children, disabled children and indigenous children. Access for children in general is, if at all, only marginally mentioned.

In countries with lower levels of development, deprivation of children of all basic necessities is often so extreme, that almost all children are vulnerable, whereas several particular groups are extremely vulnerable, such as orphans, refugee children, HIV/AIDS infected children and children living on the street. All in all, the right of children to non-discrimination as laid down in article 2 CRC is key to realizing the highest attainable standard of health of the child.

The second focus of the recommendations made by the Committee is the mentioning of concrete measures to ensure the health of infants and young children. This is exemplified by the type of services that are prioritized: maternal, postnatal and primary health care services and also in the requirement to provide for baby-friendly hospitals. It must be clearly understood that in many countries hospitals are the first line of health care encountered for women delivering their baby. One of the key characteristics of baby-friendly hospitals is that mothers are stimulated to breastfeed their children from the very beginning and to continue doing so for at least six months. Other interventions include the supplementation of nutritional deficits (e.g. iron deficiency) and the prevention, early identification, intervention and rehabilitation for easily preventable diseases and injuries.[684]

3.7.2. RELATING THE CRC FRAMEWORK TO THE CONCLUDING OBSERVATIONS OF THE COMMITTEE

The right to health of the child has been extensively elaborated in article 24 CRC and the interpretative General Comments issued by the Committee on the Rights of the Child. This paragraph answers the question whether the Recommendations made by the Committee in the Concluding Observations reflect the priorities set in the legal framework on the right to health of the child as elaborated in chapter II.

Over the last decade, the legal framework on the right to health of the child in the CRC has increasingly developed towards a community-based approach in which many different actors, including the child, its parents, extended family, medical professionals and a variety of private actors such as NGOs and private companies are identified as important stakeholders, contributors or violators of the right to health of the child. The active contribution of children and their families is sought in the identification and prioritization of the key elements of the right to health. General Comment 15 to the CRC makes ample reference to the need to actively involve all stakeholders in the implementation of the right to health of the child, including an elaborated list of items on which children's input must be sought (see paragraph 5.8.2). However, the active involvement of children and their parents or other caretakers is only marginally addressed in the Concluding Observations. Furthermore, the Concluding Observations do not reflect the opinions of the relevant stakeholders on the level of realization of their

---

684 Baby-Friendly Hospital Initiative, WHO and UNICEF, 2009. Available at: www.who.int/nutrition/publications/infantfeeding/bfhi_trainingcourse/en/.

own rights. There is very limited inclusion of the actual level of realization of the right to health of the child in the countries assessed by the Committee and the reports suffer from a fairly high level of abstraction. Still, the need to actively seek children's input in the reporting procedure to the Committee is evident, since they are the only ones who can truly testify how they experience their own health status. Such involvement would furthermore allow for a more specified and locally adjusted monitoring practice, in which children, their parents and or caretakers acquire more influence in the fulfilment of their own right to health.

The need to define a concrete framework of reference for States on which to base their health policy is found both in General Comment 15 and in the Concluding Observations. The Committee in the Concluding Observations does give specific recommendations to be better able to perform an accurate assessment of the progress made by the State in implementing the right to health of the child. These priorities are:

I. Establish a national plan with strategic budget lines.
II. Identify the responsible government departments responsible for the right to health of the child.
III. Set clear, time-bound and measurable targets.
IV. Ensure disaggregated data collection and analysis.

General Comment 15 elaborates on these requirements by establishing that children's health must be integrated in all policies and that interaction with civil society must be sought in the development of a sustainable national plan. Furthermore, the newly adopted General Comment 15 offers a more elaborated framework for assessing the measures taken, including the specification of the different levels of health care that should be provided, the health problems that must be addressed, the health interventions that must be made and the medicines that must be provided as a minimum. Not surprisingly, these recommendations have not found their way to the Concluding Observations yet, since General Comment 15 was adopted in March 2013, after the assessment of the most recent Country Reports in January 2013.

Both article 24 CRC and General Comment 15 to the CRC clearly prioritize the need to prevent health problems. This focus on prevention is reflected most remarkably in the Concluding Observations in the discussion of several subthemes, namely the need to ensure access to the underlying determinants of health and to primary health care and the need to provide for (sexual and reproductive) health education. However, not all elements of prevention that are distinguished in General Comment 15 (combating malnutrition and easily preventable diseases, early identification & intervention, awareness of health risks through education and promoting healthy lifestyles) are visibly assessed by the Committee in its Concluding Observations.

The Concluding Observations of the Committee are directed towards States. Although several references are made of the role of other non-state actors, these references are very limited. Only in the latest Concluding Observations does the Committee point to the role of the private sector. Similarly, scarce attention is given to the role of the family in providing for examples of healthy behaviour to their children. Both article 24.2 (d and f) CRC, focusing on the need to educate families about children's health and the prevention of health problems through healthy behaviour ánd General Comment 15 acknowledges the need to engage all different stakeholders in the implementation process on children's right to health.

Lastly, General Comment 15 establishes that the realization of children's right to health requires a high degree of flexibility and adaptability of measures taken to the changing needs of children and the changing circumstances in which children live, grow and develop. This general requirement is sporadically reflected in concrete recommendations on the need to establish mobile clinics for children who do not have access to regular health services. However, modern issues such as urbanization and welfare diseases do call for a more elaborated response, including a multisectoral approach as well as the direct involvement of all stakeholders, including children and their families in assessing their rights and needs. The involvement of stakeholders in the reporting procedure could be beneficial for better reflecting the differing health problems that children encounter.

3.7.3. RECOMMENDATIONS TO THE CRC COMMITTEE

The actual task of the CRC Committee with respect to realizing children's right to health is threefold:

I) Assessment of the available data

In the first place, a thorough assessment of all efforts and challenges of countries to implement the right to health of the child in daily practice is required. Hereto, a well-functioning method of disaggregated data collection that is based on child-centred statistics must be established which can be used by the Committee as a basis for assessing the status of children's rights in a country. The resulting Concluding Observations should contain measurable and timebound indicators that can be used as a reference for governments to base its policy on, for measuring progress over time and between countries with similar levels of human development. Existing schemes of indicators for assessing the status of children's right to health and the budget allocated to it, deriving both from qualitative[685] as

[685] See for an extensive example of health indicators: G. Backman, P. Hunt a.o., 'Health systems and the right to health: an assessment of 194 countries', *The Lancet* 2008, Volume 372,

well as from quantitative studies can be used as a basis for further elaboration. Experience in State Parties with establishing schemes of indicators, for example by children's Ombudspersons, can be useful to assessing the Country Reports delivered to the CRC Committee. Furthermore, significantly more efforts must be made to stimulate State Parties to involve children in the gathering of data and the construction of reports submitted to the CRC Committee. In addition to the concretization of targets, the attribution of responsibilities to different governmental departments and other responsible actors must be clearly identified to allow for establishing accountability for the (lack of) progress achieved in the realization of the right to the highest attainable standard of health of the child.

With respect to the reporting procedure on the realization of children's right to the highest attainable standard of health, this process should at least include the involvement of children with chronic diseases and regular contacts in hospitals[686] as well as healthy children on their vision and wishes on what is required in their living circumstances to be a healthy or healthier child and what aspects of health care are important to them and what changes they would like to see. In the words of the Committee: 'In many cases, only children themselves are in the position to indicate whether their rights are being fully recognized and realized.'[687] To enable (sick) children to be involved in this process, interviews and other communication methods should be available within the medical facilities. Furthermore, the best interests of the child should be guiding, so that interviews are only held when the child feels well enough to communicate and not when the moment fits best into the agenda of the interviewer. Sometimes, it is required to postpone interviews after undergoing the treatment. Possibly, the communication procedure for children and their representatives as laid down in Optional Protocol III tot the CRC (see chapter 6), provides for an additional avenue to bring such issues under the attention of the CRC Committee.

II) Monitoring of budget allocated, legislative measures taken and implemented

The second task of the CRC Committee with respect to the right to the highest attainable standard of health of the child consists of the monitoring of the organizational structure of the relevant actors involved, including medical professionals, on their particular roles and responsibilities in ensuring children's right to health. All Concluding Observations analysed contain paragraphs on

---

pp. 2047–2085, most specifically pp. 2057 and 2058. In this article, 72 indicators are proposed for assessing the progressive realization of the right to health and for monitoring health systems. This list must be adapted to meet the specific needs of assessing *children's* right to health.

686 See for a example of research involving children in research and medical treatment the dissertation of C. Dedding, 'Delen in macht en onmacht: Kindparticipatie in de (alledaagse) diabeteszorg', University of Amsterdam, 30 September 2009.

687 U.N. Doc. CRC/GC/2003/3, General Comment 3 on HIV/AIDS and the rights of the child, 17 March 2003, § 1–3.

the necessity to train professionals working with and for children, including health professionals, on the implications of the CRC for their work activities. The challenge of translating the recommendations of the Committee to the daily medical practice in local situations is thereby partly attributed to the professionals directly working with children in the health sector. In doing this, practical problems will be encountered for which concrete, practical solutions must be sought, partially depending on the local situation and the particular context of those problems. Medical professionals, being closer to the patients, have a more realistic insight into the actual needs of sick children. As a next step, medical professionals need to give feedback to the Committee on their assessment of the practical applicability of the Committee's recommendations in individual countries and to identify barriers encountered in ensuring the right to the highest attainable standard of health of the child. This can be done directly or through mediation of medical associations, NGOs, Ombudspersons and governmental bodies.

III) Interpretation and development of the rights of the child

The third task of the Committee entails the further development and interpretation of the health related rights in the Convention. The recent adoption of General Comment 15 to the CRC on the right to the highest attainable standard of health of the child is an example of this influential function. The CRC Committee is in a central position to receive and share experiences from countries all over the world in the interpretation and implementation of the right to the highest attainable standard of health of the child. When the acquired knowledge is digested, new insights from one country may help to find solutions for realizing the different elements of children's right to health in another country. The Committee is therefore in the position to give valuable recommendations to countries on the progressive steps to be taken to realize the right to the highest attainable standard of health, for example with a view to raising the standard of the health services provided to obtain the predicate of child-friendly health care. This should at least involve insights obtained from both the legal domain and from (young) children themselves.[688] The CRC Committee can also play a role in identifying ways in which more developed countries can contribute to developing the right to the highest attainable standard of health in other countries, without losing sight of the achievements made on the realization of the right to health of the child within its own borders. This includes questions over the prioritization between realizing the right to health on the domestic or on the international level as is specified in article 24.4 and article 4 CRC. Although ways to (re-)allocate budget to the health

[688] Ennew quite righteously comments that the requirement to perceive children's rights (such as the highest attainable standard of health) as a positively formulated target, is more motivating for countries, so that they will feel less inclined to compile defensive reports. This can result in a more constructive basis for improvement. See supra note 519 p. 137.

of children in both national and international situations, it should be kept in mind that there are many more effective ways to share best practices and valuable experiences between children, parents and professionals in the realization of the right to the highest attainable standard of health, such as the sharing of knowledge and human resources with less developed countries to develop the necessary health services for children.

Given the enormous burden of the CRC Committee to evaluate the actual progress of the 194 States that have ratified the UNCRC on a large number of themes that must be progressively achieved, the requirement to assess the progress achieved in the realization of the right to the highest attainable standard of health of the child constitutes a big challenge. Close cooperation with other UN Committees, (I) NGOs, State Parties, youth organizations and other institutions is not only required in the consultation session, but also in the preparation phase of the Concluding Reports. This requires the opportunity for NGOs to work independently and report on their findings to the CRC Committee. The Committee will therefore need to criticize a State not hesitantly if it limits people and organizations in working and reporting freely on the achievements in implementing children's right to health. Individuals and private organizations must have the opportunity to safely report to the Committee (for example through safe internet connections, private meetings, Facebook etc.). On the other hand, the CRC Committee has the opportunity to identify violations of children's rights by private companies.

Although not falling within the direct mandate of the CRC Committee, it is highly recommendable for NGOs working in the field of children's rights to clearly coordinate which organization focuses on what children's rights, to prevent overlap in reporting on a limited number of rights and neglecting other rights.

Through the combination of measures, the CRC Committee should produce Concluding Observations that contain measurable and time bound targets in its recommendations that can be used as practical tools for countries and medical or children's rights organizations to clearly determine who is responsible for realizing the separate elements of the right to health of the child and through what stepwise and progressive plan this can be achieved. In such a way the right to health as laid down in the UNCRC can be further developed and translated for implementation in the daily lives of children.

Lastly, given the limited possibility of the Committee to hold States accountable for complying with the CRC, it should stimulate the incorporation of the provisions of the CRC in regional treaties and in national legislation to ensure that any violations of children's right to health can be brought before the existing regional or national courts. In the future, the communications procedure for children before the CRC is expected to become a valuable additional tool for holding States accountable for their achievements in the realization of children's right to health.

IV. THE RIGHT TO HEALTH OF THE CHILD IN INTERNATIONAL HEALTH AND HUMAN RIGHTS LAW: ADDING A HUMAN VOICE?

4.1. INTRODUCTION

The right of the child to enjoy the highest attainable standard of health is laid down in article 24 of the Convention on the Rights of the Child (CRC). In addition, article 41 CRC provides that 'Nothing in the present Convention shall affect any provisions which are more conducive to the realization of the rights of the child and which may be contained in (a) The law of a State party; or (b) International law in force for that State.' This means that provisions in other (international) law sources that provide for a more extensive guarantee of children's right to health should be taken into account when applying children's right to health. This chapter seeks to investigate the additional value of the provisions in international health and human rights law other than the CRC for interpreting the right to the highest attainable standard of health of the child as enshrined in article 24 CRC. After an analysis of the key sources on children's right to health in international law in section 2, the key features of the general right to health with be discussed in section 3. Specifically, the framework of **A**vailability, **A**ccessibility, **A**cceptability and **Q**uality as laid down in General Comment 14 to the ICESCR will be assessed for its child-specificity. In section 4, participation is discussed as a key constituent element of the right of the child to the highest attainable standard of health. Section 5 recognizes the importance of the international dimension of the highest attainable standard of health. In section 6, the key features of child's rights-based health system will be identified.

4.2. AN ANALYSIS OF THE KEY SOURCES ON CHILDREN'S RIGHT TO HEALTH IN INTERNATIONAL HEALTH LAW

4.2.1. THE RIGHT TO HEALTH IN THE UDHR, ICESCR, WHO CONSTITUTION

Several international legal documents have qualified the right to health as a fundamental human right.[689] The language of the declarations and treaties varies widely, but it has become customary to refer to the provisions collectively as 'the right to health'.[690]

The preamble of the WHO Constitution states that the enjoyment of the highest attainable standard of health is 'one of the fundamental human rights of every human being without distinction of race, religion, political belief, economic or social condition'.[691] Article 25.1 of the Universal Declaration of Human Rights[692] locates the right to health in its context, as it declares that the standard of living is determinative for fulfilling the right to health by stating that 'everyone has the right to a standard of living adequate for the health and well-being of himself and his family, including food, clothing, housing and medical care and necessary social services.' The right to health as laid down in international law thus encompasses both the right to health care services and the right to a wide range of factors conducive to leading a healthy life; the underlying determinants of health, such as safe and potable drinking water, adequate nutrition, sanitation, housing, healthy working and environmental conditions and health related education and information.[693]

---

689 See article 25 of the Universal Declaration of Human Rights (U.N. Doc. A/810, 1948), and article 12 of the International Covenant on Economic, Social and Cultural Rights and article 12 of the Convention on the Elimination of Discrimination against Women.

690 V.A. Leary, 'The right to health in international human rights law', *Health and Human Rights* 1994, Volume 1, no. 1, p. 26.

691 The WHO Constitution was adopted by the International Health Conference held in New York from 19 June to 22 July 1946, signed on 22 July 1946 by the representatives of 61 States (Official Records of the World Health Organization, 2, 100), and entered into force on 7 April 1948. Amendments adopted by the Twenty-sixth, Twenty-ninth, Thirty-ninth and Fifty-first World Health Assemblies (resolutions WHA 26.37, WHA 29.38, WHA 39.6 and WHA 51.23) came into force on 3 February 1977, 20 January 1984, 11 July 1994 and 15 September 2005 respectively and are incorporated in the present text.

692 The Universal Declaration on Human Rights was initially a 'common standard of achievement for all peoples and all nations'. However, it has become an instrument exerting strong moral, legal and political influence on the development and implementation of fundamental human rights, for example by serving as a model for the development of domestic constitutions, laws, regulations and policies. Also, many of the UDHR's provisions have become part of international customary law. See for example: H. Hannum, 'The UDHR in national and international law', *Health and Human Rights* 1998, Volume 3, Number 2, pp. 145–158.

693 WHO Factsheet No. 31 on the Right to Health, Office of the United Nations High Commissioner for Human Rights, Geneva, June 2008, p. 1.

The right to health does not mean that States must ensure that their citizens are healthy, because they are not in a position to fully influence and be responsible for the biological make-up of persons nor for the level of health risks they take in their behaviour.[694] At best, they can undertake public campaigns to make people aware of the risks of for instance smoking and alcohol abuse and various measures to prevent these risks e.g. by a prohibition of smoking in public places and limitations on the sale of tobacco and alcohol. Furthermore, they can provide for vaccination campaigns for children and stimulate safe traffic behaviour. Article 25.1 UDHR establishes that the right to health of the individual (e.g. the child) is explicitly related to the health of his family. Although not explicated in the article itself, this relation may for example become visible in the role that parents have in providing examples of (non-)healthy behaviour to their children, in deciding for the child to go to the doctor and also in the distribution of underlying determinants of health among the different members of the (extended) family. The right to health of the child may also be at stake when other family members have health problems. This is for example the case when parents or other caregivers have serious health problems, such as HIV/AIDS, psychiatric diseases or chronic and terminal diseases, seriously reducing their capacity to ensure their children's right to health. Also, the relation between the health of the child and his or her family becomes clear when a sibling has a serious health problem demanding much attention from the parents or other primary caregivers. Lastly, other family issues, such as unemployment of one or both of the parents, may significantly reduce the family budget to be able to afford nutritious foods, clothing and access to medical care.

Some scholars commented that the right to health does not belong to the body of international customary law, as there is little domestic or international jurisprudence on the implementation of the right to health that would constitute an indication of the existence of an *opinio iuris*.[695, 696] However, others have provided a clear overview of the right to health in national and international jurisprudence, mounting to different sets of core state obligations to respect, protect and ensure the right to health.[697] More importantly, the Committee

---

694 General Comment No. 14 (2000) The right to the highest attainable standard of health: 11/08/2000. E/C.12/2000/4. CESCR, § 8 and 9.

695 H. Hannum, 'The UDHR in national and international law', *Health and Human Rights* 1998, Volume 3, Number 2, p. 153.

696 Sandhu argues that there are three levels of rights: moral, aspirational and legal. Problems at the legal level concerning the right to health are, according to Sandhu, threefold: indeterminacy (how to characterize it?), justifiability (how to enforce it?) and progressive realization (how to raise the standard over time?). Sandhu argues that the right to health does not go beyond the aspirational level, stating that 'I have a right to health care, but no means of enforcement.' See: P.K. Sandhu, 'A legal right to health care: what can the United States learn from foreign models of health rights jurisprudence?', *California Law Review* 2007, Volume 95, Issue 115, p. 1158.

697 A. Hendriks, 'The right to health in national and international jurisprudence', *European Journal of Health Law* 1998, Volume 5, pp. 389–408. See for a further discussion of state obligations deriving from the right to health paragraph 4.4 of this contribution.

on Economic, Social and Cultural Rights has established that the provision of 'essential primary health care is part of the minimum core obligations deriving from the right to health' and is as such applicable to all member states to the International Covenant on Economic, Social and Cultural Rights.[698] Riedel argues that although 'strictly speaking the international instruments providing for the right to health are not legally binding, the mere fact that these instruments have been followed by states as if they were binding,[699] has illustrated that they form an important component within the international movement to promote and protect the physical and mental health of all persons worldwide'.[700] The growing link between health and human rights and the growing appreciation of the right to health itself is increasingly recognized for its humanitarian importance as well as for its national security interest and its interdependence with global public health interests.[701]

Article 12.1 of the International Covenant on Economic, Social and Cultural Rights[702] elaborates on the fundamental right to health by stating that 'States Parties recognize the right of everyone to the enjoyment of the highest attainable standard of physical and mental health'. The concept of 'the highest attainable standard of health' is first introduced here in an international treaty. Article 12.2 specifies four targets to be realized out of which two are particularly relevant for realizing children's rights to health, namely (a) the provision for the reduction of the stillbirth-rate and of infant mortality and for the healthy development of the child and (d) the creation of conditions which would assure to all medical service and medical attention in the event of sickness.[703]

The central notion of 'the highest attainable standard of health' in article 12 of the ICESCR has been further elaborated in General Comment No. 14 of the Economic and Social Council.[704] The highest attainable standard of health of

698 Committee on Economic, Social and Cultural Rights, General Comment No. 3 (1990), reprinted in *Compilation of General Comments and General Recommendations Adopted by Human Rights Treaty Bodies*, U.N. Doc. HRI/GEN/1/Rev.3 (1997), § 10.

699 Some states have included the right to health in their domestic legislation, such as South-Africa and India. See: C.F. Kinney & B. Clark, 'Provisions for Health and Health Care in the Constitutions of the Countries of the World', *Cornell International Law Journal* 2004, Issue 37, pp. 285–355.

700 E. Riedel, 'The Human Right to Health: Conceptual Foundations', in: A. Clapham & M. Robinson, *Realizing the Right to Health*, Swiss Human Rights Book 2009, Volume 3, Ruffer & Rub, pp. 21–39.

701 L. Oldring, 'Advancing a Human Rights Approach on the Global Health Agenda', in: A. Clapham & M. Robinson, *Realizing the Right to Health*, Swiss Human Rights Book 2009, Volume 3, Ruffer & Rub, p. 101–102.

702 International Covenant on Economic, Social and Cultural Rights, Adopted and opened for signature, ratification and accession by General Assembly resolution 2200A (XXI) of 16 December 1966 entry into force 3 January 1976.

703 The other two specified targets in article 12.2 ICESCR are (b) the improvement of all aspects of industrial and environmental hygiene and (c) the prevention, treatment and control of epidemic, endemic, occupational and other diseases.

704 General Comment No. 14 (2000) The right to the highest attainable standard of health: 11/08/2000. E/C.12/2000/4. CESCR.

an individual depends on personal factors, such as genetics, susceptibility to ill health and unhealthy or risky lifestyles, on socio-economic preconditions and on a State's available resources.[705] The individual factors may play an important role in an individual's health, but they are generally beyond a State's control. The right to the highest attainable standard of health must therefore be understood as a right to the enjoyment of a variety of facilities, goods, services and conditions that are necessary for the realization of the highest attainable standard of health.[706]

4.2.2. THE RIGHT TO HEALTH OF THE CHILD IN INTERNATIONAL HEALTH LAW

The Preamble of the World Health Organization (the WHO)[707] states that 'the healthy development of the child is of basic importance' and that 'the ability to live harmoniously in a changing total environment is essential to such development' is one of the basic principles for the happiness, harmonious relations and security of all people'. Article 2-l, furthermore, specifies that one of the key functions of the WHO is 'to promote maternal and child health and welfare and to foster the ability to live harmoniously in a changing environment'. Although not explicitly directed at children, the provision in article 2-e elaborates that the WHO shall assist in providing health services and facilities to special groups. Given the specific requirements necessary for ensuring access to healthcare for children[708] and the fact that children are identified as special groups in need of specific attention,[709] this article is also relevant for understanding the children's right to health. This relevance is further reflected in the elaboration that the right to health should be exercised without discrimination of any kind.[710] Children, as reflected in the WHO Constitution, are thus seen as vulnerable actors in need of protection in light of the 'changing circumstances'. Not specified is what these changing circumstances are exactly, but it is logical to assume that this phrase covers at least the regular economic and political developments in a country,

---

705 Ibidem supra note 685.

706 General Comment No. 14 (2000) The right to the highest attainable standard of health: 11/08/2000. E/C.12/2000/4. CESCR, § 9.

707 The WHO Constitution was adopted by the International Health Conference held in New York from 19 June to 22 July 1946, signed on 22 July 1946 by the representatives of 61 States (Official Records of the World Health Organization, 2, 100), and entered into force on 7 April 1948. Amendments adopted by the Twenty-sixth, Twenty-ninth, Thirty-ninth and Fifty-first World Health Assemblies (resolutions WHA26.37, WHA29.38, WHA39.6 and WHA51.23) came into force on 3 February 1977, 20 January 1984, 11 July 1994 and 15 September 2005 respectively and are incorporated in the present text.

708 See chapter 2.

709 See for example General Comment No. 14 (2000) The right to the highest attainable standard of health: 11/08/2000. E/C.12/2000/4. CESCR, § 12b.

710 General Comment No. 14 (2000) The right to the highest attainable standard of health: 11/08/2000. E/C.12/2000/4. CESCR, § 30.

including those in times of economic recession. Furthermore, this provision is particularly relevant for children, since they are heavily affected by poverty.

The principle of non-retrogressive measures is relevant in this context, namely that States Parties have the burden of proving that any retrogressive measures – in casu with respect to children's right to the enjoyment of the highest attainable standard of health – deliberately taken, have been introduced after the most careful consideration of all alternatives and that they are duly justified by reference to the totality of the rights provided for in the Covenant in the context of the full use of the State party's maximum available resources.[711] Although the highest attainable standard of health differs according to available resources and situational circumstances, it has been elaborated that retrogressive measures are not permissible, notwithstanding the financial resources available in a country.[712] This means that once a certain standard of health has been achieved, only exceptional circumstances, such as the 2011 earthquake, tsunami and nuclear threat in Japan, are accepted as an excuse by the Committee on Economic Social and Cultural Rights for any setbacks in the standard of health in a country. If retrogression in the realization of the right to health occurs, governments have the burden of prove to demonstrate that all possible alternatives have been considered and that all efforts are made to reduce the impacts of such extreme circumstances and try to restore the earlier achieved health status as soon as possible.[713] Therefore, even in changing circumstances, the promotion of maternal and child health as laid down in article 2.1 of the WHO Constitution and in article 12.2a ICESCR should remain a priority that can not be easily derogated from. The need to protect children in changing circumstances is especially important, since children are disproportionally affected by poverty, environmental pollution, natural disasters and conflict.[714] The reasons for this are that children have less capacities to flee from a disaster area and that any harmful consequences affect not only their actual health status but also their future development and opportunities. In many developing countries, children make up more than 40% of the total population.

---

711 General Comment No. 14 (2000) The right to the highest attainable standard of health: 11/08/2000. E/C.12/2000/4. CESCR, § 32.

712 Ibidem supra note 694.

713 General Comment No. 14 (2000) The right to the highest attainable standard of health: 11/08/2000. E/C.12/2000/4. CESCR, § 32.

714 See for example the documentary 'Children of the tsunami' on the 2011 disaster in Japan and the effects of the meltdown of Fukushima on the health of children http://vimeo.com/40005340. Furthermore, as a result of the 2010 earthquake in Haïti 1.5 million children were affected (dead, injured, displaced, deprived of basic necessities and schools), out of which 720.000 between 6 and 12 and 494600 under 5. Office of the UN Secretary-General's Special Advisor on community medicine and special lessons form Haïti, available at: www.lessonsfromhaiti.org/relief-and-recovery/key-statistics/. Thirdly, in Syria it was estimated in late 2012, that 2 million out of 4 million affected people were children and 800.000 out of a total of 2 million were displaced. Syria's children: a lost generation? UNICEF Crisis Report March 2011-March 2013.

The most detailed and authoritative source further elaborating on children's right to health in international health law is General Comment 14 of the CESCR. Article 12.2 (a) ICESCR specifies that States have to take steps to ensure 'the provision for the reduction of the stillbirth rate and of infant mortality and for the healthy development of the child' as laid down in article 12.2. According to the CESCR this may be understood as 'requiring measures to improve child and maternal health, sexual and reproductive health services, including access to family planning, pre- and postnatal health care, emergency obstetric services and access to information, as well as to resources necessary to act on that information'. The relevance of the Convention on the Rights of the Child is mentioned in paragraph 22 of General Comment 14 to the CESCR, dealing with the right to health of children and adolescents. It focuses on the duty of States to ensure access to essential health care services for the child and his or her family. Interestingly, General Comment 14 to the CESCR refers to the presumed link in the Convention on the Rights of the Child between access to essential health care and access to child-friendly information about preventive and health-promoting behaviour and support to families and communities in implementing these practices.[715] In this phrasing, the General Comment explicitly introduces and explains the term child-friendly (health) information.[716] More importantly, the requirement of child-friendly health information as a prerequisite to ensure access to essential health services for the child and his family is made even more explicit than it is in the children's rights domain. Whereas the CRC does make mention of the right of children to be informed and supported in the use of basic knowledge of child health and nutrition, the explicit link between the need to receive child-friendly health information to acquiring access to health services is not mentioned. General Comment 4 only addresses the need to provide information on access to sexual and reproductive health services. General Comment 15 significantly elaborates on the requirement to inform and educate children within the regular school curriculum and in medical settings 'in all aspects of health to enable them to make informed choices in relation to their lifestyle and access to health services'.[717] The information required extends 'to a broad range of health issues, including: healthy eating and the promotion of physical activity, sports and recreation; accident and injury prevention; sanitation, hand washing and other personal hygiene practices; and the dangers of alcohol, tobacco and psychoactive substance use.' With regard to sexual and reproductive health, 'education should include self-awareness and knowledge about the body, including anatomical,

715 General Comment No. 14 (2000) The right to the highest attainable standard of health: 11/08/2000. E/C.12/2000/4. CESCR, § 22.

716 U.N. Doc. CRC/GC/2003/A, 1 July 2003, General Comment 4 to the Convention on the Rights of the Child on adolescent health, § 11 and 26–33. See also paragraph 2.5 for a further discussion on children's right to information in health.

717 U.N. Doc. CRC/C/GC/2013/15, General Comment 15 on the right of the child to enjoy the highest attainable standard of health, § 58–61.

physiological and emotional aspects and it should include content related to sexual health and well-being, such as information about body changes and maturation processes.' Education should also include information about how and where to access health information and services. However, in practice, it has been found that the basic knowledge on the opportunities to obtain access to health care for (minor) patients and the way in which referrals are communicated, is crucial in ensuring that these patients do actually reach the referred medical professional.[718] Unawareness of these opportunities jeopardizes the continuity of care for children, because subsequent steps in the medical treatment cannot be (adequately) followed. The explicit connection mentioned in General Comment 14 ICESCR between ensuring access to essential health services for children and families on the one hand and the requirement to ensure access to child-friendly information about preventive and health promotional behaviour is thus of additional value to the interpretation of the children's right to health.[719]

The concept of child-friendly information on health care is thus highlighted in General Comment 14. Age-friendly health care for minors is also put forward in relation to the provision of adequate health services for adolescents. Specifically referred is to youth-friendly health care, requiring at least respect for confidentiality and privacy and the 'opportunity to participate in decisions affecting their health, build life skills, acquire appropriate information, receive counselling, and negotiate health-behaviour choices.[720] Although the specific focus on adolescents seems to exclude younger children from these principles of 'youth-friendly' health care, referral in the following paragraph to the best interests of both children and adolescents as a primary consideration in health care gives room for the application of these principles to children of all ages. This could lead to the conclusion that young children must also have the opportunity to have their privacy respected and have the opportunity for confidential counselling, and participate in health-related decisions, if this is in their best interests.[721] However, especially for younger children, the role of parents is usually more dominant, given the direct dependence of children on their care.

A third element that is central in article 12.2 ICESCR in General Comment 14 is the principle of non-discrimination that is highlighted in ensuring access to

[718] For example in the Netherlands, it was documented that children, their parents and health professionals are not always aware of the way in which they can acquire access to health services. Also letters of referral are required for children without a residence permit though doctors sometimes forget to give these or patients are unaware of the importance and do not understand at all that they were referred to another doctor. See Report of Pharos Foundation, 'Undocumented children and access to hospital care', June 2010. Available at: www.medimmigrant.be/uploads/Gezondheidszorg%20per%20verblijfsstatuut/Eindrapport_Ongedocumenteerde_kinderen_en_de_toegang_tot_ziekenhuiszorg.pdf.

[719] See again article 41 CRC on the application of provisions in international law that are more conducive than the provisions in the CRC.

[720] General Comment No. 14 (2000) The right to the highest attainable standard of health: 11/08/2000. E/C.12/2000/4. CESCR, § 23.

[721] See for a further discussion on this topic § 2.5.

both the underlying determinants of health as well as physical and mental health services for children. Specific mention is made of the rights of girls to have equal access to all components of the right to health, their need to be protected against harmful traditional practices and the need to provide children with disabilities the opportunity to enjoy a decent and fulfilling life and participate meaningfully in their community.[722]

It thus becomes clear from the elaboration of the right to health in the WHO Constitution, the ICESCR and General Comment 14, that access to essential health services for children and adolescents without discrimination forms part of the minimum core content of the international right to health.[723] This legal obligation is further explained as requiring access to child-friendly health information, involving the need to ensure respect for privacy and provide for the opportunity to have confidential counselling and to participate in health-related decisions, particularly if this in the best interests of the child. In a later chapter, it will be investigated whether and if so when and why, the child-friendly aspect of health care is an essential component of acquiring access to health care in general.[724]

Read in conjunction, the priorities mentioned in § 43-a of General Comment 14, ensure the right to have access to health facilities, goods and services on a non-discriminatory basis, especially for vulnerable or marginalized groups and in § 44-a, ensure reproductive, maternal (pre- as well as postnatal) and child health care, almost literally phrase this core obligation deriving from the general right to health. Non-discriminative access to health care is thus focused upon as one of the relatively small amounts of core obligations deriving from the right to health, because this is resource-independent.[725] Toebes discusses the fact that articles 2(2) and 3 ICESCR on non-discrimination have immediate effect, given the fact that they contain the terms 'to ensure' and 'to guarantee'.[726] However, Klerk

[722] General Comment No. 14 (2000) The right to the highest attainable standard of health: 11/08/2000. E/C.12/2000/4. CESCR, § 22.

[723] General Comment No. 14 (2000) The right to the highest attainable standard of health: 11/08/2000. E/C.12/2000/4. CESCR, § 43-a and 44-a.

[724] Not only is assumed that child-friendliness is always in the best interests of the child, but that under circumstances child-friendliness is an essential requirement for acquiring adequate access to health care, for example when children are not taken care of by adults at all, as may be the case with orphans, unaccompanied minor asylum seekers, children living in child-headed households and children living in the streets. It may also be the case that children hold important health information that their parents and other caretakers are unaware of (for example acquired or experienced in peer-to-peer contacts), or that an adult tries to conceal information (for example on child maltreatment, abuse or neglect) that the child is only able to communicate in the absence of this adult. The term child-oriented health care may therefore be more appropriate then child-friendly health care, as child-friendliness assumes some level of voluntariness, whereas child orientation can be interpreted as an essential prerequisite to obtaining adequate access to health care.

[725] Riedel, supra note 700, p. 30.

[726] See also B.C.A. Toebes, *The Right to Health as a Human Right in International Law*, Groningen/Oxford: Intersentia/Hart, pp. 292 and 296.

distinguishes between de iure and de facto modes of discrimination, arguing that legislative measures may have discriminative effect, but that non-legislative measures may need to be taken gradually, obliging States to take affirmative action to prohibit practices of discrimination in horizontal relations.[727] Examples of such discriminative situations are when families tend to systematically prioritize sons or fathers in acquiring access to health facilities or when unmarried pregnant women are not provided with the nutrition and drinking water that they need.

The environmental component of the definition of health can be met by acknowledging that one of the key targets of the right to health is 'to live harmoniously in a total environment' and that this must be achieved in light of any 'changing circumstances'. These circumstances may include climate change, emergency situations due to conflict or natural disasters, financial hardship or economic crises, processes of privatization and decentralization and other policy measures such as the building of roads, railways, chemical factories or nuclear power-stations in the vicinity of children's living environments, potentially impacting upon the realization of the highest attainable standard of their health. Therefore, any measures or developments that have potential negative consequences for the realization of children's right to the highest attainable standard of health should be preceded by health impact assessments, elucidating the effects on the realization of the highest attainable standard of health of children.

4.3. KEY FEATURES OF THE RIGHT TO HEALTH OF THE CHILD IN INTERNATIONAL HEALTH LAW

The concept of 'the highest attainable standard of health' is highly debated, because it is questionable whether one universal standard can be applied across different countries, regions, cultures and situations.[728, 729] Another criticism is whether defining a minimum core content of the right to health, would instigate governments and other actors involved in realizing the right to health to stop investing as soon as that minimum standard of health has been achieved. Therefore, it is important to clarify that the minimum core content of the right to

727 Y. Klerk, 'Working on Article 2(2) and Article 3 of the International Covenant on Economic, Social and Cultural Rights', *Human Rights Quarterly* 1987, Volume 9, pp. 250–267.

728 For a further discussion on the universality of the right to the highest attainable standard of health, see chapter 5 on the right of the child in Europe.

729 See for a discussion on the challenge for child rights advocates to 'achieve universal protection of children's rights and at the same time preserve the cultural integrity of the communities that subscribe to the normative order' T. Kaime, ''Vernacularising the Convention on the Rights of the Child: Rights and Culture as Analytic Tools', *International Journal on Children's Rights* 2010, Volume 18, pp. 637–653.

health is only a first step in a continuing process,[730] being followed by intermediate stages in ensuring the right to health, until the highest attainable standard of health has been achieved.[731]

The first level of 'minimum essential levels of goods and services' has been clearly established in international law, including as a minimum core content 'certain categories of primary health care services, including immunizations and nutritional programs; the obligation to provide certain free services where necessary; adequate information; the availability of skilled health professionals; essential medicines and technologies; and the adoption and implementation of a national strategy and plan of action' these minimum essential levels will necessarily evolve in accordance with increased budget made available, medical and scientific developments and situational developments.[732,733,734,735] Furthermore, the principle of non-discrimination has immediate effect as well as the obligation of States to adopt national health plans.[736] This means that the allocation of (limited) resources must be done in an equitable manner, in a transparent and participatory process in which particular attention is given to marginalized and disadvantaged groups of children. The principle of non-discrimination must be taken into account in States' acts as well as in processes of privatization and decentralization.[737]

---

730 See General Comment 3 to the International Covenant on Economic, Social and Cultural Rights on the nature of States' Parties obligations, 14 December 1990, § 10.

731 See General Comment 3 to the International Covenant on Economic, Social and Cultural Rights on the nature of States' Parties obligations, 14 December 1990, § 9. It states that 'the fact that realization over time, or in other words progressively, is foreseen under the Covenant should not be misinterpreted as depriving the obligation of all meaningful content. It is on the one hand a necessary flexibility device, reflecting the realities of the real world and the difficulties involved for any country in ensuring full realization of economic, social and cultural rights. On the other hand, the phrase must be read in the light of the overall objective, indeed the *raison d'être*, of the Covenant which is to establish clear obligations for States parties in respect of the full realization of the rights in question. It thus imposes an obligation to move as expeditiously and effectively as possible towards that goal.'

732 See General Comment 3 to the International Covenant on Economic, Social and Cultural Rights on the nature of States' Parties obligations, 14 December 1990.

733 United Nations Special Rapporteur on the Right to the Highest Attainable Standard of Health, initial report on sources and content of the Right to Health U.N. Doc. E/CN.4/2003/58.

734 United Nations Special Rapporteur on the Right to the Highest Attainable Standard of Health, report on progress and obstacles to the health and human rights movement, in addition to cases on the right to health and other health-related rights U.N. Doc. A/HRC/4/28.

735 See also various training toolkits on the right to health, such as the Manual on the right to the highest attainable standard of health of the Human Rights Centre of the University of Essex and the International Federation of Health and Human Rights Organisations, available at: www.paho.org/hr-ecourse-e/assets/_pdf/Module2/Lesson1/M2_L1_4.pdf. See also *The Right to Health: a Resource Manual for NGOs* Asher, Judith, 2004, available at: www.shr.aaas.org/Right_to_Health_Manual/index.shtml.

736 See U.N. Doc. E/C.12/GC/20, General Comment 20 to the International Covenant on Economic, Social and Cultural Rights on the nature of States' Parties obligations, 2 July 2009, § 7.

737 See for a discussion of the relation between privatization of the Dutch health care system and the key elements of the right to the highest attainable standard of health: B.C.A. Toebes, 'The

The right to health as identified in the CESCR contains certain freedoms, such as the right to be free from non-consensual treatment and medical research and the right to be free from torture and other cruel, inhuman, degrading treatments.[738, 739] This includes child maltreatment, sexual abuse and traditional harmful practices such as female genital mutilation. The right to health also contains certain entitlements, such as the right to prevention, treatment and control of diseases, equal and timely access to basic health care, access to essential medicines and participation of the population in health related decisions at national, community and individual level.[740] The identified requirement to arrange for child-friendly health information is crucial for ensuring children's right to meaningfully participate in health decisions.

General Comment 14 to the ICESCR identifies four key elements that must be established in realizing the right to health in the provision of (basic) health services, goods and facilities: availability, accessibility, acceptability and good quality.[741] The approach of identifying key elements for interpreting a social right was initially developed by Katarina Tomasevski, the UN Special Rapporteur on the right to education.[742] However, the list of four was slightly different and not considered to be definitive. The list included the concept of adaptability, which is defined as 'the ability to evolve with changing needs of society, contribute to challenging inequalities, be locally applied and adapted to the specific context'. The element of adaptability is very useful for the interpretation of the right to health, since health needs differ widely across different regions and localities. Furthermore, in the context of the interpretation of the right to health, additional elements have been suggested including accountability, participation, patient satisfaction and effectiveness,[743] although this last one has also been identified as

right to health and the privatization of national health systems: a case study of the Netherlands', *Health and Human Rights* 2006; Volume 9, Issue 1, pp. 102–127.

738 General Comment No. 14 (2000) The right to the highest attainable standard of health: 11/08/2000. E/C.12/2000/4. CESCR, § 34–37.

739 Riedel (supra note 683, p. 26) distinguishes between the 'freedom dimension' and the 'entitlement dimension'. These issues are highly relevant for structuring the right to health of the child, as the tension between children's autonomy, i.e. their right to participation, always has to be balanced against their right to health and their right to protection, aiming to result in the best possible outcome with regard to the best interests of the child.

740 General Comment No. 14 (2000) The right to the highest attainable standard of health: 11/08/2000. E/C.12/2000/4. CESCR, § 34–37.

741 General Comment No. 14 (2000) The right to the highest attainable standard of health: 11/08/2000. E/C.12/2000/4. CESCR, § 12.

742 K. Tomasevski, *Human Rights Obligations: Making Education. Availability, Accessibility, Acceptability and Adaptability*, Gothenburg: RTE Primers, January 2001.

743 See B. Toebes, A. Hendriks & K. Stronks, 'Health inequalities and the social determinants of health', in: *Health and Human Rights in Europe*, edited by Toebes, Hartlev, Hendriks and Herrman, Groningen: Intersentia 2012, pp. 227–247, particularly p. 218.
See also example the submissions of E. Kabengele Mpinga and P. Chastonay of the University of Geneva and of Nolan, E. Yamin, and B.M. Meier for the preparation of General Comment 14 to the CRC on children's right to health, available at: www2.ohchr.org/english/bodies/crc/callsubmissionsCRC_received.htm.

an element of the principle of quality.[744] All elements relate to both the underlying determinants of health and to the health care services itself. Below, the identified factors included in General Comment 14 to the ICESCR are specifically explained for interpreting children's right to health.[745] Consequently, the other elements are discussed for their usefulness in interpreting the right to the highest attainable standard of health.

4.3.1 AVAILABILITY

Availability means that underlying determinants of health and functioning health services must be available in sufficient quantities.[746] This refers to the absolute number of health institutions and professionals in a country and also to the distribution of infrastructure and medical services over geographical areas. A high number of hospitals in the capital does not mean that sufficient medical services are available in rural areas nor in all areas of the city. For example, it may occur that certain areas can benefit from high quality medical services, whereas others lack even the most basic services. Applied to children, the requirement of availability also means that there must be sufficient health services and health professionals specifically trained for delivering child-appropriate health care available. Given the explanation of the provisions in article 12.2a ICESCR to ensure pre- and postnatal health care, as well as emergency obstetric care, this means that pregnant women should be able to reach such health facilities within a limited period of time. Research in the Netherlands has indicated that when pregnant women have to travel more than 20 minutes to a hospital, infant mortality rates significantly increase.[747] Therefore, the distance to obstetric health care should maximally be 15 minutes and that women should be treated promptly upon arrival in the hospital.

The principle of availability also refers to the availability of appropriate drugs and to the underlying determinants of health for children. With respect to the availability of drugs that are appropriate for children, it must be noted that even

---

744 See for example the submissions of Harm Reduction International: www2.ohchr.org/english/bodies/crc/docs/CallSubmissions_Art24/HRI_YouthRISE_EHRN.pdf.

745 The Committee on the Rights of the Child has endorsed the AAAQ-framework in U.N. Doc. CRC/GC/2003/A, 1 July 2003, General Comment 4 to the Convention on the Rights of the Child on adolescent health, § 41.

746 General Comment No. 14 (2000) The right to the highest attainable standard of health: 11/08/2000. E/C.12/2000/4. CESCR, § 12a.

747 In May 2012, the Dutch media reported on the closure of hospitals in some rural parts of the Netherlands, thereby increasing the travel time for women in labour to more than 40 minutes. This is a serious violation of children's right to health, as it poses increased risk to infant death in case of emergencies during pregnancy or delivery. See: www.ad.nl/ad/nl/4560/Gezond/article/detail/3252971/2012/05/09/Kleinste-ziekenhuis-van-Nederland-boos-over-sluiting-geboortezorg.dhtml.

in developed countries, limited research is done on the child-appropriateness of drugs for children, resulting in limited availability of appropriate drugs.[748, 749]

4.3.2. ACCESSIBILITY

4.3.2.1. No de iure and de facto discrimination

The second factor of the right to health is accessibility, consisting of four dimensions.[750] The first dimension entails that accessibility of health services means that there should not be any *de iure* or *de facto* discriminative barriers in place, excluding certain (vulnerable) groups such as disabled children, girls, children from minority groups or children without official residence permits from having access to health care services. Specifically for children, the prevention of any instances of discrimination may entail the provision of age-adapted services and waiting areas. For example, children have indicated that they value low reception desks, so that they can see the person they are talking to.[751] Also, as children often have school hours to adhere to, the opening hours of health are influential to their inclination to visit a doctor.[752] Lastly, as children are largely dependent on their parents or caretakers, they should not be blamed for any actions of their parents, for example when the family resides illegally in a country or when parents are in jail and are not able to take their children to a doctor. Also, the ability of parents to take their children to a doctor during working hours contribute to better accessibility of health services for children.

---

748 In order to tackle the problem of the limited availability of information on child-appropriate drugs and in line with EU Regulation 1901/2006, an expert group of pediatricians has been established in the Netherlands in 2006. Also, the Dutch Ministry of Health has funded the Dutch Knowledge Centre for Pharmacotherapy in children (NKFK-Nederlands Kenniscentrum voor Farmacotherapie bij kinderen) to develop national guidelines for prescribing medicines for children and developing a teaching module on pharmacotherapy in children for pediatricians. See for more information on the NKFK: http://nkfk.nl/.

749 It was recognized by the Dutch Minister on Health in January 2011 that pharmaceutical companies do also have a responsibility in ensuring sufficient research on the appropriate medicines for children. See letter of the Minister of Health of the 21st January 2011 in reply to parliamentary questions on medicine use in children, reference GMT-U-3036517. This standpoint is in line with the recommendations in paragraph 55 and 56 in General Comment 14 of the Committee on Economic, Social and Cultural Rights, specifying that States Parties should take steps to ensure that the private business sector considers the importance of the right to health in their activities.

750 General Comment No. 14 (2000) The right to the highest attainable standard of health: 11/08/2000. E/C.12/2000/4. CESCR, § 12b.

751 U. Kilkelly & M. Donnelly, 'The Child's Right to be heard in the Healthcare Setting: perspectives of children, parents and health professionals', Office of the Minister of Children of Ireland, The National Children's Strategy Research Series, October 2006, pp. 37–46.

752 M. Whitehead, 'The concepts and principles of equity and health', *Health Promotion International* 1991, Volume 6, no. 3, Oxford University Press, p. 221.

4.3.2.2. *Economic accessibility*

The second dimension of accessibility is economic accessibility. This dimension requires that all health services must be affordable to all, including socially disadvantaged groups. With respect to children, the prevention of *de facto* or substantial discrimination in having economic accessibility requires specific attention for children without official birth registration or residence permits limiting access to health insurances, for children whose parents are not adequately insured and may therefore lack the necessary documents to gain access to health facilities and last but not least for children who don't have parents or guardians at all to ensure the payment for their health care services. In conjunction with the dimension of non-discrimination, the dimension of economic accessibility thus entails that financial support systems should not exclude certain groups of children from health care insurances, thereby indirectly limiting access to health care services.

As phrased in General Comment 14 on the right to the highest attainable standard of health 'Equity demands that poorer households should not be disproportionately burdened with health expenses as compared to richer households.'[753, 754, 755, 756] Whitehead has identified seven determinants of health 1. natural variation, 2. health-damaging behaviour such as high risk sports, 3. health-promoting behaviour of one group over another (eating fruit and vegetables and sporting), 4. health-damaging behaviour resulting from limited choices, for

753 General Comment No. 14 (2000) The right to the highest attainable standard of health: 11/08/2000. E/C.12/2000/4. CESCR, § 12.

754 The WHO definition of equity in health is that this 'implies that ideally everyone should have a fair opportunity to attain their full health potential and, more pragmatically, that no one should be disadvantaged from achieving this potential, if it can be avoided.' WHO 1986a Social Justice and Equity in Health: Report on a WHO Meeting, Leeds, United Kingdom, 1985.

755 Whitehead defines the concept of equity in health care as 'Differences or variations in health statistics that are unnecessary and unavoidable and in addition are also unfair and unjust.' See: M. Whitehead, 'The concepts and principles of equity and health', *Health Promotion International* 1991, Volume 6, Number 3, Oxford University Press, pp. 219–220.

756 Ernest Gruenberg argued in 1968 that there is in our society 'a pattern in which the prevalence of illness is an inverse function of family income, while the volume of medical care received is a direct function of family income'. Whereas governments in the west have increasingly recognized that such inequalities, give rise to inequities, they are now faced with the almost unbearable costs of their health systems. For example, in the Netherlands, the expenditure on health constitutes the largest post on the governmental budget for 2012. Also in the USA, health care spending as a share of U.S. Economic Output has been rising steadily over the past 45 years (5% of GDP in 1960 – 15% of GDP in 2002), so that increases in income between 2020–2009 have been almost completely wiped out by increases in health costs. See: D.P. Goldman, E.A. McGlynn, *U.S.Health care, Facts about costs, access and quality*, 2005, p. 3. Available at: www.rand.org/pubs/corporate_pubs/2005/RAND_CP484.1.pdf.
Between 2001–2010, health insurance premiums in the USA increased by 178%. See for example: S.S. Jones, J. Caloyeras & S. Mattke, *Power to the People: The Role of Consumer-Controlled Personal Health Management Systems in the Evolution of Employer-Based Health Care Benefits*, p. iii. Available at: www.rand.org/content/dam/rand/pubs/occasional_papers/2011/RAND_OP352.pdf.

example limited available services in ones living environment 5. unhealthy living or working situations, 6. inadequate access to health services, 7. health-related social mobility, involving the tendency of sick people to move down the social scale.[757] Whitehead argues that the first three factors are generally not considered as inequities, whereas the last four are considered to be either avoidable or unjust. However, healthy behaviour (#3) is also influenced by a lack of resources and by the level of education of people. Therefore, it can be argued that also this factor contributes to the level to which the right to health of the child is attained.

It appears from these health determinants that having a free choice and structural vulnerability are thus crucial aspects that guide the qualification of health related practices as equitable. This leads to the suggestion that actions to improve the right to health of children must focus on enhancing both their, and their parents capacity, to adopt healthy lifestyles. In order to achieve this, three different pathways must be involved. In the first place, it must be ensured that families with lower incomes are provided with sufficient resources to pay for their medical costs and for the underlying determinants necessary to engage in healthy lifestyles, either directly or indirectly through medical and other social insurances.[758] Secondly, children and their families must be provided with health related information to actually enable them to understand their health status and make healthy choices.[759] Thirdly, they must be given the structural opportunity to participate in medical program development so that they can indicate what the most important (health) challenges encountered in their daily lives are, supported by indicators on the actual health status of (vulnerable) groups of children.[760] Only through active involvement of seemingly helpless or vulnerable children and families, will they be able to take ownership of their own health status and

---

757 M. Whitehead, 'The concepts and principles of equity and health', *Health Promotion International* 1991, Volume 6, no. 3, Oxford University Press, p. 219.

758 Szasz argues that the State can protect and promote the interests of the sick either by coercing physicians to serve patients or by creating moral, economic and political circumstances to provide the conditions necessary for the exercise of free and responsible individual choices. According to Szasz, these modes of operation reflect underlying presumptions about the role of the State in ensuring the right to health being either highly dominant and directive or on the other hand limiting its own power to provide room for society to fill in this duty. See: T.S. Szasz, 'The Right to Health', *The Georgetown Law Journal* 1968–1969, Volume 57, pp. 734–751.

759 In addition to the rights-based arguments to enhance children's and families' level of basic health knowledge, arguments are also found on the economic level; as a response to the rising costs of health care in many wealthier countries, the costs and potential benefits of personally controlled health management systems are increasingly investigated. See for example: S.S. Jones, J. Caloyeras & S. Mattke, *Power to the People: The Role of Consumer-Controlled Personal Health Management Systems in the Evolution of Employer-Based Health Care Benefits*. See also the initiative: *Helping families raise healthy children*, available at: www.rand.org/health/projects/healthy-children.html.

760 General Comment No. 14 (2000) The right to the highest attainable standard of health: 11/08/2000. E/C.12/2000/4. CESCR, § 57–58.

develop into independent actors in improving their own and their community's health status.[761]

The concept of economic accessibility extends to making a balance between budget allocation to respond to individual health claims and financing public health programs. General Comment 14 elaborates that the principle of economic accessibility entails that 'health resource allocations should not favor expensive curative care at the expense of preventive public care, benefiting a larger population.[762] In this respect, MacNaughton distinguishes the concepts of one-to-one equality, applicable to every individual identically, such as the right to have a name and bloc equality, requiring equality between blocs such as boys and girls or different groups of vulnerable children having the right to equal access to health, but not necessarily within the different blocs.[763]

A common institutionalization of bloc discrimination is seen in the dichotomy between public and private insurance systems, sometimes resulting in entirely separate health care systems wherein the wealthier benefit from more extensive health services than the poor do, being dependent on the public system. Whitehead even states that 'in general, those most in need of medical care, including preventive care, are least likely to receive high standards of services'.[764] Especially with respect to children, there is no legal basis to justify such discriminatory health care systems.[765]

In international human rights law, focus is usually placed on bloc equality, for example equality between children from different socio-economic groups.[766] Violations of one-to-one equality may arise before a Court when an individual claimant receives a benefit that others do not receive.[767] When such benefits are structurally granted on the basis of individual claims for the right to health, this may also lead to violations of bloc-equality, as wealthier families usually have better access to the judicial system through both financial and social resources and therefore have a better chance of obtaining individual benefits for ensuring their right to health at the expense of health costs being allocated to public health

761 L. London, 'What is a human-rights based approach to health and does it matter?', *International Journal on health and human rights* 2008, Volume 10, no. 1, p. 68.

762 General Comment No. 14 (2000) The right to the highest attainable standard of health: 11/08/2000. E/C.12/2000/4. CESCR, § 19.

763 MacNaughton, 'Untangling equality and non-discrimination to promote the right to health care for all', *Health and Human Rights* 2009, Volume 11, no. 2, p. 47–63.

764 M. Whitehead, 'The concepts and principles of equity and health', *Health Promotion International* 1991, Volume 6, no. 3, Oxford University Press, p. 218.

765 In unifying the benefits of the different health systems, the Court of Colombia decided that priority had to be given to children and then progressively to adults. See: *Corte Constitutional de la República de Colombia, Sala Segundo de Revisión* (2008), Constitutional Court of Colombia, Sentencia, No. T-760 de 2008.

766 Ibidem supra note 763, MacNaughton.

767 General Comment 14 states that any person or group victim of a violation of the right to health should have access to effective judicial or other appropriate remedies at both national and international levels through reparation, such as restitution, satisfaction or guarantess of non-repetition.

programs for poor families, 'given that resources are always scarce in relation to the health needs of the population as a whole'.[768] Therefore, individuals who manage to get access to the court and who are on that basis granted access to health services are privileged over others who do not manage to start a litigation procedure.[769] This is especially troublesome for children without parents taking care of them, as they often have no opportunity to go to Court at all, even if they are aware of the possibility. Some therefore argue that claims based on the right to health should only be undertaken collectively.[770] Motta Ferrez argues that such actions would lead to enormous numbers of claimants and consequently to unmanageable costs and that it would be more effective to prevent that individual claims rise to an unlimited level of medical care seems to be more in line with reality.[771] Given the seemingly limitless growth in medical opportunities and concomitant medical costs, this option seems to give room to a more equitable solution, in which the core content of the right to health, namely access to primary health care for all can and should be achieved as a priority. Current debates on the price-setting for highly specific, though scarcely used medicines are relevant in this context,[772] because extremely high costs for individuals may pose an enormous barrier to ensuring economic accessibility to basic levels of health care for many others.

MacNaughton argues that protecting one-to-one equality provides 'the balance between the collective right to equality in health care and individual claims for health benefits by requiring that benefits available to one be available to all'.[773] Interesting about this standpoint is that it places individuals and their actual enjoyment of health care at the heart of the health system. Unclear however

---

768 O.L. Motta Ferraz, 'The right to health in the courts of Brazil: worsening health inequities?', *International Journal on Health and Human Rights* 2009, Volume 11, no. 2, p. 33.

769 Ibidem supra note 768. Motta Ferraz demonstrates that this phenomenon is widespread in Brazil and growing to 'significant levels in terms of volume and costs', (p. 36). He concluded that such a model of litigation therefore has potential negative effects on health equity. The result is a 'lack of opportunity to achieve good health because of factors beyond individual control such as discrimination and severe poverty, as opposed to personal free choices'. This is exemplified by higher infant and child mortality rates in families with lower incomes.

770 F. Hoffman & F. Bentes, 'Accountability for social and economic rights in Brazil', in: V. Gauri & D. Brinks, *Courting Social Justice: Judicial Enforcement of Social and Economic Rights in the Developing World*, Cambridge University Press 2008, pp. 100–145.

771 Ibidem supra note 768, p. 41.

772 In the Netherlands, the discussion over the price-setting of extremely expensive medicines was instigated after the appearance of two concept-advices to the Dutch Minister of Health by the College for Health Insurances the 'College Zorgverzekeringen', on the financing of medicines for the Pompe and Fabry diseases. See: http://content1a.omroep.nl/3dfedaca6f632 8b38f6fbc84d3840caf/501fafa4/nos/docs/290712_pompe.pdf. See also the comments made by professor in ethics Dupuis on the Dutch Radio, stating that it is necessary to draw lines in the public financing of medicines, because many new and highly expensive medicines will appear on the market in the near future, whereas the costs for these medicines would significantly increase the total costs of health care and thereby subvert the functioning of the entire society. Interview in 'Dichtbij Nederland' on 3 August 2012, available at: http://dichtbijnederland.nps.nl/page/detail/794371/%27In+Nederland+was+Friso+al+opgegeven%27.

773 Ibidem supra note 746, MacNaughton, p. 56.

remains how poor, orphaned children are informed about their right to get such a benefit for individual health.

4.3.2.3. *Physical accessibility*

The third dimension of accessibility, namely physical accessibility, requires that the location of the health services can be easily and safely reached by all. This means that health services must be within a reasonable distance from families and their children, also in rural, mountainous or distant regions, that transport is physically accessible (e.g. for children in wheelchairs, blind children) and affordable to take (sick or injured) children timely to a health facility and that parents or other caregivers are given the opportunity to take their child to hospital when they are ill. This requires for example that parents are allowed to leave work when their child needs to go to a health facility, especially when no other persons are available to take them there.

4.3.2.4. *Information accessibility*

The fourth dimension of accessibility is information accessibility. This dimension provides that people have 'the right to seek, receive and impart information and ideas concerning health issues.'[774] Specifically for children, this means that leaflets are written in understandable language and supported by age-appropriate pictures, so that they will be able to understand their medical condition and prognosis and support them in making choices for the preferred medical treatment. It is also required to directly speak to children to explain their medical conditions, prognosis and options available for them. The right to information accessibility however, should not limit children's right to medical confidentiality and privacy; whereas children's medical data must be easily available for the children themselves, the provision must be done with high prudence, so that only the children (and their parents or caretakers) obtain access. Information accessibility is thus limited to the actors that are directly involved with a child's medical treatment.

As clarified from the analysis of General Comment 14, child-friendly, or child-oriented information often is an essential requirement to ensure access to health care at all: without understandable and relevant information, many children will not be able to reach their doctor.

774 General Comment No. 14 (2000) The right to the highest attainable standard of health: 11/08/2000. E/C.12/2000/4. CESCR, § 12.

4.3.2.5. *Organizational accessibility*

In 2008, the World Health Organization renewed its interest in the importance of the primary health care approach as laid down in the Declaration of Alma-Ata (1978).[775] As part of the Declaration, the WHO developed the concept of 'organizational accessibility'. This concept refers to convenient office hours, out-of office hours, the possibility to have distance consultations and consultations by phone or through internet, short waiting times and the possibility of home visits. Although not included in General Comment 14 to the ICESCR, the practical value of these aspects of the element of access, makes it highly relevant for the interpretation of children's right to health, although it does need adaptation to meet the particular needs of children. For example, office hours should be adapted to school hours. Another suggestion is to ensure the location of medical services in close proximity to schools and day care facilities for children.

4.3.3. ACCEPTABILITY

The factor of acceptability requires respect for medical ethics and cultural and gender-sensitive aspects of health care.[776] Interestingly, § 12 of General Comment 14 of the ECOSOC Committee specifically mentions the requirement that health facilities must be sensitive to 'life-cycle requirements'. This unmistakably involves the requirement to ensure that health services respect the rights and needs of children of all ages, especially since the 'right to maternal, child and reproductive health' is explicitly mentioned in § 12.2 (a). This can be interpreted as such that health facilities must be responsive to the needs of children of different ages and also as such that they must be responsive to the needs of children in different phases of a chronic or terminal disease. For example, a 7-year old that is infected with HIV/AIDS or a 5-year old who suffers from leukaemia, may be at the end of his or her entire life cycle. Therefore, health facilities must simultaneously apply for both 'age- ánd stage (or phase)' associated needs of children. Secondly, given the particular mentioning of the need to respect for confidentiality in health care, it can be concluded that health care that is sensitive to life-cycle requirements, must also ensure children's right to informed consent and that this may require additional efforts to enable children to be effectively involved. Thirdly, § 12 establishes that all health facilities, goods and services must be respectful of the culture of individuals, minorities, peoples and communities. Girls must preferably be examined by female doctors or at least in the presence of female employees in order to prevent any risks of abuse. Furthermore, the health care offered to

[775] *The World Health Report 2008, Primary Health Care – Now More Than Ever*, Geneva, World Health Organization, 2008. Available at: www.who.int/whr/2008/en/index.html.

[776] General Comment No. 14 (2000) The right to the highest attainable standard of health: 11/08/2000. E/C.12/2000/4. CESCR, § 12-c.

children must take into account as much as possible the wishes and traditions of (parents of) children from different cultures and religions, as long as these do not harm the best interests of the child, as may be the case with female genital mutilation. Sensitive discussions arise when alternative views on (children's) health in a society clash with more dominant health views as is the case when parents in the Netherlands refuse to vaccinate their children against the major childhood diseases as is laid down in the National Vaccination Program.[777]

Last but not least, the element of acceptability requires that health facilities must be designed to improve the health status of those concerned. This provision is in line with the medical ethical principle of 'primum non nocere', or 'doing no harm', which brings about that medical treatments may only be performed for improving the individuals' health status. It is thus not permitted to perform medical treatments that have no beneficial effect to the individual undergoing the treatment in order to acquire academic insights that potentially benefit the treatments of others with similar medical conditions (in the future), as this would not improve the health status of the individual concerned.

4.3.4. QUALITY

The fourth factor requires that health facilities, goods and services are of good quality. In the phrasing of § 13 of General Comment 14 to the ECOSOC Committee, this means that health facilities, goods and services must be scientifically and medically appropriate and of good quality. The key elements of this factor of health have been identified as effectiveness, efficiency, safety and patient-satisfaction.[778]

Applied to the provision of health care for children, the element of quality requires that professionals are adequately trained to diagnose, treat and communicate with children of all ages, that drugs are unexpired and scientifically tested and approved for children and that hospitals have adequate equipment, drinking water and sanitation.

[777] The National Vaccination Program for children in the Netherlands (het Rijksvaccinatieprogramma) was established by the Dutch Government in 1957 and aims to protect all children from dangerous or deadly infectious diseases. Vaccinations against 12 major diseases are offered without any costs for the parents: 1. cervical cancer for girls, 2. mumps, 3. diphtheria, 4. disease due to Haemophilus influenza type B (Hib), 5. hepatitis B, 6. pertussis (whooping-cough), 7. measles, 8. Meningococcal disease due to serogroup C, 9. pneumococcal disease, 10. poliomyelitis, 11. rubella, 12. tetanus. While participation is not compulsory, over 95% of parents consent to having their children vaccinated. See for more information: www.rivm.nl/Onderwerpen/Onderwerpen/R/Rijksvaccinatieprogramma/National_Immunisation_Programme.

[778] Lecture of Director UNICEF Europe, Steven Allen on the occasion of the adoption of the Guidelines on child-friendly healthcare by the Council of Europe Member States in Lisbon, September 2011.

With respect to the applicability of medicines for children, it was found in the Netherlands that 40–80% of the drugs are not specifically tested for children.[779] The exact percentage differs per age group, mode of admission and type of disease and is the lowest for newly born children and infants.[780] Even if medicines are specifically registered for children, the form in which they are registered (e.g. relatively big capsules) may only be suitable for older children, whereas younger children prefer other modes of admission (small and tasteful capsules). Unavailability of such pills affects therapy compliance and the effectiveness of therapies prescribed.

For now, doctors often prescribe medicines as a percentage of the adult body weight. There is as such not an evidence-based, but an experience-based medical treatment applied. Exemplified by the expression that 'Children are no small adults', this establishes the risk that children suffer from unforeseen side-effects and ineffective treatments. This can lead to longer hospital stays, additional treatments to reduce negative (side-)effects, ineffective treatments as well as preventable infant deaths.[781] Therefore, more research is required upon the potential (side-effects) of medicines on children. In doing so, it is necessary to find a better balance between the need to protect minors against the potential harmful effects of unregistered medicines on the one hand and the need to increase knowledge on the other hand.[782, 783] Although recent developments are intended to create more room to undertake research on the appropriateness of medicines for children, medical professionals have urged that it remains crucial to minimize any potential negative effects for children, especially when a treatment proposed

---

779 Report ZonMw 'In-depth study 'Goed Gebruik Geneesmiddelen', 11 June 2010 carried out for the Ministery of Health subsequent to a preliminary report of 20 July 2009.

780 Ibidem supra note 779.

781 It was found in the Netherlands that 2,5% of the hospital admissions of children are caused by medicine intake, of which an estimated 30% was preventable. Ibidem supra note 78.

782 In the Netherlands, the Commission Doek came to the conclusion that the actual Dutch legislation poses too many limits for conducting research on medicines for children. It proposed to change the basic principle from 'no, unless' to 'yes, unless'. In deciding upon a potential intervention for children, the potential risks for the individual child must be balanced against the potential benefits of the research. The Commission suggested that intervention research with children should be allowed if there is to be expected any direct advantage for the test person or the group of children with a similar medical condition. See: Commissie-Doek, *Advies medisch-wetenschappelijk onderzoek met kinderen*, Den Haag, 26 November 2009.

783 In the European Union, the Pediatric Regulation came into force on 26 January 2007. The new paediatric legislation comprises Regulation (EC) No 1901/2006 and the amending Regulation (EC) No 1902/2006 and obliges pharmaceutical companies to specifically test medicines for children. Aims of the regulation are 1) to facilitate the development and availability of medicines for children aged 0 to 17 years, 2) to ensure that medicines for use in children are of high quality, ethically researched and authorised appropriately and 3) to improve the availability of information on the use of medicines for children, all without subjecting children to unnecessary trials. The regulation has resulted in an increase in applications to the pediatric committee of the European Medicines Agency (PDCO) and in an increase in registrations of medicines for children. For more information see: www.ema.europa.eu/ema/index.jsp?curl=pages/special_topics/general/general_content_000302.jsp&mid=WC0b01ac058002d4ea.

does not directly benefit the health of the child who undergoes the treatment.[784] Only when such stringent requirements are respected, can individual children be protected against heavily burdensome medical treatments.

4.4. PATIENT INVOLVEMENT AS A KEY CONSTITUENT ELEMENT OF THE RIGHT TO HEALTH

The identification of the 'AAAQ-structure' as a basis for analysing the right to health has been established in General Comment 14 to the ICESCR.[785] Increasingly, the principles of 'accountability' and 'participation' are recognized as constituting key elements of the right to the highest attainable standard of health.[786] Accountability has been described by Potts as 'the process that requires the government to show, explain and justify how it has discharged its obligations regarding the right to the highest attainable standard of health. It is thus about holding all responsible actors accountable for their human rights violations, but also, and more constructively about assessing the progress made in realizing the highest attainable standard of health. Five distinct forms of accountability have been distinguished, namely judicial, quasi-judicial, administrative, political and social.[787] All these forms are interlinked and thereby lead to a community wide process for involving all stakeholders in the realization of children's right to health. A further discussion of the role of all relevant stakeholders in the realization of the right to health of the child will be presented in chapter 6.

The principle of participation aims to involve the individual patients and the population at large in the health-decision making process. Potts argues that 'an important purpose of participation in the context of the right to health is to recognise and respect differences and diversity within the population, and to ensure inclusiveness in the development of health policy'. As such, involving children in a participatory manner in their own health care is an essential step in revealing and including their particular needs in the organisation of their

[784] F. van Agt, L. Damen & F. Huysmans, 'Jonge proefpersonen zijn kwetsbaar' [Young test persons are vulnerable], *Medisch Contact* 2010, 65 no. 13, 1 April, p. 629. The authors advocate for a twofold ethical basis that 1) it is authorized to involve children in research if it can only be exercised with children and if the risks and negative side-effects are minimal. 2). This condition is not applicable if participation in the clinical research directly benefits the children, for as far as negative (side-)effects are part of the regular treatment. This means that terminally ill children may undergo a new medical treatment, if there is a chance that this treatment will be beneficial to their medical condition and prospects.

[785] General Comment No. 14 (2000) The right to the highest attainable standard of health: 11/08/2000. E/C.12/2000/4. CESCR, § 12.

[786] H. Potts, *Participation and the Right to the Highest Attainable Standard of Health* and *Accountability and the Right to the Highest Attainable Standard of Health*, University of Essex, Human Rights Centre/Open Society Institute, 2008. See also Riedel, supra note 678.

[787] See supra note 769, Potts and Riedel supra note 683, Riedel.

health care and in the health-care decision making process. Potts gives several examples of how this element of participation can be realized in practice, including interviews, focus group discussions, forums, conferences, local health committees and public meetings.[788] Other options would be to allow children to create children's newspapers, perform role or theatre plays, poems, songs, photos, drawings and other ways of artistic expression.

General Comment 15 has included the AAAQ-structure for the children's rights domain, as was suggested by various experts in the preparation phase of this General Comment.[789] It therefore is a valid structure to follow in analysing the level of realization of the right to health of the child. In addition, the principle of 'patient-satisfaction' has been introduced as a key element of the right to the highest attainable standard of health of the child in the contribution of the University of Geneva.[790] This principle of 'patient-satisfaction' has been analysed for its applicability to measure the realization of the right to the highest attainable standard of health.[791] It was found that there is a high correspondence between the recommended or collected items for patient satisfaction and the other four key constituent elements (AAAQ) of the right to health as defined by General Comment 14 to the ICESCR. The authors therefore conclude that patient satisfaction could prove a 'natural' right to health indicator, covering all other key constituent elements of the right to health.[792]

Applying patient satisfaction as a key element of the right to health has several advantages. In the first place, it tackles the problems of limited or contradicting data collection on the other constituent elements of the right to health and of inadequate monitoring or reporting by States, because 'patient satisfaction studies are frequently implemented in health services throughout the world'.[793] Furthermore, integrating the component of 'patient satisfaction' as a constituent element in the AAAQ-structure of the right to health, allows for applying a patient-centred approach to health care, involving the views, experiences and psychological dimensions of patients in assessing and improving the right to the highest attainable standard of health. Such a patient-centred approach could be translated to a child-centred approach in children's health care. In such a way, ensuring the best interests of the child and the right to participation of children

788 Ibidem supra note 769.

789 See for example the submissions of the Royal Australian College of Physicians, the submission of Professor A. Nolan a.o., the Committee for Human Rights Sweden, Harm Reduction International a.o., the International Planned Parenthood Federation and Spronk. www2.ohchr.org/english/bodies/crc/callsubmissionsCRC_received.htm.

790 See the contribution made by Professor E. Kabengele Mpinga and Professor P. Chastonay of the University of Geneva to the call for submissions on the interpretation of children's right to health, available at: www2.ohchr.org/english/bodies/crc/docs/CallSubmissions_Art24/UniversityofGeneva.pdf.

791 E. Kabengele Mpinga, & P. Chastonay, 'Satisfaction of patients: A Right to health indicator?', *Health Policy* 2011, 100, pp. 144–150.

792 Ibidem supra note 774.

793 Ibidem supra note 774.

in medical care can be integrated in the general framework of the right to health of the child.

Kabengele Mpinga and Chastonnay present several arguments in favour of applying patient satisfaction as a right to health indicator:[794]

> '– From a *legal point of view*, patient satisfaction has become a legal obligation in many states and is often considered as an element of the quality of care.'
>
> '– From *the point of view of implementing the right to health* in the health systems, patient satisfaction does integrate the recommended "participative approach" as identified by the Special-Representative on the Right to Health Paul Hunt.[795]'

Criticisms on applying patient satisfaction as a constituent element of the right to health point to the lack of consensus on the concept of patient satisfaction, the intrinsic subjectivity and the strong clinical orientation of patient satisfaction studies.[796] International consensus on the concept of patient satisfaction as an element of the right to health should be reached in order to allow for international comparison of studies on patient satisfaction and thereby possibly on assessing the level of realization of the right to the highest attainable standard of health of patients. Defining such a concept should account for any possible unpredictability due to the intrinsic subjectivity of the concept of patient satisfaction. However, it is exactly the acceptance of a certain degree of unpredictability that allows for patient involvement in assessing and raising the standard of the right to health. By taking the voice of the patient into account in the setup of medical services and in the selection of medical treatments, the concept of the highest attainable standard of health will be more responsive to patient needs. Whereas it has previously been acknowledged that the highest attainable standard of health is dependent upon

794 Ibidem supra note 774. Other arguments presented include: 'From *a political point of view* it is a democratic necessity to listen to the opinions of patients in accordance with the concept of participation as a central feature to the harmonious functioning of modern societies. Some argue that participation of patients is assumed to restore confidence in health services and that it strengthens the power of patients and facilitates their integration into the decision making process.' See also: H. Vuori, 'Patient satisfaction – does it matter?', *International Journal of Quality in Health Care* 1991, 3, pp. 183–189. See also: R. Chambers, C. Drinkwater & E. Boath, 'Involving patients and the public: How to do better?', *Radcliffe Medical Press* 2003, Abingdon, p. 158. 'From a sociological point of view, the technical, social and economic evolutions have transformed the relationship between patients and health professionals with new expectations from both parties; therefore integrating the opinion of patients into the therapeutic strategy strengthens the partnership dimension of care weakening the obsolete paternalistic approach, which once was (too often still is) the key feature of the therapeutic relationship.' See also: K. Taylor Paternalism, 'Participation and partnership-the evolution of patient centeredness in the consultation', *Patient Education and Counseling 2009*, 74, pp. 150–155.

795 P. Hunt & G. Backman, 'Health systems and the right to the highest attainable standard of health', *International Journal on Health and Human Rights* 2008, Volume 10, no. 1.

796 Ibidem supra note 791. See also: K.D. Hekkert, S. Cihangri a.o., 'Patient satisfaction revisited: a multilevel approach', *Social Science and Medicine* 2009, pp. 68–75. See also: L. Gill & L. White, 'A critical review of patient satisfaction', *Leadership in Health Services* 2009, 22(1), pp. 8–19.

financial and human resources, political will to realize such a standard and local circumstances, the individual perceptions and health choices of patients play a significant role in defining and achieving the highest standard of health.[797] For example, some terminally ill people wish to continue their medical treatments to prolong life with some months or years. Others, on the other hand, choose for a termination of medical treatments and accept the risk of more rapid deterioration of their physical health status. Individual health choices therefore do certainly impact upon the attainment of the highest attainable standard of health that is actually reached in terms of for example, infant, child and maternal mortality rates and life expectancy. The central role attributed to the individual patient (and his/her parents) is specifically acknowledged in the definition of health as introduced by Huber (see chapter 1), in which self-management by the individual and adaptability are two constituent parts.

The standard of health that is attained can be measured on the basis of objective criteria, such as number of available health services, staff and medicines, but this may still lead to unsatisfied patients. When, on the other hand, objective criteria are combined with the subjective element of patient satisfaction, seemingly less favourable health outcomes may be better assessed by the patients that have (not) undergone certain treatments, because, e.g. there was more attention and time available for personal consultations or palliative care and more room for discussing issues of concern to the patient. Items that could be measured in patient-satisfaction assessments could include timely provision of health care,[798] having enough time and attention during the care provided, transparency and coherency in the health care process and in the communication, having the opportunity to ask questions, to discuss alternative medical treatments, fears and hesitations, value for money, availability of supportive care such as massages,[799] counselling and palliative care,[800] having the opportunity to stay with or see

---

797 General Comment No. 14 (2000) The right to the highest attainable standard of health: 11/08/2000. E/C.12/2000/4. CESCR, § 9.

798 See for an example of possible items for measuring patient satisfaction the Patient Satisfaction Questionnaire of Rand Health, available at: www.rand.org/health/surveys_tools/psq.html. 'The PSQ-III is a 50-item survey that taps global satisfaction with medical care as well as satisfaction with six aspects of care: technical quality, interpersonal manner, communication, financial aspects of care, time spent with doctor, and accessibility of care.' The original version was developed by Ware and colleagues in 1974 and it has been repeatedly validated and adapted since then. RAND aims to collect and analyze health data to assess and follow health conditions in the USA and worldwide. 'RAND research on children covers the prenatal period up to age 18 and includes areas such as child health and the role of the family unit, neighborhoods, and communities in influencing child well-being.'

799 For a further motivation of the importance of providing massages as a way to improve children's health and well-being see the submission of the Massages in School Association to the UN Committee on the Rights of the Child to the development of a General Comment on children's right to health. www2.ohchr.org/english/bodies/crc/callsubmissionsCRC_received.htm.

800 For a further motivation of the need to ensure palliative care for children see the submission of the International children's palliative care network to the UN Committee on the Rights of the

family and friends in private and to refuse treatments or hospitalization if the individual does not wish to undergo a certain (series of) medical treatments. These items are by no means exhaustive and could be further developed by taking a look at previously conducted patient-satisfaction assessments in the medical sector. Particularly for children, the proposed element of patient satisfaction can be further interpreted by taking the body of law of the Convention on the Rights of the Child into account and any applicable regional treaties and medical guidelines, such as the Guidelines of the Council of Europe on Child-Friendly Health Care.[801]

4.5. A SYNTHESIS

In ensuring health facilities, several key elements are useful for assessing the level of realization of the right to the highest attainable standard of health in a given context. General Comment 14 to the ICESCR establishes several key elements that concomitantly provide for a useful legal framework to shape, assess and improve the realization of the right to the highest attainable standard of health. This framework consists of the elements of availability, accessibility, acceptability and quality, applying to both the underlying determinants of health and to the actual health care services itself. The concomitant structure that arises is strongly focused upon the requirements of the right to health to ensure 'physical health'. However, as discussed in introductory chapter 1, the WHO-definition of health goes beyond the strictly physical dimension of health by defining health as 'a state of complete physical, psychological ánd social well-being and not merely the absence of disease or disability'.[802] Therefore, the identified legal framework of the right to health as laid down in the ICESCR is deficient when comparing this to the definition of health of the WHO and the definition of Huber. In order to allow for the integration, assessment and improvement of the 'highest attainable standard of health', it would be necessary to incorporate a constituent element that allows for assessing the psychological and social well-being of patients. Hereto, it is recommendable to include the concept of patient-satisfaction as an additional key constituent element of the right to health. This allows for a more nuanced assessment of the 'highest attainable standard of health' by taking both objective criteria and personal experiences into account. The resulting highest attainable standard of health should fulfil all separate elements in the model below. For as

Child to the development of a General Comment on children's right to health. www2.ohchr.org/english/bodies/crc/callsubmissionsCRC_received.htm.

801 The Guidelines on child-friendly health care were adopted in Lisbon on 28 September 2011 in the context of the Strategy 'Building a Europe for and with children' 2009–2011.

802 Preamble to the Constitution of the World Health Organization as adopted by the International Health Conference, New York, 19–22 June 1946; signed on 22 July 1946 by the representatives of 61 States (Official Records of the World Health Organization, no. 2, p. 100) and entered into force on 7 April 1948.

long as States Parties to the ICESCR have not fulfilled the requirements of the constituent elements of the right to health, there remains room for improvement. Furthermore, new insights and developments may urge a continuous redefinition of the highest attainable standard of health of the child.

Figure 1. Key constituent elements of the right to the highest attainable standard of health of the child

	Underlying determinants of health	Health services
Availability	# and regional spread of safe drinking water, nutritious foods, sanitation and infrastructure (e.g. transport): within reasonable distance of living environment.	# and regional spread of health professionals, medical facilities and medicines
Accessibility	Non-discrimination: de facto and de iure access, economic, physical and information accessibility	Non-discrimination: de facto and de iure access, economic, physical and information accessibility
Acceptability	drinking water, nutritious foods, sanitation and infrastructure must respect traditional and cultural norms of local inhabitants.	Care and medicines provided must be respectful of medical ethics, culture, gender and life-cycle requirements.
Quality	drinking water, nutritious foods, sanitation and infrastructure must be of good quality and safe.	Care and medicines provided must be scientifically and medically tested and safe, well-trained medical professionals.
Patient-Satisfaction/ Participation	Patients indicate that they are satisfied with the drinking water, nutritious foods, sanitation and infrastructure that they use.	Patients indicate that they are satisfied with the health care received ánd with other factors relevant to their well-being, e.g.: – information, privacy and involvement in (medical) decisions – timely provision of health care – having enough time and attention – transparency in health care process and communication – coherency of health care process – opportunity to ask questions, discuss alternative treatments, fears and hesitations – supportive care and counselling (e.g. massage and palliative care) – contact with friends and family – provide health education – right to refuse medical treatments and hospitalization – value for money

	Underlying determinants of health	Health services
Adaptability	Provision of Underlying Determinants is adapted to changing needs and circumstances	Provision is adapted to changing needs and circumstances: – individual needs of children and family (beliefs and experiences, health knowledge, family composition, culture, religion) – life course (age, level of development) – stage of disease (prevention, curation, rehabilitation, palliative) – medical knowledge – needs of different groups of children – changing circumstances
Accountability	The government has shown how it meets its obligations through judicial, quasi-judicial, administrative, political and social procedures.	The government has shown how it meets its obligations through judicial, quasi-judicial, administrative, political and social procedures.

Applying a legal framework on the basis of which both objective and subjective elements can be assessed, creates the opportunity to acquire additional insights into potential mismatches between the objective elements of the right to health that are realized and the experiences of patients in receiving health care. This is of vital importance to ensuring the right to the highest attainable standard of health, because it is the physical, psychological and social well-being of the individual patients that is the primary object of the right to health. Also for children, the need to integrate children's experiences in health care assessments is crucially important, since they are generally less involved in shaping and organizing health care than adults are. Integrating the voice of children as an element of the right to health of the child, will therefore allow for rights-based improvements of the health services provided in the future and place children at the heart of the health care provided to them.

4.6. KEY FEATURES OF A HEALTH SYSTEM FOR CHILDREN BASED ON THE RIGHT TO HEALTH

In April 2002, the mandate of the UN Special Rapporteur on the right of everyone to the enjoyment of the highest attainable standard of physical and mental health was established by the Commission on Human Rights.[803] In 2008, this Rapporteur presented a report in which the key features of an effective and integrated health

[803] U.N. Doc. E/2002/23- E/CN.4/2002/200, Commission on Human Rights resolution 2002/31 on the right to the highest attainable standard of physical and mental health. The mandate was endorsed and extended by the Human Rights Council by its resolution 6/29 of 14 December 2007. For more information on the activities of the UN Special Rapporteur on the Right to Health see: www.ohchr.org/EN/Issues/Health/Pages/SRRightHealthIndex.aspx.

system were identified.[804, 805] This report provided for the translation of the right to health to essential building blocks of a human rights based health system and therefore poses a useful structure for translating the right to health of children as laid down in the children's rights domain into essential building blocks of health systems. The Rapporteur (Paul Hunt) claims that a health system that is based on human rights lies at the heart of the right to the highest attainable standard of health, being responsive to both national and local priorities and accessible to all.[806] More specifically, he claims that 'Health systems are central to children's right to health'.[807] According to Nolan and others, 'Health systems can too frequently exacerbate inequalities, stigmatization, and marginalization, and these forms of exclusion disproportionately affect children.'[808] The realization of the right to the highest attainable standard of health is thus largely dependent on the way in which health systems are structured.

In the Report, it is recommended that the key features of a rights based health system must be applied across the different building blocks of a health system.[809] All building blocks must be assessed for the separate key features of a rights-based health system. In the following, the key aspects that are most relevant for involving children in their own health care will be discussed, namely person centeredness (1), transparency (3), participation (4), respect for different (youth) cultures (6), equity (5) and continuous health care (11).[810]

---

804 U.N. Doc. No. A/HRC/7/11, 2008, Report of the UN Special Rapporteur on the right of everyone to the Enjoyment of the Highest Attainable Standard of Physical and Mental Health. All key features identified are already found in some health systems, recognized in international legal documents or advocated for in health literature.

805 It is interesting to realize that the highly organized level of health systems is barely 100 years old, even in industrialized countries. See Everybody's Business: Strengtening Health Systems to Improve Health Outcomes, WHO, 2007, p. 2, available at: http://who.int/healthsystems/strategy/everybodys_business.pdf).

806 Ibidem supra note 778, p. 2. The importance of an effective health system for the realization of the right to health is compared to the importance of a fair justice system and accessible courts for the realization of the right to a fair trial.

807 P. Hunt & G. Backman, 'Health systems and the right to the highest attainable standard of health', *Health and Human Rights* 2008, 10; and Report of the Special Rapporteur on the right of everyone to the enjoyment of the highest attainable standard of physical and mental health, UN Doc. A/HRC/7/11, 31 January 2008.

808 Ibidem supra note 778.

809 Ibidem supra note 778. p. 18. The building blocks of a rights-based health system have been identified as i. the health services, ii. the health workforce, iii. the health information system, iv. medical products, vaccines and technologies, v. health financing, vi. leadership and governance.

810 In total, 17 key features of a rights-based health system are identified in the Report: 1. the well-being of people at the centre; 2. not only outcomes, but also processes; 3. transparency; 4. participation; 5. equity, equality and non-discrimination; 6. respect for cultural differences; 7. medical care and the underlying determinants of health; 8. progressive realization and resource constraints; 9. core obligations (i. national health plan, ii. access to health-services on a non-discriminatory basis, iii. equitable distribution of health services, iv. mechanisms of accountability); 10. quality; 11. a continuum of prevention and care; 12. disease-specific or integrated health interventions; 13. coordination between sectors; 14. international

The principal element identified of a rights-based health system is its focus on the well-being of individuals, communities and populations: key feature 1 is to put patients at the centre of the health care system. Stressed is that health systems should not become 'impersonal, top down and dominated by experts'.[811] Thereto, the influence of health professionals on determining the medical treatment for children should be balanced by the voice-raising of children and their families. In achieving this, medical professionals must be able to step back and provide meaningful opportunities for children to speak up and have their say over their own bodies and treatments. Secondly, focus should not be placed only on diseases, as is now often the case, but on the patient as a whole. This element is especially important for the provision of health care to children, as children face a fourfold vulnerability: in the first place in their capacity as being a child, often being subordinate to the will and directives of their parents or other adults and in the second place as being subordinate in their capacity as being a patient with – presumably – less technical medical knowledge than their doctors.[812] Furthermore, sick children often lack the energy to stand up for their rights during their medical treatment. Lastly, medical treatments affect not only their present but also their future medical condition. The right to health of the child therefore is a good pretext to ensure that children are placed central in the health care process. Hereto, several other elements identified are supportive, such as transparency, participation, a focus on processes in addition to outcomes and respect for different (youth) cultures.[813]

The additional principles can add to a child-oriented way of organizing health care; transparency requires that children have access to health information (for example at school), so that they can become involved in promoting their own good health by eating healthy, stop smoking and start sporting.[814] This requires that the information is understandable for children of different ages and that different modalities of information transmission are used, e.g. cartoons or explanations with teddy bears and dolls. Transparency is also relevant for the continuum of prevention and care: a health system should have an appropriate mix of primary, secondary and tertiary care, including effective referrals between these different phases in the health care system and between the alternative and mainstream health sector.[815] Especially for children, the feature of transparency requires supportive guidance and patience in explaining about possible referrals that they may undergo during the health care process. It would therefore be very useful if

---

cooperation; 15. balances between different human rights; 16. monitoring and accountability; 17. legal obligation.

811 P. Hunt & G. Backman, 'Health systems and the right to the highest attainable standard of health', *International Journal on Health and Human Rights* 2008, Volume 10, no. 1, p. 83.

812 G. Brichner, 'Children in the Hospital: Issues of Power and Vulnerability', *Pediatric nursing* 2000, May-June; 26(3), pp. 277–82.

813 Ibidem supra note 810.

814 Ibidem supra note 810, p. 83.

815 Ibidem supra note 810, p. 85.

special health care coaches would guide children through the entire health care process, be it necessary for just a few visits in case of temporal medical problems or for many more sessions in the course of treatment of chronic or long-term diseases. Such a coach should guard the best interests of the child, being broader than only the physical and emotional well-being, but also involving the interests of the child in other life domains, such as family life, school life and maintaining contacts with friends and continuing leisure activities if they wish to.

Transparency enables children to participate in their own health care process. Only if they have clear and understandable information, can they make solidly motivated choices concerning their health and treatment. Through this active participatory process in which children's ideas and experiences are central, the interests of the child as a child are placed at the heart of the health care process, as is required under the first and principal element of a rights based health system.[816] This would furthermore ensure that not only the outcome of the health treatment (namely curation or not), but also the process itself is attentive of children's interests (key feature # 2). The need to ensure children's rights during the entire health care process is especially relevant for children who can not be cured completely, such as children with chronic diseases, disabled children and children with life-threatening diseases.[817] For example, in many, especially developing countries, there is no or insufficient palliative care for children, especially babies and neonates.[818] The reason given for this situation is that 'most adults have an inherent disbelief that children should not die and therefore ignore the needs of these children.'[819] Secondly, it is identified that because (young) children have limited communication skills, 'their pain and suffering are often left unnoticed and untreated'.[820] Though it is important to ensure a child-appropriate health care process for its own sake, it may be assumed that such a process will also result in a better outcome, as children and their parents will be more inclined to follow the treatment if their wishes are taken into account. Also, attention for the interests and opinions of the child during the treatment will likely reduce feelings of anxiety and helplessness over their own health.

Another important aspect of a child centred health care system is derived from the key feature of respect for different cultures.[821] It has been observed that cultural sensitivity leads 'to higher levels of programme acceptance and ownership by the community, and programme sustainability'. It can be assumed that including features of specific child and youth cultures has a beneficial effect

---

816 Ibidem supra note 810.

817 See the submission of the International children's palliative care network in response to the call for submissions of the UN Committee on the Rights of the Child for the development on a General Comment on children's right to health.

818 Ibidem supra note 810.

819 Ibidem supra note 810.

820 Ibidem supra note 810.

821 Ibidem supra note 810.

on the likelihood that children and youth will feel more attracted to such health information materials and advices from medical professionals.

A rights based health care system requires effective coordination among various sectors and departments such as health, environment, water, sanitation, food, shelter, transport and education.[822] The equal distribution of health services could be done on the basis of demographic statistics: the more children live in a specific area, the more child health services must be available. It could also be spread in coordination with the regional distribution of schools: many examples have shown that when children are provided with healthy meals, they are more likely to go to school. A similar connection could be achieved by locating primary health services in or near the schools they are going to. Problems of accessibility of schools and health care services can thereby be solved in conjunction, for example by building a road from a village to another where children can go to school and visit a doctor when they are sick. In doing so, however, children's right to privacy must be guaranteed, in order to avoid issues of stigmatization, for example, in the case of HIV/AIDS tests for children.

Last but not least, a health system that is based on children's right to the highest attainable standard of health should progressively realize the priorities that can be derived from that right. Remarkable is that the basic components of the right to the highest attainable standard of health, such as access to health care and to the underlying determinants of health concomitantly focus on achieving health for as many individuals as possible. Therefore, the social justice (or horizontal) component is much stronger than the vertical component, aiming at progressive achievement of a better health status for just a limited number of people. As this key characteristic of the right to health calls for involving *all people*, and thus *all children* without discrimination, it is necessary to determine who is actually responsible for ensuring health for all. It has been identified that community participation is crucial, given the extent of the legal obligation, which is far beyond the reach of governmental institutions. Community participation, for a start, is partly dependent on the initiatives taken within the community. A government can evoke and stimulate communities to take responsibility and be involved in the realization of the health of its children. However, it cannot and should not force communities to do so, since this would result in a top-down process, that thus does not address the capabilities of individuals to make their best contributions.

How should the responsibilities of adults, i.e. parents or other caretakers be balanced against the responsibilities of the State and other actors involved? Secondly, in order to measure progress in achieving the highest attainable standard of health over time, it is necessary to use indicators and benchmarks on children's right to health. Thirdly, to assess the level of progress in achieving the highest attainable standard of health over time, independent monitoring

822 Ibidem supra note 736.

and accountability mechanisms are crucial elements of a rights-based health system. These questions on accountability will be discussed in chapter VI on the realization of the right to health of the child.

4.7. CONCLUSION

In this concluding section the question is addressed what the additional value of the right to the highest attainable standard of health as formulated in international health and human rights law is for interpreting the right to the highest attainable standard of health of the child in the children's rights domain. Article 24 and 41 CRC concomitantly create the opportunity for elaborating the right to the highest attainable standard of health of the child in the CRC by looking at legal documents other than those in the children's rights domain.

The concept of the highest attainable standard of health of the child cannot be easily defined, because it depends on continuously moving, sometimes even conflicting conditions:

- Individual needs and viewpoints of children and their families: e.g. based on personal beliefs and experiences, level of health education, religion, culture and family composition vary. This influences the health seeking behaviour.
- Children's health needs change continuously based on their life course, age and levels of development. These varying needs require consequent health services that are adaptive to those needs: maternal, antenatal, obstetric, new-born, infant and child healthcare.
- The varying stages of diseases require primary, secondary or tertiary prevention, curation, rehabilitation and palliative care.
- The developing insights of medical science and available technologies constantly create new opportunities for medical treatment and therefore raise the highest attainable standard of health.
- The varying needs of (vulnerable) groups of children: e.g. children in early childhood, girls, immigrant children, indigenous children, orphaned children, street children require different modes of communication and adaptation of health education to their living world and level of understanding. This is reinforced by the requirement to stimulate community participation: to be able to respond to the plurality of community initiatives, health services must be flexible.
- The circumstances in which children live: e.g. socioeconomic conditions, economic crisis, humanitarian situation and climate change require continuous restructuring and re-evaluation of existing health services.
- Changing health challenges due to increasing numbers of international travellers, awareness of health problems and solutions in other areas of the world instigate continuous development.

Although it follows from the identified factors of uncertainty that one universal standard for the highest attainable standard of health is impossible to establish, several elements are considered as priorities, deriving from international health and human rights other than the CRC domain, of the right to health of the child.

1. Right to underlying determinants of health, including:
   - safe drinking water;
   - adequate nutrition;
   - sanitation;
   - housing;
   - healthy living environment;
   - health information and education;
   - vaccination campaigns.
2. Right to a variety of facilities, goods, services and conditions that are necessary for the attainment of the highest attainable standard of health:
   - Child and maternal health measures;
   - Sexual and reproductive health services, including:
     a. Access to family planning;
     b. Pre- and postnatal health care;
     c. Emergency obstetric services;
     d. Access to health information;
     e. Resources necessary to act on the health information.
   - Access to essential health care services for children and their family.
3. Child-friendly health information for prevention and promotion.
4. Inclusion of vulnerable groups through community participation.
5. Skilled health professionals.
6. Essential medicines and technologies.
7. Adoption of a national strategy or plan of action.

The provision of underlying determinants can be better met by increasing the available budget. General Comment 14 further establishes that the identified health services should be in line with the key constituent elements of the right to health in order to achieve the highest attainable standard of health: availability, accessibility, acceptability and quality. The AAAQ structure for structuring and assessing the level of realization of the general right to health offers significant insight into the way in which the highest attainable standard of health of the child can be achieved. The framework applies to both the underlying determinants of health and to the provision of medical care itself. The steps that must be taken should therefore progressively realize all the identified aspects of the key constituent elements of the AAAQ structure as depicted in figure 1. Also, in case of retrogressive measures with respect to a particular constituent element of the realized right to health in a country, alternative options must be considered in order to restore the previously realized health status of children.

However, several new trends have been discerned, which require a further development of the traditional AAAQ structure as laid down in General Comment 14 to the ICESCR: inclusion of the elements of adaptability, accountability and participation (or patient-satisfaction) in the traditional AAAQ framework. Such inclusion would be responsive to the current trend to better involve patients in their own health process. It would furthermore allow for a more flexible and adaptive health system that places the best interests of the child and its family at the heart instead of the functionalities of medical organizations. This requires approaching the child as a whole and not only as an object in need of medical physical treatment. Secondly, it allows for focusing not only on the health outcome of the medical care provided, but also on the health process. Such an approach to health care would be in line with the right to participation and with the best interests of children as laid down in articles 12 and 3 of the CRC.

So how can such a flexible and adaptive health system be realized in practice? Paragraph 12 of General Comment 14 particularly establishes the link between ensuring child friendly health information about preventive and health-promoting behaviour for children and their families in order to gain access to essential health services. Having access to understandable health information enables both children and their families to become personally involved in improving and ensuring their own level of good health. In this way, every individual gradually becomes an active participant in achieving the right to the highest attainable standard of health of children.

Secondly, a rights-based health system for children must ensure effective coordination between health services, schools and the provision of safe drinking water, food, sanitary facilities and housing. Access to those facilities must be non-discriminative, transparent, sensitive to the particular needs and (youth) cultures of different children and targeted to individual children, communities and populations. Such inclusive access requires the involvement of all community members, so that children's needs can be identified by their caretakers living in their direct vicinity.

Last but not least, the highest attainable standard of health is not confined to the limited borders of States. States have extraterritorial obligations to ensure the right to the highest attainable standard of health for children in developing countries. Key requirements for meeting these obligations are the identification of shared international health standards and indicators and the assessment of foreign policies through child health impact assessments. Coordination and realigning of existing health structures can be instigated by engaging into health diplomacy: identifying and negotiating mutual health needs and finding common grounds on which health policies can be based. The minimum requirements deriving from the right to the highest attainable standard of health as identified above are legally grounded and offer a useful starting point for engaging with such international coordination.

V. REGIONAL INTERPRETATIONS OF THE RIGHT TO HEALTH OF THE CHILD: A FOCUS ON EUROPE

5.1. INTRODUCTION

The Vienna Declaration on Human Rights provides that all human rights are universal, indivisible, interdependent and interrelated. Kinney argues that 'the right to health must be the same for all nations and people, to have meaning'.[823] However, this seems to be an unrealistic requirement, because the actual implementation of the right to health is dependent upon resources, budget allocation, cultural values and health policies in individual countries and communities. This vision is mirrored by the Committee on Economic, Social and Cultural Rights, which recognizes the relevance of the local context by stating that the precise application of the elements identified in General Comment 14 to the ICESCR, 'will depend on the conditions prevailing in a particular State party thereby demonstrating a high level of local context sensitivity'.[824] Similarly, the vision of the European Association for Children in Hospital that the right to health in countries must be evaluated in the context of the health care services available to them in their home country, better reflects the actual reality of implementing children's right to health in the daily lives of children.[825]

This chapter seeks to investigate what the States priorities are in realizing the highest attainable standard of health of children in Europe. In this region, many developments are taking place that guide the interpretation of the concept of 'the highest attainable standard of health' of the child. Therefore, the analysis of the key elements of child-friendly healthcare as elaborated in European legislation may give additional insight into the key research question 'what the key elements of the right to the highest attainable standard of health of the child are and whether there are different, progressive standards to realize this right'.

---

823 E.D. Kinney, 'International Human Right to health: what does it mean for our nation and the world?', *Indiana Law Review* 2001, p. 1457. Accessed on 16 May 2012 at: http://heinonline.org/HOL/Page?handle=hein.journals/indilr34&collection=journals.

824 General Comment No. 14 (2000) The right to the highest attainable standard of health: 11/08/2000. E/C.12/2000/4. CESCR, § 12.

825 'A Guide to General Comment 7: Implementing Child Rights in Early Childhood', produced by Bernard van Leer Foundation and UNICEF, 2006, p. 74.

After providing an introduction into the debate on universalism versus local interpretations of children's rights, the interpretation of the highest attainable standard of health of the child in Europe will be looked at by analysing the European Social Charter, the relevant law of the European Union and the recent guidelines on child-friendly health care as adopted by the Council of Europe as a point of reference. In this way, the developments within the European region illustrate that the interpretation of the right to health of the child in one particular region of the world. This region has been chosen, because considerable developments have taken place between 2010–2015 in elaborating guidelines on child-friendly healthcare. However, it must be taken into account that these guidelines are strongly oriented towards the right to health of the child in the medical sector itself, whereas the realization of this right strongly depends on social, biological and environmental factors. More research is required on interpretations in other regions.

5.2. UNIVERSALISM IN A LOCAL CONTEXT

The formal discussion on the universality of human rights arose in the period of the adoption of the Universal Declaration of Human Rights by the United Nations in 1948. Based on the belief in a universal human nature, several fundamental rights were laid down, applicable to every human being, notwithstanding their age, sex, sexual orientation, ethnic, religious or political background.[826] The guiding idea of universalists is that every person has equal human rights based on his inherent humanity, even if there are cultural differences between people. In that view, similarity must prevail over cultural differences with respect to ensuring human rights.[827] Critics on the other hand put forward that this perspective is 'lacking empirical validity, and is historically and culturally imperialistic'.[828] Relativists put forward that western values have been masqueraded as universal values.[829] These criticisms have also been made with respect to the Convention on the Rights of the Child.[830] The debate between universalists and relativists thus arises from the translation of human rights values into different cultures, more particularly in this case, on translating the meaning of the right to health of the child into different local contexts.

Criticism on the universal applicability of children's rights has been fierce. Some scholars have even stated that international human rights norms and

826 E. Brems, 'Universele grondrechten', *NJB* 2010, no. 6, pp. 19–21.

827 L.S. Bell, 'Introduction: Culture and human rights', in: L.S. Bell, L.S (a.o.), *Negotiating culture and human rights*, New York: Columbia University Press 2001, pp. 1–15.

828 Ibidem supra note 825.

829 Ibidem supra note 825.

830 S. Goonesekere, 'Introduction', in: *Protecting the World's Children, Impact of the Convention on the Rights of the Child in Diverse Legal Systems*, UNICEF 2007, Cambridge University Press, p. 1.

children's rights in particular do not acknowledge traditional values and conceptions of human rights.[831] Arts on the other hand, provides several arguments for the statement that the Children's Rights Convention gives opportunity for a culturally sensitive interpretation of (several of) its provisions. She argues that the Children's Rights Convention was particularly designed to be implemented in the variable circumstances of different countries, cultures, legal, economic and political systems and that the involvement of countries from all continents in the negotiation process[832] and the wide support for the Convention proofs the success in achieving this purpose.[833] She furthermore points to the possible advantages of a flexible interpretation technique, including the potential for a more realistic implementation of children's rights and therefore for wider support for the Convention. On the other hand, she points to the potential for abuse, misinterpretation and withdrawal of obligations.[834] However, her statement that the advantages seem to outnumber the disadvantages is not supported with practical examples.

Kaime thoroughly delves into the issue of the cultural legitimacy of the CRC.[835] He identifies that there is a tension between the merits of adopting a universal legal framework and the wish to protect cultural diversity.[836] However, he affirms that culture is not a static, unchangeable concept, but that it is shaped and transformed by the actions and perceptions of individual actors.[837] Therefore, he establishes that if the principles enshrined in the CRC are to be implemented in different cultures and local practices, this requires the acceptance of these principles across the communities in which children live.[838] This is also necessary for societies where people from multiple cultures live together. Further investigation into the interaction between the CRC principles and the involvement of children, family members, medical professionals and other actors for the realization of the right to health of the child will be presented in chapter 6.

831 A.P. Preis, 'Human rights as cultural practice: an anthropological critique', *Human Rights Quarterly* 1995, Volume 18, p. 286. Reproduced in: T. Kaime, *The African Charter on the Rights and Welfare of the Child; A socio-legal perspective'*, Cape Town: Pretoria University Press 2009, p. 3.

832 Countries participating in the negotiation process included 19 western, 6 eastern-European, 15 Asian, 9 African and 8 Latin-American Countries. See: D. Johnson, 'Cultural and Regional Pluralism in the drafting of the UN Convention on the Rights of the Child', in: M. Freeman & P. Veerman (red.), *The ideologies of Children's Rights*, Dordrecht: Martinus Nijhoff Publishers 1992, p. 96. Retrieved from Arts, supra note 827.

833 K. Arts, Inaugural lecture: 'Coming of Age in a world of diversity? An assessment of the UN Convention on the Rights of the Child', 18 November 2011, p. 13. See also: K. Arts, '21 Jaar VN-Verdrag voor de Rechten van het Kind: Een volwassen bijdrage aan kinderrechten in de wereld?', *International Spectator* 2011, year 65, no. 6, June, p. 336.

834 Ibidem supra note 832, p. 339.

835 T. Kaime, *The Convention on the Rights of the Child: A Cultural Legitimacy Critique*, Europa Law Publishing 2011.

836 Ibidem supra note 834, p. 29.

837 Ibidem supra note 834, p. 41.

838 Ibidem supra note 834, p. 48.

5.2.1. UNIVERSALISM AND THE RIGHT TO HEALTH OF THE CHILD

Two different dimensions for interpretation of the highest attainable standard of health of the child can be identified in translating human rights across cultures, namely variations deriving from thematic and variations deriving from regional differences. Whereas the ideal of equality was intended to benefit every individual person, the UDHR was predominantly constituted by white, heterosexual, Christian males.[839] Therefore, the needs of particular subgroups, such as women, children and people from minority cultural or religious groups have not been fully taken into consideration in formulating 'universal principles' of human rights in general.[840] For example, infants are fully dependent on others to survive. Their need for care and protection, e.g. in the family context, in armed conflicts or in humanitarian situations is different from that of adults. Also, children do not regularly participate in democratic processes. The inclusion of their interests in mainstream policy decisions therefore requires special measures and representation by others.

Universal claims are thus primarily based on the opinions of one dominant subgroup of the international community in that period.[841] In later years, several subgroups have asked for attention for the specific protection needed of their particular human rights, which may differ from the core content as determined in the initial discussions. This has resulted in the adoption of separate conventions, such as the Convention on the Rights of the Child (CRC) and the Convention on the Elimination of Discrimination Against Women (CEDAW) specifying the particular human rights violations of the groups involved and in the renewed interpretation of traditional human rights provisions.[842] Brems has further demonstrated that the inclusion of the protection of minority groups under human rights law has broadened the reach and protection level of human rights, but at the same time complicated their interdependence and explanatory value. She gives the example that a national judge deciding upon a case involving a foreign refugee girl, has to combine insights from the domain of children's, women's and minority rights. This is further complicated by the different levels of (sometimes conflicting) national, regional and international legislation applicable, increasingly developing at regional and international levels. Similarly, with respect to achieving the highest attainable standard of health of this girl, considerations deriving from international health law and medical ethics must also be taken into account. Also, the existence of the regional treaties itself reemphasizes the question whether the original universal human rights have universal value.

839 Ibidem supra note 825, Brems.
840 Ibidem supra note 825, Brems.
841 Ibidem supra note 825, Brems.
842 Ibidem supra note 825, Brems.

In addition to these identified thematic restraints to a universal application of human rights, other problems may arise from local differences in applying children's right to health. For example, when discussing the role of parents or the family in ensuring the right of the child to the highest attainable standard of health, the composition of a family strongly affects the influence of parents on their children's health. In the European Union for example, most children live in nuclear families, whereas this picture is changing due to increased levels of divorces in some areas and the influx of broken families and unaccompanied asylum seeking children in others.[843, 844] In other continents, such as Africa, children live in extended families where different family members are de facto considered responsible for realizing children's health and well-being.[845, 846] Heavily influenced by the large-scale HIV/AIDS epidemic, children are cared for by different family members by migrating across the country from family to family.[847] This influences their opportunities to see the same doctor and have access to qualitative health care facilities over time. Also, increasing migration streams between different continents influence the way in which children's health is viewed upon. For example, when children from non-Dutch origin are present at the school doctor with mental health problems, explanations range from a biomedical cause to the influence of spirits or ancestors. These differences must be taken into account when considering medical treatments.

Differences in interpretations of the right to health of the child demonstrate the influence of the (absent) family structures in which children live on the ways in which the right to health is interpreted and implemented. However, Freeman warns against focusing too much on the family by commenting that: 'Children suffer from ideological idealization of the family that assumes that parents love and nurture their children. The case for children's rights is based on the fact that many children do not live in such conditions'.[848] Freeman thus highlights that not all children live in a loving family. Although not explicated, this can be explained as referring to children who are not living in a family at all and of children who are living in a family in which children's best interests are not fully taken into account. The hesitance to approach the realization of children's right to health predominantly from a focus on the family, also becomes apparent in the analysis

843 Heywood, Colin, *A History of Childhood: Children and Childhood in the West from Medieval to Modern Times*, Cambridge, UK: Polity Press 2001.

844 M. Daly, 'Changing family life in Europe: Significance for state and society', *European Societies* 2005, Volume 7, Issue 3, pp. 379–398.

845 L. Blerk & N. Ansell, 'Children's experiences of migration: moving in the wake of AIDS in southern Africa', *Environment and Planning D: Society and Space* 2006, volume 24, pp. 449–471.

846 G. Foster, 'The capacity of the extended family safety net for orphans in Africa', *Psychology, Health & Medicine* 2000, Volume 5, Issue 1, pp. 55–62.

847 L. Young & N. Ansell, 'Fluid Households, Complex Families: The Impacts of Children's Migration as a Response to HIV/AIDS in Southern Africa', *The Professional Geographer* 2003, Volume 55, Issue 4, November, pp. 464–476.

848 M. Freeman, *Human rights, an interdisciplinary approach*, Polity Press 2011, p. 152.

made by Nolan, who argues that the particular inclusion of children's right to health offers a more far reaching protection of this right than when the right to health of the child is strongly related to the rights of the parents and the family.[849] Therefore, the child should be considered as a subject of the right to health in its own right. With respect to the interpretation of the role of the family as clarified in the CRC, Nolan identifies that although there is a strong emphasis on the role of the family in ensuring children's rights, 'it sets out a wide range of rights for children, and makes clear that the best interests of the child are to be accorded priority in all actions concerning them'. On the basis of the rights in the CRC, the rights of the child are thus centrally important, while being grounded in the broader context of the family.

Other differences in interpretations of children's right to health across the world result from different visions on childhood and vulnerability. Whereas in many western countries there is a strict (age) limit between childhood and adulthood, for example by protecting children against child labour, in other cultures taking responsibilities and participating in daily work activities is part of the upbringing process and often a necessary requirement to survive. Instead of a clear-cut age limit there is thus a more fluent transition phase for delineating childhood from adulthood.

Brems concludes that universality does not require uniformity. This implies that whereas children's right to health has to be applied universally in every country of the world, the way in which this right is put into practice can be adjusted to the requirements of the local circumstances. Whereas it is desirable to find the common denominators of human rights across cultures, flexibility and inter-cultural awareness are required in establishing the highest attainable standard of health that can be attained in the local context.[850]

The question then rises, what the margin of appreciation of countries is in setting priorities in the implementation of the right to the highest attainable standard of health in the local context. No clear guidelines exist yet in international law on this issue.[851] In any case, there should be a continuous dialogue on the different possible interpretations within and between different cultures and countries, so that mutual understanding can be enhanced and existing international legal norms developed. This requires an open attitude to listen to people with different visions on children's health upbringing and the willingness to adapt normative frameworks and usual behaviours. Such will necessarily require the input of children, parents, medical professionals and other caretakers, as is becoming

[849] A. Nolan, 'The child's rights to health and the courts', in: J. Harrington. M. Stuttaford (a.o.), *Global Health and human rights, legal and philosphical perspectives*, London: Routledge 2010, p. 146.

[850] M. Obemeyer, 'A cross-cultural perspective on reproductive rights' in: *Human Rights Quarterly* 1995, Issue 17, pp. 366–368. Reproduced in T. Kaime, *The African Charter on the Rights and Welfare of the Child; A socio-legal perspective*', Cape Town: Pretoria University Press 2009, p. 18.

[851] E. Brems, 'Universele grondrechten', *NJB* 2010, no. 6.

clear by the inclusion of the principles of accountability and participation into the basic AAAQ scheme as elaborated in chapter 4. Furthermore, current legal developments in the European region increasingly take into account the explicit role that (individual) children and their families can play in realizing the highest attainable standard of health of the child.

5.3. CHILDREN'S RIGHT TO HEALTH IN EUROPE

In Europe, children's right to health has been extensively elaborated. Both within the European Union and in the Council of Europe, developments have taken place that ground the right to health of all citizens and those of children in particular in different legal documents. Most far-reaching, though non-binding are the recently adopted Guidelines on Child-Friendly Health Care of the Council of Europe as adopted by the Committee of Health Ministers on 21 September 2011 in Lisbon. In this chapter it will be investigated what priorities are set in the elaboration of the right to the highest attainable standard of health of the child in the European region by looking at the relevant legal documents in the European Union and the Council of Europe, including relevant case law of the European Court on Human Rights (ECHR)[852] and interpretative legal instruments such as the Conclusions of the European Committee on Economic and Social Rights.[853]

5.3.1. THE RIGHT TO HEALTH OF THE CHILD IN THE EUROPEAN UNION

The right to health in the EU is laid down in article 35 of the Charter on the Fundamental Rights in the European Union, stating that: 'Everyone has the right of access to preventive health care and the right to benefit from medical treatment under the conditions established by national laws and practices. A high level of human health protection shall be ensured in the definition and implementation of all Union policies and activities'.[854] In the phrasing of this provision, the importance attached to prevention and protection is clear. Furthermore, access to both preventive health care and to medical treatments is prioritized. However, the provision of access is not oriented towards basic health services, such as in the CRC or in the European Social Charter, but towards medical treatments 'under

852 Cases of the ECHR relevant to children were retrieved through using the Theseus Database: www.coe.int/t/dg3/children/caselaw/CaseLawChild_en.asp.

853 The European Committee of Social Rights (ECSR) was set up to judge the conformity of national law and practice with the Charter. It is composed of independent members elected by the Committee of Ministers for a period of six years.

854 Charter of fundamental rights of the European Union, Doc. 2000/C 364/01. available at: www.europarl.europa.eu/charter/pdf/text_en.pdf.

the conditions established by national laws and practices'. The provision thus gives room for individual European Countries to take measures to achieve the highest attainable standard of health of children by referring to their national laws and practices. Examples of elaborated health care standards of individual countries can thus be indicative of the highest attainable standard of health within the European Union.[855]

The opportunity for individual countries to elaborate its own health policy is further elaborated in the very extensive article 168 Treaty on the Functioning of the European Union (TFEU), replacing the previous article 152 of the EC Treaty. Under this new article 168, a strong focus is placed on preventing health problems by stating in paragraph 1 that 'A high level of human health protection shall be ensured in the definition and implementation of all Union policies and activities.' In doing so, paragraph 168(7) provides that the Union 'shall respect the responsibilities of the Member States for the definition of their health policy and for the organization and delivery of health services and medical care. The responsibilities of the Member States shall include the management of health services and medical care and the allocation of the resources assigned to them.' The primary responsibility for ensuring health care thus lies with the Member States. In addition, Union actions shall 'complement national policies' and cooperation between Member States is encouraged 'to improve the complementarity of their health services in cross-border areas'. The key phrase 'a high level of human health protection' in article 35 of the European Charter particularly indicates the intention to go beyond ensuring basic or even intermediate levels of health care. The same phrase is also the starting point of article 168 of the TFEU. Paragraph 5 further expands the phrase by not only referring to 'protect human health' but by also referring to 'improve human health'. The provision thus seems to entail not only an obligation to protect, but also an obligation to actively fulfil. In addition, paragraph 5 not only phrases to protect 'human health' but also to protect 'public health'. The difference lies in a distinctive focus on individual health on the one hand and collective or public health on the other.

In the remainder of article 168 TFEU, several measures are specified that guide the interpretation of the highest level of 'human health protection'. Paragraph 1 provides that all Union actions 'shall be directed towards improving public health, preventing physical and mental illness and diseases, and obviating sources of danger to physical and mental health. Such action shall cover the fight against the major health scourges, by promoting research into their causes, their

[855] See for an actual overview of health systems the European Observatory on Health systems and policies, available at: www.euro.who.int/en/who-we-are/partners/observatory/health-systems-in-transition-hit-series/countries. See also Joint Report on Health systems, prepared by the European Commission and the Economic Policy Committee, 2010. Available at: http://ec.europa.eu/economy_finance/publications/occasional_paper/2010/pdf/ocp74_en.pdf and Working paper on Health systems in the European Union: a comparative study by the European Parliament, 1998. Available at: www.europarl.europa.eu/workingpapers/saco/pdf/101_en.pdf.

transmission and their prevention, as well as health information and education, and monitoring, early warning of and combating serious cross-border threats to health.' From this enumeration, it appears that again a strong focus is placed on preventive measures. On this basis, it seems logical to assume that prioritizing children's right to health is a legitimate focus for realizing the right to health of the general public. This vision is shared by the WHO Regional Office for Europe, which acknowledges that 'The period between birth and 5–6 years of age is critical.'[856] The report elaborates that:

> 'Childhood is the best period in which to act. This is when action is most effective in both promoting good health and preventing ill health in childhood and later life. Health in childhood determines health over the total lifespan and into the next generation. The first years of life lay the foundations for people's achievement of their health potential. How the brain develops in early life determines whether people have the skills to cope with disease risk in later life. Problems in early childhood development have a strong relationship to NCDs in adult life. Health promotion is most effective in the early years of life. Further, disease prevention and control should counter the negative influences on health as early as possible in life, to keep problems from passing into later stages of development. To a large extent, each stage in the development of a child prepares the way for the next. That is why it is important to anticipate risks as and when they are likely to emerge. This means that the wisest policies on children's health focus on early and well-targeted interventions.[857]

Article 24 of the Charter of Fundamental Rights of the EU focuses on the rights of children. In the phrasing of this article, the connection between this article and the CRC is identifiable:

> 1. Children shall have the right to such protection and care as is necessary for their well-being. They may express their views freely. Such views shall be taken into consideration on matters which concern them in accordance with their age and maturity.
> 2. In all actions relating to children, whether taken by public authorities or private institutions, the child's best interests must be a primary consideration.
> 3. Every child shall have the right to maintain on a regular basis a personal relationship and direct contact with both his or her parents, unless that is contrary to his or her interests.

The vision of the child as an individual in need of protection is visible in the words 'the right to such protection and care as is necessary for their well-being' is balanced in paragraph 1 with the view of the child as a capable individual in 'they

[856] WHO Regional Office for Europe, *The European Health Report 2005, Public health action for healthier children and populations*, Copenhagen 2005, p. IX.
[857] Ibidem supra note 855, p. 47.

may express their views freely'. The concepts of 'developing capacities' (§ 1) and of the 'best interests of the child' (§ 2) are primary considerations in all actions relating to children. Aasen comments that these elements are relevant for the medical sector as well as for 'a wide range of measures and services to protect children's health in a broad sense'.[858] For example, children's health is at stake in the youth protection sector, in schools and in institutions for juvenile justice. Aasen argues that ministries of health could play a leadership role in order to streamline activities to protect children's health in these different sectors.[859] On an organizational level this is true, although empowering children and parents also means that they take ownership of their own health.

Following the Treaty of Lisbon, the European Union is under a legal obligation to accede to the European Convention on Human Rights.[860] The Treaty introduces the protection of children's rights among the EU's objectives and internal and external policies. However, as will be elaborated further below, the ECHR does not contain a provision on the right to health. Its accession thus has a limited value for ensuring children's right to health in the EU. All in all, there is a need to investigate other channels to clarify the interpretation of the highest attainable standard of health of the child in the European Union. In the following, the EU strategies, ESC, EACH and Guidelines on Child-Friendly Healthcare will be analysed.

5.3.2. THE EU STRATEGY ON THE RIGHTS OF THE CHILD IN EUROPE

In 2008, the European Parliament adopted a Resolution on a EU strategy on the rights of the child.[861] In this Resolution, subparagraphs 157–170 directly address the right to health of the child and 171–177 are indirectly relevant, such as the paragraph on children's right to be registered at birth. The EU Resolution ensures that pregnant and lactating mothers have the right to access to 'quality pre- and postnatal health care in the public sector to reduce maternal and infant mortality and to prevent transmission of diseases from mother to child.' (no. 159). The principle of non-discrimination is highlighted in the provisions (nos. 166 and 174)

858 H.S. Aasen, 'Children and the right to health protection' in: Toebes, Hartlev, Hendriks & Herrman, *Health and Human Rights in Europe*, Groningen: Intersentia 2012, pp. 227–247, p. 243.

859 Ibidem supra note 857.

860 The European Union's accession to the European Convention on Human Rights is required under Article 6 of the Lisbon Treaty and foreseen by Article 59 of the ECHR as amended by Protocol 14, whose aim is to guarantee the long-term efficiency of the Court by optimizing the filtering and processing of applications entered into force on 1 June 2010.

861 OJ 2009 C41E/24OJ 2009 C41E/24, Towards an EU strategy on the rights of the child – European Parliament resolution of 16 January 2008. Available at: www.europarl.europa.eu/sides/getDoc.do?type=TA&reference=P6-TA-2008-0012&language=EN.

stating that the access to health care must be equal for children of both genders and that particular attention must be given to disadvantaged children and to children of ethnic and social minorities. In order to achieve this equal access for all children, conditions must be created that 'enable every child to have access to all kinds and levels of health services and where necessary to take positive measures to enable disadvantaged groups to benefit from healthcare service options from which they would otherwise remain excluded' (no. 168). Also, the fact is highlighted that invisibility of unregistered children increases their vulnerability and the likelihood that violations of their rights will go unnoticed (no. 171) and more particularly that the absence of a birth certificate may prevent children from gaining access to healthcare services and material assistance from the State (no. 175). Therefore, every child must be legally recognized by being registered at birth (nos. 171 and 173) by 'establishing permanent registration systems operating from the national to village level, available free of charge to the entire population including those living in remote areas, through the provision of, inter alia, mobile registration units where appropriate, adequate training for civil registrars and the allocation of sufficient resources to finance these initiatives (no. 176). For as long as (groups of) children do not have a birth certificate and legal recognition, measures must be taken to ensure that health services are universally provided to all children until the official registration process has been established (no. 175) to prevent children from being excluded from necessary medical care.

The recommendations in the Strategy that are focused on children's health pay extensive attention to sex education, reproduction (pregnancy and lactating) and the prevention of sexually transmitted diseases (nos. 161–165, 167, 169). Reflective of the high living standards and the concomitant welfare diseases in the European Union Member States, is the inclusion of recommendations to address the problems of obesity (no. 157), alcohol-related health problems in children and (pregnant) mothers (no. 167) environmental health and pollution (nos. 158 and 170).

The provisions in the EU Resolution on an EU strategy on the rights of the child thus establish several important benefits to children additional to the existing framework on public health in the TFEU. Most specifically it elaborates upon the region specific health challenges, such as obesity, alcohol, drug and tobacco abuse However, it must be noted that the identified provisions only constitute an obligation of effort and not of result by phrasing that 'measures must be taken'. In line with article 35 in the EU Charter, in which access for everyone is highlighted, the principle of non-discrimination is elaborated extensively in the EU Resolution on a strategy on the rights of the child, thereby ensuring access to all vulnerable groups of children, notwithstanding their official status.

5.3.3. THE WHO STRATEGY ON THE RIGHTS OF THE CHILD IN EUROPE

The WHO Office for Europe has elaborated on the concept of 'access to people-centred health care'. This approach renews the focus on primary health care as laid down in the Declaration of Alma-Ata (1978).[862] This approach goes beyond the narrow medical care concept and takes a holistic view on health as a starting point.[863] It implies a fundamental change in service delivery to enable people-centred care, being characterized as 'coordinated, integrated, comprehensive and continuous and accessible to all'.[864] This approach attaches great importance to the continuity of care. This concept has several dimensions, namely practically, the follow-up from one visit to another,[865] informational continuity, meaning the routine keeping of medical records for each child and visit over the entire time-span and across all different sectors involved in the health care of the child, longitudinal continuity in the place where the health care is provided and last but not least interpersonal continuity, being defined as 'a continuing personal relationship between the patient and the care provider characterized by personal trust and respect'.[866] This continuous relation between patient and medical professional can go as far as integrating preventive, curative, rehabilitative and palliative care activities all with one primary health care provider that is close to the child and its family.[867] Such an approach could be highly beneficial for children because it increases the transparency and the personal attention of the medical trajectory.

The WHO Office for Europe has furthermore developed a strategy for child and adolescent health in 2005.[868] This strategy is not binding, but it offers support to countries in providing best practices and measures to realize children's right to health. The strategy takes four principles as a starting point: 1. taking a life-course approach from prenatal life to adolescence; 2. it recognizes the need for equity and policies to address it; 3. it promotes intersectoral action and addressing the

---

862 See chapter I.

863 The WHO renewed its commitment to this holistic approach to health in The World health report 2008. *The world health report 2008, Primary health care – Now more than ever*, Geneva, World Health Organization, 2008, Available at: www.searo.who.int/LinkFiles/Reports_whr08_en.pdf.

864 *The world health report 2008, Primary health care – Now more than ever*, Geneva, World Health Organization, 2008, Available at: www.searo.who.int/LinkFiles/Reports_whr08_en.pdf.

865 Starfield (a.o.), 'Continuity and coordination in primary care: their achievement and utility', *Medical Care* 1976, Issue 14, pp. 625–636.

866 J.W. Saultz, 'Defining and measuring interpersonal continuity of care', *Annals of Family Medicine* 2003, Issue 1, pp. 134–143. Available at: www.annfammed.org/cgi/content/full/1/3/134.

867 WHO Office for Europe, European Health Report 2009 Health and Health systems, p. 122. Available at: www.euro.who.int/__data/assets/pdf_file/0009/82386/E93103.pdf.

868 U.N. Doc. EUR/05/5048378, WHO Regional Office for Europe, *European strategy for child and adolescent health and development. From resolution to action*, Copenhagen 2005. Available at: www.euro.who.int/__data/assets/pdf_file/0020/79400/E87710.pdf.

fundamental determinants of health; 4. it promotes participation and the need to involve young people in decisions about their own services. Paragraph 14 sets out the overall goal, which is 'to enable children and adolescents in the European Region to realize their full potential for health and development and to reduce the burden of avoidable disease and mortality.' This goal is to be achieved by taking a life-course approach which sets out in detail the different provisions required during the different phases of a child's life, starting with the pre-conception period, pregnancy, during delivery. During the first four weeks of life, during the first year of life, early childhood, late childhood and adolescence.[869] In addition to outlining the possible activities that can be undertaken by different sectors,[870] the Report elaborates on the role that children can play themselves in ensuring their right to health by stating that 'Experience has shown that the participation of children and adolescents is crucial to the successful development and implementation of strategies, policies and services focused on this population group. Participation needs to be more than lip service; it requires the genuine engagement of young people.'[871] With respect to the participation of young children, the report elaborates that 'younger children may not have the skills to be directly involved in policy-making and planning, it is, nevertheless, still possible to include advocates on their behalf, such as adults with particular expertise in and understanding of young children's needs.' It even appears that life-style interventions are more effective if they have been developed with the involvement of children and young children.[872]

5.3.4. THE ROLE OF CHILDREN IN ENSURING THE HIGHEST ATTAINABLE STANDARD OF HEALTH OF THE CHILD IN THE EUROPEAN UNION

The opportunity of individuals to become involved in realizing the highest attainable standard of health of children in the European Union can only indirectly be derived from article 168 TFEU, which speaks of 'health information and education'. Still, it is not formulated as a separate right or duty of individuals, but as a general measure that should be taken by States. Several EU Documents offer additional insight into the potential role of individuals in realizing the highest attainable standard of health of children in the European Union.

The Council's conclusions on early detection and treatment of communication disorders, such as an impairment in hearing, vision and speech, in children

[869] Ibidem supra note 825, pp. 7–12.
[870] See for a further elaboration chapter 6 on the responsibilities of the different actors in involved in realizing the right to health of the child.
[871] Ibidem supra note 861, p. 17, § 83.
[872] Ibidem supra note 861, p. 17, § 84. See also Chapter II on General Comments 7 and 12 to the CRC.

establishes the link between children's health and their opportunities in life by stating in paragraph 2 that 'each EU citizen, and children in particular, should have equal opportunities to develop.[873] This should be done by making accessible the appropriate tools and procedures to prevent, detect, treat and to monitor health problems'. Paragraph 7 furthermore establishes the importance of children's health for their future life and development by stating that 'children's good health is fundamental for their proper development and influences their quality of life and social and economical situation in the future'.[874] Thereto, *particularly crucial for children* is that 'prevention, early detection, monitoring and active surveillance play a significant role in warding off the development of diseases and disorders.' The prevention of health problems at the earliest possible stage, during childhood, is thus set as a priority.

This focus on early intervention for preventing future health problems is also found in the Council's conclusions on preventing chronic respiratory diseases in children.[875] Paragraph 15 emphasizes that 'conditions before birth and in early childhood influence health in adult life.' Thereto, both 'children and pregnant women must be protected against negative influences of environmental factors.' The role of pregnant women in ensuring their children's future health is thereby explicitly recognized. Similarly, the role of pregnant women and young mothers in influencing the health of their children by choosing the nutrition of their newborn children is acknowledged in the Guideline on infant formulae, elaborating that Member States must take appropriate measures to provide information that ensures adequate use of artificial nutrition, meanwhile promoting the use of breast feeding.[876]

The central role for children in managing their own health status is expressly highlighted in several instances. For example, in the Council's conclusions on preventing chronic respiratory diseases in children, it is recognized that there are several 'important elements for the prevention and treatment of respiratory diseases in children', namely children's ability for 'self-management, their participation in decisions affecting them, taking into account their age and

---

873 EU Document 2011/C 361/4, Council conclusions of 2 December 2011 on early detection and treatment of communication disorders in children, including the use of e-Health tools and innovative solutions. Published in the Official Journal of the European Union on 10th December 2011. Available at: http://eur-lex.europa.eu/LexUriServ/LexUriServ.do?uri=OJ:C:2011:361:0009:0010:EN:PDF. Article 8 defines a communication disorder as an impairment in hearing, vision or speech that influences the ability to comprehend and receive information.

874 Ibidem supra note 872.

875 EU Document 2011/C 361/5, Council conclusions of 2 December 2011 on prevention, early diagnosis and treatment of chronic respiratory diseases in children. Published in the Official Journal of the European Union on 10 December 2011. Available at: http://eur-lex.europa.eu/LexUriServ/LexUriServ.do?uri=OJ:C:2011:361:0009:0010:EN:PDF.

876 EU Document Commission directive 2006/141/EC of 22 December 2006 on infant formulae and follow-on formulae and amending Directive 1999/21/EC, § 28. Published in the Official Journal of the European Union on 31 December 2006, L 401/1. Available at: http://eur-lex.europa.eu/LexUriServ/LexUriServ.do?uri=OJ:L:2006:401:0001:0001:EN:PDF.

maturity, as well as the active involvement of the parents and family.'[877] Both the active involvement of children themselves and of their parents is thus expressly required. According to paragraphs 16 and 19, this active involvement is to be achieved by 'continuous health education of children, parents, teachers and training of health professionals' in preventing and responding to chronic respiratory diseases.[878] Furthermore, paragraph 20 requires that 'health professionals' and patients' organizations are engaged to work towards more patient empowerment in the process of prevention, early diagnosis and treatment of chronic respiratory diseases.' Children and parents thus do not stand alone in the process of empowerment in health. They must be enabled and supported by professionals that are active in the health care field.

Similarly, the need to actively involve children and their family in managing children's mental health status is highlighted by the European Parliament, stating that 'any future proposal by the Commission should involve partnership and consultation with and the participation of those who have experienced or are experiencing mental health problems, their families and carers and advocacy NGOs, associations of family members and other interested parties, so as to make decision-making processes more representative and inclusive, and should promote networking among members of the families of psychiatric patients'.[879] The role of children themselves in managing their own health status is reinforced in paragraph 55, stating that it is essential to apply 'individualised methods of promoting mental health, taking into account the particular needs of individuals and target groups'. With regard to improving adolescents' health, possible measures to stimulate adolescents to take responsibility for their own health are communicated in the Council's conclusions on the health and well-being of young people.[880] These include the involvement of young people 'in the development and implementation of health-related initiatives, particularly by peer learning', 'in all areas' as well as by 'strengthening the partnership with young people and their organizations' and by 'promoting the 'youth' dimension in health-related initiatives and the implementation of measures for the health of

877 EU Document 2011/C 361/5, Council conclusions of 2 December 2011 on prevention, early diagnosis and treatment of chronic respiratory diseases in children. Published in the Official Journal of the European Union on 10th December 2012. Available at: http://eur-lex.europa.eu/LexUriServ/LexUriServ.do?uri=OJ:C:2011:361:0009:0010:EN:PDF.

878 The issue of health education of all actors involved, including vulnerable groups of children, health professionals and others is also mentioned in the Council's Conclusion on the prevention of injury and the promotion of safety. EU Document 2007/C 164/01, p. 3. Available at: http://eur-lex.europa.eu/LexUriServ/LexUriServ.do?uri=OJ:C:2007:164:0001:0002:EN:PDF.

879 EU Document 2006/C 305 E/148. Resolution of the European Parliament on improving the mental health of the population. Towards a strategy on mental health for the European Union (2006/2058(INI)). Published in the Officical Journal of the European Union on 14 December 2006. Available at: http://eur-lex.europa.eu/LexUriServ/LexUriServ.do?uri=OJ:C:2006:305E:0148:0155:EN:PDF.

880 EU Document 2008/C 319/01, Resolution of the Council and the Representatives of the Governments of the Member States, meeting within the Council of 20 November 2008 on the health and well-being of young people.

young people'. In doing so, it is believed, that not only will young people be better able to take responsibility over their own health, but this will also raise their self-esteem and increase their autonomy, in particular by raising young people's awareness of the positive effects of a healthy lifestyle and of the risks related to their health'. The notion that children should be involved in the design of health services and strategies is also put forward in the European Health Report, stating that 'Implementation strategies are most successful when they are based on comprehensive national planning that involves children themselves, utilizes the contributions of families and communities, schools, the mass media, the health system and governments'.[881]

In the discussion on children and the right to health protection in the European context, Aasen focuses on the need to tackle inequalities in health. It has been established that socio-economic living conditions have a strong linkage to the increasing numbers of obesity in school children, alcohol and drug abuse, mental health problems and chronic respiratory conditions or allergies. Aasen comments that strategies at the individual level are not sufficient and that public health initiatives are urgently required.[882] Although this is a legitimate claim, caution must be taken by approaching children as one or several groups of vulnerable children that are reached by many gross-scale standardized measures. In developing and applying such measures, the view of the child as an independent holder of human rights must be kept at the forefront and also as a person in its own right must be respected. Different children have different experiences, views and needs which must be taken into account in determining the highest attainable standard of health and the health measures that are required to achieve this standard of health.

5.3.5. THE ROLE OF FAMILIES IN ENSURING THE HIGHEST ATTAINABLE STANDARD OF HEALTH OF THE CHILD

The Guideline on early detection and treatment of communication disorders in children, stipulates that 'Awareness of the problem, integrated and coordinated multidisciplinary approaches, which must be accompanied by active parental involvement during the whole process of child development and across healthcare and educational settings, are of significant importance.'[883] Both in the context

---

[881] WHO Regional Office for Europe, *The European Health Report 2005, Public health action for healthier children and populations*, Copenhagen 2005, p. 80.

[882] H.S. Aasen, 'Children and the right to health protection', in: Toebes, Hartlev, Hendriks & Herrman, *Health and Human Rights in Europe*, Groningen: Intersentia 2012, pp. 227–247, particularly p. 230.

[883] EU Document 2011/C 361/4, § 11, Council conclusions of 2 December 2011 on early detection and treatment of communication disorders in children, including the use of e-Health tools and innovative solutions. Published in the Official Journal of the European Union on 10 December

of ensuring the health of adolescents[884] and in improving the mental health of the population[885] the significant influence of family members for preventing, mitigating and responding to mental health problems is signalled in different life stages, such as early childhood (§ 18, 19 and 22), childhood, adolescence (§ 20) generally (§ 56) by acknowledging that 'whereas the precondition for good mental health is an upbringing in a healthy family environment providing both material and psychological security and parental love' (§ 18) and that 'mental health problems commonly have their roots in early childhood', (§ 22), urged is for 'support for mothers during the prenatal and postnatal periods in order to prevent depression' (§ 19), because good mental health of mothers and parents helps children to develop without hindrance and grow into healthy adults'. In this phrasing, the future health of children is directly linked to the (mental) health of their parents or caretakers during the upbringing of their children.

5.3.6. THE ROLE OF MEDICAL PROFESSIONALS

The role of professionals in responding to health problems in children is also addressed. Particularly with respect to children, a multidisciplinary and multi-agency approach is propagated for supporting children or adolescents with developmental or behavioural problems or eating disorders.[886] Thereto, continuous training for intermediaries and family practitioners is required,[887] as well as a critical reflection over the appropriate treatments for children, which extend to medicines that are particularly suitable for children, although the term treatment should extent to influencing psychosocial and environmental factors, because 'particularly in the case of children and young people, the growing medicalisation and pathologisation of life stages, without a comprehensive search for causes is criticized'.[888] Therefore, factors such as personal experiences, family, social support and living and working conditions must be taken into account in determining the causes of mental health problems, whereas an appropriate social

2012. Available at: http://eur-lex.europa.eu/LexUriServ/LexUriServ.do?uri=OJ:C:2011:361:0009:0010:EN:PDF.

884 EU Document 2008/C 319/01, Resolution of the Council and the Representatives of the Governments of the Member States, meeting within the Council of 20 November 2008 on the health and well-being of young people. In point 6 is noted that 'parents play a vital role in the well-being and healthy environment of young people and further measures should therefore be taken to support them.'

885 EU Document 2006/C 305 E/148. Resolution of the European Parliament on improving the mental health of the population. Towards a strategy on mental health for the European Union (2006/2058(INI)). Published in the Official Journal of the European Union on 14 December 2006. Available at: http://eur-lex.europa.eu/LexUriServ/LexUriServ.do?uri=OJ:C:2006:305E:0148:0155:EN:PDF.

886 Ibidem supra note 883, § 20.

887 Ibidem supra note 883, § 23 and 39.

888 Ibidem supra note 883, § 48.

and work environment as well as family and community support is required to provide support to people with mental health problems.[889]

5.4. THE INTERPRETATION OF THE RIGHT TO HEALTH OF THE CHILD BY THE COUNCIL OF EUROPE

This paragraph will discuss the relevant treaties and recommendations of the Council of Europe on the right to health of the child. The next paragraph will address the Guidelines on child-friendly health care separately, because these constitute a significant step forward in the elaboration of the concept of the highest attainable standard of health of the child.

5.4.1. INTERPRETATION OF THE RIGHT TO HEALTH OF THE CHILD IN THE EUROPEAN SOCIAL CHARTER

The European Social Charter[890] is central in ensuring children's rights in Europe through two channels: firstly, it addresses social rights directly relevant for children, such as article 8 ESC, (special protection for employed pregnant women), article 16 (the right of the family to social, legal and economic protection), article 11 (the right to protection of health) and article 13 (the right to adequate assistance, in particular by benefits under a social security system, in case of sickness for all nationals and people on the territory). Article 19 furthermore ensures that services for health, medical attention and good hygienic conditions must be provided for migrant workers and their families. In these articles, children's rights are intrinsically related to the rights of their families. A dual focus is found on providing protection on the one hand and on providing health services and adequate assistance on the other hand.

Secondly, the European Social Charter contains specific rights relating exclusively to children, such as article 7 (the right of children and young persons to protection) and article 17 (the right of children and young persons to social, legal and economic protection).[891] Articles 7–9 of the ESH, persons under 18 years of age and pregnant women are provided with protection rights in their working environment. Particularly relevant to the right to health of the child, article 8

---

889 Ibidem supra note 883, § 47–48.

890 The European Social Charter ensures economic and social human rights, such as the right to housing, health, social protection and non-discrimination. It was adopted in 1961 and revised in 1996, being signed by 47 member states of the Council and ratified by 39.

891 Children's rights under the European Social Charter, Information document prepared by the secretariat of the ESC, March 2009, p. 1 and 2. See also the revised European Social Charter ETS 163, 3.V.1996.

of the European Social Charter provides protection to pregnant women, thus also affecting their unborn children. This protection includes the right of the mother to paid maternity leave of at least 14 weeks, the right to maternity pay, the prohibition of dismissal during pregnancy, the provision of sufficient time and regulations for nursing and healthy working conditions. Article 11 provides for an elaborated framework of measures required to ensure the right to health, namely the removal of the causes of ill-health, the establishment of advisory and educational facilities for the promotion of health and for the encouragement of individual responsibility and the prevention of accidents, epidemic, endemic and other diseases. Although both the family-related rights as well as the child-specific rights have a strong focus on children's right to protection (of their health), there is also explicit attention for the role of individuals in taking responsibility over their own health, being supported by the provision of educational facilities for health promotion to enable them to take the individual responsibility for their own health.

Under the European Social Charter States have the duty to ensure 'the best possible state of health for the population according to existing knowledge'.[892] This implies that existing knowledge is determinative in establishing the 'best possible state of health'. Furthermore, as explained in the information materials of the Secretariat of the European Social Council, this phrase means that avoidable health risks must be prevented as indicated by important health indicators such as life expectancy and principal causes of death, as compared to the European averages. Infant and maternal mortality must be reduced to rates as close to zero as possible.[893] Health measures to achieve these targets can generally be divided in health promotion and health provision initiatives.[894] Health promotion includes preventive measures (environmental health, immunisation, prevention of accidents), education (personal and public behaviour and health education at school) and the implementation of health regulations (occupational health, children's, women's and elderly persons' health). Mikkola asserts that health education for children is only sufficient if this is part of the school curricula and continued throughout basic education.[895]

The section on health provision most specifically implies the right to have adequate access to health for the entire population. Furthermore, health care must be available to all children without discrimination, including refugee children

[892] The right to health and the European Social Charter, Information document prepared by the secretariat of the ESC, March 2009, p. 9. Conclusions XV-2, Denmark, pp. 126–129 and United Kingdom, p. 599.

[893] Conclusions 2003, Romania, p. 390.
45 Conclusions XV-2, Belgium, pp. 93–96; Conclusions 2003, France, p. 146.

[894] The right to health and the European Social Charter, Information document prepared by the secretariat of the ESC, March 2009, pp. 2–10.

[895] M. Mikkola, *Social Human Rights of Europe*, Karelactio 2010, p. 485.

and undocumented children.[896] Also, vaccination programmes must be widely accessible and there must be high vaccination coverage rates.[897] This right to have access to health care has four central implications:[898]

1) the cost of health care should be borne, at least in part, by the community as a whole;[899]
2) health costs should not place an excessive burden on individuals; hereto measures must be taken so that medical costs are not only carried by people from disadvantaged populations;[900]
3) access to treatment must be based on transparent criteria, not causing unnecessary delay while assessing a patient's need for medical help. These criteria should address the risk of deterioration of the health status in both clinical (immediate) and quality of life terms;[901]
4) there must be an adequate number of health care professionals and equipment (at least 3 beds per thousand population).[902]

It appears from these implications, that whereas the total costs should be borne by the entire community, 'no excessive burden' should be placed on individuals. The particular position of individuals is thus taken into account in a protective sense. Furthermore, preventive and primary health care measures are prioritized for achieving health for all. This should give all individuals the opportunity to realize a basic level of health care. Involvement of individuals in ensuring their own level of health is stimulated by organizing health education.

The broadly elaborated article 17 ESC, lastly, provides that States Parties take all necessary measures to ensure that children 'have the care, the assistance, the education and the training they need' (§ 1a) and that states undertake 'to protect children against negligence, violence or exploitation' (§ 1b) and 'provide protection and special aid for children temporarily or definitively deprived of their family's support' (§ 1c). The phrasing in § 1a obliges States to protect children against the detrimental (health) consequences of negligence and violence against children. This is important, because medical professionals are often the first to

---

896 See International Federation of Human Rights Leagues (FIDH) v. France, Complaint No. 14/2003.

897 See Belgium and Turkey, where the situation was found to be in breach of Article 11§ 3 owing to insufficient coverage rates for certain diseases (ECSR, Conclusions XV-2). Reproduced in the Factsheet on the right to health and the European Social Charter, Information document prepared by the secretariat of the ESC, March 2009, p. 5.

898 The right to health and the European Social Charter, Information document prepared by the secretariat of the ESC, March 2009, pp. 9–10.

899 Conclusions I, pp. 59–60, Statement of Interpretation on Article 11; Conclusions XV-2, Addendum, Cyprus, pp. 26–28.

900 Conclusions XVII-2, Portugal, pp. 680–683.

901 Conclusions XV-2, United Kingdom, p. 599.

902 Conclusions XV-2, Addendum, Turkey, p. 257.

signal instances of child abuse and neglect, because they are allowed to conduct physical examinations on children.

5.4.2. THE BIOMEDICAL CONVENTION

The ESC takes a broader approach by focusing on both health care and underlying determinants of health than the other health-related convention of the Council of Europe, the Biomedical Convention.[903] The Biomedical Convention focuses more narrowly on the protection of human dignity in the field of biology and medicine.[904] As such, it focuses on the provisions of health care access by stipulating in article 3 that 'Parties, taking into account health needs and available resources, shall take appropriate measures with a view to providing, within their jurisdiction, equitable access to health care of appropriate quality.' In doing so, article 2 stipulates that 'the primacy of the human being shall prevail over the sole interest of society or science'. With respect to children, it is furthermore elaborated in article 6, 17 and 20 BC respectively that whereas authorization for a medical treatment, for inclusion in medical research or for organ donation may be given by the representative of a minor, 'the opinion of the minor shall be taken into consideration as an increasingly determining factor in proportion to his or her age and degree of maturity.' With respect to medical research, this must further be beneficial for the health of the child and the child must not object, whereas organ donation by children is forbidden unless several strict conditions are met.[905]

The Explanatory Memorandum to the Biomedicine Convention elaborates that healthcare must be of a fitting standard and that it must be subject to continuous quality assessment.[906] Aassen argues that this must be viewed in relation to children's particular vulnerabilities and needs.[907]

---

903 The Convention for the protection of Human Rights and Dignity of the Human Being with regard to the Application of Biology and Medicine: Convention on Human Rights and Biomedicine CETS No. 164 entered into force on 1 December 1999.

904 H.S. Aasen, 'Children and the right to health protection', in: Toebes, Hartlev, Hendriks & Herrman (a.o), *Health and Human Rights in Europe*, Groningen: Intersentia 2012, p. 233.

905 Article 20 Biomedicine Convention sets several conditions which must be met before organ donation by a minor is allowed. These include 1. there is no compatible donor available who has the capacity to consent; 2. the recipient is a brother or sister of the donor; 3. the donation must have the potential to be life-saving for the recipient; 4. the potential donor does not object.

906 Explanatory Memorandum to the Biomedicine Convention, § 24–25, Council of Europe 1996.

907 H.S. Aasen, 'Children and the right to health protection', in: Toebes, Hartlev, Hendriks & Herrman (a.o.), *Health and Human Rights in Europe*, Groningen: Intersentia 2012, p. 233.

5.4.3. KEY HEALTH ISSUES IN THE RECOMMENDATIONS OF THE COUNCIL OF EUROPE

The Council of Ministers and the Parliamentary Assembly of the Council of Europe have also adopted several non-binding recommendations on the health of children and adolescents. A broad range of topics have dealt with the interaction between children, their family and the state in ensuring the (right to) health of children. Relevant health issues addressed include the safeguarding of children and young people against obesity and diabetes II,[908] the health issues of teenagers in distress,[909] the safeguarding of the health of children living in single parent families,[910] the treatment of children with ADHD[911] and the care of children from birth until age eight.[912]

In the contents of the recommendations of the Council of Europe, a development can be discerned in which the role of the child is strengthened over the years. Whereas the child was already regarded as an individual in his own right in 1981, its active involvement in determining his own lifestyle is becoming increasingly dominant. For example, in the recommendation of the Parliamentary Assembly on controlling the diagnosis and treatment of hyperactive children in Europe (2002),[913] most elements address the responsibilities of the 'medical, scientific and pharmaceutical industry' in (§ 7) as well as the international organizations and member states involved (§ 8). Only in the last paragraph (§ 8-3-c) is mentioned that 'the Committee of Ministers is recommended...to invite the governments of the member states...to produce information material designed for *parents* of hyperactive children explaining what possibilities exist for improving their condition'. No mention is made of the role of children or teenagers themselves in managing their own hyperactivity, although they are the first who suffer from its existence and who may benefit from any improvements.

In more recent recommendations, the Council of Europe has acknowledged that 'there is a greater awareness than before of children as individuals with their

908 Recommendation of the Council of Ministers of the Council of Europe. 'Safeguarding children and young people against obesity and diabetes II', (1966) 2011. See also Resolution 1804 (2011) of the Parliamentary Assembly on Safeguarding children and young people from obesity and type 2 diabetes.

909 Recommendation of the Parliamentary Assembly of the Council of Europe. 'Teenagers in distress: a social and health-based approach to youth malaise', REC (1632) 2003.

910 Recommendation of the Council of Ministers of the Council of Europe. 'On securing and promoting the health of single-parent families', REC (4) 1997.

911 Recommendation of the Parliamentary Assembly of the Council of Europe. 'Controlling the diagnosis and treatment of hyperactive children in Europe, REC (1562) 2002.

912 Recommendation of the Council of Ministers of the Council of Europe. 'Concerning the care and education of children from birth to the age of eight, REC (3) 1981. See also the Recommendation of the Council of Ministers of the Council of Europe. 'On child day-care', REC (8) 2002.

913 Resolution 1804 (2011) of the Parliamentary Assembly on Safeguarding children and young people from obesity and type 2 diabetes.

own rights'.[914] Thereto, it is elaborated that 'children need to be able to grow up and develop according to their own capacities and to receive acknowledgement for that, the need for security, stability and confidence in their environment and their relationships, and the need for unconditional love and acceptance; the need to create possibilities for children to make their opinions heard on matters concerning them, and to ensure that their views are taken into account in decision-making processes, respecting parents as the first educators of the child'.[915] In this vision on children, both the direct involvement of children and the primary responsibility of parents in caring for their children is apparent.

The important role of the family was already acknowledged in 1981 by stating that 'the child will normally depend primarily on his family to recognize and secure these rights. It also becomes evident from the health-related recommendations for children growing up in single-parent families. The recommendation on securing health in single-parent families qualifies living in a single parent family as 'a major public health problem', because the heavy burden goes hand in hand with psychological and physical stress. Therefore, many measures are suggested for preventing and mitigating the negative health impacts on children by growing up in a single parent family, such as the early identification of specific health problems, strengthening of personal skills, the provision of self-help groups and counselling services and day centres that are adjusted to the working hours of single-parents and that can respond to the needs of single parents when their children are sick. In doing so, it is furthermore recommended that in establishing such services, single parent families must be consulted and involved in the design of services so that these will best respond to their needs. To counter the risk of stigma, the Council of Europe stipulates in part I.2 that 'The health policy should respect the current diversity of family structures, make efforts to integrate them, accept the changing quality and content of family life and afford equal treatment to different types of family.'

The family thus operates within a wider social framework from which it should be able to obtain the support it needs to fulfil its obligations. In providing such support, care should be taken not to undermine parental responsibilities towards the child.'[916] With respect to the functioning of the health sector, it is established that 'health services should work with, and through, the family to provide continuity of experience for the child.'[917] In addition, the state is charged with the responsibility 'to assist parents and others responsible for the child to secure the conditions necessary for the child's development' and to ensure that

914 Ibidem supra note 911.

915 Ibidem supra note 911.

916 Recommendation of the Council of Ministers of the Council of Europe. 'Concerning the care and education of children from birth to the age of eight, REC (3) 1981, § I.A.

917 Ibidem supra note 915.

'services responsible for the care and protection of children conform to standards established by competent authorities, particularly in the area of health'.[918]

In the 2003 recommendation that deals with the issues of teenagers in distress,[919] more attention is paid to the role of the individual youngsters themselves, by stating in § 9 that 'to strengthen the ability of young people to cope with the uncertainty and unpredictability of their future, programs to foster resilience should be made an integral part of general youth policies'. At the same time, the necessity to establish a supporting social network is clearly established by indicating 'the supportive role of the family' (§ 5), the need to ensure 'access to advice and counseling in a friendly and supportive environment' (§ 8) and 'to devise health education programs' (§ 10-4-b), giving evidence of a balance between strengthening the role of teenagers and establishing a strong and supporting social network.

In a more recent recommendation, it appears that the Parliamentary Assembly aims to empower the child to take responsibility over the realization of its own right to health. For example, resolution 1804 on safeguarding children against obesity and diabetes II, contains several provisions that call for educational measures to inform children and young people (and their parents) about (5.4) 'the benefits of healthy eating habits, as well as the dangers and the long-term consequences of nutritionally unbalanced fast-food consumption and the risks of poor health due to induced obesity;' Furthermore, measures are propagated to (6.2) promote active behaviour and provide for opportunities to become active and to (6.1) raise awareness among children about the nutritional value of food instead of regarding it as a way of comforting themselves when they experience negative emotions. Full participation of children is furthermore stimulated in active behaviour (6.6) as well as in (10) the design of public health programs.

The last step in the increasing recognition of children's right to involvement by the Council of Europe is the adoption of the Recommendation on Promoting the participation by children in decisions affecting them.[920] Paragraph 3 mentions that children should be involved, ranging from dialogues with decision-makers at all levels to individual decisions that concern children. It particularly mentions health, medical care and family policy (§ 3) as well as in programs for violence prevention (§ 8).

---

918 Ibidem supra note 909.

919 Recommendation of the Parliamentary Assembly of the Council of Europe. 'Teenagers in distress: a social and health-based approach to youth malaise', REC (1632) 2003.

920 EU Doc. 12080, Recommendation 1864, on Promoting the participation by children in decisions affecting them, adopted at the 1069th meeting of the Ministers' Deputies, 4 November 2009.

5.4.4. THE EUROPEAN CONVENTION ON HUMAN RIGHTS

The right to health as such is not incorporated in the European Convention on Human Rights. However, 'the protection of health' is mentioned in article 8-2 as a possible justification for interfering with the right to respect for family life as laid down in article 8-1 ECHR. This means that the protection of health, under circumstances, can be prioritized over the protection of the family life.

Although the right to health is not included in the European Convention on Human Rights, the right to health for children has been explained by the European Committee on Social Rights (ECSR): it has been established that medical services must exist at schools and periodical medical examinations must be carried out throughout schooling.[921] Examples include health education in nurseries and infant schools on 'respect for the body' and training in high school on ways to decrease high risk behaviour among adolescents. However, the Committee identified that some of the programs were not integrated in the regular curriculum and dependent on the initiative of individual teachers.

The European Court of Human Rights has considered children's right to health in a limited number of cases. All cases dealt with procedural issues related to medical care around childbirth.[922] The European Court on Human Rights applies the doctrine of the 'margin of appreciation' to take into account differences in cultural interpretations of the provisions in the ECHR and the ESC.[923] The margin of appreciation is applied to distinguish between matters that are left to national discretion and matters that are of such importance that similar conditions are required for countries with different cultural or ideological standpoints.[924] Although case law is not particularly consistent on the determination of the

[921] Belgium and France, European Committee on Social Rights, Conclusions XV-2 (2001), pp. 96–97 and 208–209.

[922] For cases involving children's right to health see:
- *Tysiąc v. Poland*, 20 March 2007: "Lawful therapeutic abortion in Poland";
- *Byrzykowski v. Poland*, 27 June 2006: "Death of a woman during childbirth and her child's ensuing health problems";
- *Yardimci v. Turkey*, 5 January 2010: "Child suffering infirmity attributable, according to its parents, to inappropriate medical treatment during childbirth, in Turkey";
- *Oyal v. Turkey*, 23 March 2010: "Child contaminated by HIV when given blood transfusions immediately after his birth, in Turkey".

[923] The doctrine of the margin of appreciation was first addressed in the *Belgian Linguistics Case* – 'In the case "relating to certain aspects of the laws on the use of languages in education in Belgium" v Belgium', Application no 1474/62; 1677/62; 1691/62; 1769/63; 1994/63; 2126/64 and further elaborated in *Handyside v. United Kingdom*, Application no. 5493/72, 7 December 1976. In this second case the Court judged that it had limited competence to control the Treaty Parties to ECHR and judged that article 10 ECHR had not been violated. Following this judgement, the doctrine of the margin of appreciation of countries was then applied to other provisions.

[924] F. Mahony, 'Marvellous richness of Diversity or Individious Cultural Relativism', *Human Rights Law Journal* 1998, Issue 19, p. 1.

margin of appreciation,[925] several elements have been identified to influence the decisions of the Court on this matter,[926] namely the level of consensus on the matter between European countries, the nature of the protected objective and thirdly, the interests of the complainant. Last but not least the socio-economic policy of the State Party is taken into account.[927] Especially from the last element, it appears that there is room to take the interests of the complainant into account in interpreting their right to health. Furthermore, it appears from the cases that have been dealt with by the Court, that prevention of health problems is prioritized by making medical services and regular examinations particularly available for children.

5.5. CHILD-FRIENDLY HEALTH CARE: A STEP FORWARD?

5.5.1. THE GUIDELINES ON CHILD-FRIENDLY HEALTHCARE: A FOCUS ON CHILDREN AND THEIR FAMILIES

Holistic interpretation of the different CRC provisions implies a more far reaching standard for achieving children's right to health than the isolated application of article 24 CRC. For European countries this more far reaching standard has recently been concretized in the Guidelines of the Committee of Ministers of the Council of Europe on child-friendly health care.[928] As such, it establishes an explicit legal framework for determining the peculiarities of child-friendly health care in the European context.

These Guidelines provide for a comprehensive framework on children's rights in health care. The Guidelines have been developed in the context of the Council of Europe Program 'Building a Europe for and with children',[929] the 2009–2011

925 J. van de Lanotte & Y. Haeck, *Handboek EVRM. Deel 1 Algemene beginselen*, Antwerpen-Oxford: Intersentia 2005, p. 220.

926 J. Gerards, 'Methoden en beginselen van interpretatie en toetsing, inclusief de margin of appreciation-doctrine', in: J.H. Gerards, H.J. Janssen & J. van der Velde (red.), *EVRM Rechtspraak en Commentaar*, Den Haag: SDU 2010, aanv. 88 (part 2.1), pp. 56–87. See also: J.H. Gerards, 'Pluralism, Deference and the Margin of Appreciation Doctrine', *European Law Journal* 2011, Volume 17, no. 1, pp. 80–120.

927 Ibidem supra note 911.

928 The Guidelines on child-friendly health care were adopted in Lisbon on 28st September 2011 in the context of the Strategy 'Building a Europe for and with children' 2009–2011.

929 The program 'Building a Europe for and with children' was implemented in 2005 after the 3rd Summit of Heads of State and Government of the Council of Europe I Warshaw and comprises two strands: the promotion of children's rights and the protection of children against violence. See for more information: www.coe.int/t/dg3/children. The Program contains several projects including child-friendly social services, children's participation, child-friendly justice and child-friendly health care. See also www.coe.int/t/dg3/children/participation/Newdefault_en.asp. and www.coe.int/t/dghl/standardsetting/childjustice.

Strategy for the Rights of the Child[930] and the current 2012–2015 Strategy for the Rights of the Child. They build on previously existing Recommendations of the Council of Europe, the previously adopted Guidelines on child friendly justice,[931] as well as on the CRC and relevant documents issued by the health sector itself. In addition to basic provisions on children's right to health, protection and social security, progress has been made in developing a legal framework to achieving not only regular health care, but also to child-friendly health care.

Some argue that the term 'child-friendly' health care should be replaced by the term 'child-oriented' or child-appropriate health care, because these expressions would better reflect the necessary character of integrating the different aspects of children's rights in health care. Defining health care as 'child-friendly' is perceived to be too voluntarily, whereas a specific orientation of health care towards children is claimed to be essential for ensuring adequate health care. In this thesis I opt for the term 'child-friendly' health care, being in line with the applied terminology in the Guidelines of the Council of Europe on children's rights in justice and in health care, although I do support the idea that ensuring children's rights in health care is more than a luxury and that it is crucial in establishing health care that is truly beneficial for children's health.

The Guidelines of the Council of Europe define child-friendly health care as 'Health care policy and practice that are centered on children's rights, needs, characteristics, assets and evolving capacities, taking into account their own opinion'.[932, 933]Also, the concept of child-friendly health care includes the notion of family-friendly health care, defined as 'facilitating bonding between newborn babies and their mothers/parents, facilitating contacts between the child and his or her family and preventing the separation of the child from his or her family unless it is in the best interests of the child'.[934] In establishing a relation with children, medical professionals thus have to intrinsically take into account the influence and role of parents in guiding their children through the health care system, although the best interests of the child should remain a priority.

Within the European region, the guidelines on child-friendly health care pose an interesting example of a legal framework that is developed to reach the highest attainable standard of health within the health sector. The guidelines are extensive and in the drafting process medical professionals were intensively involved. Furthermore, information was obtained of more than 2200 children and

930 The 2009–2011 Strategy prioritized vulnerable children, focusing on children without parents, children with disabilities and children in or at risk of poverty and social exclusion. See: www.coe.int/t/dg3/children/news/200911Strategy_en.asp.

931 Guidelines of the Council of Europe on child-friendly justice, adopted on 17 November 2010.

932 See for example § 3 of the Guidelines on child-friendly healthcare.

933 Elsewhere, namely in footnote 19 of the Explanatory Memorandum, the child friendly health care approach is defined as 'integrating the principles of participation, promotion, protection and prevention into a practical framework of provision based on pathways to guide the planning, delivery and improvement of children's services.'

934 § 21 of the Guidelines on child-friendly healthcare.

adolescents from a large online survey in several member states of the Council of Europe.[935]

Child-friendly health care is required for several reasons. In the first place, it aims to protect sick children, because they have plural vulnerabilities: in the first place for being dependent on adults in their quality of being a child and in the second place for being dependent on medical professionals who are better informed and experienced on the (highly technical) medical treatments that they may undergo.[936] Thirdly, children are in development, which means that any infections, diseases, treatments and possible complications not only impact upon them at present, but possibly also in the future. Fourthly, since children are sick, they have less energy and resilience they have less energy to stand up for their rights in the course of their medical treatments. Aasen furthermore acknowledges that 'children are not only vulnerable due to their physical and mental conditions, but also because of their physical and social environments'.[937] Fifthly, medical treatments can make enormous infringements on the physical integrity of the child, thereby potentially causing a lot of harm if this happens against the will or best interests of the child or if it does not respect medical professional standards. In the society at large and specifically from the part of the medical professionals, there is increasing awareness and call for guidance on applying children's rights in health care.[938] Last but not least, the common principle in international health law to 'progressively realize the right to health' (of children) as found both in the Convention on the Rights of the Child and in the International Covenant on Economic, Social and Cultural Rights offers a strong argument for further developing the right to health of the child. It must be noted that the guidelines on child-friendly healthcare focus on children's rights within the health care sector, indicating the strong medical orientation of looking at children's health in contrast to the focus on basic health measures and underlying determinants of health in article 24 CRC and 12 ICESCR.

---

935 It is questionable to what extent the views are representative of the particular vulnerable youth population. Unclear is whether children within the hospital, undergoing medical treatments or marginalized children, such as refugee children or others who do not have internet at their disposal, were able to have access to the survey. It appears from the report that only a small percentage of children under 10 were involved in the research. As part of the study, the Irish National Ombudsman for children did conduct qualitative research with children, but the results of this study can not be simply transposed to children under 10 in other countries, because health systems differ widely, as well as underlying presumptions on children, health and health care.

936 G. Bricher, 'Children in the Hospital: Issues of Power and Vulnerability', *Pediatric Nursing* 2000, May, available at: http://findarticles.com/p/articles/mi_m0FSZ/is_3_26/ai_n18610056/.

937 H.S. Aasen, 'Children and the right to health protection', in: Toebes, Hartlev, Hendriks & Herrman, *Health and Human Rights in Europe*, Groningen: Intersentia 2012, p. 230.

938 The Guidelines of the Council of Europe were developed in close cooperation with pediatricians from a variety of member States. In the Netherlands, the 33rd Yearly Conference of Pediatricians organized two symposia on children's rights in health care in November 2011.

5.5.2. KEY ELEMENTS OF CHILD-FRIENDLY HEALTH CARE

The question now is what encompasses the notion of child-friendly health care. How is it elaborated in the newly established Guidelines of the Council of Europe and what role is attributed to children and their families in realizing the right to the highest attainable standard of health of the child?

The central aim of the Guidelines on child-friendly practice is to improve the quality of child health care by focusing on effectiveness, efficiency, equity, patient safety and satisfaction.[939] The Preamble of the Guidelines on child-friendly health care reiterates relevant international legal treaties[940] and relevant texts adopted by the Committee of Ministers on children and[941] on health care.[942] By adhering to the basic principles in international law, the guidelines integrate the concepts of non-discrimination, dignity, participation, equitable access and the best interests of the child,[943] concomitantly constituting 'an integrated conceptual and operational framework[944] which fully respects children's rights, health needs and resources'.[945]

---

939 See § 29 of the Guidelines on child-friendly healthcare.

940
- The United Nations Covenant on Economic, Social and Cultural Rights (1966), and in particular its Article 12 on the right to the highest attainable standard of health;
- the United Nations Convention on the Rights of the Child (1989);
- the United Nations Convention on the Rights of Persons with Disabilities (2006);
- the Convention for the Protection of Human Rights and Fundamental Freedoms (1950, ETS No. 5);
- the European Social Charter (1961, ETS No. 35) and the revised European Social Charter (1996, ETS No. 163);
- the European Convention on the Exercise of Children's Rights (1996, ETS No. 160);
- the European Convention for the Prevention of Torture and Inhuman or Degrading Treatment or Punishment (1987, ETS No. 126);
- the Council of Europe Convention on the Protection of Children against Sexual Exploitation and Sexual Abuse (2007, CETS No. 201);
- the Convention for the Protection of Human Rights and Dignity of the Human Being with regard to the Application of Biology and Medicine: Convention on Human Rights and Biomedicine (1997, ETS No. 164), in particular Article 6.

941
- Guidelines on Child-friendly Justice, adopted on 17 November 2010;
- Recommendation CM/Rec(2010)2 on deinstitutionalisation and community living of children with disabilities;
- Recommendation CM/Rec(2009)10 on integrated national strategies for the protection of children from violence;
- Recommendation Rec(98)8 on children's participation in family and social life.

942
- Recommendation Rec(2006)7 on management of patient safety and prevention of adverse events in health care;
- Recommendation Rec(2006)5 on the Council of Europe Action Plan to promote the rights and full participation of people with disabilities in society: improving the quality of life of people with disabilities in Europe 2006–2015;
- Recommendation Rec(2000)5 on the development of structures for citizen and patient participation in the decision-making process affecting health care.

943 See § 6–16 of the Guidelines on child-friendly healthcare.

944 The Guidelines are intended to provide a practical framework that drives cultural change in the medical domain. See § 20 of the Guidelines on child-friendly healthcare.

945 See § 17 of the Guidelines on child-friendly healthcare.

It takes into account the changing epidemiology of childhood,[946] the rising costs of health care and unacceptable variations in the quality of health care services for children and their families and it aims to achieve a continuum of care between the primary, secondary and tertiary health care organizations consequently and simultaneously involving health, education, social care and justice systems in public, private and voluntary sectors.[947] All in all, the child-friendly health care approach must be designed around children and their families.[948]

The scope of child-friendly health care as laid down in the guidelines is thus very broad, including both different levels of health care as different disciplines relevant to children's health status. This can be confusing and non-transparent for children. Therefore, it would be helpful for children to be guided by a 'child health advocate', an independent professional who guides the child through the health care process by explaining the role of the different doctors and organizations the child encounters in the process. Furthermore, the child health advocate can help to ensure that the child's interests are put central during the entire process and support the child in balancing its rights and the rights of the parents and support the child in balancing its rights *vis-à-vis* its parents and medical professionals.[949]

Although the large plurality of legal treaties and conventions relevant to the right to health of the child offers a starting point for understanding the highest attainable standard of health of the child, the guidelines have an additional value. This added value is created by elaborating its basic principles to be applied in the medical practice. The involvement of a wide range of experts, including paediatricians has undoubtedly added to this practical applicability.[950] As argued above, a good start has been made to involving children in the development of the guidelines, but more in-depth research is required to get further insights into the interaction between the realization of children's rights in health care and the visions of children upon these rights. The underlying principle of satisfaction in

946 See for example U.N. Doc. WHO (2010), Millennium Development Goals in the WHO European Region: A situational analysis at the eve of the 5-year countdown. Copenhagen, WHO Regional Office for Europe.

947 Examples of services involved that are enumerated in the Explanatory Memorandum, range from screening and immunization programs to neonatal intensive care and heart-lung transplantations to other interventions such as anti-bullying campaigns, health promoting schools, social care support organizations in cases of child maltreatment and the voluntary sector supporting children with disabilities or chronic diseases and access to housing, safe drinking water and sanitation.

948 Explanatory Memorandum to the Guidelines on child-friendly health care, § 17 and 21.5.

949 According to the Guidelines on child-friendly health care, the health care domain is divided into several pathways. These will be further discussed in the remainder of this paragraph.

950 The Committee of Experts was composed of 15 independent specialists who were selected by the European Health Committee. The request was to prepare guidelines on child-friendly healthcare, proposing a practical approach to assist member states to improve their health care systems. In addition, a wide range of observers, including representatives of leading intergovernmental and non-governmental organizations such as UNICEF, the WHO, the European Youth Forum, the European Patient Forum, the European Pediatric Association, the European Public Health Alliance, Schools for Health in Europe, the Royal College of Nursing and the European Network of Ombudspeople for Children also contributed.

the guidelines offers a legal basis for grounding such research because satisfaction can only be established by taking into account the views and experiences of children themselves. Such an approach allows for a full evaluation of the health care provided, because it integrates the experiences of children in health care assessments with more solid criteria such as medical outcome statistics, costs and other measureable criteria. In that way, the views and opinions of children are integrated in the elaboration of the highest attainable standard of health of the child.

5.5.3. PRACTICAL RELEVANCE OF THE GUIDELINES

The practical orientation of the guidelines is reflected by its distinction of the different pathways that exist within the health care system. In addition to the individual journey in health care, defined as 'the individual experience of the health services', a group of similar journeys constitutes a 'pathway' of which individual parts are delivered by a team of professionals. Three pathways are distinguished, each consisting of the four components Prevention, Identification, Assessment and Interventions.[951]

- initial pathway: The development, identification, initial assessment and management of the medical condition of the child.
- cyclical pathway: The regular review of the medical condition of the child with a focus on the best management of the condition and prevention of complications or other morbidities.
- transition pathway: The transition to the normal situation if the condition is cured, to adult health care or to palliative care if there is further deterioration likely to result in death.

Multidisciplinary collaboration within and between these pathways must create synergy and alignment between the policy level, the service level and the individual level, so that an integrated health system is established that takes into account the various actors and factors involved.[952] As set out in figure 1 below, this integrated health system, the child-friendly health care approach, is characterized

---

[951] See § 30–31 of the Guidelines on child-friendly healthcare. See also the Explanatory Memorandum, § 49–59.

[952] See § 33 and 37 of the Guidelines on child-friendly healthcare. See also supra note 58.

by the '5 P's':[953] Participation,[954] Promotion,[955] Protection,[956] Prevention[957] and Provision.[958] The 5 P's concomitantly place the needs of children and their families at the heart.

Figure 1. Overview by the Committee of Experts on child-friendly health care, 2011[959]

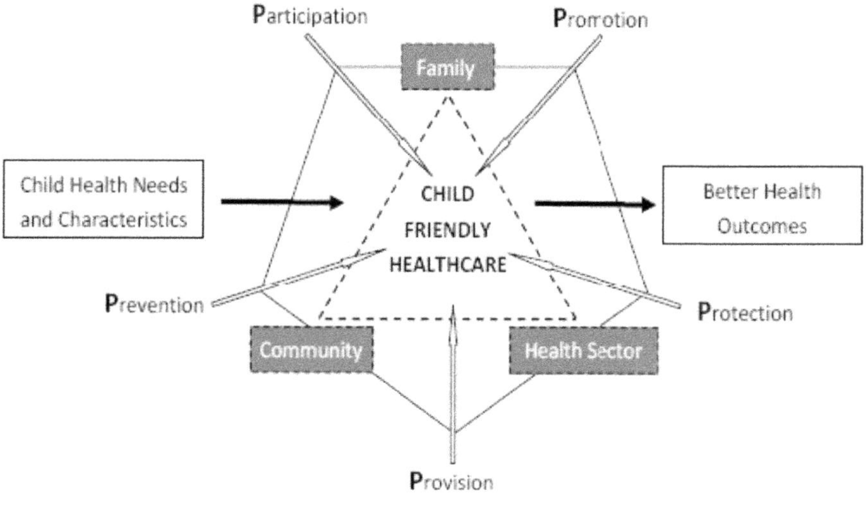

953 The 5 P's are laid down in § 23–28 of the Guidelines and further explained in § 41–54 and in the Explanatory Memorandum, pp. 16–17.

954 Participation in the health field is divided between giving free and informed consent on the one hand and taking part in social decision-making processes on health care issues, including the assessment, planning and improvement of health care services, on the other hand. Children are recognized as active stakeholders and rights bearers and the level of participation depends on their age, evolving capacities, maturity and on the importance of the decision being taken. See § 11, 12, 23 and 24 of the Guidelines on child-friendly healthcare.

955 Promotion is defined in § 25 of the Guidelines as 'The process of enabling people to increase control over their health and its determinants and thereby improve their health'. This definition is drawn from the WHO Health Promotion Glossary, 1998. The Guidelines further explain promotion as 'including all actions that allow children to become more involved in their own health and increase their exposure to positive determinants of health. It involves activities at family and community level and factors in health care services and settings.

956 Protection is defined in § 26 of the Guidelines on child-friendly healthcare as 'all actions that either limit or avoid children's exposure to hazards in families, communities or health services'.

957 Prevention is defined in § 27 of the Guidelines on child-friendly healthcare and 'refers to any service which contributes to the health and well-being of children and families and therefore includes more than just the traditional health services'.

958 Provision is defined in § 28 of the Guidelines on child-friendly healthcare and 'refers to any service which contributes to the health and well-being of children and families and therefore includes more than just the traditional health services.

959 The model was taken from the preparatory document on child-friendly health care for and with children in Europe by J.A. Diaz Huertas and A.I.F. Guerreiro, Council of Europe Document No. MSN (2011) 4E.

The concept of Promotion as a central element to children's health care is additional to the '4 P's' that are central in the Convention on the Rights of the Child, although health promotional activities are inexplicitly mentioned in article 24 CRC and in the Guidelines on Reporting[960] on article 24 CRC as well.

Overall, the child-friendly health care approach is characterized by the so-called 5-4-3-2-1 approach: there are 5 basic principles (the 5 P's), 4 components of the different pathways of the principle P-rovision (prevention, identification, assessment and interventions), 3 pathways (initial, cyclical and transitional), 2 driving forces (alignment between services and coupling measures, feedback and action) and one central aim (improvement in outcomes and impact).[961] This system appears to be somewhat artificial. Furthermore, because the guidelines and explanatory memorandum are complementary, addressing different elements of the 5 P's in the child-friendly health care approach, the resulting schedule of the guidelines is somewhat chaotic. Therefore, figure 3 integrates all elements in one scheme. Figure 3 demonstrates the integrated health system[962] based on the different pathways and elements of the child-friendly health care approach discerned.

Figure 2. Key concepts of child-friendly health care based on the 5-P-rinciples

1.	PARTICIPATION in:
a.	*individual decision-making* (consultation, informed consent and confidentiality)
b.	*feedback* on children's experiences in the services provided;
c.	involvement and priority setting in service *planning and policy.*
d.	research
2.	PROMOTION by:
a.	general support directed towards *all children*: health promotion programmes, such as child-friendly healthcare, schools and sporting facilities and financial arrangements;
b.	additional targeted support directed towards (socially, emotionally or financially) *vulnerable children*;
c.	*children* (repeatedly) *using health services*: chronically ill, recovering from trauma
3.	PROTECTION of:
a.	general protection for all children against environmental hazards, physical, social, emotional or financial harm, racism. E.g. improving parental skills and support for families with low incomes, legislation on equal access and child protection measures).
b.	special protection for vulnerable children, such as refugee and minority children, disabled children or children with rare chronic diseases.
c.	children using health services, e.g. by ensuring a patient-safety policy framework and feedback mechanisms.
4	PREVENTION levels:

960 U.N. Doc. HRI/GEN/2/Rev.6, 3 June 2009.

961 See Appendix II to the Explanatory Memorandum.

962 The WHO defines health systems as 'all organizations, people and actions whose primary intent is to promote, restore or maintain health'. See: www.who.int/alliance-hpsr/resources/9789241563895/en/index.html.

a.	primary: population-based interventions (vaccinations, water fluoridation).
b.	secondary: early detection (neonatal screening for health problems).
c.	tertiary: prevent secondary disabilities or deficiencies (use of asthma inhalers).
d.	quaternary: avoid harm through the contact with the health system itself (e.g. by separation of parents, disruption of social network, unnecessary medical treatments and lack of information).
5	PROVISION of health care through:
a.	individual journeys and collective pathways, provided by networks of medical professionals and consisting of prevention-identification-assessment-intervention.
b.	evidence-based, user-friendly, readily accessible, competent practitioners, appropriate care environment, timely
c.	measurement, feedback, continuous learning

5.5.4. THE CHARTER OF THE EUROPEAN ASSOCIATION ON CHILDREN'S RIGHTS

Before adoption of the Guidelines on child-friendly health care, the European Association for Children in Hospitals (EACH), an umbrella organization for non-governmental and non-profit associations from 18 European member states that are involved in the welfare of children in hospital, had already established an ethical foundation for the care of children in hospital.[963]

The EACH Association was founded by 12 European voluntary organizations to address the needs of children in hospital, who were found to suffer from the detrimental effects of health care in hospitals, largely because of the (long-term) separation from their families resulting in long-lasting emotional disturbances. The EACH Charter was adopted in Leiden in 1988, preceding corresponding and binding rights in the UN Convention on the Rights of the Child and addressing all sick children between 0–18 years.

The Charter applies to all sick children, 'regardless of their illness or age or disability, their origin or their social or cultural background, or of any possible reason for treatment or forms or places of treatment, whether as in-patients or out-patients.'[964] The principle of non-discrimination is thus specifically highlighted in implementing the right to health of children in the EACH Charter. On the other hand, the focus selectively on 'sick children' is narrower than that of the Guidelines on child-friendly health care. Therein, three categories of children are distinguished for targeting health related activities, namely 'children in general', 'sick children' and other groups of 'vulnerable children'.

The EACH Charter contains 10 fundamental principles. Furthermore, the Association identifies 16 (sub-) rights of the UN Children's Rights Convention that are relevant to implementing children's right to health, namely article 8, 24,

963 See the website of EACH: www.actionforsickchildren.org/index.asp?ID=186.

964 See the EACH website: www.each-for-sick-children.org/each-charter. Last accessed on 25 July 2011.

3-1 and 3-3, 5, 9-1, 12-1, 16, 17, 18, 19, 23-3 and 23-4, 25, 28, 29-1a and c, 30 and 31.[965]

Despite the fact that the EACH Charter has not been adopted by a formal legislative organ, the specificity of the provisions relevant to children's right to health is helpful in elaborating upon children's right to health as laid down in other international legal documents, especially in the European context. Its direct relevance is justified by the close involvement of medical professionals in its elaboration, giving it practical relevance. Furthermore, the relevance of the EACH Charter has been reconfirmed in the Preamble of the Guidelines of the Committee of Ministers of the Council of Europe on child-friendly health care.[966] The rights enshrined in the EACH Charter are generally divided into three categories:[967]

- Rights to resources and care – good hospital care, food, warmth, safety, parents' loving care;
- Rights to protection from harm – from neglect and abuse, from fear, pain and loneliness, from too many medical interventions or the neglect of being denied necessary treatment;
- Rights to self determination, dignity, respect, integrity, non-interference, the right to make informed personal decisions.

Especially the third category is often criticized by adults, arguing that children would refuse all treatments if they are allowed to decide for themselves. However, such a point of view is heavily prejudicial towards the understanding and capacities of (young) children. Alderson identifies several age-assumptions that have been proven wrong about children undergoing medical care, including 'children under 3 years old do not understand explanations' and 'young children do not mind that their privacy is being disregarded', 'children of 5/6 years are too young to participate in complex medical decisions' and 'adolescents do not want close mothering care'.[968] These examples demonstrate that seeking children's views is essential in interpreting the type of health care they wish to receive and the standard of health they wish to attain. Even when children are not capable of expressing their own views, parents or other representatives may be able to provide additional insights into their particular point of view and medical

965 Presumably the drafters of the EACH Charter were informed about the drafting process of the Convention on the Rights of the Child, as they did already refer to the contents of this Convention before it was officially adopted.

966 Guidelines of the Committee of Ministers of the Council of Europe on child-friendly health care, adopted by the Committee of Ministers on 21st September 2011 at the 1121st meeting of the Ministers' Deputies explicitly refer to the relevance of the EACH Charter in its Preamble.

967 P. Alderson, 'European Charter of Children's Rights', *Bulletin of Medical Ethics*, October 1993, p. 13–15.

968 P. Alderson, 'European Charter of Children's Rights', *Bulletin of Medical Ethics*, October 1993, p. 13–15.

situation, which are indispensable to providing the highest attainable standard of health.[969]

In order to allow parents and children to be involved in the medical treatment, medical professionals must be able to clearly explain and motivate the choices made in treating children. This requirement not only involves the question what is the least invasive treatment available, but also the question whether it is really necessary to perform a medical intervention and if so, whether it is really necessary to admit the child to hospital. The right to health of children thus also encompasses the right *not* to be treated. Especially in high-tech hospitals, with highly educated and sometimes intimidating doctors, it is important to give children and their families the opportunity to question and criticize the possible benefits of medical interventions.[970] Evidence has even been found about the paradox that 'the more professionals believe they have provided a safe haven for children in hospital, the bigger the risk is that questions will be seen as negative and ungrateful, so that their right to make informed choices is threatened.[971] Also, history has shown that many children have resided much longer than required in medical institutions (far) away from their homes and families.[972] This residential staying disturbs their daily eating, sleeping and relaxing routines more than necessary, hinders the contacts with family and friends and also places an additional burden on family members having to travel for hours a day to see their child.

On the website of the European Association for Children in Hospital additional explanations of the 10 fundamental principles is provided.[973] The central idea of the principles is to reduce the negative psychological impact of medical treatments on children as much as possible. In the first place (article 1), this must be achieved by minimizing the hospitalization of children as much as possible by enabling their parents to take care of their children themselves -if possible at home- by providing them all necessary information, assistance and support and by regularly reviewing the type of care that is provided to the child to prevent unnecessary hospital stays. In the second place (article 2), if hospitalization of the child is absolutely necessary and unavoidable, all efforts must be made to keep the child and its parents together during all possible phases, such as during the night, during treatments and examinations, during periods of coma and immediately after recovery. To achieve this (article 3), parents must be provided with, explicitly invited to and supported by the staff to reside close to their children in free accommodation with – at a minimum – a bed, the availability of a bathroom,

---

969 U.N. Doc. CRC/C/GC/7/Rev.1, General Comment 7 on Child rights in early childhood, 20 September 2006, § 27.

970 P. Alderson, 'European Charter of Children's Rights', *Bulletin of Medical Ethics*, October 1993, pp. 13–15.

971 B. Mayall, 'Learning from well children', in: P. Alderson (ed.), *Children's decisions in health care and research*, In press, London: Institute of Education. Reproduced in: P. Alderson, 'European Charter of Children's Rights', *Bulletin of Medical Ethics*, October 1993, pp. 13–15.

972 M. Bonn, 'The effects of hospitalization on children: a review', *Curationis* 1994, Jun; 17(2): 20-4.

973 Http://each-for-sick-children.org/each-charter/charter-and-annotations?showall=1.

sitting and dining facilities and a storage space for personal belongings.[974] Parents and children must also be provided the opportunity for private and undisturbed communication and association (article 10).

Furthermore, according to EACH Charter, parents may not be charged financially for staying overnight and eating in the hospital, they should be given the opportunity to have paid leave from work during the illness of their child and they should be financially compensated for loss of income due to the fulltime care of their child or the supervision over healthy siblings by others. Whereas it remains unclear in the Charter how these targets must be achieved, it may be possible to achieve this through specialized medical legislation for extraordinary medical costs. In the Netherlands, for example, special medical costs for long-term hospitalization and professional support at home are covered by the AWBZ (Algemene Wet Bijzondere Ziektekosten – General Law Special Health Costs). However, this law does not cover all the entitlements found in the EACH Charter. Also, given the current economic crisis and the steadily increasing costs of health care, it seems unlikely to become a priority in the health care policy of the near future.[975] On the other hand, prevention of hospitalization of children would significantly improve children's well-being ánd be cost-effective in the long-term.[976, 977, 978] An example of reduction of hospital stays in the United States with only half a day was estimated to account for a reduction in costs of $725 (per half a day).[979] It has been estimated that the average hospital rate in the Netherlands is significantly higher than in other OECD and EU countries and than the United States.[980] Considerable cost reductions should therefore be possible. The reductions

[974] Recent developments in the Netherlands demonstrate that such measures are successful in improving the health care provided to children. To assess the progress made by hospitals in establishing such child-friendly health care unites, the foundation Child & Hospital (Kind & Ziekenhuis), member of the European Association on Children in Hospital has established a system of 'smileys' that are granted to hospitals that are qualified as child-friendly. A distinction is made between the requirements of the departments of neonatal care, daycare and the children's department.

[975] See for the Netherlands a notification by the Central Bureau on Statistics on the increasing costs in health care as a percentage of the GDP, 20 May 2010. (www.cbs.nl/nl-NL/menu/themas/gezondheid-welzijn/publicaties/artikelen/archief/2010/2010-039-pb.htm.) See for an overview of measures on reducing health care costs: www.lvg.org/digi/2011/24/euro.htm.

[976] S.C. Schimpff, *The Future of Medicine: Megatrends in Medicine that Will Improve Your Health Care & Your Quality of Life*, Nashville: Thomas Nelson Publishers 2007. Schimpff argues that 'Prevention is the key to both better health and lower healthcare costs over the long haul.'

[977] R. Keren, 'Direct Medical Cost of Influenza-Related Hospitalizations in Children', *Pediatrics* 2006, Volume 118, no. 5, November 1, pp. e1321–132.

[978] V. Sazonov Kozevar, 'Variations in Pediatric Asthma Hospitalization Rates and Costs Between and Within Nordic Countries', *Chest* 2004, 125, pp. 1680–1684.

[979] M. Raut (et al.), 'Estimating the economic impact of a half-day reduction in length of hospital stay among patients with community-acquired pneumonia in the US', *Current Medical Research and Opinion* 2009, 25 (9), p. 2151–2157, Available at: www.ncbi.nlm.nih.gov/pubmed/19601711.

[980] I. Borghmans (et al.), 'Benchmarking and reducing length of stay in Dutch hospitals', *BMC Health Services Research* 2008, Volume 8, p. 220. Available at: www.biomedcentral.com/1472-6963/8/220/.

possible are dependent on the type of disease and the actual benchmark of length of hospital stay, which varies considerably.

When hospitalization of the child can not be prevented, all efforts must be made to ensure that the environment in which children reside is child-friendly. This means that enough possibilities must exist for play, recreation and education suited for the different age groups, developmental stages, gender and possible medical limitations. This applies to the decoration and furnishing in all areas where children reside and are treated, for the time available and the staff supporting the children (article 7). Also, children must be cared for along with children with similar developmental and medical needs (article 6.1) and no age restrictions must be put in place to receive friends, siblings or other visitors (article 6.2).

Within the category of protection of children against (medical) harm and in order to reduce the invasiveness of medical treatments, children must be protected against unnecessary treatments (article 5.2), for example when no beneficial effects can be expected. Furthermore, steps must be taken to mitigate physical and emotional stress (article 4.2) by granting sufficient periods of rest between treatments, by avoiding isolation and the use of restraints, by providing psychological support to children and their parents, by supporting parents whose children are receiving palliative care (article 4.2) and by deploying staff (article 8) that is well-trained and sensitive to respond to the physical, emotional and developmental needs of children and families. In all medical interventions, specifically trained staff must be involved and there must be continuity in the staff caring for the child (article 9). This requires good team work and communication by a limited number of professionals, extending to those caring for the child when it returns home.

To allow children and their parents to be genuinely involved in their medical treatment, good communication with both parents and their children is essential, meaning that all information must be continuously and openly shared in a confidential atmosphere and without time pressure, to enable parents to care for their children (article 3.3), to make informed medical decisions extending to their medical situation, possible treatments, side-effects, risks and outcomes and to integrate this knowledge in the existing knowledge (article 5.1) and while respecting the autonomy and privacy of the child also *vis-à-vis* his parents (article 10). The information must be child-friendly ánd at the same time understandable for the parents, considerate of the cultural and religious backgrounds and both the child and its parents must be encouraged to ask questions and given the opportunity to express their views. This open and well-informed communication and decision-making process requires that medical professionals are given enough time and training for communicating with their patients.

5.5.5. RELATION BETWEEN THE EACH CHARTER AND THE GUIDELINES ON CHILD-FRIENDLY HEALTH CARE

Whereas the EACH Charter is referred to in the Guidelines on child-friendly healthcare, both sets of principles codifying children's rights in health care show some overlaps and distinctions. In the first place, it is remarkable that both sets of principles are practically oriented while simultaneously suffering from a considerable degree of inconsistency. The EACH Charter, being much less elaborate than the Guidelines, contains 10 principles that are categorized in a somewhat non-logical and random order. For example, principles 3.3, 4.1, 5.1 ánd 10 all address issues of communication that could have been better dealt with in comprehension. Similarly, principles 4.2 and 5.2 aim to mitigate emotional and physical stress and prevent unnecessary medical treatments and principles 8 and 9 both refer to the role and training of medical staff. A better structure would have been beneficial to the clarity of the principles. The same is true to an even larger extent for the Guidelines of the EU Committee on child-friendly health care. Several different ways of structuring the basic principles are elaborated in the '5-4-3-2-1' structure,[981] as appears from Annex II to the Guidelines. However, this ordering does not appear very clearly from the Guidelines themselves and seems to be somewhat artificial. Furthermore, the Explanatory Memorandum to the Guidelines does not follow the order in which the Guidelines are structured: the three pathways and the elaboration of the 5 P-rinciples are reversed, further complicating the already limited transparency of the prioritization of the different ordering structures. Furthermore, whereas 4 P-rinciples are divided in 3 different categories, P-rovision is organized in 3 × 3 different categories, without clearly explaining this difference and the relation to the 3 pathways and the 4 stages therein. It can be deduced by carefully considering the pictograms in the Explanatory Memorandum, but many questions (e.g. how do primary, secondary and tertiary prevention relate to the transitional pathway? How do the stages of prevention, identification, assessment and intervention relate to protective or promotional activities?) remain unclear. Notwithstanding the importance of the issues addressed, better streamlining of the different values and structuring systems would have definitely benefited the transparency of the Guidelines and thereby also the practical applicability.

A difference between the two sets of principles lays in the scope. Whereas the Guidelines are enormously broad,[982] covering not only medical, but also socio-economic, schooling and housing aspects of children's right to child-friendly health care, the EACH Charter is more particularly focused on ensuring children's rights in the strict medical domain. The main focus of the EACH Charter is

[981] See supra § 5.2.3 and figure 2.

[982] See supra § 5.2.3 for a further discussion of all parties and organizations involved.

thereby oriented towards prevention of harm resulting from medical treatments and possible hospital stays during those treatments, whereas the Guidelines also cover preventive, promotional and provisional aspects of health care policy. Both sets of principles emphasize the importance of providing information on and ensuring participation of children in medical treatment, but these concepts are elaborated more extensively in the Guidelines.

Last but not least, the documents have a different focus *vis-à-vis* the children that are primarily targeted. In line with the broad, both medically and society-oriented approach of the Guidelines, the focus distinguishes children as a general group, sick children and vulnerable groups of children, whereas the EACH Charter focuses only on sick children.[983]

The additional value of the EACH Charter for the Guidelines on child-friendly health care is that the annotations are particularly concrete, making the 10 basic principles practically applicable and demonstrating a thorough insight in the daily reality of children's lives in medical care. This can be of additional value to interpreting and implementing the Guidelines on service and individual levels.

5.6. CONCLUSION

5.6.1. THE MARGIN OF APPRECIATION ON CHILDREN'S RIGHT TO HEALTH IN EUROPE

Two distinct concepts are discerned in determining the margin of discretion of European States in implementing the right to health of the child. Within the European Union, the CFREU provides that access to preventive health care and medical treatments must be established under the conditions established by national laws and practices. Member States thus have the room to define the health measures that they deem appropriate in their national legislation. On the basis of article 168 TFEU, Member States retain their primary responsibility for defining their health policy and for the organization and delivery of medical services. Both the management and the allocation of resources fall under the responsibility of the Member States. However, 168 TFEU instigates that both the Union actions and the activities of individual member States in cross-border areas complement national policies. In that way, European countries can support each other to raise their health standards.

Under the European Social Charter States have the duty to ensure 'the best possible state of health for the population according to existing knowledge'. In addition to measures established by national law, existing knowledge is

[983] See supra § 5.2.3 for the division of targeted children: general measures targeted towards all children in society, special measures for vulnerable children and special measures for children in medical care.

determinative for establishing the 'best possible state of health'. This phrasing gives room for more flexible interpretation of existing legal provisions, since medical knowledge is in constant motion.

Several areas of particular concern to the European region are identified, including sexual and reproductive health, maternal and child healthcare, obesity, diabetes II, teenagers in distress, mental health problems (ADHD), alcohol, drug and tobacco abuse and children in their early childhood (0–8). The margin of discretion enables countries to prioritize health measures on the basis of the specific health indicators in the country. This practice is in line with the requirement as established by the UN Committee on the Rights of the Child that national health policies must be based on disaggregated health data. In addition, the priorities mentioned in the following paragraphs derive from European human rights law.

5.6.2. FOCUS ON PREVENTION OF HEALTH PROBLEMS

Both from the perspective of the EU and from the Council of Europe, a clear focus is visible on the need to prevent health problems from the very beginning: before conception, during pregnancy, birth and in the earliest years of life going on in school years and through adolescence. Measures must be directed both at individual and public health (art. 35 CFREU) so that a high level of human health protection is achieved. Preventive measures include the following (art. 168 TFEU):

- Promote research into the causes of disease;
- Prevent transmission of disease;
- Provide health information and education;
- Ensure monitoring and early warning;
- Combat serious cross-border threats;
- Ensure non-discriminatory access to health services. The EU strategy specifies measures to ensure that all children receive birth certificates:
  1. Birth registration must be free of charge;
  2. Civil servants must be well-trained;
  3. Permanent and if necessary mobile birth registration units must be available;
  4. Sufficient resources must be allocated.

Article 24 of the Charter of the Fundamental Freedoms specifically focuses on the need to prevent health problems in children. Immunizations, healthy lifestyles, prevention of injuries and prevention of violence against children are all crucial components of the comprehensive approach to reach the highest attainable standard of health of the child.

5.6.3. CHILD-CENTRED HEALTH CARE

The Guidelines on child friendly healthcare of the Council of Europe establish that health care must be centred around the rights, needs and characteristics of children. The identification of these elements requires taking into account their own opinion as well as the role and influence of their parents/family.

Both the Guidelines on child friendly healthcare and the WHO strategy establish that child-centred healthcare requires a coordinated, integrated, comprehensive and continuous approach. The Guidelines speak of child friendly healthcare and the WHO of people-centred health care. The Guidelines specify that such an approach should address:

- The changing epidemiology of childhood.
- Resources and rising costs of health care.
- Variations in the quality of care.
- Multidisciplinary cooperation.
- Continuity of care between primary, secondary and tertiary health services *or* continuity of care in the initial, cyclical and transitional pathway. The WHO strategy for Europe offers additional insight into the concept of continuity by elaborating that continuity of care consists of four elements:
  i. Follow-up between subsequent visits (life course approach).
  ii. Informational continuity.
  iii. Longitudinal continuity.
  iv. Interpersonal continuity: the WHO suggests that preventive, curative, rehabilitative and palliative care should be provided as much as possible by one provider, so that transparency and personal attention are maximized.

5.6.4. FAMILY FRIENDLY HEALTH CARE

Creating a healthy family environment in which children can grow up safely is crucial to ensuring both the health of children and the health of adults in the future. Therefore, many of the identified interventions can and should be taken at the level of the family (art. 8, 13, 16, 17, 19 ESC and the Guidelines on Child Friendly Healthcare). The Guidelines not only speak about child-friendly but also about family-friendly health care. These Guidelines establish that healthcare must be designed around children and their families. The idea is that when health services work through families, this creates continuity of experience for the child. Three central aims are specified:

- Facilitate bonding between new-borns and their parents.
- Facilitate bonding between children and their family members.
- Prevent separation of children from their parents.

Although this child and family-centred approach can have many benefits for realizing the right to health of the child, caution must be taken not to submerge the interests of the child in the broader set of family-oriented rights and interests.

5.6.5. EMPOWERMENT

The Council of Europe and the WHO emphasize that health measures must be taken to enable children to reach their full potential for health and development and reduce the burden of disease and mortality. Hereto, individuals must be stimulated to take responsibility over their own health.

The central role of children in managing their own health status is expressly highlighted in several instances. Children's ability for self-management and their participation in decisions affecting them, taking into account their age and maturity, as well as the active involvement of the parents and family' must be stimulated. In order to increase this ability of children to ensure their own health, continuous health education of children through incorporation of health education in school curricula, parents, teachers and training of health professionals' is required (ESC Conclusions). To ensure that children have access to regular medical check- ups, the ESC provides that medical services must exist at schools so that children can receive periodical examinations. Furthermore, health professionals' and patients' organizations must be involved in the empowerment of children and parents in the health care field.

The importance of approaching children as individual holders of human rights is central in the Guidelines on Child-Friendly Healthcare of the Council of Europe. Children need to grow up and develop according to their capacities and receive acknowledgement for that. In the design of the health care process, both in individual health decisions and in an abstract sense, children and their families must be directly consulted. Hereto, more research into the interaction between the realization of children's rights in health care and the visions of children upon these rights is necessary. The underlying principle of satisfaction in the Guidelines on Child-Friendly Health care, offers a basis for grounding such research, because satisfaction necessarily requires taking into account the views and experiences of children themselves. In such a way, interventions aimed at realizing the highest attainable standard of health will not only be more effective, but they give children and their families the opportunity to raise the highest attainable standard of health to a level that they value and personally contribute to.

5.6.6. DISCUSSION

The body of law in the children's rights domain and in international health and human rights law takes very basic health measures as a starting point, including the provision of basic health services. This chapter illustrates that the legal frameworks in the European region focus more on the way in which the different levels of health services are organized. Also, many are more oriented towards specific subthemes, so-called welfare diseases, which are relevant in the European region, including obesity, mental health problems and alcohol and drug abuse.

More in-depth analyses can be made for other regions, such as the Americas, Africa, the Middle-East and Asia. The next chapter will take a closer look at the interaction between the legal provision on the right to health of the child and the role of the different actors involved in its implementation. Investigated is how this interaction influences the way in which the right to health of the child is interpreted in different communities.

VI. REALIZING THE RIGHT TO HEALTH OF THE CHILD

6.1. INTRODUCTION

The question in this chapter is how and by whom the right to health of the child can be realized in practice and how the process of realization influences upon the interpretation of the right to the highest attainable standard of health of the child.

Whereas the children's right to health has been laid down in numerous international and regional treaties, the realization of this right is largely dependent on the modes of enforcement that have been established.[984] For example, the realization or 'home-coming' of human rights,[985] requires the necessary translation of human rights principles into national law systems, more specifically in the legal response to violations of children's right to health in domestic cases. Secondly, the realization of children's right to health requires translation of its key constituent elements to non-legal work fields, such as the medical and child protection sectors, school systems, the housing sector, the activities of private companies that impact upon children's health[986, 987, 988] and many other stakeholders. The 'hard' or normative rules of children's right to health have to be translated into solid policies which ultimately lead to a comprehensive health system that is rooted in the children's rights framework and to the application of soft or child-sensitive skills of (medical) professionals working with children.

---

984 U.N. Doc. CRC/GC/2003/5, 27 November 2003. General Comment 5 to the Convention on the Rights of the Child on General Measures of Implementation defines implementation as 'the process whereby States parties take action to ensure the realization of all rights in the Convention for all children in their jurisdiction.'

985 B. Oomen, Inaugural lecture, Utrecht University chair in the 'Sociology of Human Rights', *Small places: the home-coming of human rights*, delivered at Utrecht University Roosevelt Academy in Middelburg, the Netherlands on 2 December 2011.

986 See U.N. Doc. CRC/C/GC/16, 17 April 2013 General Comment 16 on State obligations regarding the impact of the business sector on children's rights.

987 For the UN Guiding Principles on Business and Human Rights see: www.crin.org/docs/FileManager/ruggie_guiding_principles_21-mar_2011_1.pdf. For an interpretative guide of Guiding Principles by the Office of the High Commissioner of Human Rights see: www.ohchr.org/Documents/Issues/Business/RtRInterpretativeGuide.pdf.

988 GlaxoSmithKline, the biggest pharmaceutical company, in 2012 settled charges for 3 billion dollars in the United States for illegal marketing of dangerous antidepressant drugs to children that made them suicidal and that had not been approved by safety regulators. See: www.independent.co.uk/news/business/news/glaxosmithkline-pays-3bn-for-illegally-marketing-depression-drug-7904555.html. Website last accessed on 9 July 2014.

This contribution discusses the possible modes of enforcement of the right to health of the child. Paragraph 6.2 locates the right to the highest attainable standard of health of the child in the social reality in which children live. It discusses recent interdisciplinary approaches to the realization of children's rights, more particularly of the right to health of the child. Paragraph 6.3 discusses the obligations of the state in realizing the right to the highest attainable standard of health of the child. It does so by focusing on the concepts of 'available resources' and 'all appropriate measures' as specified in article 4 CRC and by looking at the implementation of the right to health in Dutch domestic cases. The possibilities of implementing the right to health of the child depend on the justiciability of social rights.[989, 990] The question will be discussed whether these entitlements of children to the right to health amount to States' obligations of effort or of result. Paragraph 6.4 will identify non-state actors that (can) have an impact on the realization of the right to health of the child. It addresses the way in which non-state actors can be held responsible for (non-)interfering with the right to health of the child. In paragraph 6.5, the obligations of States for international cooperation in realizing the right to health of children his discussed. As a measure of last resort, the additional value of the newly adopted Optional Protocol to the Convention on the Rights of the Child on a Communications Procedure for realizing the right to the highest attainable standard of health for children is discussed in paragraph 6.5. In the concluding paragraph 6.6, the question will be discussed how the process of realization influences the interpretation of the highest attainable standard of health of the child.

6.2. CHILDREN'S RIGHT TO HEALTH AND THE SOCIAL REALITY IN WHICH CHILDREN LIVE

In 2010 a comment was published in the Lancet that 'despite important gains, there is a substantial gap between ideals aspired to by human rights advocates

989 The distinction between civil and political rights on the one hand and economic, social and cultural rights on the other, is reflected in the two basic international human rights law treaties: the International Covenant on Civil and Political Rights (ICCPR), which entails freedom rights such as the right to freedom of speech, the right to private property and the right to a fair trial and the International covenant on Economic, social and Cultural Rights (ICESCR). However, both the Committee on Economic, Social and Cultural Rights and the Committee on the Rights of the Child acknowledge that both sets of rights are indivisible and interdependent. See supra note 989 and 990.

990 See for example a discussion on enforcing social rights for children and their families Sachs, A., 'Enforcement of Economic, Social and Cultural Rights', American University International Law Review, Volume 22, Issue 5, 2007, pp. 673–708. Available at: http://heinonline.org/HOL/Page?handle=hein.journals/amuilr22&div=35&collection=journals&set_as_cursor=6&men_tab=srchresults.

and realities on the ground.'[991] Amartya Sen similarly states that 'More attention has been paid to 'niti' = development of rules and behavioural norms of justice, than to 'nyaya' = the actual social realisations of justice – the lives people lead, regardless of whether or not the institutional architecture and laws have been perfectly rendered.'[992] This process of realization thus goes beyond the strictly legal domain, as is also acknowledged by UNICEF commentators in stating that 'Legal measures and abstract principles provide scant guidance for real-world decision making around resource allocation and programme strategies.'[993] Legal provisions must be translated to practical tools and guidelines that are accepted and integrated in daily work practices. Thereto, the involvement of actors directly affected by the rules and procedures such as children, their families and medical professionals in the translation and implementation process of children's rights in health systems and practices is essential to ensure acceptance and adjustment of the rights to the medical reality in which the actors operate. Sen and others speak of 'a continual process of public engagement and rational analysis to improve the lives of the most vulnerable'.[994] Hanson goes even further by introducing the concept of 'living rights'. In his words, 'The concept of living rights highlights that children, while making use of notions of rights, shape what these rights are – and become – in the social world. The concept challenges the idea that children's rights are exclusively those defined by international institutions or States. We look at children's rights as a 'living practice' shaped by children's everyday concerns.'[995] He speaks of a cyclical process in which children's rights are implemented and thereby impact upon the social reality which in its turn impacts upon the ways in which children's rights are further developed and implemented.[996] This process thus integrates the social reality as a constitutive element of the development of children's rights. Obviously, this would have the consequence that different social realities in different countries all have a different impact on the implementation of the same standardized children's rights provisions as laid down in the Convention on the Rights of the Child. Hanson acknowledges this effect and elaborates that 'rights are put into effect through social practices in particular contexts and time

991 Comment made by Asha George, Mickey Chopra, Daniel Seymour, Paolo Marchi, working for UNICEF Health Section and Gender and Rights Unit, New York, in: *the Lancet* 2010, Volume 375, May 22, p. 1764, available at: www.sum.uio.no/english/research/doctoral-degree/doctoral-courses/2012/the-political-determinants-of-health/syllabus/a-george-etal-hu-rts-of-h-workers-lancet-2010.pdf.

992 A. Sen, *The idea of justice*, Cambridge, MA: Harvard University Press 2009.

993 Ibidem supra note 991.

994 Ibidem supra note 991.

995 'Reconceptualizing children's rights in International Development', edited by Karl Hanson and Olga Nieuwenhuys, 2013, Cambridge University Press, introduction.

996 Lecture by prof.dr. K. Hanson in the International Interdisciplinary Course: Human Rights for Development at the University of Antwerp, 17 August 2012. In this lecture, he referred to the book 'Reconceptualizing children's rights', edited by Karl Hanson and Olga Nieuwenhuys, 2013, Cambridge University Press.

frames and that they therefore do not always carry the same meaning.'[997, 998] Also, he suggests a change of paradigm in contemplating children's rights from an abstract top down exercise to a permanent bottom-up development in children's minds and day to day activities, which is more empowering towards children. In his words, 'children engage with, interpret and give meaning to their rights: it is from this perspective that rights can be seen as living'. Therefore, Hanson claims, that children should be part of the shaping and implementation process instead of being passive recipients of rights. In approaching rights as a living reality that is influenced by the beneficiaries themselves, the interaction of children as 'interdependent agents' in their families and broader social structures must be taken into account, because, as argued by Hanson, 'Children become aware of their rights as they struggle with their families and communities to give meaning to their daily existence'.[999] However, one of the main questions that rise is what the additional value is of the universally phrased articles in the CRC if their implementation is so dependent on the actual realities in which they are realized. Secondly, the influence that can be exercised on the development of children's rights by very young children is limited. As clarified in section 4, this influence is present, although not deliberately oriented towards the development and implementation of children's rights, but resulting from their direct and indirect behaviour in health care settings and at home.

Vice versa, the implementation of child rights in its turn effects on the social reality of children's lives, being defined as 'the actual daily situation of people and the way they experience the standards and their implementation'.[1000] Whereas the mutual influencing between written provisions and social realities may occur both consciously by making deliberate choices (e.g. medical professionals who actively involve children and their parents in the medical decision-making process) and unconsciously (e.g. doctors who primarily address the parents without taking into account the opinion of the child) it is important to make the actors involved aware of their potential to impact upon their own treatment.[1001] Therefore, in order to ensure the lived through and conscious acceptance of children's rights,

997 K. Hanson, 'Does practice also work in theory?', in: A. Alen, H. Bosly, M. De Bie, J. Van de Lanotte (Eds.), *The UN Children's Rights Convention: Theory meets practice. Proceedings of the International Interdisciplinary Conference on Children's Rights, 18–19 May 2006, Ghent, Belgium*, Antwerp/Oxford: Intersentia 2007, p. 642.

998 Ibidem supra note 996. Hanson elaborates that 'children's rights have multiple geographical centres. Even if they are undeniably codified in international and national legal documents and further specified in international jurisprudence and development programmes, they were already alive in the minds and lived realities of children throughout the globe before that'.

999 Ibidem supra note 996.

1000 Ibidem supra note 996, p. 638.

1001 Depending on the particular context an enormous variety of examples can be given of this distinction, such as: the deliberate in- or exclusion of groups of (marginalized) children in programs to overcome access to primary health care facilities.

the implementation process must take into account the opinions of those actors involved.[1002]

Tobin provides for an elaborate motivation for the need to involve beneficiaries of the right to health in the implementation process. He argues that the identified elements of the right to health – availability, accessibility, acceptability and quality – remain at a fairly high level of abstraction and that States are therefore free to exercise their margin of appreciation in determining the measures that are required to meet the requirements under those four elements of the right to health.[1003] Tobin therefore argues that the involvement of beneficiaries themselves in determining the most appropriate measures for realizing children's right to health is required. He states that 'the process of identification, design, construction, and delivery of services to address the health needs of various groups within a state must be based on a collaborative process which engages not just health care providers and medical practitioners but also the intended beneficiaries themselves (or their advocates) to determine both the nature and form that specialist facilities should take'.[1004] This notion is also found in article 12 CRC and in General Comment 12 to the CRC, which deals with the obligation to involve children in all matters affecting them as well as in General Comment 14 to the ICESCR, noting that 'an important aspect of the right to health is the participation of the population in all health-related decision-making at the community, national and international levels'.[1005] Tobin acknowledges that 'the requirement to involve beneficiaries of health care services and the associated determinants of health will challenge dominant social and cultural expectations within elements of the interpretative community of the right to health (...) to not only consent to but also refuse medical treatment.'[1006] Therefore, notwithstanding any explicit or intrinsic refusal from medical professionals to engage children in the structuring and provision of their health care, such hesitance should not be tolerated if the outcome of children's deliberations run contrary to the dominant views of medical professionals, e.g. if children persistently refuse a medical treatment. UNICEF similarly encourages health professionals to internalize human rights, more particularly the right to health, and operationalize its elements in their daily health programming challenges.[1007] An example is when clinicians develop routine strategies for asking their juvenile patients about pain

1002 Ibidem supra note 995.

1003 Tobin, *The right to health in international law*, Oxford Scholarship Online, January 2012, Chapter 4, p. 35.

1004 Ibidem supra note 1002, p. 37.

1005 General Comment No. 14 (2000) The right to the highest attainable standard of health: 11/08/2000. E/C.12/2000/4. CESCR, § 11.

1006 Tobin, *The right to health in international law*, Oxford Scholarship Online, January 2012, Chapter 4, p. 48. In line with this statement, UNICEF emphasized that the role of power relations as a mitigating factor for recognition of children's rights must be acknowledged. Supra note 990.

1007 Ibidem supra note 990.

and noting this in their medical records. Parents and from a certain age children themselves can contribute by noting all pain episodes in a diary.[1008] Also, the design of a model that includes children or their representatives in the decision-making process should be sensitive towards any wishes of children *not* to be involved. Some children indicate that they would rather have limited information and just surrender to the medical process they are undergoing. For example, in a recent interview with a 19-year old girl who had been treated for cancer as a child, she explained that she didn't want to hear much about her chances for survival, but preferred to maintain her hope for the future. In hindsight, she recalled that it helped her to undergo the treatment step by step.[1009] Such wishes should be clearly respected. However, caution must be taken to ensure that children are withheld medical information or treatment only if they indicate so themselves instead of being denied access to medical information or treatment by their parents or legal representatives as may be the case in strictly religious families.[1010] The particular capabilities of very young children and their parents to shape the medical health care they are provided with is discussed in paragraph 6.3.4 on the opportunities of non-state actors in realizing the right to health of the child.

This section has elucidated that the involvement of the beneficiaries of health services is crucial to realizing the highest attainable standard of health of the child (e.g. in the identification, design, construction and delivery of health services). In fact and in response to subquestion (a) of this thesis, it appears that the social reality in which children live is a constitutive element of the right to health of the child. In response to subquestion (b), it appears that the social reality is part of a continuous process in which the right to health of the child is translated into daily practice and in which the daily practice in its turn influences the interpretation of the right to health of the child. As such, the right to health of the child is dependent on a particular context and time. Furthermore, it appears that children are active participants in the process of realizing their own right to health, because they consciously or unconsciously influence the way in which their own right to health is interpreted. The particular role of children and other actors involved will be further elaborated in section 4 of this chapter.

1008 K. Herr, *Pain Assessment in the Patient Unable to Self-Report, Position Statement with Clinical Practice Recommendations*, American Society for Pain Management Nursing, July 2011, Available at: www.aspmn.org/organization/documents/UPDATED_NonverbalRevisionFinalWEB.pdf.

1009 The interview was conducted on Wednesday 17 October 2012 in the Hague. Previously, the now 19 year old girl had been successfully treated for a large tumor in her back in the Sophia Children's Hospital in Rotterdam.

1010 See for example: S. Asser & R. Swan, 'Child Fatalities From Religion-motivated Medical Neglect', *Pediatrics* 1998, Volume 101, no. 4, April. Available at: http://childrenshealthcare.org/wp-content/uploads/2010/07/Pediatricsarticle.pdf.

6.3. THE ROLE OF THE STATE IN REALIZING THE RIGHT TO HEALTH OF CHILDREN

6.3.1. THE RIGHT TO HEALTH OF CHILDREN: REALIZING ECONOMIC, SOCIAL, CULTURAL RIGHTS

Although several domestic and international courts have dealt with the issue of enforcing economic, social and cultural rights, Langford and Clark comment that the legal principles developed, predominantly set the boundaries for enforcing these rights and that little is said on actual actions and inactions to be executed by the States involved.[1011] States therefore have a fairly broad margin of appreciation in prioritizing the measures to realize the different elements of children's right to the highest attainable standard of health. The question of enforceability of these rights is still subject to much debate, notwithstanding repeated confirmations of both the Committee on Economic, Social and Cultural Rights and the Committee on the Rights of the Child, that both categories of rights are indivisible and interdependent[1012, 1013] and that 'economic, social and cultural rights, as well as civil and political rights, should be regarded as justiciable'.[1014, 1015]

As laid down in article 4 CRC, two elements are central in the assessment of the level of realization of economic, social and cultural rights, such as the right to the highest attainable standard of health of the child, namely the concept of the 'available resources' of a country to realize that standard of health and the prioritization of 'appropriate measures' that can be taken to achieve that standard of health. These concepts will be further discussed in the following. Article 24 CRC furthermore speaks of the concept of 'progressive realization' in relation to international cooperation with a view to achieving progressively the full realization of the right to health of the child.

1011 Langford & Clark, 'The new kid on the block: A complaints procedure for the Convention on the Rights of the Child', Working Paper, no.1, Socio-Economic Rights Programme, Norwegian Centre for Human Rights, University of Oslo, January 2010. Available at: www.jus.uio.no/smr/english/people/aca/malcolml/new-kid-on-the-block-langford-clark.pdf.

1012 General Comment 2 to the ICESCR on International technical assistance measures, 2 February 1990, § 6.

1013 U.N. Doc. CRC/GC/5/2003/5, 27 November 2003, § 6. In General Comment 5, it is discussed that although the distinction in article 4 CRC implies a division between economic, social and cultural rights and civil and political rights, 'There is no simple or authoritative division of human rights in general or of Convention rights into the two categories'. It is specifically noted that 'Enjoyment of economic, social and cultural rights is inextricably intertwined with enjoyment of civil and political rights.'

1014 Ibidem supra note 1012, § 6.

1015 In the Preamble of Optional Protocol III to the Convention on the Rights of the Child, the universality, indivisibility, interdependence and interrelatedness of all human rights and fundamental freedoms is reaffirmed.

6.3.2. 'AVAILABLE RESOURCES'

Article 4 CRC elaborates that 'the maximum extent of the available resources of States Parties', must guide the measures taken to realize economic, social and cultural rights. Also, as identified in chapter III, the Committee on the Rights of the Child systematically recommends States Parties to the Convention on the Rights of the Child to ensure sufficient budget allocation to ensure equal access to basic services for all (vulnerable) groups of children in all areas and regions of a country. In doing so, providing access to health is prioritized among other social rights.[1016]

The question therefore is how the available resources of a country for realizing the highest attainable standard of health of the child can be determined. This question can be answered by looking at the total de facto domestic budget of a country or by looking at the partial budget that has been allocated to human rights, more particularly to children's right to health.[1017] The phrasing in article 4 that '*the maximum extent* of available resources' must be made available implies that all efforts must be made to increase the available budget for children's rights beyond the budget that has already been allocated to children's rights. The recommendations of the Committee on the Rights of the Child to reallocate budget from military expenditure towards children's rights, support this conclusion. Vandenhole has indicated that the total available resources in a country are generally sufficient to realize all children's rights.[1018] It is the allocation of resources that creates discrepancies between the resources available and the resources required for the realization of children's rights. Guideline 10 of the Maastricht Guidelines on Violations of Economic, Social and Cultural Rights identifies that compliance with the obligations deriving from economic, social and cultural rights may be undertaken by most States with relative ease, and without significant resource implications.[1019] It furthermore emphasizes that 'resource scarcity does not relieve States of certain minimum obligations in respect of the implementation of economic, social and cultural rights.' This provision is

1016 See also chapter 3.5.2 on the Recommendations of the Committee on the Rights of the Child on making available sufficient resources to realize children's rights.

1017 See M. Rishmawi, *A Commentary on the United Nations Convention on the Rights of the Child, Article 4: The Nature of States Parties' Obligations*, Martinus Nijhof Publishers 2006, p. 28, § 74.

1018 Lecture by W. Vandenhole at the Tobias Asser Institute in the Hague as a keynote speaker at the Research Seminar on Economic, Social and Cultural Rights: Vehicles for Social Justice?, organized by the Working Group on Economic, Social and Cultural Rights, The Netherlands School of Human Rights Research, 21 November 2012. See also: S. Skogly, 'The requirement of Using the Maximum Available Resources' for Human Rights Realisation: A Question of Quality as well as Quantity?', *Human Rights Law Review* 2012, pp. 1–28.

1019 The Maastricht Guidelines on Violations of Economic, Social and Cultural rights were adopted on the occasion of the 10th anniversary of the Limburg Principles on the Implementation of the International Covenant on Economic, Social and Cultural Rights. A group of experts met in January 1997 and unanimously agreed on the adoption of the guidelines. Available at: wwwl.umn.edu/humanrts/instree/Maastrichtguidelines_.html.

important because it establishes that countries are under the obligation to ensure the minimum core content (see chapter 4) of the right to health when they have signed the relevant treaties and thereby accepted the legal obligation to do so.

Approaching the question of the available resources from the side of children's needs, the available resources can be balanced against the resources required to realize the highest attainable standard of health of children in a country. The absence of 'a maximum of resources' that must be provided to ensure the highest attainable standard of health seems to suggest that 'the sky is the limit' for countries with (hypothetically) unlimited resources.[1020] Nolan has demonstrated that the lack of clarity of standards in implementing economic, social and cultural rights weakens the relevance of budget analyses of resources allocated to economic, social and cultural rights and the legal obligations of States.[1021] Conclusions of budgetary practitioners consequently remain rather broad and unspecified. Additionally, Nolan establishes that this lack of clear standard constitutes a problem for advocates that intend to use the Convention on the Rights of the Child as a standard for monitoring and for holding governments accountable.[1022]

Several targets can be suggested for determining a minimum level of resources that should be required. First of all, the absolute amount of resources that is necessary for ensuring the minimum core content of the right to health of children must be calculated.[1023] In calculating the exact budget required in a particular country, both the number and spread of children living in the country and in its different regions must be taken into account, as well as their basic health needs and the costs for ensuring the different components of their right to health. For example, the total health costs must be calculated for ensuring access to underlying determinants of health, access to primary health care, emergency health care and perinatal health care, an immunization campaign covering all children and the provision of health education about easily preventable diseases and family planning. This target is in line with the viewpoint of the Committee that children should be prioritized in allocating the maximum extent of available resources. Hereby, universal protection of children and access to basic but good

---

1020 In absolute terms, all countries have limited resources, but countries such as Norway and Qatar, have so many resources at their disposal, that the concept of the 'highest attainable standard of health' can be stretched beyond actual levels within their own national borders. However, when looking at health from an international perspective, article 4 CRC indicates that States Parties have an obligation to contribute to the realization of the right to health of the child within the framework of international cooperation. It may be argued therefore, that the highest attainable standard of health can be extended to including the right to health in other, less affluent countries.

1021 A. Nolan, 'Economic, social and cultural rights, budgets and the CRC', in: *International Journal of Children's Rights*, Martinus Nijhoff Publishers, 2013, Volume 21, issue 3, p. 270.

1022 Ibidem supra note 1020.

1023 See chapter V on the right to health of the child in international health and human rights for a discussion of the core content of the right to health of children.

quality social services must be guaranteed.[1024] Even in circumstances in which the available resources are inadequate, the Committee on the Rights of the Child reiterates that States retain the obligation to ensure the widest possible enjoyment of the relevant rights under the prevailing circumstances, notwithstanding the availability of limited resources.[1025] The rationale behind this is that countries have deliberately signed the Convention and that they are thereby under the obligation to do everything they can to ensure its provisions. This obligation even extends to situations as the current political or economic crisis or emergency situations.[1026]

In order to evaluate a country's preparedness to realize the right to health of children, comparisons can be made with countries with similar levels of development.[1027] This can be helpful in making a distinction between a country's inability and either its unwillingness to realize children's right to health. A division as made in chapter 4 can be helpful by integrating several relevant comparative factors, including gross domestic product, income per capita, a long and healthy life, access to knowledge and a decent standard of living. In making comparisons between countries periodical reviews based on data and indicators should be enriched by including the opinions of children, parents and other caretakers in the assessment.[1028] In this way, any possible instances of (large-scale) manipulation of data can be better signalled. Also, it gives room for individuals to ventilate their experiences and take up their own responsibility, so that every citizen can contribute to the development of the health care system. It can contribute to increasing the awareness of all actors involved in the realization process of the right to health of the child and in enforcing their own role in reflecting upon the way in which the health care system takes into account their preferences.

As a second step, given the fact that available resources are generally limited, policy choices must be made by local, regional or national governments over the allocation of resources to different regions and to high quality (and often more expensive) health care for a limited number of individuals or either to a much bigger number of individuals that only have basic health care requirements. On the basis of article 24 CRC, prioritizing basic levels of health requirements and access to health care, read in conjunction with the core principle of non-discrimination in article 2 CRC, the choice for allocating the available resources to basic health

1024 CRC Committee, 10th Anniversary Commemorative Meeting (UN Doc. CRC/C/87, 1999, Annex IV, § 291).

1025 See conclusion made by: M. Rishmawi, *A Commentary on the United Nations Convention on the Rights of the Child, Article 4: The Nature of States Parties' Obligations*, Martinus Nijhof Publishers 2006, note 1066.

1026 U.N. Doc. CRC/C/GC/15 on the right of the child to the enjoyment of the highest attainable standard of health, 14 March, § 74.

1027 Ibidem supra note 1024, notes 1058, 1073–1074.

1028 U.N. Doc. CRC/GC/2003/5, 27 November 2003, General Comment 5 to the CRC on General measures of implementation of the Convention on the Rights of the Child, 27 November 2003, § 50.

care facilities seems to be favourable. However, when judges are confronted with individual children who are in need of high quality health care, the decision becomes much more troublesome. Refusing such a child a necessary treatment, may lead to further deterioration of his health condition and potential chances for survival. It thereby jeopardizes the highest attainable standard of health of the individual child's right to health and its right to life and survival. Sachs, a retired judge in South-Africa commenting upon this dilemma from experience, even transfers the responsibility of making such difficult medical choices and 'to have ethical standards and criteria for making those determinations' to 'the medical community, in conjunction with the families and individuals concerned '.[1029] However, for medical professionals it can be highly awkward to refuse medical care to patients in need, especially since they have a duty to care and because they have direct encounters with the patients concerned. Also, individual medical ethical decisions will often conflict with ethical choices on a macro level.[1030] Therefore, a more direct relation is necessary for identifying the implications of abstract policy choices on allocation of resources for child health for the real and daily lives of individual people and the professionals who are responsible for communicating such implications in practice. Also, this close relation requires the involvement of health care providers and (representatives of) patients in deciding upon the resources allocated to children's health care to ensure practical applicability and integrating a human voice in the decision-making process. Such a link could for example be strengthened by providing people the choice to opt for different treatments under their health insurance.

In allocating budget for the realization of the right to health of the child, the question comes into play whether budget should be allocated to one overall, integrated children's rights program or whether the budget should be divided over all different governmental Departments that are involved in realizing children's rights, such as Departments of Health, Education, Justice and Family. Rishmawi draws attention to several comments made by the Committee in its Concluding Observations in which concern is expressed that the total budget allocated to

1029 A. Sachs, 'Enforcement of social and economic rights', *American University International Law Review* 2007, Volume 22, Issue 5, p. 679. Available at: http://heinonline.org/HOL/Page?handle=hein.journals/amuilr22&div=35&collection=journals&set_as_cursor=6&men_tab=srchresults. The example is discussed of the case of Soobramoney (1998) in which an applicant with chronic renal failure was refused access to health care by the hospital because 'it deemed that the best use of a limited amount of equipment would be to serve others that had better chances of benefiting from renal transplants'. The Court ruled that 'the selection process used was not discriminatory, except on pure health grounds and that it could not order the hospital to act otherwise'. Sachs adds that 'moving the applicant to the head of the queue would be to prejudice other people who had greater health claims, by saying that government must take money away from dealing with HIV, immunizing children, health education programs, victims of trauma, and all other diseases such as cancer and tuberculosis. We decided that, as judges, we could not interfere with the priorities in that particular area'.

1030 See the discussion instigated by Motta Ferraz and elaborated in chapter 5 on balancing the costs of individual lawsuits versus costs of ensuring access to health care for a large proportion of the population.

children is insufficient or that there is no integrated budget for children.[1031] This thus seems to point to the recommendation that States must ensure that there is a designated department that specifically looks after the interests of children. The answer to this question is also related to the question which actors and departments are responsible for taking the distinctive appropriate measures that are required to realize children's right to health. This question is discussed in the following section.

In addition to financial resources, States must ensure that sufficient human resources are made available to realizing the right to health of the child. Sufficient medical professionals must be available in all types of urban and rural health facilities and they must be adequately trained to ensure the key components of the right to health of the child.

In this section it was identified that States must allocate sufficient budget to realizing the right to health of the child. Hereto, the total costs for realizing the minimum core content of the right to health must be calculated. This includes the costs for (§ 43 and 44 GC 14 ICESCR):

1. Non-discriminatory access to essential primary health care.
2. Access to nutritious and safe food.
3. Access to shelter, housing, sanitation and safe and potable drinking water.
4. Access to essential drugs.
5. Equal distribution of health facilities, goods and services.
6. Adopt and implement a national public health strategy and plan of action.
7. Ensure reproductive, maternal and child health care.
8. Ensure immunization against the major infectious diseases.
9. Measures to prevent, treat and control epidemic and endemic diseases.
10. Provide education and access to health information.
11. Provide appropriate training for health personnel.
12. Provide international assistance and cooperation.

As a next step, the available resources must be allocated to address the most pressing health problems. This logically differs per country and region and thus depends on the particular context in which the measures are taken. Periodical reviews of both statistical data and personal assessments must be done to assess whether the measures prioritized by a country contribute to realizing the envisaged effect.

[1031] Concluding Observations of the CRC Committee on Chile, U.N. Doc. CRC/C/15Add.173, 2002, § 14; Burkina Faso U.N. Doc. CRC/C/15 Add.193, 2002, § 16(a) and Republic of Korea, U.N. Doc. CRC/C/15 Add 197, 2003, § 13; Poland U.N. Doc. CRC/C/15 Add. 194, 2002, § 17 and Sri Lanka, U.N. Doc. CRC/C/15 Add. 207, 2003, § 17. See also: M. Rishmawi, *A Commentary on the United Nations Convention on the Rights of the Child, Article 4: The Nature of States Parties' Obligations*, Martinus Nijhoff Publishers 2006, p. 31.

The implementation of general measures to realize the right to health must be attributed to one designated governmental department. This department must coordinate the different programs in place that concomitantly contribute to realizing the right to health of the child, such as the departments that deal with education (health education), traffic safety (prevention of accidents), social affairs (provision of social protection and underlying determinants of health) and care (health care and prevention of violence).

6.3.3. APPROPRIATE MEASURES

The second question that should be answered in identifying the steps to be taken by States to realize the right to the highest attainable standard of health of the child is what measures are deemed appropriate in relation to the available resources. Article 4 of the Convention states that: 'States Parties shall undertake all appropriate legislative, administrative, and other measures for the implementation of the rights recognized in the present Convention.' Article 10.4 of the Optional Protocol on a communications procedure for children furthermore states that: 'When examining communications alleging violations of economic, social or cultural rights, the Committee shall consider the reasonableness of the steps taken by the State party in accordance with article 4 of the Convention. In doing so, the Committee shall bear in mind that the State party may adopt a range of possible policy measures for the implementation of the economic, social and cultural rights in the Convention.' From these provisions, it appears that States have a broad range of possible legislative, administrative and policy measures that can be taken to ensure children's right to health and that they should pass the test of 'reasonableness'. Sachs comments that 'reasonableness is a concept that lawyers are very familiar with, although they are not familiar with the concepts of 'available resources' and 'progressive realization''.[1032] Sachs argues that a minimum standard of reasonableness should include 'appropriate arrangements for people in situations of extreme scarcity – such as flood or fire victims, people who for one reason or another have got nothing at all'.[1033] A similar reference is found in paragraph 18 of General Comment 14 to the ICESCR, stating that 'even in times of severe resource constraints, the vulnerable members of society must be protected by the adoption of relatively low-cost targeted programmes.'[1034] These vulnerable people clearly include children under five. Sachs furthermore

---

1032 A. Sachs, 'Enforcement of social and economic rights', *American University International Law Review* 2007, Volume 22, Issue 5, p. 679. Available at: http://heinonline.org/HOL/Page?handle=hein.journals/amuilr22&div=35&collection=journals&set_as_cursor=6&men_tab=srchresults.

1033 Ibidem supra note 1031.

1034 The same is noted by: H.S. Aasen in 'Children and the Right to Health Protection', *Health and Human Rights in Europe*, Groningen: Intersentia 2012, January, p. 236.

argues that in judging upon the possible measures that are taken by governments to ensure social rights, a legal obligation is imposed upon governments to develop a reasonable program, within a reasonable time to meet reasonable obligations.[1035] Three elements are thus discerned for assessing the reasonableness of measures taken to realize the right to health of the child. In the following, only the concepts of reasonable time and reasonable program will be discussed, because these obligations have been discussed in the previous chapters.

6.3.3.1. Within a reasonable time

The element of reasonable time is dependent on the qualification of the obligations to achieve the right to health of the child. Nolan distinguishes between obligations of immediate and obligations of progressive nature.[1036] The obligations to protect and to respect the right to health of the child can generally be qualified as obligations of an immediate nature. The obligation to fulfil has elements of both categories. However, as identified by Rishmawi, 'the obligation to take steps to progressively realize economic, social and cultural rights is an immediate one'.[1037] States thus have an obligation of result to make progress in the realization of the right to health of the child. However, there is a broad margin of appreciation in determining the steps that lead to that progress. These steps all relate to the duty to protect, respect and fulfil the right to health of the child.

Although the right to health of the child as laid down in the Convention on the Rights of the Child is qualified as a provisional right, interpretation in line with the other CRC articles and with the elaboration of the right to health in international human rights law (see chapter 5), also reveals protective and participatory elements, such as children's right to be protected against harmful medical practices (e.g. art. 24.3 CRC, art. 19 CRC) and the right to refrain from a medical treatment. The realization of these protective and participatory elements of children's right to the highest attainable standard of health does not need to pose an enormous burden on States' available resources. Therefore, these elements should fall within the scope of States' immediate obligation of result. The provisional aspects of the right to health of the child however, such as the provision of health services to reduce infant and maternal mortality, the provision of health education, healthy food and drinking water, require proactive measures to be realized and thus place a larger burden on a States' available resources. The wide array of possible measures to fulfil children's right to the highest attainable standard of health include giving medicines or providing affordable health care (direct or through freely accessible insurances) to people and to building medical facilities.

[1035] Ibidem supra note 1031.

[1036] A. Nolan, 'The child's right to health and the courts', in: J. Harrington & M. Stuttaford, *Global Health and Human Rights*, Routledge 2012, p. 140.

[1037] Ibidem supra note 1016, p. 28.

Nolan has argued that not only the regulatory role of States in preventing and punishing violations of the right to health of the child by non-state actors must be considered by the Committee on the Rights of the Child, but also its potential to stimulate non-state actors to provide for health-related goods and services.[1038] In this way, more actors can take ownership and become involved in realizing children's right to health, which will increase the overall capacity to reach the highest attainable standard of health for children.

Although the obligation to fulfil must be realized progressively, the obligation to ensure the minimum core content of the right to health of the child is an obligation of immediate nature. The requirement to take measures within a reasonable time thus only applies to measures that go beyond the minimum core content of the right to health of the child towards the *full* realization of the highest attainable standard of health, because those are the rights that are dependent upon progressive realization instead of immediate realization.

The element of reasonable time also appears in various domestic law systems. As such, the concept has been criticized for being too vague and subjective.[1039] Whereas the concept must become clear in the particular context in which it is applied, this poses a particular challenge in international law, because people can argue for a variety of time frames and they have done so in litigation in both national and international courts.[1040] Therefore, it would be recommendable to specify further guidelines on what constitutes a reasonable time or either to give specific deadlines for some of the main health measures that must be taken, such as within 1, 5, 10 or 20 years time. This could help governments to develop a realistic plan to progressively realize the separate elements of the right to health of the child to which they can be held accountable. However, in achieving transnational uniformity of the application of the concept of reasonable time, agreement must be reached on a common baseline or yardstick from which progress in realizing the right to health of the child can be measured, e.g. the status quo.[1041]

In private law, the concept of the reasonable time has been interpreted by courts in light of the nature (i.e. particular health condition at stake), purpose (realize good health in one particular child or group of children) and

---

1038 Ibidem supra note 1012. See also submission for the development of CRC General Comment 15 on the right to health of the child by Nolan, Eli Yamin and Meier, p. 3. Available at: www2.ohchr.org/english/bodies/crc/docs/CallSubmissions_Art24/ProfNolan-DurhamUniversity-ProfElyYamin-HarvardUniversityandProfMeier-UniversityofNorthCarolina.docx.

1039 S.E. Smith, *In law, what is reasonable time?*, 2013. Available at: www.wisegeek.com/in-law-what-is-reasonable-time.htm.

1040 Ibidem supra note 1038. For a further discussion of the concept of 'reasonable time in international and various domestic law systems see: C. Baasch Andersen, *Reasonable Time in Article 39(1) of the CISG – Is Article 39(1) Truly a Uniform Provision?*, University of Copenhagen, 1998, available at: www.cisg.law.pace.edu/cisg/biblio/andersen.html. CISG = United Nations Convention on Contracts for the International Sale of Goods. Generally, the actual meaning of reasonable time is determined by the application of the provision in International Courts and Tribunals.

1041 Ibidem supra note 1038 and 1039, chapter VI.2.

circumstances (e.g. depending on country, region, health situation, situation of war/peace, other infrastructure and climate) of the case as well as the intentions of the parties when signing the contract.[1042] Other considerations that can be made in assessing the reasonable time include the damage that is caused by not taking the particular health measure at stake (maternal, infant and child mortality rates, lost DALYs or QALYs,[1043] burden of disease and lost work force), deliberations on prior delays in taking health measures, and comparing a situation to results in other countries. Baasch Andersen argues that the list of factors that can influence the reasonableness or unreasonableness of time is not exhaustive, but that it falls under the discretion of Courts and Tribunals to include them in the assessment of reasonableness, as long as the factors are relevant to the objective of the measures at stake.[1044] In determining the reasonableness, it can be argued that the reasonable time extends 'so long as the delay is attributable to causes beyond the control of the State and that the State has neither acted negligently or unreasonably'.[1045] On the basis of guideline 13 of the Maastricht Guidelines States have the burden of proof in demonstrating that causes for non-compliance lie beyond their control.[1046] Causes beyond the control of the State may include natural disasters or infectious diseases that impact upon the health of its population. However, such circumstances do not dismiss States from taken all measures required to mitigate or prevent the harmful impact of such events.

6.3.3.2. Reasonable program

The second element of reasonableness is the requirement to develop a reasonable program. On the basis of articles 4 and 24 CRC such a program should include at least all appropriate legislative, administrative and other measures. The element

---

1042 The concept of reasonable time is a Reasonable Time Law and legal definition, uslegal.com, available at: http://definitions.uslegal.com/r/reasonable-time/.

1043 The disability-adjusted life year (DALY) is a measure of overall disease burden, expressed as the number of years lost due to ill-health, disability or early death. Potential years lost due to premature death are combined with the healthy years lost due to disease or disability. Both the concept of mortality and morbidity are therefore integrated in one single parameter of health, which is increasingly used in public health. The quality-adjusted life year (QALY) is a measure of disease burden, including both the quality and the quantity of life lived. It is used in assessing the value for money of a medical intervention. The QALY is based on the number of years of life that would be added by the intervention. Each year in perfect health is assigned the value of 1.0 down to a value of 0.0 for being dead. Years lived with deficits are assigned a value between 1.0 and 0.0 dependent on the loss of the quality of life. See also 'Measuring effectiveness and cost effectiveness', National Institute for Health and Clinical Excellence: www.nice.org.uk/newsroom/features/measuringeffectivenessandcosteffectivenesstheqaly.jsp.

1044 Ibidem supra note 1038.

1045 Ibidem supra note 1017, guideline 13. The example is given that the closure of educational facilities may be justified in the event of an earthquake. The same can be argued for the closure of medical facilities. However, if the State neglected to take preventive measures to mitigate the impact of an earthquake or refrained from warning people timely, the measures that could have been taken should be qualified as falling in the control of the State.

1046 Ibidem supra note 1018.

'other measures' has been incorporated to include any possible measures that contribute to realizing the rights of children, including their right to health.[1047] Such measures may go beyond legislation and include all child-specific measures and practices.

General Comment 5 to the CRC on General Measures of Implementation and the General Guidelines provide for a wide array of possible measures, including the provision of information i) any comprehensive review of domestic legislation, ii) the adoption of new laws or codes or amendments made to existing ones, iii) the status of the CRC in domestic law, including the recognition of the CRC in the constitution or in other legislation and the status of the CRC in the event of conflict with national legislation, iv) the possibility of invoking the CRC in national courts and v) the conclusion of any bilateral or multilateral agreements in the field of children's rights.[1048, 1049]

From these recommended measures, it appears that the Committee focuses on the one hand on the explicit recognition of the provisions of the CRC in the constitution or in one comprehensive children's law and on the other hand in the different sectorial laws that codify domestic children's rights.[1050] Children's rights must thus be integrated on all possible levels and in all relevant sectors. With respect to the realization of the right to health of the child, the holistic character of the CRC thus requires the integration of provisions in national health law, housing law, social security law, protection law, environmental law and other fields of law. Hereto, a full review of all existing and proposed national legislation is required as well as consideration of any applicable customary or religious laws in a country.[1051] Furthermore, the review of legislation must be continuous and cover all different levels of the government, such as the national, federal and provincial levels.[1052]

Although administrative and other measures cannot be spelt out in full detail, the Committee provides several guidelines for effective implementation. Key in these guidelines is the need for cross-sectorial coordination between different levels of the government and civil society, in particular children themselves.[1053]

1047 See also: M. Rishmawi, *A Commentary on the United Nations Convention on the Rights of the Child, Article 4: The Nature of States Parties' Obligations*, Martinus Nijhof Publishers 2006, p. 4.

1048 U.N.Doc, CRC/C/GC5, CRC Committee General Comment 5 on General Measures of Implementation, § 18–22.

1049 UN Doc. CRC/C/58/Rev.1, 29 November 2005. General Guidelines regarding the form and content of periodic reports to be submitted by States Parties under article 44, § 44, 1b of the CRC, Adopted by the Committee at its thirty-ninth session on 3 June 2005. Available at: www.unhchr.ch/tbs/doc.nsf/898586b1dc7b4043c1256a450044f331/af20808817648df4c12570fa002ba893/$FILE/G0545289.pdf.

1050 In General Comment 5 the Committee welcomes the adoption of consolidated children's rights statutes, but also reminds States of the need to ensure that all relevant sectoral laws reflect consistently the principles and standards of the Convention. See § 22.

1051 Ibidem supra note 1049, § 20.

1052 Ibidem supra note 1049, § 5. See also ibidem supra note 30, § 18.

1053 Ibidem supra note 1049, § 27.

Secondly, the need for monitoring of implementation by the government itself, national human rights institutions and NGOs is deemed highly important.[1054] Furthermore, the Committee has specified several priority measures that should be integrated in the realization process.[1055] In these measures, several specific references are made to ensuring children's health. First of all, in developing a national strategy on children's health, specific goals for sectoral action plans must be set. Such a sectoral plan on health must contain time bound and measurable targets, implementation measures, specification of human and financial resources allocated and mechanisms for monitoring, review, updates and periodic reporting. Although prioritization of policy targets is necessary, these priorities must include the minimum requirements as laid down in the CRC.[1056] Under the Reporting Guidelines States Parties are furthermore expected to identify the impact of the measures taken on the actual realization of economic, social and cultural rights by providing a wide set of indicators on health. With respect to children's health, data must be included about the budget allocated to health, the number of health professionals that have been trained in children's rights and a large variety of other health indicators, including, infant, child and maternal mortality rates, the proportion of children with low birth weight, the number of children that is immunized, the proportion of children that have access to safe drinking water and sanitation, the number of pregnant women who have access to perinatal health care, the number of children born in hospital and the number of children receiving exclusive breastfeeding.[1057] States are further held to set appropriate standards for the private sector in the area of health, such as the number and suitability of staff and the establishment of permanent monitoring mechanisms. The effectiveness of child rights education to both professionals and children and their families must not only be reviewed for knowledge transmission, but also for changes in practice and attitudes.[1058]

1054 Ibidem supra note 1049, § 27.

1055 Measures include: A. adoption of a comprehensive national plan that is endorsed by all governmental levels; B. coordination of implementation measures; C. ensuring sufficient allocation of resources in decentralization and delegation; D. engagement of the private sector; E. the monitoring of the implementation by child impact assessments and evaluations; F. quantitative and qualitative data collection to get a complete picture of progress, including by engaging children in the process as interviewers and researchers; G. identify the proportion of the budgets that are allocated to children; H. Training and capacity building for children, caretakers and professionals; I. cooperation with civil society; J. international cooperation; K. Independent human rights institutions.

1056 Ibidem supra note 1049, § 28.

1057 UN Doc. CRC/C/58/Rev.2, 23 November 2010, Reporting Guidelines Treaty-specific guidelines regarding the form and content of periodic reports to be submitted by States parties under article 44, paragraph 1(b), of the Convention on the Rights of the Child, adopted by the Committee at its fifty-fifth session (13 September–1 October 2010). See Annex for an overview of the statistical data that are required, specifically § 3b, 4d, C1c&f, F. Other indicators include the number of children infected with HIV/AIDS and the proportion of those that receives medical care and counselling, different health problems in adolescents and the available health services to tackle those problems.

1058 Ibidem supra note 1049, § 55.

Generally, children must be considered as independent rights holders.[1059] Therefore, the involvement of beneficiaries of health, young children or de facto their caretakers or representatives, must be sought in all phases of the realization process, including the development of a national plan, the implementation measures, data collection, monitoring and evaluation, for example by integrating data gained from interviews with children in the monitoring reports.[1060] The Committee on the Rights of the Child therefore recommends that there should be a continuous process of child impact assessments and child impact evaluations, which consequently predict and evaluate the effects of proposed laws, policies or budget allocations.[1061] The Committee places great emphasis on the involvement of children in data collection and interviewing them, so that their interests are directly reflected.[1062] With respect to the involvement of very young children, this requires age-appropriate interview techniques as well as interviewing their parents.

6.3.4. JUSTICIABILITY OF CHILDREN'S RIGHT TO HEALTH IN DOMESTIC COURTS

In addition to the obligation to take legislative and policy measures, States must ensure that effective remedies are in place for children or their representatives to effectuate their right to health. Effective remedies in the domestic law of States Parties are essential in ensuring the effective implementation of children's right to health at the national level. Therefore, States Parties must provide information on the remedies available and their accessibility towards children.[1063] The provisions of the CRC must be directly applicable and appropriately enforced. The Committee on the Rights of the Child has established that legislation should meet several criteria to be directly applicable. In addition, the Committee has elaborated that effective remedies have a child rights based approach and that these remedies are widely published and accessible to all children, including those of marginalized groups.[1064] The child rights based approach requires as a minimum that child-friendly procedures are in place, that child-friendly information and legal assistance is provided and that appropriate reparation, including compensation, physical and psychological recovery, rehabilitation and reintegration, as required by article 39 are provided.[1065]

1059 Ibidem supra note 1049, § 21, 66–70.
1060 Ibidem supra note 1049, § 29, 46, 50, 54 and 58.
1061 Ibidem supra note 1049, § 45.
1062 Ibidem supra note 1049, § 50.
1063 Ibidem supra note 1049, § 14.
1064 Ibidem supra note 1049, § 24 and 66–69.
1065 Ibidem supra note 1049, § 24.

Nolan notes that worldwide, a growing tendency is discerned in which economic, social and cultural rights are incorporated in the national constitution.[1066] She establishes that out of a survey of 86 national constitutions, 18 explicitly contain a provision on children's right to health. Also, plural constitutions contain a reference to the child's right to protection, which contains components that relate to the right to health of the child.[1067] Sloth-Nielsen identifies a similar development in the recently adopted constitutions of several African countries.[1068] However, she also points out that although children's rights have increasingly been integrated in national constitutions, the actual realization of these rights sets a working agenda at least for the coming 30 years.[1069]

6.3.4.1. Application of the right to health in Dutch domestic law cases

In an analysis of the application of children's rights principles in Dutch domestic courts, Pulles has argued that the provisions of the CRC can be directly applied because they provide for a clear and precise standard and because they are very similar to provisions in other human rights treaties, such as the ICESCR that are applied directly.[1070] However, there still is a highly diversified application of CRC provisions in Dutch domestic courts.[1071] Although this diversified application of CRC provisions was previously attributed to the relatively new status of the CRC as an interpretative tool, this argument is increasingly becoming outdated, because the CRC is becoming increasingly well-known among different professionals.[1072] The recent research conducted by the Centre on Children's Rights Amsterdam (CCRA) has provided additional insight into the possibilities of and the ways in which children's rights, most particularly children's right to health, are applied in domestic cases. Although it is concluded that a relatively positive development can be discerned with respect to the direct application of CRC provisions in Dutch

1066 A. Nolan, 'The child's right to health and the courts', in: J. Harrington & M. Stuttaford (eds.), *Global Health and Human Rights,* Routledge 2012, p. 142. Nolan establishes that out of a survey of 86 national constitutions, 18 explicitly contain a provision on children's right to health.

1067 Ibidem supra note 1065, p. 142.

1068 Lecture delivered by Professor Sloth-Nielsen on 19 November 2012 on the occasion of the inauguration of professor Ton Liefaard at the University of Leiden.

1069 Ibidem supra note 1065.

1070 G. Pulles, 'Onduidelijkheid over de rechtstreekse werking van het VN-kinderrechtenverdrag', *Nederlands Juristenblad* 2011, Volume 4, 28 January 2011, p. 233. Differences identified sometimes raised the level of child protection.

1071 The finding that the direct application of CRC provisions in Dutch courts is very variable, has been reaffirmed and well-established in an extensive research by the Centre for Children's Rights in Amsterdam on the application of CRC provisions in Dutch law cases between 1 January 2002 and 1 September 2011. See: J. de Graaf & M.M.C. Limbeek, *De toepassing van het Internationaal Verdrag inzake de Rechten van het Kind in de Nederlandse Rechtspraak*, Nijmegen: Ars Aequi Libri 2012, p. 275. Available at: www.defenceforchildren.nl/images/20/2073.pdf.

1072 Ibidem supra note 1070, p. 234.

domestic law, this conclusion is explicitly not true for the right to health.[1073] In all different legal sections researched and in all cases in which article 24 CRC was evoked, the Court implicitly (by not referring to article 24) or explicitly decided that the right to health of the child as laid down in article 24 CRC is not directly applicable.[1074] In one case, the Court elaborated that 'article 24 CRC cannot be directly applied, because it addresses the State Party and not the individual citizen'.[1075] Similarly, the Court in Zwolle stated that Article 24 CRC provides for generally described social targets, from which no unconditional and precisely defined individual rights can be derived.[1076] In yet another case the Court held that 'Given the phrasing, nature and scope of the right to health of the child as laid down in article 24, it cannot be directly applied, nor can other rights be derived from it'.[1077] The case involved a Romanian family that was removed from the house in which they were illegally living. The family argued that their only option was to go back to Romania, where there would be no adequate medical treatment available for their child. Although the court did not consider article 24 CRC directly applicable, it did consider the question whether an immediate emergency situation resulted from the removal. It found that that would not be the case. Whereas article 24 was not considered directly applicable, its contents did influence the consideration of the child's situation in this case. This influence of article 24 CRC is discerned in several other cases across the different legal disciplines researched. For example, in an immigrant law case, the court decided that a previous decision made by the IND (immigration body that decides upon the admission of asylum seekers to the Netherlands), did not sufficiently take into account the interest of the severely sick child.[1078] The Court held that a heavier duty of motivation is required when sending back children to their home country and that this duty is even heavier with respect to a severely sick child.[1079] Therefore, the

1073 Ibidem supra note 1070, pp. 77–79.

1074 Ibidem supra note 1070, pp. 62–64, 90–92, 142–145 and 194–196. Legal sectors researched included civil and family law, immigrant law, administrative law and juvenile law. See law cases Rb. Alkmaar 20 July 2005, LJN AT 9598, Rb. Rotterdam, 6 September 2010, *LJN* BO1013, Rb. Zwolle-Lelystad (vzr), 9 June 2011, LJN BR 3569, ABRvS 12 April 07, LJN BA 3394, Rb. Den Haag, 24 February 2008, LJN BF 0906, Rb. Den Haag, 2 March 2010, LJN BM 2383, Rb. Den Haag, 19 December 2005, AWB 04/19508, Rb. Zwolle-Lelystad, 19 April 2011, LJN BQ 3967, CRvB 20 October 2010, LJN BO 3581 and Rb. Utrecht (vzr) 6 April 2010, LJN BM 0846.

1075 Rb. Alkmaar, 20 July 2005, LJN AT 9598. The case involved a single mother who had given permission to perform a medical treatment on her daughter on the basis of her right to health. However, it was decided that the lack of permission by the father was not justified, *inter alia* because the right to health of the child is not directly applicable.

1076 Rb. Zwolle-Lelystad, 19 April 2011, LJN BQ 3967.

1077 Rb. Zwolle-Lelystad (vzr), 9 June 2011, LJN BR 3569. The case involved a Romanian family that was removed from the house in which they were illegally living. The family argued that their only option was to go back to Romania, where there would be no adequate medical treatment available for their child. Although the judge did not consider article 24 CRC directly applicable, it did consider the question whether an immediate emergency situation resulted from the removal. It found that that would not be the case.

1078 Rb. Den Haag, 19 December 2005, AWB 04/19508.

1079 Ibidem supra note 1077.

health of the child did play a role in the consideration of the case. Lastly, the Court of Utrecht held that providing emergency housing to an asylum seeking woman and her child, who suffered from asthma and epilepsy, was essential in ensuring the human dignity of the child.[1080] All these examples show that the lack of direct applicability of the right to health of the child in Dutch court practice, thus does not lead to the conclusion that there is no additional value of the right to health of the child in individual cases. Interpretation in conformity with the CRC did give prove of the additional value of the right to health of the child in the CRC in explaining the treaty in domestic procedures as well as in taking children's health situation into account in decisions.[1081] De Graaf identifies that in order to increase the opportunity that children's rights are taken into account, referral to the facts and circumstances underlying the case often greatly contribute.[1082] Thus, it is the daily circumstances in which children live that greatly influence the interpretation and effectuation of the right to health of the child.

Although the abovementioned examples of Dutch domestic law show that there may be some room for involving article 24 CRC in the interpretation of domestic cases, it is also clear that the Dutch State retains its primary responsibility for ensuring children's right to health. Therefore, its activities in realizing the right to health must be primarily considered by judicial and quasi-judicial institutions. So what is this role of the judiciary and how does it influence the interpretation of children's right to the highest attainable standard of health?

6.3.4.2. Judicial and quasi-judicial decision-making

Nolan has identified the role played by judicial and quasi-judicial decision-making bodies in evaluating the efforts made by states to take adequate positive steps to fulfil the right to health of the child, e.g. by allocating sufficient resources. She argues that a somewhat protective role is taken up by the courts,[1083] because children are excluded from the democratic process, that political organs therefore aren't held sufficiently accountable and that therefore 'they are less likely to be attentive to the rights and needs of children'.[1084] She therefore comes to the conclusion that evidence from international and domestic legislation shows that both drafters of human rights instruments and courts are more inclined to impose obligations on States with regard to the realization of the right to health

---

1080 Rb. Utrecht (vzr), 6 April 2010, LJN BM 0846.

1081 Ibidem supra note 1070, pp. 275–280.

1082 Ibidem supra note 1070, pp. 275–280.

1083 An example of this protective orientation towards children is found in the Constitution of South-Africa, in which elaborates that the right to health is dependent on available resources. However, with respect to children, this condition is left out, so that children benefit from a better, namely a less conditioned right to health than adults.

1084 A. Nolan, 'The child's right to health and the courts', in: J. Harrington & M. Stuttaford, *Global Health and Human Rights*, Rotledge 2012, p. 138.

of children than of adults.[1085] This particular position of courts *vis-à-vis* children is remarkable, given the often heard criticism that courts should be careful in judging upon the justiciability of economic, social and cultural rights, because this would involve them in budgetary or policy matters which would be a violation of the separation of powers in the trias politica.[1086, 1087] Another significant criticism against justiciability of the right to health of the child follows from the argument made by Yash and Gill.[1088] Although Nolan argues that courts have a role to play in the delineation of the right to health and its enforceability, Yash and Gill's argument that justiciability of economic, social and cultural rights may detract from other ways of social enforcement is particularly true for the realization of children's right to health. When courts consider the efforts made by States to realize children's right to health, they determine the reasonableness of health measures taken and they do not consider possible alternatives. Especially with respect to the realization of children's right to health, many other non-legal measures are possible to ensure that children have access to underlying determinants of health and to health care. Also, many non-state actors are better equipped and more closely connected to the child and its family than States Parties to take such measures. In order to establish progressive standards for the realization of the highest attainable standard of health of the child that are rooted in the daily lives of children and their families, involvement of all public and private actors that operate close to the child is therefore required. Furthermore, as indicated previously, accepting justiciability of children's right to health may result in a flood of litigation, which could detract resources from the actual implementation of children's right to health.[1089] Therefore, it should be kept in mind that court intervention should remain a last resort in the realization process of children's right to health.

However, the importance of primarily considering non-judicial measures in ensuring children's right to health does not entail that the right to health in itself is or should be meaningless. On the contrary, as established by Nolan, the integration of the right to health of the child in national constitutions shifts the

1085 Ibidem supra note 1083, p. 146.

1086 Y. Ghai & J. Cottrell, 'The role of the Courts in the protection of Economic, Social and Cultural Rights', in: *Economic, Social and Cultural Rights in Practice, The Role of Judges in Implementing Economic, Social and Cultural Rights*, Interights 2004, p. 65.

1087 For a clear overview of pro and contra arguments on the justiciability of economic, social and cultural rights, see: Maite San Giorgi, *The Human Rights to Equal Access to Health Care*, Intersentia 2012, pp. 80–84.

1088 Ibidem supra note 1085.

1089 The current 'tsunami' of cases that constitutes a real challenge for the functioning of the European Court on Human Rights is an example of this considerable and genuine threat. See: J.P. Costa, *Current Challenges for the European Court on Human Rights*, lecture delivered at the University of Leiden on 10 December 2011 as part of the series of Raymond and Beverly Sackler Distinguished Lectures in Human Rights at Leiden Law School.

discussion from 'is the right to health of the child enforceable?' to 'how can this right be enforced?'.[1090]

Last but not least, when remedies against violations of children's right to health are in fact sought, States must ensure that effective, child-sensitive procedures are available to children and their representatives, which include the provision of child-friendly information, advice, advocacy and legal and other assistance when seeking access to independent complaints procedures and to the courts.[1091] With respect to the application of cases concerning the right to health of the child, special attention must therein be given to children who are physically unable to leave the medical facilities due to their medical condition or of parents who have difficulty in visiting their children in hospital and also attending law suits.

In addition to the formal legal procedures, Kaime argues that the realization of children's rights should not only entail the incorporation of these rights in national legislation and policy measures, but also the translation of these rights to local circumstances, i.e. the effective influence on children's daily realities.[1092] Kaime identifies that in addition to the formal ways to legally enforce children's rights, such as state courts and other law enforcement mechanisms, the effectuation of children's rights norms in daily life requires active deliberation with local institutions, authorities and other influential actors such as the elders in a family.[1093] However, in the negotiation process to transform the CRC principles into lived realities of children, it is important to identify and ensure that children, women and other traditionally less dominant groups are included in the decision-making processes.[1094] The discussion on the way in which they contribute and how children's rights are put into practice has in itself an awareness-raising effect.

Kaime acknowledges that different communities all have different structures, legal procedures and institutions and that the involvement of different local actors in the realization of children's rights thus also takes many different forms. However, he does identify a few guidelines that should be taken into account when translating children's rights to the local practice:[1095]

1. Understand the basic structure of the institution that is sought to be involved. This includes the identification of key actors that have a role in gatekeeping and in introducing and influencing decision-making processes.
2. Understand basic procedures and structure any new proposal in terms that conform to the standard procedures. The introduction of new ideas will be more likely to be accepted.

1090 A. Nolan, 'The child's right to health and the courts', in: J. Harrington & M. Stuttaford, *Global Health and Human Rights*, Routledge 2012, pp. 152–153.

1091 Ibidem supra note 1007, § 5.

1092 T. Kaime, *The Convention on the Rights of the Child: A Cultural Legitimacy Critique*, Europa Law Publishing 2011, pp. 137–140.

1093 Ibidem supra note 1091, pp. 137–140 and 148.

1094 Ibidem supra note 1091, p. 149.

1095 Ibidem supra note 1091, pp. 151–153.

3. Understand the sphere of influence of the institutions involved and its relation to the realization of children's rights. This enable advocates of children's rights to engage with the institution that has the biggest impact on the improvement of children's rights implementation.
4. Respect local customs and traditions and show sincere interest. The process of building trust often requires less talking and more listening.

Kaime establishes that by respecting these guidelines, a more organic and locally accepted way of implementing children's rights can be achieved, which in the long term has a more lasting effect on the improvement on the lived reality of children.[1096] He concludes by stating that the involvement of local institutions in addition to formal and more centralized legal enforcement mechanisms increases the accessibility, the affordability and the legitimacy.[1097] In my opinion, these guidelines have significant added value in bridging the gap between the rights of children as written down in international and national legislation and the effectuation of these rights in the daily lives of children.

In this section the justiciability of the right to health of the child was discussed. Although this right is increasingly laid down in national legislations, the possibility of direct application of the right to health in individual law cases is not clear cut. Direct applicability may be assumed in cases in which a State did not meet its obligation to respect and to protect. However, a study on the application of children's rights in the Netherlands showed that whereas many rights are directly applied, this is explicitly not the case for the right to health of the child. This points to the conclusion that the justiciability of the right to health of the child is limited to the duties to respect and to protect.

The second issue discussed is whether it is desirable to directly apply the right to health of the child. It was concluded that this should be a measure of last resort, since law suits detract resources from the allocation of resources to actual health care measures and that there are alternative ways to enforce the right to health that benefit the right to health more directly, such as through quasi-judicial institutions that are more closely connected to the daily realities in which children live or through the efforts made by private actors.

6.3.5. INTERNATIONAL COOPERATION FOR ENSURING THE RIGHT TO HEALTH OF THE CHILD

Health crosses borders. Not only do infectious diseases easily overcome manmade boundaries between countries and regions, the enormous flows of travellers due to

[1096] Ibidem supra note 1091, p. 153.
[1097] Ibidem supra note 1091, p. 153.

tourism, business, immigration and refugee flows enable viruses to quickly spread among and infect people in virtually all corners of the world. This phenomenon simply obliges States to collaborate and mutually define the steps required to mitigate the impact of potentially life threating viruses that spread the world on the basis of their own want for survival.[1098] Following the outbreak of a new strain of avian flu in 2004, the WHO issued the International Health Regulations (IHL 2005), which set international rules for responding to international outbreaks of infectious diseases.[1099] In addition, with respect to the right to health of the child in the international children's rights domain, article 24.4 CRC specifically obliges States Parties to promote and encourage international cooperation with a view to progressively achieving the right to health of the child. Such cooperation can be divided in regular development aid and emergency care in humanitarian situations such as natural disasters and conflict situations.

International cooperation involves donor countries and recipient countries. However, as identified by Wabwile, there is no definition of developing countries in international law and macro-economic indicators for ranking states are not static.[1100] Therefore, the identification of donor or developing countries is not simply determined. With respect to children's health, developing countries are generally characterized by low government investments in health infrastructure resulting in high numbers of ill health, infant and child mortality rates and malnutrition. It has been found that child deaths from easily preventable causes amount to 49% of the total number of child deaths. Also, high rates of population growth are often reported.[1101] Article 4 CRC elaborates that all measures for realizing economic, social and cultural rights must be taken to the maximum extent of the available resources of the States Parties and 'where needed, within

1098 In response to the outbreak of swine flu in 2009, the Director-General of the WHO declared a public health emergency of international concern and established an Emergency Committee. This outbreak of swine or Mexican flu posed particular challenges for newborns and young children, because they had never experienced a previous, similar strain if flu that had spread the world several decades earlier.

1099 World Health Organization [WHO], *International Health Regulations 2005*, (2nd ed. 2008), *at* http://whqlibdoc.who.int/publications/2008/9789241580410_eng.pdf. See also *See* David P. Fidler, *Global Outbreak of Avian Influenza A (H5N1) and International Law*, ASIL Insights, Jan. 2004, at www.asil.org/insigh125.cfm. The IHL 2005 authorize the Director-General of the WHO to declare a state of public emergency of international concern under article 12 (1), which is defined in article 1 IHL 2005 as 'an extraordinary event which is determined ... (i) to constitute a public health risk to other States through the international spread of disease and (ii) to potentially require a coordinated international response'. Consequently, on the basis of articles 15 and 18 IHL 2005, the Director-General must issue temporary recommendations, which depend on the nature of the threat and may include surveillance and reporting new incidents of the disease to WHO, information-sharing, travel and trade restrictions. Although the guidelines are authoritative, they are not binding on States Parties.

1100 M. Wabwile, 'Implementing the Social and Economic Rights of Children in Developing countries: the place of international assistance and cooperation', *International Journal on Children's Rights* 2010, Volume 18, pp. 357–358.

1101 UNICEF Children in an Urban World: The State of the World's Children 2012. See also: Todaro & Smith, *Economic Development*, London: Pearson Addison Wesley 2006, pp. 65–66.

the framework of international co-operation.' Article 24.4 CRC speaks of the obligation to progressively achieve the full realization of the right to health of children and to take particular account of the needs of developing countries. Both articles thus refer to the obligation to gradually fulfil the right to health of the child, if necessary with support of the international community. Therefore, in order to tackle pressing health problems in children, developing countries primarily have the obligation to maximize their domestic available resources and secondly to actively seek assistance from the international community.[1102] Also, the Committee on the Rights of the Child encourages recipient countries to allocate a substantive part of the international aid and assistance it receives to children and to yearly indicate the amount and proportion that has been allocated for the implementation of children's rights.[1103] The Committee on the Rights of the Child endorses the 20/20 initiative, which entails that recipient countries must allocate at least 20 percent of its public expenditure to realize universal access to basic social services.[1104] On the other side, developed countries must allocate at least 20 percent of foreign aid to human priority goals such as primary health care, education and the provision of underlying determinants of health.[1105] In doing so, the Committee advises developed countries to apply the Convention on the Rights of the Child as the framework for international development.[1106] The Committee furthermore endorses agreements reached that States Parties need to allocate at least 0.7% of their GDP to foreign aid.

Vandenhole has convincingly established that the extraterritorial obligations of States Parties to realize the right to health of the child in other, less developed countries include the duties to respect and protect, though not to fulfil the right to health.[1107] This means that States should not interfere with economic, social and cultural rights in other countries. Also, it means that States should refrain from embargos that target water, food, medicines or medical equipment.[1108] Furthermore, it means that States should prevent third parties under their control to interfere with children's right to health. Given the jurisdiction clause as expressed by the CRC Committee, this includes activities within the territory of the State, but also activities in other States by individuals who are subject to the States' jurisdiction.[1109] With respect to the duty to fulfil the right to health of the child in other countries, the duty of States is complementary to the domestic

[1102] Ibidem supra note 1099, pp. 367–368.
[1103] Ibidem supra note 1047, § 61.
[1104] Ibidem supra note 1047, § 62. For a further discussion of the 20/20 initiative see *Implementing the 20/20 initiative*, 1998.
[1105] Ibidem supra note 1100.
[1106] Ibidem supra note 1017, § 61.
[1107] Vandenhole, 'Economic, Social and Cultural Rights in the CRC: Is there a legal obligation to cooperate internationally for development?', *International Journal on Children's Rights* 2009, Volume 17, pp. 23–63.
[1108] Ibidem supra note 1106, Vandenhole, p. 53. See also Committee on ESCR 1999b, par. 37.
[1109] U.N.Doc, CRC/C/GC5, CRC Committee General Comment 5 on General Measures of Implementation, § 12.

State obligations.[1110] This means that all measures should only be taken with the approval of the recipient State. Interestingly, although no general legal obligation has been established for States to engage in international cooperation, there is a shared responsibility between donor and recipient countries to exchange information on preventive health care and treatment of disabled children and the right to the highest attainable standard of health.[1111]

Although measures to fulfil the right to health need to include measures to improve access to health facilities and underlying determinants of health, many other measures in other sectors should be considered that can significantly influence the health status of children. Such measures could include the creation of employment opportunities, making available investments through microcredits, investments in infrastructure, debt relief, stimulating commercial activities and private-public partnerships and through bilateral and multilateral agreements. More developed countries therefore have the responsibility to strengthen the capacity of developing countries to progressively realize the right to health of the child by providing funding, sharing knowledge and experiences. In doing so, caution must be taken to ensure that developing countries do not become fully dependent upon external aid.[1112] In conclusion, all States Parties to the CRC have the obligation to cooperate to progressively realize the right to health of the child.

6.4. RESPONSIBILITIES FOR NON-STATE ACTORS TO CONTRIBUTE TO REALIZING THE RIGHT TO THE HIGHEST ATTAINABLE STANDARD OF HEALTH OF THE CHILD

The Committee on the Rights of the Child has acknowledged that the realization of children's rights is achieved by the public sector, the private sector and voluntary actors concomitantly. For example, General Comment 5 establishes that the States task to realize children's rights needs to engage all sectors of society and, of course, children themselves.[1113] Therefore, the Committee has repeatedly requested States to provide insight into the division of responsibilities and into the allocation of resources to the different sectors involved in the provision of services to children.[1114] Specifically, both the CESCR Committee and the Committee on the Rights of the child have indicated that all members of society, including medical

1110 Ibidem supra note 1106, Vandenhole, p. 53.

1111 Ibidem supra note 1106, pp. 34 and 61, see also *Travaux Préparatires*, Working Group 1985.

1112 UN Doc CRC/C/15/Add.177, § 11 and 12.

1113 Ibidem supra note 1047, § 1.

1114 M. Rishmawi, *A Commentary on the United Nations Convention on the Rights of the Child, Article 4: The Nature of States Parties' Obligations*, Martinus Nijhoff Publishers 2006, p. 32, § 84.

professionals, families, local communities, (i)NGOs, civil society organizations, private companies and individuals, all have responsibilities in realizing the right to health.[1115] However, in involving non-state actors in the realization process of children's rights, the Committee has explicitly cautioned against delegating responsibilities to NGOs without providing them with the necessary resources to meet those responsibilities.[1116]

This section takes a bottom-up approach by analysing how all actors involved, including children and their families themselves, can contribute to realizing the right to health of children in their daily lives. It starts with the discussion of the extent to which very young patients can be involved in their own health situation and it continues with discussing the role of their parents or other caretakers and other actors in their direct environment. Thirdly, the role of medical professionals is discussed for as far as they do not operate as a representative of the state.

6.4.1. THE INVOLVEMENT OF CHILDREN IN THE MEDICAL PROCESS

Children, in the first place, are the holders of the right to health and the other connected rights as laid down in varying international legal documents on the right to health, most predominantly the Convention on the Rights of the Child.[1117] In international health law, namely the Constitution of the World Health Organization and the International Covenant on Economic, Social and Cultural Rights, the concept of the child focuses on its vulnerability and on its dependence on especially the mother. This is exemplified by the concomitant incorporation of the necessity to take measures to ensure 'children's ánd maternal health'. For example, the elaboration of the right to health in General Comment 14 ICESCR, article 12.2 (a), elaborates that 'the provision for the reduction of the stillbirth rate and of infant mortality and for the healthy development of the child' as laid down in the ICESCR 'may be understood as requiring measures to improve *child and maternal health*, sexual and reproductive health services, including access to family planning, pre- and post-natal care, emergency obstetric services and access to information, as well as to resources necessary to act on that information.' Child and maternal health are thus closely connected and focus is primarily placed on the services required during pregnancy and in the period immediately surrounding childbirth. This connection is especially relevant in the realization

1115 Ibidem supra note 1047, § 56. See also General Comment No. 14 (2000) The right to the highest attainable standard of health: 11/08/2000. E/C.12/2000/4. CESCR, § 2.

1116 UN Doc CRC/C/87, CRC Committee, Report on the 21st session, Annex IV, § 291.

1117 See for two contrasting views on the issue of children as rights-holders: L. Purdy, 'Why children shouldn't have equal rights', *International Journal of Children's Rights* 1994, Volume 2, pp. 223–241 and A. McGillivray, 'Why children do have equal rights: In reply to Laura Purdy', in: *International Journal on Children's Rights* 1994, Volume 2, pp. 243–258.

of the right to health of very young children who are fully or to a very large extent dependent on both the health and care-taking of their mothers and other primary caretakers.

On the other hand, notwithstanding the vulnerability of the very young ones, there is an increasing call for empowerment of vulnerable children in general, such as girls, children from minority or indigenous groups, street children etcetera. Whereas very young children are only vulnerable on the basis of their level of development, they do have the capability to grow into healthy and empowered adults. Therefore, there is no reason to withhold a minimum level of empowerment from children that inspires and stimulates their potential for growth and development. Even more, it is essential for children to grow and develop in good health and to be listened to from the very beginning. Furthermore, by taking the innate capabilities of children as a starting point, their empowerment can be achieved gradually in the course of their lifetime. This idea is in line with the notion laid down in article 12 CRC, which provides that children's views must be heard in all matters affecting the child and that these views must be given due weight in accordance with the age and maturity of the child. No maximum or minimum age limit is specified, so that children of all ages, including the youngest ones must be – literally – heard in the realization process of their rights.

Similarly, the Committee on the Rights of the Child has indicated that it is essential to hear children's voices or the voices of their representatives in order to assess how their rights have been implemented. For example, the Committee has established that 'While it is the State which takes on obligations under the Convention, its task of implementation – of making reality of the human rights of children – needs to engage all sectors of society and, of course, children themselves.'[1118] Hereto, the Committee has established that there must be continuous child impact assessments and evaluations on any laws, policy or budget allocation that impacts upon the actual implementation of children's right to health.[1119] However, with respect to the opportunities of children in their early childhood to be involved in their medical treatment, significant limitations are clear as a result of their limited verbal and cognitive capacities. Therefore, this paragraph undertakes to identify the abilities of very young children to influence and be informed about their medical condition and possible treatments and the ways in which the views of very young children can and should be taken into account in realizing the right to health of children.

Although, infants and toddlers clearly have limited verbal capacities to express themselves, their physical appearance as well as other ways of expression can be highly indicative of discomfort such as incessant crying, sleeping and withdrawal, restlessness, irritability, lack of interest or appetite and unnatural

---

1118 Ibidem supra note 1047, § 1.

1119 Ibidem supra note 1047, § 45.

clinging to the parents.[1120] Facial expressions in babies have shown that they clearly have the capacity to experience and communicate feelings of comfort and discomfort or pain.[1121] Thereby, they are able to directly and non-verbally influence the behaviour of the people around them, with their parents at the forefront.[1122]Also, by means of forcefully and persistently refusing medicines, they are able to influence the actual treatment they receive.

In earlier years, and still in some areas of the world, presumptions were held that infants and neonates are not able to experience pain. However, as demonstrated in more recent researches, infants often have a more intense experience of pain than adults do.[1123] Nevertheless, due to the difficulties in reading the body language of young children and infants, their pain often remains undertreated. Several scales have been developed to identify the level of pain experienced by this group of very young patients. However, in premature children and severely ill children, these scales are not always adequate, because they are unable to produce a robust cry due to their lack of physical strength.[1124] However, findings from older children than those in their infancy show that also children below the age of 5 should be carefully listened to in the medical process. Not only because this is respectful of their rights and shows them that they are taken seriously from the very beginning, but also because young children do have additional information that can be crucial in establishing an accurate diagnosis.[1125] For example, children aged 2 are increasingly able to report and localize pain, although they are not yet capable of rating the intensity of their pain.[1126] Children who develop rapidly have been proven able to quantify pain at the age of 3 using simple and creative pain assessment tools, such as pictures with facial expressions or different amounts of coins to explain the intensity of pain.[1127] However, in children aged 3–5 years, report bias is still very common, which complicates the interpretation of their pain scores. Specific communication methods can add to ensuring maximum

---

1120 B.F. Fuller, 'Infant behaviors as indicators of established acute pain', *Journal of the Society of Pediatric Nurses: JSPN* 2001, *6*(3), pp. 109–115.

1121 McGrath (a.o), 'Core outcome domains and measures for pediatric acute and chronic/recurrent pain clinical trials: PedIMMPACT recommendations', *The Journal of Pain: Official Journal of the American Pain Society* 2008, *9*(9), pp. 771–783.

1122 K.D. Craig & K.M. Prkachin, 'Expressing pain: The communication and interpretation of facial pain signals', *Journal of nonverbal behavior* 1995, Volume 19, Issue 4, p. 191–205.

1123 S. Ratnapalan, R. Srouji & S. Schneeweiss, 'Pain in Children: Assessment and Nonpharmacological Management', *International Journal of Pediatrics* 2010, Volume 2010, Article ID 474838, 11 pages doi:10.1155/2010/474838. Available at: www.hindawi.com/journals/ijped/2010/474838/.

1124 Ibidem supra note 1121.

1125 P.J. Mesko, 'Use of picture communication aids to assess pain location in pediatric postoperative patients', *Journal of Perianesthesia Nursing* 2011, 26, 6, December, pp. 395–404. Available at: www.jopan.org/article/S1089-9472(11)00421-7/abstract.

1126 Pain Measurement in Children, in: Clinical updates on Pain, Volume III, Issue 2, International Association for the Study of Pain, July 1995, available at: www.iasp-pain.org/AM/AMTemplate.cfm?Section=Home&TEMPLATE=/CM/ContentDisplay.cfm&SECTION=Home&CONTENTID=2549.

1127 Ibidem supra note 1122.

reliability of their answers, for example by posing open questions instead of implying or broadly explaining medical problems as a result of which children will often feel inclined to confirm.

As laid down in articles 12 and 13 CRC, children 'shall be provided the opportunity to be heard in any proceeding affecting the child, either directly or through a representative or an appropriate body' on the basis of article 12-2 CRC and the child shall have the freedom to receive information, either orally, in writing or in print, in the form of art, or through any other media of the child's choice. Even very young children have the right to be directly informed about the medical treatment they are undergoing, even in very short wordings. Therefore, challenges in establishing reliable answers, should not be used as a pretext for not informing and not involving children in their own medical treatments. It should be used as a motivational factor to further elaborate on the communication skills and techniques in medical care to very young children.

Furthermore, dependent on their level of development and comprehension, they either have a direct influence on the medical process through their own visions or behaviour (e.g. refusal) and indirectly through a representative, such as the parents, the medical professional or a third party who particularly envisages the best interests of the child in the determination of the medical treatment he or she is undergoing. By accurately observing the behaviour of (very) young children in the medical context, indications can be obtained over the way in which child-friendly health care services should be designed. In doing so, observations and communication methods must go far beyond verbal and written communications, but pay particular attention to body language, behaviour and reporting by children, parents and other proxy caregivers of the young child. For example, children can be given the opportunity to signal if they want a medical treatment to be stopped or interrupted when they feel they cannot bear the pain. Furthermore, the ideas and primary responsibility of parents or primary caretakers for the health and well-being of the child as laid down in articles 5 and 18 CRC should be taken seriously in the health care process, because they have day-to-day interaction with their children and generally know best whether their children appear sicker or better than they normally do. The abilities and responsibilities of parents and primary caretakers to identify the health needs of their children will be discussed in the following paragraph.

6.4.2. THE RESPONSIBILITIES OF PARENTS

As laid down in articles 5 and 18 CRC, parents and if applicable the extended family and communities of the child, have the primary responsibility to ensure the health of their children by providing the underlying determinants of health and ensuring a healthy lifestyle and a healthy living environment. In the preamble to the Convention on the Rights of the Child the family is defined as 'the fundamental group of society and the natural environment for the growth and well-being of all its members and particularly children'. In General Comment 7 on the rights of children in early childhood, the Committee elaborates on the concept by recognizing that 'family' refers to a variety of arrangements that can provide for young children's care, nurturance and development, including the nuclear family, the extended family, and other traditional and modern community-based arrangements, provided these are consistent with children's rights and best interests.[1128] Both article 5 CRC and the interpretations made by the CRC Committee thus explicitly acknowledge that worldwide there is a wide variety of family arrangements in which children grow up and which thus have the possibility to directly influence the level of realization of the right to health of children.

A established in chapter 2 of this thesis, the health of the mother directly influences the health of the unborn and the new-born child and indirectly the rest of the child's lifespan.

Article 18 CRC establishes that both parents have the primary responsibility for the upbringing and (healthy) development of the child. The focus of this provision thus makes a shift from the exclusive focus on the relation between the child's health and the health of the mother to a focus on the role of both the mother and the father or the legal guardians. After birth, both parents are primarily responsible for their children's health by ensuring the provision of healthy and nutritious foods, drinking water, prevention of accidents and a hygienic and smoke- free environment within the home and in other places where children spend time. Also, the health behaviour of both parents plays a crucial role in the example-setting and subsequent health behaviour of their children. Article 18 CRC provides that States 'shall use their best efforts to ensure recognition of the principle that both parents have common responsibilities for the upbringing and development of the child.' It is therefore remarkable that article 24 CRC only addresses the need to prevent maternal mortality.

Whereas the health of the child is heavily influenced by the health status of both parents, the way in which other family members treat the mother, by sharing nutritious food with her, taking over potential harmful work and treating her with respect (e.g. no domestic violence) also has a very important impact on the healthy development of the foetus. In the second place, parents play a central role in seeking access to health care for their children, including preventive and basic health care, mental health care, specialized health care, dental health care and more. Thirdly, parents have the responsibility to ensure and advocate for a healthy living environment of their children in a broader sense: they may need to advocate for a healthy and hygienic living environment in schools, recreation facilities and outdoor playgrounds where their children spend time. However, due

[1128] U.N. Doc. CRC/C/GC/7/Rev.1, General Comment 7 on Child rights in early childhood, 20 September 2006, § 14.

to limits in the level of health-related knowledge, personal incapacity, financial means or other resources, the State has the additional responsibility under article 18 CRC to ensure the development of institutions, facilities and services for the care of children.

It was repeatedly found that educating mothers, significantly increases children's health status and survival, as they are thereby enabled to apply basic knowledge on healthy nutrition, hygiene, prevention of accidents and infections to preventing health problems of their children.[1129, 1130]

In addition to ensuring the necessary health facilities for children, prevention of health problems starts with enabling parents to take good care of their children. This requires enabling them to continuously adapt to the changing life cycle and stages of development of their children, both physically and mentally. For example, when a toddler learns to walk, parents must be more alert on preventing accidents such as falling of the stairs or running on the streets. Changing nutrition and sleep patterns, timely recognition of serious or typical child diseases and social interaction with siblings and peers will all require flexibility and empathy of the parents, especially when they have children with severe health problems or learning disorders. Therefore, specific health information must be readily available for young parents so that they can respond timely and adequately to the health needs of their children. However, the ways in which such health information can be obtained are diverse. In developing health institutions it is important to acknowledge that family and other social networks can and do make a significant contribution to shaping the ways in which necessary health information and healthy behaviour are transferred to new parents. Also, the genetic make-up of children can be partly disclosed by undertaking extensive family anamnesis on existing diseases, allergies and other relevant medical conditions in a family. This can be crucial in preventing the development or deterioration of these health problems in the children.[1131]

1129 The health of the child is inextricably linked to the health and the health practices of their mothers. The World Bank found that 'at least 20% of the burden of disease among children less than 5 years old is attributable to conditions directly associated with poor maternal health, nutrition and the quality of obstetric and newborn care.' Safe Motherhood and the World Bank: Lessons from 10 Years of Experience, Washington, D.C., World Bank, Human Development Network, Health Nutrition, and Population Division, 1999 Jun. 42, Volume 12: Available at: www.k4health.org/popline/safe-motherhood-and-world-bank-lessons-10-years-experience, information discussed in: D.L. Parker & S. Bachman, 'Economic exploitation and the health of children: Towards a rights-oriented public health approach', *Health and Human Rights*, Volume 5, no. 2, p. 100.

1130 In order to tackle problems deriving from the intricate relation between mothers and their newborn children, the Save Motherhood Initiative was launched in 1987 by the World Health Organization and other international agencies aiming to reduce the maternal and infant mortality rates caused by pre- and perinatal circumstances.

1131 For example, knowledge on the genetic predisposition for a mutation in BRCA 1 or BRCA 2 can stimulate girls to closely monitor their breasts and thereby identify any instances of breast cancer so that early intervention becomes possible.

Furthermore, in contacts with medical professionals, the primary responsibility of parents and other primary caretakers as laid down in articles 5 and 18 CRC for their children must be respected and enhanced, because they see their children most often and therefore usually know best what their children need. Therefore, especially for very young children, parents and primary caretakers must be given sufficient time and opportunity to communicate their observations on their children's health needs. By truly acknowledging this primary responsibility of parents to ensure their children's health, parents are better enabled to take responsibility over their children in the health care process.

A clear distinction thus appears between the responsibilities of the parents on the one hand, namely to provide the individual child with care and guidance and the general responsibilities of the States Parties to render assistance to all parents in their child-rearing responsibilities by providing for institutions, facilities and services for child care. Parents thus are responsible for ensuring the right to health of their individual children, whereas States Parties have the responsibility to support parents in meeting these obligations. Only in exceptional circumstances, in which parents do not or cannot meet their primary responsibility of ensuring the right to health of their children, does the State acquire the primary and direct responsibility for realizing the right to health of the child.

6.4.3. THE ROLE OF MEDICAL PROFESSIONALS IN REALIZING CHILDREN'S RIGHT TO HEALTH

In the attribution of responsibilities to the different professionals involved in children's health care, two important points of distinction are identified: the division of responsibilities between State Parties and medical professionals and the division of responsibilities between medical professionals and the child and its family.

The first intersection concerns the relation between the responsibilities of the State and the responsibilities of medical professionals in applying children's rights principles in practice. Several scholars have righteously argued that the medical approach to ensuring children's health is principally focused on clinical diagnosis and intervention, involving the identification of morbidities, such as asthma, obesitas, diabetes, infant mortality etc.[1132] The subsequent steps taken are usually also confined to the medical domain, consisting of establishing incidence, prevalence, mortality, etc. to characterize mortality. However, it has also repeatedly been demonstrated that the root causes of many childhood illnesses

[1132] Goldhagen & Mercer, 'Child Health Equity: From Theory to Reality', in: A. Invernizzi, *The Human Rights of Children*.

lay in a much wider context, involving different economic, cultural, social and political domains.[1133]

The need to approach the right to health of children from different perspectives is the domain in which States Parties have to coordinate different policy areas that all contribute to the realization of the right to health of children. At the same time, the health related articles of the CRC and its translation to the practice of medical professionals can help to expand the approach taken by medical professionals in ensuring children's right to health beyond the limited scope of the biomedical approach.

Therefore, crucial in the realization of children's rights in health care is the translation of children's rights legislation to the daily practices of medical professionals. Both from General Comment 5 of the Committee on the Rights of the Child on the General measures of implementation of the Convention (art. 4, 42 and 44.6) and from the analysis of the Concluding Observations of the Country Reports, it appears that health professionals must be continuously (re-)educated on the requirements of child-friendly health care. This can be achieved through specific education for medical students and professionals on the implications of children's rights for their daily medical practice. The role of medical professionals in realizing the highest attainable standard of health of children is crucial. When medical professionals truly apply children's rights in their daily practices, 'they become implementers and agents of social justice and human rights in the communities in which they work.'[1134] In order to enable educational institutions to provide for children's rights education to medical professionals, sufficient resources must be allocated to such education.

Equally important is the integration of children's rights and the implications following from these rights in work protocols and practices in the medical sector. For example, whereas blood values of infants in hospital can be determined at one pre-set moment, for example at 8 o'clock in the morning, the best interests of the child are usually better met when they are tested once the baby has woken up. The same goes for planning appointments for babies during their daily nap. Simple, but significant changes in daily routines can greatly contribute to putting the interests of the child first, instead of taking the working methods in the medical sector as a starting point.

It is at this second intersection between the actions, communications and responsibilities of medical professionals in the daily health care practice that the input of children and families becomes important. Whereas professionals compare the appearance of a child (e.g. colour, heart rate, blood values) with standard health or disease indicators, children and their parents are among the first to notice any changes in the normal functioning of the child. A child is the

---

1133 E. Riedel, 'The Right to Life and the Right to Health, in particular the obligation to reduce child mortality', in: C. Tomuscat, *The right to life*, Martinus Nijhoff Publishers 2010, p. 365.

1134 Ibidem supra note 1131.

first to experience pain and express this (or to become silent), whereas parents are usually well-able to compare the behaviour of the sick child with its normal behaviour. Notwithstanding standardized measurements by or impressions of the medical professionals, different children can have different more or less expressive ways to communicate their feelings of comfort or discomfort. Therefore, it is important to take parents' appraisal of their child's symptoms seriously, because they can give crucial additional information that is not directly visible or measurable and can definitely not be standardized.[1135] On the other hand, medical professionals are better able to compare the peculiarities of the symptoms with similar disease patterns in other children. They can also play a significant role in establishing good relations with children and their parents. Research findings have identified several key factors that are influential to the effectiveness of communication with children, including the personality and attitude of the health professional, sufficient time and opportunity and physical environment and the lack of training in communication skills.[1136] Research on the interaction between families and health professionals have confirmed that the dynamic between them and parents is a hugely significant factor in how they communicate with their child patients.[1137]

This section identified the role of medical professionals in realizing the right to health of the child. Whereas their work is largely confined to the strictly medical domain, they are among the first to signal instances of violations of the right to health of children. Through the interference of medical organizations such violations can be systematically identified and addressed before courts and in the (in)ternational political arena.

6.5. OPTIONAL PROTOCOL III TO THE CRC ON A COMMUNICATIONS PROCEDURE FOR CHILDREN

In the preparation phase to the third Optional Protocol to the CRC on a communications procedure for children, the Special Representative of the Secretary-General on Violence against Children commented that 'the right to an effective remedy provides the bridge between theoretical recognition and

1135 See also Recommendations on Communication between health care professionals children and their parents or carers. Available at: http://webarchive.nationalarchives.gov.uk/+/www.dh.gov.uk/en/Publicationsandstatistics/Publications/PublicationsPolicyAndGuidance/Browsable/DH_5258136.

1136 D. Kamin, 'Hospital rounds: How's the doctor-patient communication system?', *Vector* 2011. Available at: http://vectorblog.org/2011/09/hospital-rounds-hows-the-doctor-patient-communication-system/.

1137 Ibidem supra note 1135.

meaningful enforcement of human rights'.[1138] Newell phrased this same point negatively by stating that 'the gap between the obligations taken up by States and the extent to which children's rights are realized and enjoyed in reality (...) owes much to the lack of effective mechanisms at national, regional and international level to enable children and their representatives to challenge violations and gain remedies'.[1139] The Committee on the Rights of the Child had previously stated that 'for rights to have meaning, effective remedies must be available to redress violations'.[1140] The idea of the adoption of an Optional Protocol to the Convention on the Rights of the Child on a Communications procedure for children was to fill in this lacuna.

On 19 December 2011, Optional Protocol III to the Convention on the Rights of the Child on a Communications Procedure for children was adopted by the UN General Assembly.[1141] Although welcomed as an important milestone in the emancipation and acknowledgement of children's rights,[1142, 1143] there is one important deficit in the resulting document: no children were involved in its drafting process.[1144, 1145] This is at least remarkable given the qualification of the

1138 U.N. Doc. A/HRC/WG.7/1/CRP.7, 14 December 2009, Human Rights Council Working Group on an Optional Protocol to the Convention on the Rights of the Child to provide a communications procedure. Marta Santos Pais, Special Representative of the Secretary-General on Violence against children, p. 2.

1139 U.N. Doc. A/HRC/WG.7/1/CRP.2, 9 December 2009. Submission by Newell, P. to the First session of the Open-Ended Working Group of the Human Rights Council considering the possibility of elaborating an Optional Protocol to provide a communications procedure for the Convention on the Rights of the Child, § 1, p. 1.

1140 U.N. Doc. CRC/GC/2003/5, General Comment 5 General measures of implementation of the Convention on the Rights of the Child, 27 November 2003, § 24.

1141 U.N. Doc. GA/11198, 19 December 2011.

1142 Y. Lee, 'Celebrating important milestones for children and their rights', *The International Journal of Children's Rights* 2010, Volume 18, The Hague: Kluwer Law International.

1143 S. Lembrechts, 'Wiens klachtrecht? Het kind-concept in het derde Facultatief Protocol bij het Verdrag inzake de Rechten van het Kind betreffende de instelling van een communicatieprocedure', *Tijdschrift voor Jeugd- en Kinderrechten* 2012, Issue 2, p. 97.

1144 Only in a joint submission by several NGOs to the first Open-ended working groups there is included a 2-page Annex that includes a statement signed by 27 adolescents from England, Sweden and Moldova. See all documents of the drafting process of the Optional Protocol at: www.ohchr.org/EN/HRBodies/HRC/WGCRC/Pages/OpenEndedWorkingGroupIndex.aspx.

1145 The issue of involving children in the drafting process of Optional Protocol III to the Convention on the rights of the child was mentioned by several delegations and independent experts. Switzerland commented that 'article 12 is a key article in this process'; Portugal reiterated the right to be heard of children; Syria asked whether there are any best practices of how children can be involved in the drafting of legislation that includes their basic rights; Yanghee Lee, Chair of the CRC Committee said that 'General Comment 12 on the right of the child to be heard was a key introduction to pave the way for the OP'; Slovenia particularly mentioned the need for 'an innovative approach in order to make the communications procedure comprehensive and accessible' and highlighted the need to seek the views of children. This was followed by a comment made by Ireland that they 'would like to echo the comments made by Slovenia that children should be informed about the work of this working group and get their input on the drafting of a procedure, what it means and how it can be used'. See Meeting of the UN Working Group for the Communications Procedure, December 2009, available at: www.crin.org/docs/OP_CRC_WG_Meeting_Dec2009.pdf.

children's right to participation as one of the key principles in the Convention on the Rights of the Child.[1146] The same is true for the Convention on the Rights of the Child itself: no children were involved in its drafting process.[1147, 1148] Therefore, additional research is required on ways to involve children in conceptualizing and realizing their rights, including their right to health and their right to participation. Nevertheless, the adoption of Optional Protocol III to the Convention on the Rights of the Child does offer an opportunity for children to become involved in the realization of their own rights.[1149] The Protocol entered into force in January 2014, when Costa Rica was the 10th Member State to sign the Protocol.[1150]

A complaints procedure allows individuals, groups and their representatives to bring alleged violations of their rights before a competent Human Rights Committee. This is especially important when domestic or regional complaints mechanisms are insufficient or don't exist.[1151] In addition to the monitoring activities of the Committee in its Concluding Observations in the Country Reports and the issuing of General Comments and Days of General Discussion, it provides for an additional tool to put pressure on States Parties to ensure children's rights and to provide for effective remedies at the national level.[1152] Thereby, it would be a necessary tool to enhancing State accountability for ensuring children's rights.

The absence of a communications procedure for children was criticized to be discriminatory towards children, given the fact that all other Human Rights Treaties had or were in the process of obtaining a complaints mechanism,

---

1146 U.N. Doc. CRC/GC/2003/5, § 12.

1147 Legislative history of the Convention on the Rights of the Child, Volume I and II, United Nations, New York and Geneva, 2007.

1148 Detrick, *The Convention on the Rights of the Child: A Guide to the Travaux Préparatoires*, Dordrecht/Boston/London: Martinus Nijhoff Publishers 1992, p. 23. Chapter on Participants in the Drafting Process, available at: http://books.google.nl/books?hl=nl&lr=&id=65TCU0N9fksC&oi=fnd&pg=PR9&dq=guiding+principles+convention+on+the+rights+of+the+child&ots=KXLEfgVPsG&sig=fRlTjSKxGqxh2QxCN9DrXuGnqT8#v=onepage&q=guiding%20principles%20convention%20on%20the%20rights%20of%20the%20child&f=false.

1149 See article 19 of the Optional Protocol III, which stipulates that the Protocol shall entry into force three months after the deposit of the tenth instrument of ratification or accession. For States who ratify the Protocol after that moment, the Protocol shall entry into force three months after the date of the deposit of its own instrument of ratification or accession.

1150 On 28 February 2012, the Optional Protocol on a communications procedure for children was opened for signature in a ceremony in Geneva. It was signed by 20 States, including Brazil, Costa Rica, Peru, Uruguay, Chile, Spain, Italy, Portugal, Austria, Belgium, Germany, Finland, Luxembourg, the Slovak Republic, Slovenia, Serbia, Montenegro, Maroc, Mali and Maldives. Since June 2013 the Optional Protocol is ratified by 6 States: Albania, Bolivia, Gabon, Germany, Spain, Thailand, Available at: www2.ohchr.org/english/bodies/crc/OPIC_Ceremony.htm.

1151 U.N. Doc. A/HRC/WG.7.1.CRP.2, 9 December 2009, it was commented by Newell that in addition to the domestic legal procedures, requiring the provision of child-friendly information, access to courts and independent children's ombudsmen could also play a role in receiving and dealing with complaints made by children.

1152 See the arguments made in the online campaign on the children's rights information network to call for petitions: www.crin.org/petitions/petition.asp?PetID=1007.

most notably the ICESCR.[1153, 1154, 1155] Furthermore, the application of already existing procedures for children, would not take into account the entire range and holistic character of all children's rights.[1156] Therefore, there was a need adopt a communications procedure that would be child-sensitive. Furthermore, the establishment of a separate complaints procedure for children would allow for the assessment of alleged children's rights violations by Members of the CRC Committee, being experts on the rights of the child and their particular vulnerabilities.[1157] Last but not least, it was assumed that existing complaints mechanisms were hardly known among children.

6.5.1. DRAFTING HISTORY

The initiative for an Optional Protocol to the CRC on a communications procedure for children was taken in 2002 by a German NGO, Kindernothilfe.[1158] When the communications procedure to the ICESCR was adopted on 19 June 2008, the international campaign had grown to more than 400 organizations and the Committee on the Rights of the Child expressed its support in stating that 'The Committee had 'weighed the pros and cons' and was 'now inviting all stakeholders

1153 Ibidem supra note 1151.

1154 The Optional Protocol to the ICCPR entered into force on 23 March 1976; the Convention against Torture and Other Cruel, Inhuman or Degrading Treatment or Punishment allows for an inquiry procedure under article 20 and for a communications procedure under article 20. It entered into force on 26 June 1987; the International Convention on the Elimination of All Forms of Racial Discrimination contains a communication procedure in article 14, which entered into force on 4 January 1982 following acceptance of the competence of the monitoring Committee by 10 States; the Optional Protocol to the Convention on the Elimination of Discrimination against Women entered into force on 22 December 2000; the Convention on the Rights of Persons with Disabilities and its Optional Protocol, will enter into force after ratification by 10 States; the International Convention on the Protection of the Rights of All Migrant Workers and Members of Their Families contains a communication procedure under article 77; the International Convention for the Protection of All Persons from Enforced Disappearance contains a provision on a communication procedure under article 31 for which the competence of the monitoring Committee can be recognized by States. The Optional Protocol to the ICESCR was adopted by the General assembly by resolution A/RES/63/117 on 10 December 2008, available at: www2.ohchr.org/english/law/docs/a.RES.63.117_en.pdf.

1155 Several regional courts also provide for a complaints mechanism including the African Commission on Human and People's Rights under article 56 of the African Charter on Human and Peoples' Rights; the African Committee of Experts on the Rights and Welfare of the Child under article 44 of the African Charter on the Rights and Welfare of Children (individual, group or recognized organizations); the Inter-American Commission and Court of Human Rights under article 44 of the American Convention on Human Rights (individual, group and organizations); the European Court of Human Rights (individual complaint procedure) and the European Committee of Social Rights (collective complaint procedure by certain approved NGOs).

1156 Ibidem supra note 1025.

1157 Ibidem supra note 1025.

1158 See Report: U. Müller, *Children as strong as nations*, Kindernothilfe. Available at: Background, reasons and arguments for introducing a right of petition.www.crin.org/docs/Children_as_Strong_as_Nations.pdf.

to come forth and seriously work together on the drafting process'.[1159] Thereupon, they requested the General Assembly of the United Nations to establish a working group to draft such a Protocol,[1160] which was soon thereafter established by a resolution of the Human Rights Council in June 2009.[1161] The mandate was to 'explore the possibility of elaborating an Optional Protocol to the Convention on the Rights of the Child to provide a communications procedure complementary to the reporting procedure under the Convention'.[1162] After a three-day discussion with children's rights experts, NGOs, and members of the Committee on the Rights of the Child, the Working Group was mandated by a resolution of the General Assembly to write a draft for the Optional Protocol on a communications procedure for children.[1163]

The second working group was held in two parts: from 6–10 December 2010 devoted to debating the draft optional protocol as prepared by the chairperson of the working group and from 10–16 February 2011 to debate a revised version of the draft optional protocol.[1164] The session was opened by the High Commissioner for Human Rights and she informed the working group about a special expert meeting that had been organized in June 2010. The experts had acknowledged the value of existing communications procedures and they were generally in favour of an innovative protocol that suited the needs of children, that was transparent and widely disseminated to its users and that would cover the rights enshrined in the CRC and in its Optional Protocols.[1165] Furthermore, the experts were in favour of providing for both an individual and a collective communications procedure and they argued the need to allow the Committee to request interim measures in cases pending before it. Lastly, they would include 'a procedure for friendly settlements between the parties in a communication, taking into account the best interests of the children involved'. The Chairperson, who prepared the draft version of the optional protocol, clarified that his intention was to seek consistency with existing communications procedures, while taking into account the specificities of children.[1166, 1167]

1159 See CRIN: Communications procedure: Committee on the Rights of the Child endorsed campaign, www.crin.org/resources/infoDetail.asp?ID=17602&flag=news.

1160 U.N. Doc A/HRC/8/NGO/6, 26 May 2008.

1161 U.N. Doc A/HRC/RES/11/1, 17 June 2009. Resolution of the General Assembly to establish an open-ended working group on an Optional Protocol to the Convention on the Rights of the Child to provide a communications procedure, 17 June 2009.

1162 Ibidem supra note 1038, § 1.

1163 U.N. Doc General Assembly, A/HRC/RES/13/3, 14 April 2010.

1164 U.N. Doc. A/HRC/17/36, 25 May 2011, § 3.

1165 U.N. Doc. A/HRC/17/36, 25 May 2011, § 5.

1166 U.N. Doc. A/HRC/17/36, 25 May 2011, § 16.

1167 U.N. Doc. A/HRC/WG.7/1/CRP.2, 14 December 2009. Peter Newell provided for a useful overview of the provisions included in the existing communications procedures for other treaties, including the ICCPR, CEDAW, ICESCR, CRPD. See Annex II. Available at: www.ohchr.org/EN/HRBodies/HRC/WGCRC/Pages/OpenEndedWorkingGroupSession1.aspx.

Initially, the intention was to include three kinds of procedures: an individual, a collective and an interstate complaints procedure.[1168] Several arguments were made to incorporate not only an individual but also a collective complaints mechanism. First of all, it would be in line with the African Charter on the Rights and Welfare of the Child.[1169] Secondly, it would enhance the accessibility of the procedure,[1170] because it would give children the opportunity to remain anonymous in the filing of a complaint.[1171] Thirdly, it would allow for a more efficient procedure in the Committee on the Rights of the Child, having the opportunity to investigate and condemn plural violations at the same time.[1172] However, the second draft contained an 'opt-in clause', which led to much debate.[1173, 1174, 1175] This clause entailed that States should explicitly recognize the collective complaints mechanism when ratifying the Protocol.[1176] The incorporation of this clause was heavily criticized in the discussion of this second draft document in February 2011. Notwithstanding the support of NGOs, the Committee on the Rights of the Child and several children's rights experts,[1177] the strong opposition of a significant number of Member States led to the complete removal of the collective complaints procedure for children in the final draft.[1178, 1179]

Given the collective nature of economic, social and cultural rights, the removal of the collective complaints procedure for children is a serious deficit in the new Optional Protocol for realizing children's right to health. This is

---

1168 See articles 2 and 3 of the draft proposal for the Optional Protocol discussed in the open-ended working group. UN Doc. A/HRC/WG.7/2/2, 1 September 2012, available at: http://daccess-dds-ny.un.org/doc/UNDOC/GEN/G10/157/81/PDF/G1015781.pdf?OpenElement.

1169 UN General Assembly, A/HRC/WG.7/2/2, 1st September 2010.

1170 Joint NGO Submission to the Open-ended Working Group on an Optional Protocol to the Convention on the Rights of the Child to provide a Communications Procedure, October 2010, p. 6–7.

1171 C. Phillips, 'Klachtrecht bij het Comité inzake de rechten van het Kind', *Tijdschrift voor Familie- en jeugdrecht* 2012, Issue 4, April, p. 93.

1172 Ibidem supra note 1170.

1173 Langford & Clark argued that an opt-out clause would be better than an opt-in clause upon ratification of the Optional Protocol. However, ultimately, the collective complaints procedure was completely left out. See: Langford & Clark, *A complaints Procedure for the Convention on the Rights of the Child: Commentary on the Second Draft*, Norwegian Centre for Human Rights (University of Oslo), 7 February 2011, p. 4. Available at: www.ohchr.org/Documents/HRBodies/HRCouncil/WGCRC/Session2/NCHR_Commentary.pdf.

1174 Langford & Clark, *The new kid on the block: A complaints procedure for the Convention on the Rights of the Child*, Working Paper, No.1, Socio-Economic Rights Programme, Norwegian Centre for Human Rights, University of Oslo, January 2010. Available at: www.jus.uio.no/smr/english/people/aca/malcolml/new-kid-on-the-block-langford-clark.pdf.

1175 Preliminary Joint NGO Submission to the Open-ended Working Group on an Optional Protocol to the convention on the Rights of the Child to provide a communications procedure, February 2011.

1176 UN General Assembly, A/HRC/WG.7/2/4, 13 January 2011, p. 4.

1177 UN General Assembly, A/HRC/17/36, 16 May 2011, pp. 12–13.

1178 Final version of the Optional Protocol on a communications procedure for children. Available at: http://treaties.un.org/doc/source/signature/2012/CTC_4-11d.pdf.

1179 Complaints Mechanism: Summary of Final Draft Meeting www.crin.org/resources/infodetail.asp?id=24180.

especially so for the obligation to fulfil children's right to health, because it is difficult to establish the necessary health infrastructure for separate individuals. If complaints can be brought before the Committee in concomitance, it is easier to establish the possible existence of systematic or widespread violations of children's economic, social and cultural rights, including their right to health.[1180] Newell confirms this by stating that 'a collective complaints mechanism could be helpful in encouraging States to develop CRC-compliant laws as well as policies'.[1181] Although no objections were made in the Open-ended Working Group on the justiciability of economic, social and cultural rights, the participants did not translate this point of view in an actual enforcement mechanism.[1182] With respect to the more passive obligation to respect children's right to the highest attainable standard of health, the Optional Protocol may therefore be more effective than it is with respect to the enforcement of its active obligations to protect and to fulfil the right of the child to the highest attainable standard of health. Whereas individual children do have the opportunity to make an individual complaint over a breach of their personal right to health, the lack of teeth of the Protocol for enforcing economic, social and cultural rights, more particularly children's right to the highest attainable standard of health thus remains a lacuna to be filled.

6.5.2. EXHAUSTION OF NATIONAL REMEDIES

The Preamble of Optional Protocol III to the Convention on the Rights of the Child states that States Parties are encouraged 'to develop appropriate national mechanisms to enable a child whose rights have been violated to have access to effective remedies at the domestic level'. Article 7e OP III furthermore establishes that 'The Committee shall consider a communication inadmissible, when all available domestic remedies have not been exhausted.' Before acquiring access to the communications procedure for children as laid down in Optional Protocol III to the CRC, children's rights violations must be first dealt with at the national

1180 Although the specific text was debated, the first draft stated that only grave or systematic violations were justiciable in a collective communications procedure. However, now this provision was left out, the Committee on the Rights of the Child will need to keep a register of all children's rights violations, especially of a similar type within a certain country to be able to establish such a systemic, systematic or widespread practice of children's rights violations.

1181 U.N. Doc. A/HRC/WG.7/1/CRP.2, 9 December 2009. Submission by Newell, P. to the First session of the Open-Ended Working Group of the Human Rights Council, considering the possibility of elaborating an Optional Protocol to provide a communications procedure for the Convention on the Rights of the Child, § 48.

1182 Langford & Clark comment that the previous resolution of the debate had been solved in the extensive discussions on the Optional Protocol to the ICESCR. This Optional Protocol was adopted by consensus in December 2008. See: Langford & Clark, *The new kid on the block: A complaints procedure for the Convention on the Rights of the Child*, Working Paper, no. 1, Socio-Economic Rights Program, Norwegian Centre for Human Rights, University of Oslo, January 2010, p. 10. Available at: www.jus.uio.no/smr/english/people/aca/malcolml/new-kid-on-the-block-langford-clark.pdf.

level. Although the point of departure for establishing admissibility of the Committee for receiving complaints is the exhaustion of national remedies,[1183] article 7e of OP III provides for an emergency exit when 'the application of remedies is unreasonably prolonged or unlikely to bring effective relief'. Taking the health related cases in the Dutch study on enforceability of children's rights in domestic courts as an example, this means that the cases in which no direct justiciability of the right to health of the child was established, may give room to starting a communications procedure before the Committee on the Rights of the Child on the basis of a violation of the right to health of the children at hand. Another entrance may develop, when children are not granted legal capacity within domestic law. Proving this however, may constitute a significant threshold for children to make a complaint before the Committee. Especially for very young children aged 0–5, representation at both the national and the international level is required to make a case for violations of their right to health. Another option is that violations of children's rights superannuate only after a considerable period of time. Problematic, however, in this option is that present day violations may only be dealt with in the future and that children therefore continue to suffer from them. With respect to the enjoyment of the right to health, this may have long-lasting and even irrevocable consequences for the health and even the survival of the child. Therefore, it is more recommendable to ensure that procedures for addressing violations of children's right to health truly take into account the best interests of the child.

6.5.3. CHILDREN'S RIGHTS IN OPTIONAL PROTOCOL III: ROOM FOR PARTICIPATION?

Optional Protocol III to the Convention on the Rights of the Child contains 24 articles and a Preamble. The provisions are grouped in four parts. Part I entails general provisions and establishes the admissibility of the Committee in article 1, the general principles that guide the functioning of the Committee in article 2, the rules of procedure in article 3 and protection measures in article 4. It is remarkable that in this part, no separate article is included on participatory measures to involve children in the process. Given the required balancing in the Convention between the protection rights of children and their participation rights,[1184] it would have been more balanced to incorporate an explicit article on

[1183] It is considered in the Preamble that Optional Protocol III 'will reinforce and complement national and regional mechanisms allowing children to submit complaints for violations of their rights' and thereto States Parties are encouraged 'to develop appropriate national mechanisms to enable a child whose rights have been violated to have access to effective remedies at the domestic level'. Article 7e OP III furthermore establishes that 'The Committee shall consider a communication inadmissible, when all available domestic remedies have not been exhausted.'

[1184] See supra note 1139.

children's participation rights in the actual Protocol in addition to the relatively strong focus on protective measures, such as the protection measures in article 4. Although now included in paragraph 19 of the Rules of Procedure of the Committee, inclusion in the Protocol itself would have had more standing and it could have established a significant point of reference for regional and national communications procedures for children.[1185] The left-out of such a provision is a missed opportunity in enabling children to stand-up for their rights.

Part II provides for the actual communications procedure in articles 5-12. Two separate routes are possible, namely a communications procedure of individuals in article 5 and an inter-state communications procedure in article 12 OP III. On the basis of article 1 OP III, complaints are lodged against States that satisfy two conditions: the State must be a party to the CRC and to the Optional protocol III and the State must have recognized the competence of the Committee to consider complaints from individuals. In response to these distinct communications procedures, the Committee has several responses at its disposal. In the first place and under article 8 OP III, the Committee confidentially brings the complaint to the attention of the State Party, who thereupon has the opportunity 'to submit a written explanation or statement clarifying the matter or any remedy that it provided'. Article 10-4 provides that in reviewing any violations of economic, social and cultural rights, the Committee 'considers the reasonableness of the steps taken by the State, bearing in mind that the State Party may adopt a range of possible policy measures for the implementation of economic, social and cultural rights in the Convention. Secondly, the Committee has the possibility to request the State to take interim measures to avoid possible irreparable damage to the child on the basis of article 6 OP III. The rationale behind this article is that minimizing harm in children by violations of their rights may require immediate action on the basis of their developing capacities. Thirdly, the Committee has the option to settle complaints in a friendly way for complaints made by individuals in article 9 and for interstate procedures in article 12-3. In responding to individual communications, this last option poses an interesting opportunity for the Committee to support children in standing up for their own rights, while mediating between the State Party and the children who make a complaint. Through this route, children can become involved in the process of problem-solving themselves, experiencing and elaborating upon the

[1185] In preparation to the Optional Protocol on a communications procedure for children, Newell has provided an overview of the regional human rights mechanisms that are available to children. He found that there are 'African, Inter-American and European mechanisms that can be used to challenge violations of children's rights'. He furthermore commented that 'although there has been relatively little use of them by or on behalf of children, this is certainly not an indication that children are enjoying general respect for their rights, nor that they have adequate remedies at national level'. U.N. Doc. A/HRC/WG.7/1/CRP.2, 9 December 2009. Submission by P. Newell to the First session of the Open-Ended Working Group of the Human Rights Council, considering the possibility of elaborating an Optional Protocol to provide a communications procedure for the Convention on the Rights of the Child.

realization of their own rights. However, caution must be taken that children's communications are taken seriously in this route, because this route closes the initial communications procedure and because the Committee is not permitted to consider communications which it has dealt with before (article 7d). Also, this route may be difficult in situations of grave or systematic violations of children's rights as referred to in article 13 OP III, but it could be an innovative route to establish good and child-friendly practices in countries where the government is willing to collaborate and improve its policy and working methods not only to the benefit, but, more importantly, with the active involvement of its minor inhabitants. The fourth and last option that the Committee has at his disposal is to conduct an inquiry in a State under article 13 when there is reliable information that children's rights as laid down in the Convention and/or its Optional Protocols are gravely or systematically violated. If required thereto, the Committee may designate one or more of its members to conduct such an inquiry, confidentially and if necessary including a field visit. Part IV eventually contains final provisions dealing with practical issues such as signature, ratification and entry into force and also with international assistance and cooperation in article 15 OP III.

In the Preamble of OP III it is recognized that 'children's special and dependent status may create real difficulties for them in pursuing remedies for violations of their rights.' It is furthermore stated that remedies for violations of children's rights should take into account the need for child-sensitive procedures at all levels. All delegations present emphasized the need to include child-friendly procedures, as currently laid down in article 3 OP III. The specificities of these procedures are to be elaborated by the Committee on the Rights of the Child in its rules of procedure.[1186] In addition, delegations reached consensus over the inclusion of a provision to protect children within their domestic jurisdiction against human rights violations, ill-treatment or intimidation as a consequence of having submitted communications procedures.[1187] This was eventually laid down in article 4 OP III. Lembrechts argues that whereas the traditional image of childhood in the Convention on the Rights of the Child shifts along the lines of its developing capacities as laid down in article 5 CRC from an emphasis on 'the child as a passive recipient of protection and care' in article 3 CRC to 'the child as an active participant' in article 12 CRC, the interconnected nature of these three rights, is reflected in the final draft of the Optional Protocol. Especially article 2 is exemplary in mentioning elements of all three rights:

Article 2 OP III to the CRC: 'In fulfilling the functions conferred to it by the present Protocol, the Committee shall be guided by the principle of the best interests of the child. It shall also have regard for the rights and views of the child,

[1186] UN General Assembly, A/HRC/WG.7/2/4, 13 January 2011 § 29.
[1187] Ibidem supra note 1185, § 31–33.

the views of the child being given due weight in accordance with the age and maturity of the child.'

Lembrechts argues that whereas the mentioning of children's right to be heard is limited to this provision, the broad support for the participatory dimension of the child-concept in the drafting phase, reflects the intention to involve children in the communications procedure.[1188] In line with the many declarations of intent for involving children in advocating for their own rights,[1189] this intention has recently be included in paragraph 19 of the Rules of Procedure of the Committee on the Rights of the Child. Given the history of *not* involving children in the drafting of the Convention on the Rights of the Child, in its Optional Protocols nor in the General Comments or the Concluding Observations of the Committee on the Country Reports, it is time that the Committee on the Rights of the Child itself provides for a good example of involving children in the drafting of its own rules of procedure. This would be a much more convincing example of involving children in the enforcement of their own rights, than repeatedly stating that children's right to be heard should be respected.[1190]

The main issue that remains to be resolved in the Rules of Procedure is the determination of who is capable of making complaints before the Committee: children, their parents, legal guardians or other representatives. In general, article 5 OP III provides that an individual or a group of individuals whose rights as laid down in the CRC or its Optional Protocols have been violated can make a complaint. Secondly, when someone makes a complaint on behalf of an individual, this must be done with their consent or the author must be able to justify acting without the consent of that person (e.g. when acting on behalf of a baby, who is not able to give consent, but who have suffered violations of his or her rights). Newell righteously recalls that children are not the only group who may be dependent on others to bring a complaint before an international Committee. He states that 'the lack of capacity is not unique to children. It is equally true for many adult rights holders who are considered to lack the capacity to act on their own behalf – for example adults with severe learning disabilities, elderly and confused adults.'[1191] Lessons can therefore be learned from experiences of these groups to include children either directly or indirectly in the communications procedure.

1188 S. Lembrechts, 'Wiens klachtrecht? Het kind-concept in het derde Facultatief Protocol bij het Verdrag inzake de Rechten van het Kind betreffende de instelling van een communicatieprocedure', *Tijdschrift voor Jeugd- en Kinderrechten* 2012, Issue 2, p. 99–103.

1189 See supra note 1186.

1190 See for an extensive elaboration of the Committee's explanation of the right of the child to be heard, General Comment 12. U.N. Doc. CRC/C/GC/12, 20 July 2009.

1191 U.N. Doc. A/HRC/WG.7/1/CRP.2, 9 December 2009. Submission by P. Newell to the First session of the Open-Ended Working Group of the Human Rights Council considering the possibility of elaborating an Optional Protocol to provide a communications procedure for the Convention on the Rights of the Child, § 53, p. 12.

In order to genuinely involve children in the communications procedure, the modes of involvement should be taken into account. However, the requirement as laid down in article 7b OP III that complaints need to be submitted in written form poses a significant obstacle in genuinely involving children in the adjudication of violations of their rights, given the fact that many children have different modes of preferred communication, including drawing, talking or playing with dolls and communicating through music.[1192, 1193] This requirement especially poses a barrier to children or their representatives who are not able to write. Also in other respects, caution must be taken to ensure that no legal or practical barriers are established in ensuring access for children to this communications procedure. Marta Santos Pais, the Special Representative of the Secretary-General on Violence against Children, sets several conditions for ensuring a communication procedure that is child sensitive.[1194] According to her, a first requirement is that the information on the existing complaint mechanism to children and the way in which it can be used is widely disseminated to children and other actors involved, e.g. through incorporation in the school curricula of the child.[1195] Thereto, the Protocol must be issued in a child-friendly version.[1196] Thirdly, 'all relevant actors must be knowledgeable and skillful in the use of communications procedures and in the promotion of ethical principles when dealing with and supporting children in this regard'.[1197] Fourthly, the right of the child to be informed must be realized 'in a form and language that is adapted to the age and level of understanding of the child'.[1198] Last but not least, children who become involved in a communications procedure must be protected against 'any pressure

---

1192 See for example: M. Delfos, *Luister je wel naar mij? Gespreksvoering met kinderen tuseen vier en twaalf jaar*, [*Do you listen to me? Communicating with children between 4–12 years*], Amsterdam: Uitgeverij SWP 2007, pp. 149–156. Delfos establishes that for children both verbal and non-verbal modes of communication are important, as well as a combination of communication and playing techniques.

1193 See also the Guidelines on child-friendly justice of the Council of Europe, November 2010, available at: https://wcd.coe.int/ViewDoc.jsp?Ref=CM/Del/Dec(2010)1098/10.2abc&Language=lanEnglish&Ver=app6&Site=CM&BackColorInternet=C3C3C3&BackColorIntranet=EDB021&BackColorLogged=F5D383. General Principle A1 provides that children's level of maturity and any communications difficulties must be born in mind in order to make their participation meaningful. Furthermore in 3.44, it is stipulated that 'Means used for the hearing of children should be adapted to the child's level of understanding and ability to communicate and take into account the circumstances of the case'. Another example of child-friendly communications procedures is found in 5.59 'Interview methods, such as video or audio-recording or pre-trial hearings in camera, should be used and considered as admissible evidence.'

1194 In the UN Guidelines on Justice in Matters involving Child Victims and Witnessess of Crime the term 'child sensitive' is defined as: 'an approach that balances the child's right to protection and that takes into account the child's individual needs and views'. ECOSOC Resolution 2005/20, 22 July 2005.

1195 U.N. Doc. A/HRC/Wg.7/1/CRP.7, Submission of the Special Representative of the Secretary-General on Violence against Children, 14 December 2009, pp. 6–7.

1196 Ibidem supra note 1194, p. 6.

1197 Ibidem supra note 1194, p. 6.

1198 Ibidem supra note 1194, p. 6.

or manipulation, discrimination, intimidation or reprisal'.[1199] Hereto, they should be entitled to support by a legal counsel and other forms of appropriate assistance. These requirements show overlap with the requirements set by the Victims and Witnesses Unit of the ICC,[1200] such as doing video-interviews by trained professionals, using screens, face and voice distortion and holding closed sessions,[1201] in the sense that specific efforts must be made to critically evaluate and adapt the regular complaints procedures to the rights, needs and views of children. Given the qualification of the communications procedure as a quasi-judicial procedure, it is also important to prepare children and manage their expectations on the (limits of the) potential outcome of the procedure. All in all, the newly adopted Optional Protocol on a communications procedure for children is a good step forward on the way towards involving children in standing up for their rights. Receiving its 10th ratification on 14 January, Optional Protocol III has entered into force in April 2014.

6.6. CONCLUSION: HOW CAN THE HIGHEST ATTAINABLE STANDARD OF HEALTH OF THE CHILD, I.E. CHILD-CENTRED HEALTH-CARE BE REALIZED?

In this chapter the question was addressed how the process of realization influences the interpretation of the highest attainable standard of health of the child and which actors are responsible for realizing it. The right to health of the child gets meaning in the daily reality of children's lives. The interpretation of the right to health requires the active involvement of the beneficiaries as well as, in the case of children in their early childhood, their representatives. In such a way, the realization process reduces the level of abstraction and the right to health becomes a 'living right'.

From this chapter, it appears that plural actors are responsible for ensuring the right to the highest attainable standard of health of the child. These actors are States Parties and non-state actors, including children, their families and medical professionals. Furthermore, other private actors such as private companies and

1199 Ibidem supra note 1194, p. 6.

1200 ICC Rules of Procedure and Evidence U.N. Doc. PCNICC/2000/1/Add.1 (2000). See also Working Paper no 3 of the Special-Representative of the Secretary General for Children in armed conflict: Children and justice during and in the aftermath of armed conflict, September 2011, p. 17, available at: www.un.org/children/conflict/_documents/Working%20Paper%20Number%203_Children%20and%20Justice.pdf.

1201 This last requirement is in line with the provision in article 4-2 of the Optional Protocol that 'The identity of any individual or group of individuals concerned shall not be revealed publicly without their express consent.'

(I)NGOs all can play a role in realizing the highest attainable standard of health of the child.

States have an immediate obligation to realize the minimum core content of the highest attainable standard of health without discrimination of any children. States must integrate the right to health of the child both in its constitution and governmental policies as well as in sector specific legislation and policy. The sector wide implementation of children's right to health furthermore requires solid cross-sectoral coordination. Although States have a broad margin of appreciation in determining the measures that are taken to realize the highest attainable standard of health, it is required that more concrete parameters are established to assess the measures prioritized, such as the formulation of concrete implementation measures, time bound measurable targets, clear deadlines, the identification of all human and financial resources, and the identification of the responsible actors. Thereby, Courts are enabled to better assess the reasonableness of the measures taken. Furthermore, States must conduct child impact assessments beforehand and a child impact evaluation afterwards, both including interviews with children and their family members to identify the impact of the measures selected. In this way, it can be assessed whether the peculiarities of the right to the highest attainable standard actually have an impact on the daily health care of the beneficiaries.

Although the right to health of children has increasingly been laid down in national legislation, there is still much debate over its justiciability in court proceedings. The principal argument against holding States directly accountable for violations of children's right to health are the limitations of States in the available resources they have at their disposal to realize the right to the highest attainable standard of health. However, the amount of available resources can be significantly increased by reallocating budget from military or other sectors to the social sector and the health sector. Furthermore, developing countries must seek active assistance from other countries to make sufficient resources available for the realization of the right to health of the child. In doing so, the process of making more resources available does not only refer to financial resources, but also to human and informational resources.

In addition to the requirement to make legal arrangements to effectuate the right to health of the child, it is recommended to translate these rights to the local realities in which children live. Kaime provides for several useful guidelines to bridge the gap between the legal provisions of children's rights and the norms used in traditional institutions in the communities where children live. Furthermore, although States have immediate responsibilities in ensuring the necessary health infrastructure, especially primary and emergency health care, providing for basic life necessities, such as safe drinking water, food, housing and health education, many other private actors can significantly contribute to making more resources available. The highest attainable standard of health can best be achieved if every individual contributes to its realization to the maximum extent of its individual capabilities. Not only because this will help mobilize as much different resources as possible, but also because more flexibility and adaptability to the specific needs of individual children and their parents can be achieved.

In order to realize the active involvement of children and their parents, it is necessary that people take ownership for their own health and the health of their children. This conclusion is in line with articles 5 and 18 CRC that primarily hold parents accountable for the health and well-being of their children. States have the secondary responsibility in supporting parents to bring up their children in health.

The provision of health care to young children and their parents should take their capabilities for ensuring their own health as a starting point. This implies that even very young children must be respected as rights-holders. Even very young children have innate capabilities that should be stimulated so that children can grow into self-reliant, healthy adults. Therefore, they should be involved in their own health care from the very beginning. Using child-sensitive and creative methods can add significantly to bringing the best interests of very young children to the light. In practice, this means that sufficient opportunities must be created for children and their parents to ask questions, to share information and observations and to influence and criticize the decisions at hand.

All in all, the newly adopted Protocol to the CRC on a communications procedure for children, offers a significant step forward for individuals and their representatives to hold States accountable for violations of the right to the highest attainable standard of health of the child. Entering into force on 14 April 2014, it is now time for States to sign and ratify the Protocol.

VII. CONCLUSIONS

When a mother gives birth to a child, the new born has a wealth of innate opportunities that can be brought to life. Therefore, it is essential to ensure that the child is born and raised in the best possible circumstances. The right to the highest attainable standard of health of the child encompasses the key notion that children are enabled and supported from the very beginning to realize the capabilities that they value most in life. In doing so, it is essential to acknowledge that every child has its own unique combination of capabilities that it wishes to achieve in life.

In the introductory chapter it was established that the concept of the highest attainable standard of health of the child remains vague, since it depends on situational and individual circumstances, financial resources and political will. As a result, it remains unclear who has the responsibility to implement its constitutive elements and what the legal effect is of the right to health of the child. Therefore, in this thesis we analysed:

(a) What priorities derive from the concept of the highest attainable standard of health of the child, the definition and interpretation of the key constituent elements of this concept on the basis of international human rights law;
(b) How this concept should be further implemented in the light of the international human rights standards.

In order to answer these questions, a literature research was conducted of the relevant international legal documents, the *travaux préparatoires*, General Comments, Country Reports, UN documents, EU documents and relevant scientific literature. These legal documents were considered from the perspective of Amartya Sen's capability approach, which focuses on the intrinsic (or innate) opportunities that people have. The level of realization of these opportunities, referred to as peoples' 'functionings' is effectuated by the interplay of individual choices and situational circumstances. In the following sections, the priorities or key constituent elements required to realize the highest attainable standard of health of the child (the capability of the child to be healthy) as found in international law are presented. The implications of these priorities for defining the concept of the highest attainable standard of health of the child are discussed in section 7.1.4.

7.1. PRIORITIES SET TO ACHIEVE THE HIGHEST ATTAINABLE STANDARD OF HEALTH OF THE CHILD

7.1.1. PRIORITIES SET IN THE CHILDREN'S RIGHTS DOMAIN

I. What priorities relating to the right to the highest attainable standard of health of the child can be derived from the interpretations found in the international children's right domain?

II. How are these priorities explained in the Concluding Observations of the Committee on the Rights of the Child?

In analysing the right to the highest attainable standard of health of the child as laid down in article 24 CRC and elaborated in the newly adopted General Comment 15 to the CRC and interpreted for specific countries in the Concluding Observations of the Committee on the Rights of the Child, core priorities can be identified which are critical for ensuring that children can achieve a basic level of health. The approach taken in this research can also be used to identify the different standards applicable for other social rights, such as the right to education or the right to an adequate standard of living. In doing so, different balances can be expected for those responsible such as the parents, the state and other professionals.

Although the Concluding Observations are meant to contain country specific explanations of children's rights, the elaboration remains at such a high level of abstraction, that paragraphs are often identical for countries as diverse as Colombia and the Netherlands. Therefore, it is not possible to further explain the priorities identified. The identified priorities following from the right to health in the children's rights domain, i.e. the CRC and the General Comments of the Committee on the Rights of the Child, are:

1. Non-discrimination (art. 2 CRC) should be a high priority in all actions of governments in order to ensure that all children are included in health programming. Special attention should be given to all groups of vulnerable children, such as very young children, girls, sick children, orphaned children, children from minority groups, indigenous children, children with handicaps and all children living in vulnerable situations, such as street children, children living in rural areas and children living in crises. This requirement extents to all of the following elements of the right to health of the child. The principle of discrimination also prohibits discrimination of children on the basis of the status or behaviour of their parents.

2. Prevention: in establishing health programmes a first priority must be given to prevention of health problems. Several approaches are identified, namely prevention and combating malnutrition by providing for the underlying determinants of health, early identification and intervention in case of disease, combating easily preventable diseases, the provision of (sexual and reproductive) health education and health promotion.
3. Primary health care: provision of primary health care requires that health services are close to the places where children live and play. This increases the accessibility and the affordability of health services for all. Furthermore, health services must be continuously available and include as a minimum:
   - Provision of health care and information to the mother during pregnancy.
   - Obstetric health care around the birth of the child.
   - Neonatal health care for the mother and the child immediately after birth.
   - Quality health care during childhood.
4. Health education: this enables both children and their parents to adopt a healthy lifestyle. Health education should include information on hygiene, healthy nutrition, sunburn, prevention of transmission of diseases (e.g. the use of malaria bed nets) and sexual and reproductive health information. Also, education on traffic regulations and other safety measures can significantly reduce the number of injuries resulting from accidents.
5. Training on child rights: this should be provided for children, parents and medical professionals in order to ensure that children's rights are respected and implemented in the health care setting. Examples are the provision of age-appropriate, full and quality information to both the child and its parents on the diagnosis, prognosis, possible interventions and side effects of medical treatments. This enables children to practice their right to participation and to be involved in the health care process. Since medical professionals are trained in medical ethics, it is recommended to elaborate on the different implications of medical ethics and children's rights in the health care setting. Also, particular training is required on child-friendly communication, the particular needs of vulnerable groups, such as young children and children with disabilities and the prevention, identification and addressing of violence against children.
6. Birth registration must be ensured for all children, so that children can have direct access to (primary) health care services. However, if children do not have an official birth certificate, this should not exclude them from receiving medical care. Even then, birth registration is also required so that doctors can better assess the age and level of development (or stagnation in the development) of children.
7. Social security is required to ensure that the costs for the underlying determinants of health and for the provision of medical services can be borne. This right to social security of the child as laid down in articles 26 and

27 CRC is also applicable when the parents do not apply for the child. This is especially important for refugee children, orphaned children and children living on the street. Furthermore, it is required to inform children and their parents on the availability of social insurances, so that medical services are not only accessible in theory, but also in practice.

The additional value of the Concluding Observations to the CRC Convention is that several additional priorities are mentioned (points 8–11):

8. In its Concluding Observation to the Country Reports (see chapter 3) the Committee on the Rights of the Child identifies the priority to stimulate breastfeeding of infants for a minimum of six months. To realize this target, several measures are required:
   - The establishment of baby-friendly hospitals, where mothers are stimulated to breastfeed their children from the moment of birth.
   - The adoption of legislation that enables mothers to have maternity leave and to have opportunities at work to continue breastfeeding.
   - The implementation of awareness raising campaigns on the benefits of breastfeeding.
   - The implementation of the International Code of Marketing Breast milk Substitutes.
9. Governments should define a concrete and coordinated health policy. This must include:
   - The adoption of a national plan with strategic budget lines.
   - Identify the responsible governmental departments.
   - Set clear, time-bound and measurable targets.
   - Ensure disaggregated data collection on health indicators for all children.

   In the newly adopted General Comment 15 tot the CRC, the Committee has further specified that a national plan must specify as a matter of priority:
   - The different levels of health care that must be provided.
   - The health problems that need to be addressed.
   - The health interventions that must be made available.
   - The medicines that must be provided.
10. In its Concluding Observations, the Committee on the Rights of the Child gives increasing attention to the need to ensure healthy living circumstances for children. To prevent environmental pollution, sustainable development programs must be implemented. Furthermore, efforts must be made to prevent the business sector from activities that pollute the environment in which children live and to stimulate working in healthy conditions.
11. The provision of basic health care to children in humanitarian crises is found as a matter of priority in the Concluding Observations of the CRC Committee. Natural disasters and conflict impact heavily on the availability of health services for children. Also, infectious diseases, violence, malnutrition

and a rise in trauma related mental health problems significantly hamper the realization of the highest attainable standard of health of children. Furthermore, children are among the most vulnerable persons, because of their size, limited capacities to flee from sudden danger and developmental needs. Therefore, it is crucial to prioritize the provision of necessary health services to children in crisis situations. In some areas or (crisis) situations, it is necessary to set up mobile health clinics or other types of flexible health services (e.g. flying doctors) to ensure accessible health care for all.

12. The Committee also considers as a priority in General Comment 15 that all stakeholders must be involved in the implementation of the right to health. Thereby, a community based approach to realizing the right to health of the child can be established that involves many different actors, including the child, its parents, extended family, medical professionals and a variety of private actors such as NGOs and companies. States are encouraged to seek active contribution of children and their families in the identification and prioritization of the key elements of the right to health of the child. These can be obtained by regular consultations and by research with children, which is adapted to their age and maturity and which includes the possibility to do this without the parents being present. GC 15 to the CRC provides suggestions for elements on which children's opinions must be sought (see section 2.5.8.2).

The right to health of the child as laid down in article 24 CRC sets clear priorities. However, as found in the analysis of the Concluding Observations of the Committee on the Rights of the Child on the Country Reports, these priorities are best suited for countries with medium and high levels of development (see section 3.3). In countries with low levels of development and in conflict and disaster areas, even the most basic levels of health are scarcely achieved. Notwithstanding, governments – and the international community – do have the obligation to ensure the minimum level of health care to children necessary for their survival, if necessary by actively seeking support from the international community. For countries with very high levels of development, more ambition is expected to raise the health standards, in terms of health indicators, to a higher standard. An example is found in the European region (see section 7.1.3).

Resulting from the analysis of the Concluding Observations of the Committee on the Rights of the Child, three additional recommendations are relevant with regard to the functioning of the Committee:

13. The Committee on the Rights of the Child has a central role in the assessment of child-sensitive and disaggregated data on the basis of which measurable and time bound targets must be set. In doing so, it is crucial to involve children themselves and their family in the gathering and (self-)assessment of available data. In order to ensure the involvement of (chronically) ill children,

it is required that interview and communication opportunities are available within medical institutions. Furthermore, the best interests of the child must be leading, which implies that timing, duration and location of interviews must be exercised in a way that takes into account the medical condition of the child.

14. The Committee on the Rights of the Child has a central role in holding States accountable for the development of a national health plan, which specifies the way in which its health sector is organized and what budget is allocated for the different departments involved in the realization of the right to health of children.
15. Given the regular assessment of Country Reports, the Committee on the Rights of the Child has a central role in the interpretation of health related rights. New insights from one country may help to find solutions for identifying the necessary steps to realize children's right to health in another country. The Committee is therefore in the position to give valuable recommendations to countries on the progressive steps to be taken to realize the right to the highest attainable standard of health.

7.1.2. PRIORITIES SET IN INTERNATIONAL HEALTH AND HUMAN RIGHTS LAW

III. What priorities related to the right to the highest attainable standard of health of the child can be derived from the interpretation found in the international health and human rights law? What is the additional value of this body of law for the interpretation of the right to the highest attainable standard of health in the children's rights domain?

The international legal framework on health and human rights identifies several elements that can be considered as the minimum core content, i.e. the priorities to be achieved to realize the right to the highest attainable standard of health of the child (see section 4.8). These minimum essential levels can be further raised with increased budget made available.

In the first place four principles should be guiding in the interpretation and implementation of the general right to health, namely the principles of availability, accessibility, acceptability and quality (see section 4.5 for a detailed overview). A trend is visible in which the principles of participation, adaptability and accountability are increasingly taken into account. The application of these principles gives room for the development of a more flexible, adaptive health care system that places the child and its family at the heart instead of the functionalities of medical organizations. Furthermore, the application of these principles allows for an approach that focuses not only on the health outcome, but also on the health process itself. This is especially important for children who can't be cured.

The legal framework established in the international health and human rights domain has been translated in essential building blocks of a rights-based health system by the former UN Special Rapporteur on the right to health. A rights-based health system lies at the heart of the right to the highest attainable standard of health. A central priority of such a system is effective coordination between health services and schools in addition to services for the provision of safe drinking water, food, housing, transport and sanitary facilities. For example, primary health care services could be located in the vicinity of schools to improve accessibility.

A rights-based health system furthermore requires – as a matter of priority – a bottom-up approach. A bottom-up approach means that the community participation is an important factor in the process of realization of the right to health of the child. The government can invite and support communities to take healthy initiatives in a large variety of ways, which can contribute to the realization of the right to health of the child. However, the actual set up of health programs and services should be done with close consultations of local communities. In order to enable children and their families to be involved in their own health care process, the provision of child-friendly health information is required. This information must be sensitive to the special needs of children of different ages, with different cultural backgrounds and with varying needs. Furthermore, transparency in the health system and the possible referrals is required, which could be accomplished if children who have plural encounters with medical professionals are guided by one person during the entire process.

Lastly, the right to health as laid down in the international health and human rights law domain also requires international cooperation. Hereto, it is necessary to establish shared international health standards and indicators that can be used as a basis for comparison and to measure progress over time. Furthermore, national foreign policies must include health impact assessments. Improving and realigning international health agreements can be further achieved by deploying health diplomacy: identifying and negotiating mutual health needs and finding common grounds on which health policies are based on. Health diplomacy can also contribute significantly to coordinating the provision of humanitarian help and identifying the different actors responsible.

7.1.3. PRIORITIES SET IN EUROPEAN HUMAN RIGHTS LAW

IV. What priorities in the interpretation of the right to the highest attainable standard of health of the child are found in human rights law in Europe?

The elaboration of the right to health of the child in Europe provides a good example of an extended interpretation of the right to the highest attainable standard of health of the child.

Both the relevant EU legislation and the European Social Charter give room for a flexible interpretation of the right to health of the child. In the EU, access to preventive health care and medical services must be established *under the conditions established by national law and practices*. Different member states thus have a broad margin of appreciation to determine the measures that should be given high priority on the basis of their national health indicators. Such an interpretation is in line with the children's rights domain, because therein it is established that health policies for children must be based on disaggregated data. In the ESC, a flexible interpretation is made possible through the dependence of the right to health on the development of medical knowledge.

- In the European Union, a high level of human health protection is required. Prevention of health problems is obviously of clear priority and measures in this regard must include:
  - Promote research into the causes of disease.
  - Prevent transmission of disease.
  - Provide health information and education.
  - Ensure monitoring and early warning.
  - Combat serious cross-border threats.
  - Ensure immunization of children against the major childhood diseases.
  - Prevent injuries and violence against children.

- The development of child-friendly health care is another matter of priority. Guidelines have been issued which contain many suggestions or recommendations for measures inter alia to ensure that hospitalization is minimized and that health care must be organized around the rights, needs and characteristics of children. This requires a coordinated, integrated, comprehensive and continuous approach. Whereas the Guidelines take into account several changing factors (for a further specification see section 7.1.4), both the Guidelines and the WHO strategy underline the importance of continuity of health care. Usually, continuity is interpreted as the transition from primary to secondary to tertiary care. However, both the guidelines on CFHC and the WHO strategy provide for different systems to distinguish different forms of continuity in health care (see section 5.6.3).

The Guidelines on CFHC assume that a child lives in a social context. Therefore, it is a matter of priority to establish a healthy family environment and provide for family-friendly healthcare. By working through families, continuity of experience is created for the child and the bonding between the child, its parents and other family members is stimulated. Still, it is important not to submerge the best interests of the child on the broader set of family-oriented rights and interests. On the other hand, targeting children through their families with health education may increase their exposure to necessary health information. Both the Council of Europe and the WHO establish that children – and in the long term adults- must be stimulated to take responsibility for their own health. Empowerment must be achieved as a matter of priority through continuous health education that is in line with their evolving capacities.

7.1.4. THE HIGHEST ATTAINABLE STANDARD OF HEALTH IS A MOVING TARGET

The priorities necessary for achieving the highest attainable standard of health of the child have been identified in the previous part of this chapter. However, the concept of 'the highest attainable standard of health' has the inherent capability to extend beyond the basic level of health care. In fact, the concept of the 'highest attainable standard of health' varies significantly according to different personal and situational circumstances. Therefore, the highest attainable standard of health of the child is in constant motion. As such, the right to the highest attainable standard of health can be qualified as *a moving target*, because it is dependent on several changing factors. These factors are:

First of all, children are in a permanent state of development. Children's healthy growth is in itself characterized by constant change. From the moment of conception and continuing after birth, children experience the gradual development of new physical, mental and social skills. This constant change influences their nutritional needs, susceptibility to infectious diseases and abilities to cope with external stressors. The varying needs deriving from the changing life course of children require health services that are adaptive to these different phases: maternal, antenatal, obstetric, new born, infant and child and adolescent health care. Also, health services must be adaptive to the changing needs of children in different stages of disease and include primary, secondary, tertiary prevention, curation, rehabilitation and palliative care.

Secondly, all individuals are different. Some basic capabilities are necessary for survival, such as food, drinking water, shelter and basic health care. However, the amount and type of nutrition required vary per individual. In addition, there is a great interpersonal variation in the intrinsic opportunities that children have. These variations in intrinsic opportunities are augmented or mitigated by the level of health education that children receive and the circumstances in which they live. Therefore, different (groups of) children have different health needs and make different health choices. This influences the interpretation of the highest attainable standard of health and the measures required to achieve that level of health.

Thirdly, children live in continuously changing circumstances. Being healthy requires constant adaptation of the body to its natural habitat. This adaptation takes into account changes in nutrition and sleeping patterns, the prevalence of infectious diseases and other health challenges, such as seasonal cycli and challenges such as traffic, travels, stress, deprivation or crises. The Guidelines on CFHC specifically refer to the changing epidemiology of childhood.

Lastly, changing health insights continuously augment the opportunities for prevention of health problems, (early) diagnosis, treatment and mitigation of the impact of health threats. These new insights influence both the quality of health care and the total costs of health care. The highest attainable standard of health thus also changes when the availability of effective health interventions changes.

Therefore, in order to attain the highest attainable standard of health, the health care and guidance provided to children must be responsive to the changing intrinsic and extrinsic circumstances in which children live. This requires flexibility of medical professionals and ongoing involvement of both children and their caretakers.

7.2. REALIZING THE RIGHT TO THE HIGHEST ATTAINABLE STANDARD OF HEALTH

V. How does the process of realization influence the interpretation of the highest attainable standard of health of the child?

To answer this question, the role of the different actors involved in the realization of the right to health has been elucidated. Secondly, the cyclical process of law enforcement and the interaction with the social reality in which children live has been clarified.

The realization of the right of the child to the highest attainable standard of health requires the involvement of different actors, specified inter alia in General Comment 15 to the CRC and in other documents such as the Guidelines on child-friendly healthcare. The results of the findings from this research are presented below.

7.2.1. CHILDREN AS RIGHTS-HOLDERS: EMPOWERMENT

The involvement of the beneficiaries of health services is crucial to realizing the highest attainable standard of health of the child (e.g. in the identification, design, construction and delivery of health services). It appears that the social reality in which children live is a constitutive element of the right to health of the child. In response to subquestion (b) *'How should the concept of the highest attainable standard of health of the child be implemented in light of international human rights standards?'*, it appears that the social reality is part of a continuous process in which the right to health of the child is translated into daily practice and in which the daily practice in its turn influences the interpretation of the right to health of the child. As such, the interpretation of the right to health of the child is dependent on a particular context and time. Furthermore, it appears that *children are active participants in the process of realizing their own right to health*, because they consciously or unconsciously influence the way in which their own right to health is interpreted.

The position of children as rights holders requires that their own views upon their health must be taken into consideration from the beginning of their lives, notwithstanding their age or limited verbal capacities. The new concept of health as introduced by Huber is exemplary, since it takes people's abilities for self-management and adaptability to changing circumstances as a starting point. This approach to health, in which children's capabilities and evolving capacities are elementary, is crucial to realizing the right to the highest attainable standard of health as a moving target. *The right to the highest attainable standard of health of the child is in fact the ability of the child to adapt to continuously changing circumstances.*

Therefore, children must be stimulated and enabled to live harmoniously in a continuously changing environment. This requires that children gradually take ownership for their own health. This can be achieved by listening to the child and involving its views from the very beginning in the appreciation of its best interests. For children in their early childhood, the support, guidance and appreciation of their parents or caretakers is pivotal in this process. Listening to children in their early childhood is respectful of their rights and it shows them that they are taken seriously from the very beginning. Also, young children have additional information that can be crucial in establishing an accurate diagnosis. Specific age-appropriate communication methods can add to increasing the reliability of their answers and the accuracy of any diagnoses made.

Empowerment of children and their parents/caretakers is central to the realization process of the right to health of the child. This must be achieved by involving them in individual health decisions and in shaping the organization of health care services. The Committee on the Rights of the Child therefore recommends that there should be a continuous process of child impact assessments and child impact evaluations, which consequently predict and evaluate the effects of any proposed laws, policies and budget allocations. The Committee places great emphasis on the involvement of children in data collection and interviewing them, so that their interests are directly reflected. With respect to the involvement of very young children, this requires age-appropriate interview techniques as well as interviewing their parents or caretakers.

7.2.2. THE ROLE OF THE STATE IN REALIZING THE RIGHT TO HEALTH OF THE CHILD

States have a wide range of possible legislative, administrative and policy measures to meet their obligations following from the right to health of the child. Appropriate measures pass the test of reasonableness and are taken within a reasonable time. A distinction is made between obligations of immediate and obligations of progressive nature.

The obligations to respect and protect the right to health of the child require less resources than the obligation to fulfil the right to health. Therefore, the obligation to respect and the obligation to protect should fall within the scope of States' immediate obligation to fulfil. The obligation to fulfil the right to health of the child however, such as the provision of medicines and the provision of health services to reduce infant and maternal mortality, require considerable investments to be realized and thus place a larger burden on a States' available resources. This element must be realized progressively.

Although the obligation to fulfil must be realized progressively, the obligation to ensure the minimum core content of the right to health of the child is an obligation of immediate nature. The requirement to take measures within a reasonable time thus only applies to measures that go beyond the minimum core content of the right to health of the child towards the *full* realization of the highest attainable standard of health. Considerations to be made by Courts and Tribunals in assessing the reasonableness of time frames include:

- The nature and purpose of the health measure.
- The circumstances of the country.
- The intentions of the States Parties to the CRC.
- The potential damage caused by not taking the identified measure.
- The achievements made in comparable countries.

The right to health must be included in national legislation and people must be informed about it. Measures must include (General Comment 5 to the CRC):

i. The provision of information on the right to health of the child (and the CRC).
ii. A comprehensive review of existing domestic legislation.
iii. The adoption of new laws or codes or amendments made to existing ones.
iv. The status of the CRC in domestic law, including the recognition of the CRC in the constitution or in other legislation and the status of the CRC in the event of conflict with national legislation.
v. The possibility of invoking the CRC in national courts.

States have the obligation to provide for the necessary health infrastructure, health education and underlying determinants of health. These requirements can be best achieved if they are organized collectively. Furthermore, States must ensure quality and disaggregated data collection on the basis of which comprehensive and integrated national health programs can be formulated. The realization of these health programs must be enabled by allocating sufficient financial and human resources (see § 6.3.3).

The available resources must be allocated to address the most pressing health problems. This logically differs per country and region and thus depends on the particular context in which the measures are taken. Periodical reviews of both statistical data and personal assessments must be done to assess whether the measures prioritized by a country contribute to realizing the envisaged effect.

In developing a national strategy on children's health, specific goals for sectoral action plans must be set (see section 7.1.1 point 9). The implementation of general measures to realize the right to health must be attributed to one designated governmental department, that coordinates the different programs in place that contribute to realizing the right to health of the child. A national strategy should take into account the health sector, but also the activities of other sectors that impact upon the realization of the right to health of children.

In addition to providing for collective health measures and setting appropriate standards for the private sector, States must stimulate private actors to contribute to the realization of the right to health of the child. In this way, more actors can take ownership and become involved in realizing children's right to health, which will increase the overall impact of the measures taken.

To identify the impact of the measures taken, data must be gathered about the budget allocated to:

- The number of health professionals that have been trained in children's rights.
- A large variety of other health indicators, including:
  i. Infant, child and maternal mortality rates.
  ii. The proportion of children with low birth weight.
  iii. The number of children that is immunized.

iv. The proportion of children that have access to safe drinking water and sanitation.
v. The number of pregnant women who have access to perinatal health care.
vi. The number of children born in hospital.
vii. The number of children receiving exclusive breastfeeding.

7.2.2.1. Effective remedies

The right to health of the child is increasingly laid down in national legislations. However, the possibility of direct application of the right to health in individual law cases is not clear cut. Direct applicability may be assumed in cases in which a State did not meet its obligation to respect and to protect. However, a study of the application of children's rights in the Netherlands showed that whereas many rights are directly applied, this is explicitly not the case for the right to health of the child. On the other hand, the right to health of the child occasionally does influence the interpretation of this right when referral is made to the facts and circumstances of the case.

The second issue discussed is whether it is desirable to directly apply the right to health of the child. It was concluded that this should be a measure of last resort, since law suits detract resources from the allocation of resources to actual health care measures and that there are alternative ways to enforce the right to health that benefit the right to health more directly, such as through quasi-judicial institutions that are more closely connected to the daily realities in which children live. Also, many private actors are more closely connected to the daily realities in which children live and can therefore have a more direct impact on the realization of their right to health.

Notwithstanding the choices made to enforce the right to health of the child through judicial or quasi-judicial means, it is important to establish child-sensitive procedures. Special considerations may be necessary to enable children with health problems to be involved in (quasi-)judicial procedures.

Quasi-judicial effectuation of children's rights norms in daily life furthermore requires active deliberation with local institutions, authorities and other influential actors, such as the elders in a family, traditional leaders etc., in the negotiation process to transform the CRC principles into lived realities of children. Given the highly divergent circumstances in which children live, this process can take many different forms. It is important to identify and ensure that children, women and other traditionally less dominant groups are included in the decision-making processes.

As soon as Optional Protocol III to the CRC on a communications procedure for children enters into force in the different member states to the CRC, children and their representatives will have an additional remedy at their disposal to hold States accountable for not meeting their responsibilities to ensure the right to health of the child. However, given the collective nature of many health measures required to realize the right to health of the child, it is highly recommendable to enable children to apply collectively for this procedure. Furthermore, since children apply many different forms of communication to make themselves heard, it is recommended to extent the admissibility of cases beyond the submission of written complaints to better enable them to become directly involved in such procedures if they wish to.

The CRC Committee has a central role in assessing the progress achieved in the realization of the right to health of the child. Its role entails the following tasks:

I. Assessment of available data on health indicators.
II. Monitoring of measures taken and progress achieved.
III. Interpretation and development of child rights.
IV. Suggest measurable, time bound targets
V. Identify responsible actors and governmental departments.
VI. In the future: receive complaints through the communications procedure.

7.2.2.2. International cooperation

Article 24.4 CRC obliges States Parties to promote and encourage international cooperation with a view to progressively achieving the right to health of the child. Such cooperation can be divided in regular development aid and emergency care in humanitarian situations. Extraterritorial obligations of States Parties to realize the right to health of the child in other, less developed countries include the duties to respect and protect, though not to fulfil the right to health.

Developing countries primarily have the obligation to maximize their domestic available resources and secondly to actively seek assistance from the international community. The Committee on the Rights of the Child endorses the 20/20 initiative, which entails that recipient countries must allocate at least 20 percent of its public expenditure to realize universal access to basic social services, such as health.

The Committee on the Rights of the Child advices developed countries to allocate at least 20 percent of foreign aid to human priority goals such as primary health care. Measures include the creation of employment opportunities, investments through microcredits, investments in infrastructure, debt relief, stimulating commercial activities and private-public partnerships and through bilateral and multilateral agreements. The Committee furthermore endorses agreements reached that States Parties need to allocate at least 0.7% of its GDP to foreign aid within a children's rights framework. Developed countries thus have the responsibility to strengthen the capacity of developing countries to progressively realize the right to health of the child by providing funding, sharing knowledge and experiences on health.

7.2.3. ACTORS RESPONSIBLE IN THE PROCESS OF IMPLEMENTATION

7.2.3.1. Parents

Whereas States are responsible for taking collective health measures to realize the right to health of the child, the primary responsibility for realizing the right to health of the child lies with the parents and if applicable the extended family of the child. Furthermore, other actors, such as medical professionals, local communities, (i)NGOs, civil society organizations and private actors have a shared responsibility to contribute to the realization of the right to health of the child.

In international health law, the concept of the child focuses on its vulnerability and on its dependence on especially the mother. Article 18 CRC establishes that both parents have the responsibility for the upbringing and (healthy) development of the child. The focus of this provision thus makes a shift from the exclusive focus on the relation between the child's health and the health of the mother to a focus on the role of both the mother and the father or the legal guardians.

Providing parents with necessary health information and information on the rights of the child is essential to enable them to set examples of healthy behaviour, to seek medical assistance and to engage in advocacy to ensure a healthy living environment for the child. Providing such information can support parents to continuously adapt to the changing health needs and life cycle of their children.

7.2.3.2. Medical professionals

Although the root causes of many childhood illnesses lie in the wider socioeconomical context, the activities of medical professionals are largely confined to the medical domain. The health related articles of the CRC and its translation to the practice of medical professionals can help to expand the approach taken by medical professionals in ensuring children's right to health beyond the limited scope of the biomedical approach.

Crucial in the realization of children's rights in health care is the translation of children's rights legislation to the daily practices of medical professionals. This implies that health professionals must be continuously (re-)educated on the requirements of child-friendly health care, so that they can become agents of change – directly or through the involvement in medical organizations. Also, inclusion of children's rights in work protocols is essential.

The interaction between medical professionals, children and their parents is an influential factor in identifying health problems and achieving treatment compliancy. Training on effective communication which takes into account the personality, attitude and communication skills of the health professionals, the availability of sufficient time and the creation of a supporting physical environment all contribute to the establishment of constructive relations to realize the right to health of the child.

Medical professionals are among the first to signal instances of violations of the right to health of children. Through the interference of medical organizations such violations can be systematically identified and addressed before courts and in the (in)ternational political arena.

7.3. CHILDREN'S RIGHT TO HEALTH: A LIVING REALITY

The central question of my research was which priorities can be derived from the CRC, the Concluding Observations of the CRC Committee and its General Comments and from other relevant international and regional instruments for realizing the right to the highest attainable standard of health of children under twelve.

It is not easy to summarize the findings of my research given the fact that the wide variety of priorities not only emerge from these instruments but because they are also influenced by the national context in which the right to the highest attainable standard of health is implemented as is shown by the Concluding Observations of the CRC Committee. As indicated before, the right to health of the child is a moving target because children are in a permanent state of development, children are different and live in continuously changing circumstances and health insights are changing. Therefore, the right to the highest attainable standard of health of the child is qualified as a living reality.

Notwithstanding, from my research it can be concluded that States parties to the CRC should in their efforts to progressively implement the rights of the child to the highest attainable standard of health consider the following measures as priorities:

I. The implementation of a continuous and well-coordinated national health policy for children which should include legislative, administrative and social measures to develop an infrastructure of services of health care. Such a health policy should contain the following elements:
   - Domestic legislation on the right to health of the child.
   - Identify responsible actors.
   - Establish strategic budget lines.
   - A system for disaggregated data collection on health indicators for children.
   - Set clear and measurable targets on:
     - health services;

  - medicines;
  - health interventions;
  - number of health professionals trained in children's rights.
- Mechanisms for monitoring and review.

II. Prevention of health problems:
- Provide for underlying determinants of health.
- Immunization program.
- Program to stimulate breastfeeding.
- Early identification and intervention in disease.

III. Community-based Primary Health Care
- Available, accessible, affordable, acceptable and quality health services.
- In close proximity to the beneficiaries.
- Involving children, parents and community stakeholders.
- Adequate referral system.

IV. Information and training for children, parents and medical professionals
- Child-friendly health information (e.g. diagnosis, treatment, side effects).
- Child rights training in health care to ensure child-sensitive procedures (age-appropriate, specific needs, participatory modes of communication).

V. Child impact assessments and evaluations to identify:
- Most pressing health problems and solutions.
- Barriers to having access to health services.
- Impact of health interventions.
- Impact of commercial activities.
- Organization of health care (e.g. level of hospitalization, play facilities).

VI. Involvement of the private sector in:
- Identification of pressing health problems and solutions.
- Increasing availability of child-appropriate medicines, prostheses, health services and special devices for disabilities.
- Provision of healthy foods, sporting equipment, etcetera.

VII. Effective remedies
- Accessible and child-sensitive (quasi-)judicial procedures and institutions.
- Access to (non-)written complaints mechanism before the CRC Committee.

VIII. International cooperation between developing and developed countries
- 20/20 initiative (see section 7.2.2).
- 0.7% of GDP to foreign aid within children's rights framework.
- Actively seek/offer assistance, share knowledge and experiences.

REFERENCES

BOOKS

Aristotle, *On Rhetoric*, New York/Oxford: Oxford University Press, 1991 (G.A. Kennedy Translation).

K. Arts, Inaugural lecture: 'Coming of Age in a world of diversity? An assessment of the UN Convention on the Rights of the Child', 18 November 2011, p. 13.

J. Asher, *The right to health, A resource manual for NGOs*, London: Commonwealth Medical Trust 2004.

M. Bluebond-Langner, *The private worlds of dying children'*, Princeton, New Jersey: Princeton University Press 1978.

M.J. Bossuyt, *Guide to the Travaux préparatoires of the ICCPR*, Dordrecht: Martinus Nijhoff 1987.

K.C. Braat, *Ik ben er wel, maar ze zien me niet*, Amsterdam: Defence for Children International Nederland 2004.

C.F. Brockington, *Public Health in the Nineteenth Century*, London, England: Livingston 1965.

G. van Bueren, *'Child rights in Europe'*, Council of Europe Publishing 2007.

G. van Bueren, *The international law on the rights of the child*. Dordrecht: Martinus Nijhoff Publishers/Save the Children 1995.

J. Dane, *Honderd jaar kinderbescherming. Uitgave ter gelegenheid van het jubileum van de Raad voor de kinderbescherming en de Kinderwetten (1905–2005)*, Amsterdam: Uitgeverij SWP 2006.

C. Dedding, *Delen in macht en onmacht, Kinderparticipatie in de (alledaagse) diabeteszorg*, (Academic thesis/Dissertation University of Amsterdam), 30 September 2009.

M. Delfos, *Luister je wel naar mij? Gespreksvoering met kinderen tuseen vier en twaalf jaar*, [*Do you listen to me? Communicating with children between 4–12 years*], Amsterdam: Uitgeverij SWP 2007.

S. Detrick, *A Commentary on the United Nations Convention on the Rights of the child*, The Hague: Kluwer Law International and Martinus Nijhoff Publishers 1999.

S. Detrick (ed.), *The United Nations Convention on the Rights of the Child. A Guide to the 'Travaux préparatoires* (academic thesis), Dordrecht/Boston/London: Martinus Nijhoff Publishers 1992.

V.E.T. Dörenberg, *Kind en Stoornis, Een systematisch onderzoek naar de rechtspositie van minderjarigen in de kinder- en jeugdpsychiatrie*, Den Haag: Boom Juridische Uitgevers 2010.

A. Eide & W.B. Eide, *A Commentary on the UN CRC Article 24: The right to health*, Leiden: Martinus Nijhoff Publishers 2006.

M. Freeman, *A Commentary on the United Nations Convention on the Rights of the Child, Article 3: The Best Interests of the Child*, Martinus Nijhoff Publishers 2007.

S. Golombok, *Parenting, what really counts?*, London: Routledge 2000.

J. de Graaf & M.M.C. Limbeek, *De toepassing van het Internationaal Verdrag inzake de Rechten van het Kind in de Nederlandse Rechtspraak*, Nijmegen: Ars Aequi Libri 2012.

K. Hanson & O. Nieuwenhuys, *Reconceptualizing children's rights*, Cambridge University Press 2012.

J. Harris, *On cloning: thinking in action*, London: Routledge 2004.

Harris, O'Boyle & Warbrick, *Law of the European Convention on Human Rights*, Oxford University Press 2009.

R. Hart, *Children's participation: From tokenism to citizenship*, Florence: UNICEF International Child Development Centre: 1992.

R. Hart, *Children's participation, the theory and practice of involving young citizens in community development and environmental care*, London: Earthscan Publications Ltd. 1997.

C. Heywood, *A History of Childhood: Children and Childhood in the West from Medieval to Modern Times*, Cambridge, UK: Polity Press 2001.

T. Kaime, *The African Charter on the Rights and Welfare of the Child; A socio-legal perspective'*, Cape Town: Pretoria University Press 2009.

T. Kaime, *The Convention on the Rights of the Child: A Cultural Legitimacy Critique*, Europa Law Publishing 2011.

U. Kilkelly & M. Donnelly, *The Child's Right to be heard in the Healthcare Setting: perspectives of children, parents and health professionals*, Office of the Minister of Children of Ireland, The National Children's Strategy Research Series, October 2006.

E. Kübler-Ross, *On Children and death, how children and their parents can and do cope with death*, Touchstone, Simon & Schuster 1997.

G. Landsdown, *Promoting Children's Participation in Democratic Decision-Making*, Florence: UNICEF Innocenti Research Centre 2001.

G. Landsdown, *Taking Part: Children's Participation in Decision Making*, London: IPPR 1995.

G. Landsdown, C. Heykoop & S. Hart, *CRED-PRO Child Rights Curriculum for Health Professionals*, International Institute for Child Rights and Development 2008.

J. van de Lanotte & Y. Haeck, *Handboek EVRM. Deel 1 Algemene beginselen*, Antwerpen/Oxford: Intersentia 2005.

L.J. Leblanc, *The Convention on the Rights of the Child: United Nations Law Making on Human Rights*, Lincoln: University of Nebraska Press 1995.

L. Ling, *Internationale regelgeving over de rechten van het kind, het VN-kinderrechtenverdrag vergeleken met andere mensenrechten documenten*, Amsterdam: Defence for Children International Afdeling Nederland 1993.

S. Meuwese, *Handboek Internationaal Jeugdrecht*, Nijmegen: Ars Aequi Libri 2005.

M. Mikkola, *Social Human Rights of Europe*, Karelactio 2010.

K. Mink & J.P. Kleijburg, *Jaarbericht Kinderrechten 2008*, Voorburg/Amsterdam: Unicef Nederland/Defence for Children International 2008.

S. Neumann, *Die öffentliche Gesundheitspflege und das Egeintum [Public Health Care and Property]*, Berlin: Adolf Riek 1847.

S. Nicholson & A. Clarke, *Child friendly healthcare, A manual for health workers*, Nottingham: CFHI 2007.

L. Oldring, 'Advancing a Human Rights Approach on the Global Health Agenda', in: A. Clapham & M. Robinson, *Realizing the Right to Health*, Swiss Human Rights Book Volume 3, Ruffer & Rub 2009.

H. Potts, *Participation and the right to the highest attainable standard of health* and *Accountability and the right to the highest attainable standard of health*, University of Essex, Human Rights Centre/Open Society Institute, 2008.

M. Rishmawi, *A Commentary on the United Nations Convention on the Rights of the Child, Article 4: The Nature of States Parties' Obligations*, Martinus Nijhof Publishers 2006.

G. Rosen, *A History of Public Health*, Baltimore/London: The Johns Hopkins University Press 1993.

G.C.A.M. Ruitenberg, *Het internationaal kinderrechtenverdrag in the rechtspraak*, Amsterdam: SWP 2003.

M. San Giorgi, *The Human Rights to Equal Access to Health Care*, Intersentia 2012.

S.C. Schimpff, *The Future of Medicine: Megatrends in Medicine that Will Improve Your Health Care & Your Quality of Life*, Nashville: Thomas Nelson Publishers 2007.

A.K. Sen, *Commodities and Capabilities*, Amsterdam: North-Holland Publishers 1985.

A.K. Sen, *Inequality Reexamined*, Oxford: Oxford University Press 1992.

A.K. Sen, *The idea of justice*, Cambridge, MA: Harvard University Press 2009.

H.E. Sigerist, *Medicine and Human Welfare*, New Haven/London: Yale University Press/ Oxford University Press 1941.

M. Singer & H. Baer, *Introducing medical anthropology*, Lanham: AltaMira Press 2007.

A. de Swaan, *In Care of the State*, Oxford/Cambridge: Basil Blackwell/Polity Press 1988.

Todaro & Smith, *Economic Development*, London: Pearson Addison Wesley 2006.

Tobin, *The right to health in international law*, Oxford Scholarship Online, January 2012, Chapter 4, p. 35.

B.C.A. Toebes, *The Right to Health as a Human Right in International Law*, Groningen/ Oxford: Intersentia/Hart, 1999.

K. Tomasevski, *Human rights obligations: making education. Availability, accessibility, acceptability and adaptability*, Gothenburg: RTE Primers, January 2001.

UNICEF & WHO, *Immunization summary, A statistical reference containing data through 2009 (The 2011 Edition)*, New York/Geneva: UNICEF 2011.

United Nations Office of the High Commissioner for Human Rights and Save the Children Sweden (SCS), *Legislative History of the Convention on the Rights of the Child*, Volume II, New York/Geneva: United Nations 2007.

WHO, *The first ten years of the World Health Organization*, Geneva 1958.

B. Wisner, *Power and Need in Africa*, Trenton, New Jersey: Africa World Press 1989.

Legislative history of the Convention on the Rights of the Child, Volume I and II, New York/ Geneva: United Nations 2007.

CONTRIBUTION TO BOOKS

H.S. Aasen, 'Children and the right to health protection' in: Toebes, Hartlev, Hendriks & Herrman, *Health and Human Rights in Europe*, Groningen: Intersentia 2012, p. 227–247.

B. Abramson, 'Article 2 the right of non-discrimination', in the Series: *A Commentary on the United Nations Convention on the Rights of the Child*, Leiden/Boston: Martinus Nijhoff Publishers 2008.

L.S. Bell, 'Introduction: Culture and human rights', in: L.S. Bell, L.S (a.o.), *Negotiating culture and human rights*, New York: Columbia University Press 2001, p. 1–15.

F. Buffing, & R. v.d. Zanden, 'Signalen en signaleren van kindermishandeling', in: H. Baartman, H. & A. Montfoort (Red.), *Kindermishandeling. Resultaten van multidisciplinair onderzoek*, Utrecht: Bruna 1992.

S. Dodds, 'Choice and control in feminist bioethics' in: C. Mackenzie & and N. Stoljar (eds.), *Relational Autonomy: Feminist Perspectives on Autonomy, Agency and the Social Self*, New York: Oxford University Press 2000, p. 229. Reproduced in M. Donnelly & U. Kilkelly, 'Child-friendly healthcare: delivering on the right to be heard', *The Medical Law Review* 2011, 19 (1), p. 27–54.

A. Eide, 'Article 27: The Right to an Adequate Standard of Living', in Series: *A CRC Commentary on the United Nations Convention on the Rights of the Child*, Leiden: Martinus Nijhoff Publishers 2006.

A. Eide & W.B. Eide, 'Article 24, The Right to Health', in: A. Alen, J. Van de Lanotte, E. Verhellen, F. Ang, E. Berghmans & M. Verheyde (eds), *A Commentary on the United Nations Convention on the Rights of the Child*, Leiden & Boston: Martinus Nijhoff Publishers 2006.

J. Ennew, 'Has Research Improved the Human Rights of Children? Or have the Information Needs of the CRC Improved Data about Children?' in: A. Invernizzi, *The Human Rights of Children*, 2011.

J. Gerards, 'Methoden en beginselen van interpretatie en toetsing, inclusief de margin of appreciation-doctrine', in: J.H. Gerards, H.J. Janssen & J. van der Velde (red.), *EVRM Rechtspraak en Commentaar*, Den Haag: SDU 2010.

Y. Ghai & J. Cottrell, 'The role of the Courts in the protection of Economic, Social and Cultural Rights', in: *Economic, Social and Cultural Rights in Practice, The Role of Judges in Implementing Economic, Social and Cultural Rights*, Interights 2004, p. 65.

Goldhagen & Mercer, 'Child Health Equity: From Theory to Reality', in: A. Invernizzi, *The Human Rights of Children*, 2011.

S. Goonesekere, 'Introduction', in: *Protecting the World's Children, Impact of th Convention on the Rights of the Child in Diverse Legal Systems*, UNICEF 2007, Cambridge University Press, p. 1.

K. Hanson, 'Does practice also work in theory?', in: A. Alen, H. Bosly, M. De Bie, J. Van de Lanotte (Eds.), *The UN Children's Rights Convention: Theory meets practice. Proceedings of the International Interdisciplinary Conference on Children's Rights, 18–19 May 2006, Ghent, Belgium*, Antwerpen/Oxford: Intersentia 2007, p. 642.

F. Hoffman & F. Bentes, 'Accountability for social and economic rights in Brazil', in: V. Gauri & D. Brinks, *Courting social justice: judicial enforcement of social and economic rights in the developing world*, Cambridge University Press 2008, p. 100–145.

Hogan, 'The right to life and the abortion question under the European Convention on Human Rights', in: Heffernan (ed.), *Human rights: a European perspective*, 1994, p. 104.

D. Johnson, 'Cultural and Regional Pluralism in the drafting of the UN Convention on the Rights of the Child', in: M. Freeman & P. Veerman (red.), *The ideologies of Children's Rights*, Dordrecht: Martinus Nijhoff Publishers 1992, p. 96.

H.J.J. Leenen, 'Leven in wording, prenatale diagnostiek en behandeling van de foetus', in: H.J.J. Leenen & J.K.M. Gevers redacteuren, *Handboek gezondheidsrecht. Deel 1: Rechten van mensen in de gezondheidszorg*, Houten: Bohn Stafleu Van Loghum 2000. p. 152–4.

B. Mayall, 'Learning from well children', in: P. Alderson (ed.), *Children's decisions in health care and research*, In press, London: Institute of Education. Reproduced in: P. Alderson, 'European Charter of Children's Rights', *Bulletin of Medical Ethics*, October 1993, p. 13–15.

A. Nolan, 'The child's right to health and the courts', in: *Global Health and Human Rights: Legal and philosophical perspectives*, edited by J. Harrington & M. Stuttaford, London: Routledge 2010.

L. Oldring, 'Advancing a Human Rights Approach on the Global Health Agenda', in: A. Clapham & M. Robinson, *Realizing the Right to Health*, Swiss Human Rights Book 2009, Volume 3, Ruffer & Rub, p. 101–102.

E. Riedel, 'The Human Right to Health: Conceptual Foundations', in: A. Clapham & M. Robinson, *Realizing the Right to Health*, Swiss Human Rights Book 2009, Volume 3, Ruffer & Rub, p. 21–39.

E. Riedel, 'The Right to Life and the Right to Health, in particular the obligation to reduce child mortality', in: A. Invernizzi & J. Williams (eds.), *The Human Rights of children: From Visions to Implementation*, Ashgate, 2011, p. 351–369.

E. Riedel, 'The Right to Life and the Right to Health, in particular the obligation to reduce child mortality', in: C. Tomuscat, *The right to life*, Martinus Nijhoff Publishers 2010, p. 365.

H.D.C. Roscam Abbing, 'Recht op gezondheidszorg: een beschouwing over grenzen aan het stellen van grenzen (liber amicorum voor Prof. Dr. H.J.J. Leenen), in: J.K.M. Gevers & J.H. Hubben, *Grenzen aan de zorg: zorgen aan de grens*, Alphen aan de Rijn: Samsom/H.D. Tjeenk Willink 1990.

L.F. Ross, 'Health Care Decision Making by Children. Is it in their best interest?' in: *Children, Medicine and the Law*, Hastings Center Report, November-December 1997, p. 487.

G. Sreenivasan, 'Opportunity is not the Key', in: B. Steinbock, A.D. Arras & A.J. London, *Ethical Issues in Modern Medicine*, New York: McGraw-Hill 2009, p. 235.

B. Toebes, A. Hendriks & K. Stronks, 'Health inequalities and the social determinants of health', in: *Health and Human Rights in Europe*, edited by Toebes, Hartlev, Hendriks and Herrman, Groningen: Intersentia 2012, p. 227–247.

I. Thèry, 'The Interests of the Child and the Regulation of Post-Divorce Family' in: C. Smart & S. Sevenhuijsen, *Child Custody and the Politics of Gender*, London: Routledge, p. 82.

W. Vandenhole, 'The right to benefit from social security', in the Series: *A Commentary on the United Nations Convention on the Rights of the Child*, Leiden: Martinus Nijhoff Publishers 2007.

E. Webb, 'An Exploration of the Discrimination-Rights Dynamic in Relation to Children', in: A. Invernizzi & J. Williams (eds), *The Human Rights of children: From Visions to Implementation'*, Ashgate 2011, p. 287–306.

'De vrijheid en waardigheid van de zwangere vrouw en het ongeboren kind. Een gezondheidsrechtelijk dilemma' in: *Grondrechten in de gezondheidszorg*, Liber Amicorum voor prof. Mr. J.K.M. Gevers, onder redactie van A.C. Hendriks e.a., Houten: Uitgeverij Bohn Stafleu van Loghum 2010, p. 6.

ARTICLES

F. van Agt, L. Damen & F. Huysmans, 'Jonge proefpersonen zijn kwetsbaar' [Young test persons are vulnerable], *Medisch Contact* 2010, 65 nr. 13, 1st April, p. 629.

P. Alderson, 'European Charter of Children's Rights', *Bulletin of Medical Ethics*, October 1993, p. 13–15.

Appelbaum & Grisso, 'Assessing patient's capacities to consent to treatment', *New England Journal of Medicine* 1988, vol. 319, no. 25, p. 1635–1638.

K. Arts, '21 Jaar VN-Verdrag voor de Rechten van het Kind: Een volwassen bijdrage aan kinderrechten in de wereld?', *Internationale Spectator* 2011, year 65, number 6, June, p. 337.

S. Asser & R. Swan, 'Child Fatalities From Religion-motivated Medical Neglect', *Pediatrics* 1998, Volume 101, No. 4, April.

G. Backman, P. Hunt a.o., 'Health systems and the right to health: an assessment of 194 countries', *The Lancet* 2008, Volume 372, p. 2047–2085.

P. Baines, 'Medical ethics for children: applying the four principles to paediatrics', *Journal of Medical Ethics* 2008, Issue 34, p. 142.

D.J. Barker, 'Fetal Origins of Coronary Heart Disease', *British Medical Journal* 1995, 311, p. 171–174.

S.J.H. Biddle, 'Health-enhancing physical activity and sedentary behavior in children and adolescents', *Journal of Sports Sciences 2004*, Volume 22, Issue 8, p. 679–701.

A.B. Bindman, 'Preventable hospitalizations and access to health care', *Journal of the American Medical Association* 1995, Volume 274, Number 4, p. 305–311.

S.C. Bischoff, *The UN Convention on the rights of the child. A comparative study*, (PhD thesis Free University of Amsterdam), 2 March 1999.

L. Blerk & N. Ansell, 'Children's experiences of migration: moving in the wake of AIDS in southern Africa', *Environment and Planning D: Society and Space* 2006, volume 24, p. 449–471.

E. Blyth, 'To be or not to be? A critical appraisal of the welfare of children conceived through new reproductive technologies', *International Journal of Children's Rights* 2008, Issue 16, p. 505–522.

M. Bonn, 'The effects of hospitalization on children: a review', *Curationis* 1994, Jun;17(2):20-4.

I. Borghmans (a.o), 'Benchmarking and reducing length of stay in Dutch hospitals', *BMC Health Services Research* 2008, Volume 8, p. 220.

S.T. Borra a.o., 'Developing health messages: Qualitative studies with children, parents, and teachers help identify communications opportunities for healthy lifestyles and the prevention of obesity', *Journal of the America Dietetic Association* 2003, Volume 103, Issue 6, June, p. 721–728.

E. Brems, 'Universele grondrechten', *NJB* 2010, no. 6, p. 19–21.

L. Breslow, 'A Quantitative approach to the World Health Organization Definition of Health: Physical, Mental and Social Well-being', *International Journal of Epidemiology* 1972, Volume 1, Number 4.

G. Brichner, 'Children in the Hospital: Issues of Power and Vulnerability', *Pediatric nursing* 2000, May-June; 26(3): p. 277–82.

A.E. Buchanan, 'The Right to a Decent Minimum of Health Care', *Philosophy and Public Affairs* 1984, Volume 13, Number 1, p. 61.

Buchanan & Brock, 'Deciding for others: the ethics of surrogate decision making', *Cambridge University Press* 1989.

R. Chambers, C. Drinkwater & E. Boath, 'Involving patients and the public: How to do better?', *Radcliffe Medical Press* 2003, Abingdon, p. 158.

M. Cornock & H. Montgomery, 'Children's rights in and out of the womb', *International Journal on Children's Rights* 2011, Issue 19, p. 3–19.

K.D. Craig & K.M. Prkachin, 'Expressing pain: The communication and interpretation of facial pain signals', *Journal of nonverbal behavior* 1995, Volume 19, Issue 4, p. 191–205.

M. Daly, 'Changing family life in Europe: Significance for state and society', *European Societies* 2005, Volume 7, Issue 3, p. 379 – 398.

N. Davidson a.o., 'An issue of access: delivering equitable health care for newly arrived refugee children in Australia', *Paediatric Journal Child Health* 2004, Volume 40.

D.S. Diekema, 'Responding to Parental Refusals of Immunization of Children', *Pediatrics* 2005, Volume 115, Number 5, May, p. 1428–1431.

J.E. Doek, 'Children and their right to enjoy health: A brief report on the monitoring activities of the Committee on the Rights of the Child.', *Health and Human Rights* 2001, 5 (2).

M. Donnelly & U. Kilkelly, 'Child-friendly healthcare: delivering on the right to be heard', *The Medical Law Review* 2011, 19 (1), p. 27–54.

S.E. Duijs, 'Het recht op zorg én de plicht om te betalen'. [The right to health care and the duty to pay], *Dokters van de Wereld [Doctors of the World]*, July 2010.

H. Feldbaum, K. Lee & J. Michaud, 'Global health and foreign policy', *Epidemiologic reviews* 2010, Volume 32, Issue 1, p. 82–92.

D.P. Fidler, 'Geographical morality' Revisited International Relations, International law and the controversy over placebo - controlled HIV Clinical trials', *Harvard International Law Journal* 2001, Volume 42, number 2, Issue 299, p. 348.

D.P. Fidler, & N. Drager, 'Health and foreign policy', *Bulletin of the World Health Organization* 2006, September, Issue 86, Number 9, p. 687.

J. Fortin, 'Children's rights: are the courts taking them more seriously', *King's College Law Journal* 2004, Volume 15, p. 253.

G. Foster, 'The capacity of the extended family safety net for orphans in Africa', *Psychology, Health & Medicine* 2000, Volume 5, Issue 1, p. 55 - 62.

M. Freeman, 'Human rights, an interdisciplinary approach', *Polity Press* 2011, p. 152.

L. Friedman Ross, 'Health Care Decision Making by Children. Is it in their best interest?', *Hastings Center Report* 1997, Vol. 27, No. 6, p. 41–45.

B.F. Fuller, 'Infant behaviors as indicators of established acute pain', *Journal of the Society of Pediatric Nurses: JSPN* 2001, 6(3), 109–115.

Gabe a.o., 'It takes three to tango: a framework for understanding patient partnership in paediatric clinics', *Social Science Medicine* 2004, Issue, 59, p. 1071 and 1074.

J.H. Gerards, 'Pluralism, Deference and the Margin of Appreciation Doctrine', *European Law Journal* 2011, Volume 17, No. 1, p. 80–120.

L. Gill & L. White, 'A critical review of patient satisfaction', *Leadership in Health Services* 2009, 22 (1), p. 8–19.

W. Ghent, 'Family violence: guidelines for recognition and management', *Canadian Medical Association Journal* 1985, 1 March, Volume 132, p. 541–553.

J. Goldhagen, 'Children's rights and the United Nations Convention on the Rights of the Child', *Pediatrics* 2003, 112-(3), p. 742–745.

McGrath (a.o), 'Core outcome domains and measures for pediatric acute and chronic/recurrent pain clinical trials: PedIMMPACT recommendations', *The Journal of Pain: Official Journal of the American Pain Society* 2008, *9* (9), p. 771–783.

B. Gushulak & D. Macpherson, 'The basic principles of migration health: Population mobility and gaps in disease prevalence', *Emerging themes in Epidemiology*, May 2006, p. 3.

H. Hannum, 'The UDHR in national and international law', *Health and Human Rights* 1998, Volume 3, Number 2, p. 145–158.

K.L. Hanson, 'Is insurance for children enough? The link between parents' and children's health care use revisited', *Inquiry* (a journal of medical care organization, provision and financing) 1998, Volume 35, Issue 3, p. 294–302.

K.D. Hekkert, S. Cihangri a.o., 'Patient satisfaction revisited: a multilevel approach', *Social Science and Medicine* 2009, p. 68–75.

A. Hendriks, 'The right to health in national and international jurisprudence', *European Journal of Health Law* 1998, Volume 5, p. 389–408.

A. Hjern & P. Bouvier, 'Migrant children- a challenge for European paediatricians.', *Acta Paediatrica* 2004, Volume 93, 1535–1539.

Hondius, Stikker, Wenink en Honig, 'Wet BOPZ toegepast bij vroege zwangerschap van verslaafde', *Nederlands Tijdschrift voor de Geneeskunde* 2012, 156, A3818.

M. Huber a.o., 'How should we define health?', *British Medical Journal* 2011, Volume 343, number b4163.

P. Hunt & G. Backman, 'Health systems and the right to the highest attainable standard of health', *International Journal on Health and Human Rights* 2008, Volume 10, Number 1.

A.R. Jadad & L. O'Grady, 'How should health be defined?', *British Medical Journal* 2008, Volume 337, Number a2900.

E. Kabengele Mpinga, & P. Chastonay, 'Satisfaction of patients: A Right to health indicator?', *Health Policy* 2011, 100, p. 144–150.

T. Kaime, "Vernacularising the Convention on the Rights of the Child: Rights and Culture as Analytic Tools', *International Journal on Children's Rights* 2010, Volume 18, p. 637–653.

J. Kasper, 'The Relevance of U.S. Ratification of the Convention on the Rights of the Child for Child Health: A Matter of Equity and Social Justice', *Child Welfare* 2010, No. 89, Volume 5.

R. Keren, 'Direct Medical Cost of Influenza-Related Hospitalizations in Children', *Pediatrics* 2006, Volume 118, Number 5, November 1, p. e1321–132.

U. Kilkelly & M. Donnelly, 'Participation in Healthcare: The views and experiences of children and young people', *International Journal on children's rights* 2011, Issue 19, p. 107–125.

C.F. Kinney & B. Clark, 'Provisions for Health and Health Care in the Constitutions of the Countries of the World', *Cornell International Law Journal* 2004, Issue 37, p. 285–355.

E.D. Kinney, 'International Human Right to health: what does it mean for our nation and the world?', *Indiana Law Review* 2001, p. 1457.

Y. Klerk, 'Working on Article 2(2) and Article 3 of the International Covenant on Economic, Social and Cultural Rights', *Human Rights Quarterly* 1987, Volume 9, p. 250–267.

R. Korobkin, 'Determining health care rights behind a veil of ignorance', *University of Illinois Law Review* 1998, Number 3, p. 806.

J.S. Larson, 'Conceptualization of health', *Medical Care Research & Review* 1999, Issue 56, p. 124.

V.A. Leary, 'The right to health in international human rights law', *Health and Human Rights* 1994, 1 (1).

Y. Lee, 'Celebrating important milestones for children and their rights', *The International Journal of Children's Rights* 2010, Volume 18, The Hague: Kluwer Law International.

S. Lembrechts, 'Wiens klachtrecht? Het kind-concept in het derde Facultatief Protocol bij het Verdrag inzake de Rechten van het Kind betreffende de instelling van een communicatieprocedure', *Tijdschrift voor Jeugd- en Kinderrechten* 2012, Issue 2.

T. Lindberg, 'The Child's Right to Health and Treatment', *Medicine, conflict and survival* 1999, Volume 15, p. 336.

L. London, 'What is a human-rights based approach to health and does it matter?', *International Journal on health and human rights* 2008, Volume 10, Number 1, p. 68.

O. Luiz Motta Ferraz, 'The right to health in the courts of Brazil: worsening health inequities?', *Health and Human Rights* 2009, Volume 11, Number 2, p. 33–45.

MacNaughton, 'Untangling equality and non-discrimination to promote the right to health care for all', *Health and Human Rights* 2009, Volume 11, Number 2, p. 47–63.

F. Mahony, 'Marvellous richness of Diversity or Individious Cultural Relativism', *Human Rights Law Journal* 1998, Issue 19, p. 1.

D. Mannaerts, 'Minderjarigen en participatie in de gezondheidszorg', *Rechten van minderjarigen in de gezondheidszorg* 2004, Kinderrechtencoalitie Vlaanderen vzw, 1[e] jaargang, nr. 2, p. 23–37.

A. McGillivray, 'Why children do have equal rights: In reply to Laura Purdy', in: *International Journal on Children's Rights* 1994, Volume 2, p. 243–258.

F.S. Mendoza, 'The health of Latino children in the United States', *Critical health issues for children and youth* 1994, Volume 4, Number 3.

P.J. Mesko, 'Use of picture communication aids to assess pain location in pediatric postoperative patients', *Journal of Perianesthesia Nursing* 2011, 26, 6, December, p. 395–404.

B. Meyboom-de Jong, 'De huisarts als poortwachter', *Nederlands Tijdschrift voor de Geneeskunde* 1994, Volume 138, Number 53, 31 December 1994, p. 2668–2673.

F.I. Michelman, 'Forword: On Protecting the Poor Through the Fourteenth Amendment', *Harvard Law Review* 1969, Issue 7, p. 7.

S. Moses, 'Children and participation in South Africa: An overview', *The International Journal on Children's Rights* 2008, Issue 16, p. 327–328.

O.L. Motta Ferraz, 'The right to health in the courts of Brazil: worsening health inequities?', *International Journal on Health and Human Rights* 2009, Volume 11, No.2.

A.W. Musschenga & E. Borst-Eilers, 'Prioriteiten in de gezondheidszorg. Rechtvaardig verdelen, maar hoe?', *Medische Contact* 1987, Number 1, p. 13–19.

S. Nixon & L. Forman, 'Exploring synergies between human rights and public health ethics: a whole greater than the sum of its parts', *British Medical Journal on International Health and Human Rights 2008*, Volume 8, Issue 2.

A. Nolan, 'Economic, social and cultural rights, budgets and the CRC', in: *International Journal of Children's Rights*, Martinus Nijhoff Publishers, 2013, Volume 21, issue 3.

A. Nolan, 'The child's right to health and the courts', in: J. Harrington & M. Stuttaford, *Global Health and Human Rights*, Rotledge 2012, p. 140.

M. Nussbaum, 'Capabilities as fundamental entitlements: Sen and social justice', *Feminist Economics* 2003, 9(2/3), p. 33–59.

M. Obemeyer, 'A cross-cultural perspective on reproductive rights', *Human Rights Quarterly* 1995, Issue 17, p. 366–368.

M. Okada a.o., 'Influence of parents' oral health behaviour on oral health status of their school children: an exploratory study employing a causal modelling technique',

International Journal of Paediatric Dentistry 2002, volume 12, number 2, March, p. 101–108.

B. Oomen, Inaugural lecture for obtaining the Utrecht University chair in the 'Sociology of Human Rights', *Small places: the home-coming of human rights*, delivered at Utrecht University Roosevelt Academy in Middelburg, the Netherlands on 2 December 2011.

J.W. Owen & O. Roberts, 'Globalisation, health and foreign policy: emerging linkages and interests', *Global Health* 2005, Volume 1, Number 12.

K. Panter-Brick, 'Street children, human rights and public health: A Critique and Future Directions', *Annual Review of Anthropology* 2002, Volume 31, p. 147–171.

N. Peleg, 'Children and the capability approach', *International Journal of Children's Rights*, 2013, Volume 2013, Issue 3, pp. 523–542.

C.L. Perry, 'Parent involvement with children's health promotion: the Minnesota Home Team', *American Journal of Public Health* 1988, Volume 78, Issue 9, p. 1156–1160.

C. Phillips, 'Klachtrecht bij het Comité inzake de rechten van het Kind', *Tijdschrift voor Familie- en jeugdrecht* 2012, Issue 4, April, p. 93.

A.P. Preis, 'Human rights as cultural practice: an anthropological critique', *Human Rights Quarterly* 1995, Volume 18, p. 286.

G. Pulles, 'Onduidelijkheid over de rechtstreekse werking van het VN-kinderrechten-verdrag', *Nederlands Juristenblad* 2011, Volume 4, 28-01-2011, p. 233.

L. Purdy, 'Why children shouldn't have equal rights', *International Journal of Children's Rights* 1994, Volume 2, p. 223–241.

S. Ratnapalan, R. Srouji & S. Schneeweiss, 'Pain in Children: Assessment and Nonpharmacological Management', *International Journal of Pediatrics* 2010, Volume 2010, Article ID 474838.

M. Raut (a.o.), 'Estimating the economic impact of a half-day reduction in length of hospital stay among patients with community-acquired pneumonia in the US', *Current Medical Research and Opinion* 2009, 25(9), p. 2151–2157.

Rechel, Boika and Blackburn, Clare, 'Access to health care for Roma children in Central and Eastern Europe: findings from a qualitative study in Bulgaria', *International Journal for Equity in Health*, Volume 8 (Article 24), 2009.

R.L. Repetti a.o., 'Risky Families: Family Social Environments and the Mental and Physical Health of Offspring', *Psychological Bulletin* 2002, Volume 128, Number 2, 330–366.

A. Richters, 'Arts en oorlog: ethische aspecten van triage', in: J. Bierens e.a., '*Urgentiegeneeskunde en triage*', Maarssen: Elsevier Gezondheidszorg 2004, p. 55–70.

R. Romero-Ortuño, 'Access to health care for illegal immigrants in the EU: should we be concerned?', *European journal of Health Law* 2004, Volume 11, p. 245–272.

J.P. Ruger, 'Toward a Theory of a Right to Health: Capability and Incompletely Theorized Agreements', *Yale Journal of Law & the Humanities* 2006, Volume 18.

A. Sachs, 'Enforcement of Economic, Social and Cultural Rights', *American University International Law Review* 2007, Volume 22, Issue 5, p. 673–708.

W.M. Sage, 'Solidarity: Unfashionable, But Still American', *Connecting American Values with health reform* 2009, The Hastings Centre, p. 10.

D. Sanders & D. Werner, 'The Politics of Primary Health Care and Child Survival', *HealthWrights*, 1997.

P.K. Sandhu, 'A legal right to health care: what can the United States learn from foreign models of health rights jurisprudence?', *California Law Review* 2007, Volume 95, Issue 115, p. 1158.

R. Saracci, 'The world health organization needs to reconsider its definition of health', *British Medical Journal* 1997, Volume 314, Number 1409.

J.W. Saultz, 'Defining and measuring interpersonal continuity of care', *Annals of Family Medicine* 2003, Issue 1, p. 134–143.

J. Savulescu, 'Deaf lesbians, 'designer disability', and the future of medicine', *British Medical Journal* 2002, Issue 325, p. 771–773.

V. Sazonov Kozevar, 'Variations in Pediatric Asthma Hospitalization Rates and Costs Between and Within Nordic Countries', *Chest* 2004, 125, p. 1680–1684.

A.K. Sen, 'Capabilities, Lists, and Public Reason: Continuing the Conversation', *Feminist Economics* 2004, Volume 10, Number 3, p. 77–80.

C. Sepúlveda, 'The right to child health: the development of primary health services in Chile and Thailand', *UNICEF Innocenti Research Centre Occasional Paper Number 7*, April 1994.

L. Shields a.o., 'A review of the literature from developed and developing countries relating to the effects of hospitalization on children and parents', *International Council of Nurses* 2001, Number 48, p. 30.

A.E. Simon, K.S. Chan & C.B. Forrest, 'Assessment of children's quality of life in the United States with a multidimensional index', *Pediatrics* 2008, 121(1), e118– e126.

S. Skogly, 'The requirement of Using the Maximum Available Resources' for Human Rights Realisation: A Question of Quality as well as Quantity?', *Human Rights Law Review* 2012, p. 1–28.

D. Southall a.o., 'The Child-Friendly Healthcare Initiative (CFHI): Healthcare Provision in Accordance With the UN Convention on the Rights of the Child', *Pediatrics* 2000, Volume 106, Number 5, November 1, p. 1054 -1064.

Starfield (a.o.), 'Continuity and coordination in primary care: their achievement and utility', *Medical Care* 1976, Issue 14, p. 625–636.

M. Susser, 'Ethical components in the definition of health', *International Journal of Health Services* 1974, volume 4, p. 539–548.

T.S. Szasz, 'The Right to Health', *The Georgetown Law Journal* 1968–1969, Volume 57, p. 734–751.

K. Taylor Paternalism, 'Participation and partnership-the evolution of patient centeredness in the consultation', *Patient Education and Counseling 2009*, 74, p. 150–155.

B.C.A. Toebes, 'The right to health and the privatization of national health systems: a case study of the Netherlands', *Health and Human Rights* 2006; Volume 9, Issue 1, p. 102–127.

N. Thomas, 'Towards a theory of children's participation', *International Journal on Children's Rights* 2007, Issue 15, p. 199.

A. Tjon, W.E. Ten & T.W. Schulpen, 'Medical care of underage refugees', *Nederlands Tijdschrift voor de Geneeskunde* 1999, Volume 143, Number 30, p. 1569–1572.

W. Vandenhole, 'Economic, Social and Cultural rights in the CRC: Is there a legal obligation to cooperate internationally for development?', *International Journal of Children's Rights* 2009, volume 17, p. 23–63.

H. Vuori, 'Patient satisfaction – does it matter?', *International Journal of Quality in Health Care* 1991, 3, p. 183–189.

M. Wabwile, 'Implementing the Social and Economic Rights of Children in Developing Countries: The Place of International Assistance and Cooperation', *International Journal of Children's Rights* 2010, Volume 18, p. 355–385.

J. Walsh & K. Warren, 'Selective Primary Health Care: An interim Stategy for Disease Control in Developing Countries, *New England Journal of Medicine* 1979, Volume 301, number 18, p. 967–974.

L.J. Weiss & J. Bluestein, 'Faithful patients: the effect of long-term physician-patient relationships on the costs and use of health care by older Americans', *American Journal of Public Health* 1996, Issue 86, p. 1742–1747.

D. Werner, 'The Life and Death of Primary Health Care or The McDonaldization of Alma Ata', *HealthWrights*, 1997.

M. Whitehead, 'The concepts and principles of equity and health', *Health Promotion International* 1991, Volume 6, Number 3, Oxford University Press, p. 221.

World Bank, Human Development Network, Health Nutrition & Population Division, 'Safe Motherhood and the World Bank: Lessons from 10 Years of Experience', *Washington, D.C., World Bank, Human Development Network, Health Nutrition, and Population Division* 1999, Jun. 42, Volume 12.

L. Young & N. Ansell, 'Fluid Households, Complex Families: The Impacts of Children's Migration as a Response to HIV/AIDS in Southern Africa', *The Professional Geographer* 2003, Volume 55, Issue 4, November, p. 464–476.

B. Young and others, 'Managing communication with young people who have a potentially life threatening chronic illness: qualitative study of patients and parents', *British Medical Journal* 2003, p. 305.

B. Zuckerman & S. Parker, 'Preventive pediatrics: New models of providing needed health services', *Pediatrics* 1995, *95*(5), p. 758- 762.

Comment made by Asha George, Mickey Chopra, Daniel Seymour, Paolo Marchi, working for UNICEF Health Section and Gender and Rights Unit, New York, *the Lancet* 2010, Volume 375, May 22, p. 1764.

'Medical care of underage refugees', *Nederlands Tijdschrift voor de Geneeskunde* 1999, July 24; Volume 143, Number 30, p. 1569–1572.

'Pain Measurement in Children', *Clinical updates on Pain* 1995, Volume III, Issue 2, International Association for the Study of Pain, July 1995.

LEGISLATION

Additional Protocol to the American Convention on Human Rights in the Area of Economic, Social and Cultural Rights, OAS
African Charter on Human and Peoples' Rights
African Charter on the Rights and well-being of children
American Convention on Human Rights
Asian Human Rights Charter
Charter of Fundamental Rights of the European Union (Doc. 2000/C 364/01)
Constitution of the World Health Organization
Convention against Torture and Other Cruel, Inhuman or Degrading Treatment or Punishment
Constitution of South-Africa
Convention for the Protection of Human Rights and Fundamental Freedoms (1950, ETS No. 5);
Convention for the protection of Human Rights and Dignity of the Human Being with regard to the Application of Biology and Medicine: Convention on Human Rights and Biomedicine
Convention on the Elimination of all forms of Racial Discrimination
Convention on the Elimination of Discrimination against Women
Convention on the Protection of Children against Sexual Exploitation and Sexual Abuse, Council of Europe (2007, CETS No. 201).
Convention on the Rights of the Child
Covenant on the Right of the Child in Islam
Convention on the Rights of Persons with Disabilities
Declaration of Alma-Ata, International Conference on Primary Health Care, Alma-Ata, USSR, 6–12 September 1978.
Declaration of Rabat
Dutch Criminal Code
Dutch Civil Law Code
EU-Regulation 1901/2006
EU-Regulation 1902/2006
European Convention on Human Rights
European Convention for the Prevention of Torture and Inhuman or Degrading Treatment or Punishment (1987, ETS No. 126);
European Convention on the Exercise of Children's Rights (1996, ETS No. 160);
European Social Charter
Explanatory Memorandum to the Biomedicine Convention, Council of Europe 1996.
Explanatory Memorandum to the guidelines on Child-friendly Health Care, Council of Europe, 2011.
Guidelines of the Committee of Ministers of the Council of Europe on child-friendly health care, adopted on 21st September 2011 at the 1121st meeting of the Ministers' Deputies.

Guidelines of the Committee of Ministers of the Council of Europe on child-friendly justice, adopted on 17th November 2010.
Indigenous and Tribal Peoples Convention 1989 (No. 169)
International Convention for the Protection of All Persons from Enforced Disappearance
International Convention on the Protection of the Rights of All Migrant Workers and Members of Their Families
International Convention on the Elimination of All Forms of Racial Discrimination
International Covenant on Civil and Political Rights (ICCPR)
International Covenant on Economic Social and Cultural Rights (ICESCR)
Maastricht Guidelines on Violations of Economic, Social and Cultural rights.
Optional Protocol III to the Convention on the Rights of the Child on a communications procedure
Optional Protocol to the Convention on the Elimination of Discrimination against Women
Optional Protocol to the Convention on the Rights of Persons with Disabilities
Optional Protocol to the ICCPR
Optional Protocol to the ICESCR
Protocol No. 14 to the Convention for the Protection of Human Rights and Fundamental Freedoms, amending the control system of the Convention
Social Security (Minimum Standards) Convention 1952 (No. 102)/Convention concerning Minimum Standards of Social Security
Universal Declaration of Human Rights
United Nations Declaration on the Rights of Indigenous Peoples
Wet op de geneeskundige behandelingsovereenkomst (WGBO)

CASE-LAW

EUROPEAN COURT OF HUMAN RIGHTS (ECHR)

23 July 1968, *Case relating to certain aspects of the laws on the use of languages in education in Belgium*, App. No. 1474/62; 1677/62; 1691/62; 1769/63; 1994/63; 2126/64.
7 December 1976, *Handyside v. United Kingdom*, App. No. 5493/72.
13 May 1980, *Paton v. UK*, App. No. 8416/78.
19 May 1992, *H. v. Norway*, App. No. 17004/90.
5 September 2002, *Boso vs. Italy*, App. No 50490/99.
8 July 2004, *Vo v. France*, App. No. 53924/00.
27 June 2006, *Byrzykowski v. Poland*, App. No. 11562/05.
20 March 2007, *Tysiąc v. Poland*, App. No. 5410/03.
5 January 2010, *Yardimci v. Turkey*, App. No. 25266/05.
23 March 2010, *Oyal v. Turkey*, App. No. 4864/05.
16 December 2010 *A.B.C. vs. Ireland* No 25579/05.
26 May 2011 *R.R.vs. Poland*, No 27617/04.

COLOMBIA. CONSTITUTIONAL COURT, SECOND REVIEW CHAMBER

31 July 2008, No. T-760/08

GREAT BRITAIN. COURT OF APPEAL, CIVIL DIVISION

22 September 2000, *Re A. (Conjoined twins)*, Case No: B1/2000/2969

SOUTH AFRICA. CONSTITUTIONAL COURT

27 November 1997, *Soobramoney v. Minister of Health (Kwazulu-Natal)*, Case No: CCT32/97

THE NETHERLANDS

ABRvS 12 April 2007, *LJN* BA3394
CRvB 20 October 2010, *LJN* BO3581
Rb. Alkmaar 20 July 2005, *LJN* AT9598
Rb. Den Haag, 19 December 2005, *AWB* 04/19508
Rb. Den Haag, 24 February 2008, *LJN* BF0906
Rb. Den Haag, 2 March 2010, *LJN* BM2383
Rb. Utrecht (vzr) 6 April 2010, *LJN* BM0846
Rb. Rotterdam, 6 September 2010, *LJN* BO1013
Rb. Zwolle-Lelystad, 19 April 2011, *LJN* BQ3967
Rb. Zwolle-Lelystad (vzr), 9 June 2011, *LJN* BR3569

UN DOCUMENTS

GENERAL ASSEMBLY

UN General Assembly, *A World Fit for Children*, Resolution adopted by the United Nations General Assembly, Resolution, 11 October 2002, UN Doc. A/RES/S-27/2.

UN General Assembly, *Optional Protocol to the Convention on the Rights of the Child on the Sale of Children, Child Prostitution and Child Pornography*, 25 May 2000, UN Doc. A/RES/54/263.

UN General Assembly, *Optional Protocol to the International Covenant on Economic, Social and Cultural Rights: resolution / adopted by the General Assembly*, 5 March 2009, A/RES/63/117

UN General Assembly, *Resolutions adopted by the General Assembly: 44/25. Convention on the Rights of the Child*, 20 November 1989, UN Doc. A/RES/44/25.

UN General Assembly, *Report of the independent expert for the United Nations study on violence against children*, 29 August 2006, UN Doc. A/61/299.

UN General Assembly, *United Nations Declaration on the Rights of Indigenous Peoples: resolution / adopted by the General Assembly*, 2 October 2007, UN Doc. A/RES/61/295.

UN COMMITTEE ON ECONOMIC, SOCIAL AND CULTURAL RIGHTS (CESCR)

UN Committee on Economic, Social and Cultural Rights (CESCR), *Concluding Observations of the Committee on Economic, Social and Cultural Rights, India*, May 2008, UN Doc. E/C.12/IND/CO/5.

UN Committee on Economic, Social and Cultural Rights (CESCR), *General Comment No. 3: The Nature of States Parties' Obligations (Art. 2, Para. 1, of the Covenant)*, 14 December 1990, UN Doc. E/1991/23.

UN Committee on Economic, Social and Cultural Rights (CESCR), *General Comment No. 4: The Right to Adequate Housing (Art. 11 (1) of the Covenant)*, 13 December 1991, UN Doc. E/1992/23.

UN Committee on Economic, Social and Cultural Rights (CESCR), *General Comment No. 14: The right to the highest attainable standard of health*, 11 August 2000, UN Doc. E/C.12/2000/4.

UN Committee on Economic, Social and Cultural Rights (CESCR), *General comment No. 20: Non-discrimination in economic, social and cultural rights (art. 2, para. 2, of the International Covenant on Economic, Social and Cultural Rights)*, 2 July 2009, E/C.12/GC/20.

UN COMMITTEE ON THE RIGHTS OF THE CHILD (CRC)

Concluding Observations

UN Committee on the Rights of the Child (CRC), *Concluding Observations: Algeria*, 18 June 1997, UN Doc. CRC/C/15/Add.76.

UN Committee on the Rights of the Child (CRC), *Concluding Observations: Argentina*, 11 June 2010, UN Doc. CRC/C/ARG/CO/3–4.

UN Committee on the Rights of the Child (CRC), *Concluding Observations: Australia*, 20 October 2005, UN Doc. CRC/C/15/Add.268.

UN Committee on the Rights of the Child (CRC), *Concluding Observations: Bangladesh*, 27 October 2003, UN Doc. CRC/C/15/Add.221.

UN Committee on the Rights of the Child (CRC), *Concluding Observations: Bosnia and Herzegovina*, 21 September 2005, UN Doc. CRC/C/15/Add.260.

UN Committee on the Rights of the Child (CRC), *Concluding Observations: Brazil*, 3 November 2004, UN Doc. CRC/C/15/Add.241.

UN Committee on the Rights of the Child (CRC), *Concluding Observations: Bulgaria*, 23 June 2008, UN Doc. CRC/C/BGR/CO/2.

UN Committee on the Rights of the Child (CRC), *Concluding Observations: Burkina Faso*, 9 October 2002, UN Doc. CRC/C/15/Add.193.

UN Committee on the Rights of the Child (CRC), *Concluding Observations: Canada*, 27 October 2003, UN Doc. CRC/C/15/Add.215.

UN Committee on the Rights of the Child (CRC), *Concluding Observations: Chile*, 3 April 2002, CRC/C/15/Add.173.

UN Committee on the Rights of the Child (CRC), *Concluding Observations: China*, 7 June 1996, UN Doc. CRC/C/15/Add.56.

UN Committee on the Rights of the Child (CRC), *Concluding Observations: China (including Hong Kong and Macau Special Administrative Regions)*, 24 November 2005, UN Doc. CRC/C/CHN/CO/2.

UN Committee on the Rights of the Child (CRC), *Concluding Observations: Colombia*, 15 February 1995, UN Doc. CRC/C/15/Add.30.

UN Committee on the Rights of the Child (CRC), *Concluding Observations: Colombia*, 8 June 2006, UN Doc. CRC/C/COL/CO/3.

UN Committee on the Rights of the Child (CRC), *Concluding Observations: Cuba*, 18 June 1997, UN Doc. CRC/C/15/Add.72.

UN Committee on the Rights of the Child (CRC), *Concluding Observations: Czech Republic*, 18 March 2003, UN Doc. CRC/C/15/Add.201.

UN Committee on the Rights of the Child (CRC), *Concluding Observations: Democratic People's Republic of Korea*, 1 July 2004, UN Doc. CRC/C/15/Add.239.

UN Committee on the Rights of the Child (CRC), *Concluding Observations: Democratic Republic of the Congo*, 9 July 2001, UN Doc. CRC/C/15/Add.153.

UN Committee on the Rights of the Child (CRC), *Concluding Observations: Egypt*, 21 February 2001, UN Doc. CRC/C/15/Add.145.

UN Committee on the Rights of the Child (CRC), *Concluding Observations: Gabon*, 3 April 2002, UN Doc. CRC/C/15/Add.171.

UN Committee on the Rights of the Child (CRC), *Concluding Observations: Germany*, 27 November 1995, UN Doc. CRC/C/15/Add.43.

UN Committee on the Rights of the Child (CRC), *Concluding Observations: Germany*, 26 February 2004, UN Doc. CRC/C/15/Add.226.

UN Committee on the Rights of the Child (CRC), *Concluding Observations: Guatemala*, 7 June 1996, UN Doc. CRC/C/15/Add.58.

UN Committee on the Rights of the Child (CRC), *Concluding Observations: Guatemala*, 9 July 2001, UN Doc. CRC/C/15/Add.154.

UN Committee on the Rights of the Child (CRC), *Concluding Observations: Guinea Bissau*,13 June 2002, UN Doc. CRC/C/15/Add.177.

UN Committee on the Rights of the Child (CRC), *Concluding Observations: Haiti*, 18 March 2003, UN Doc. CRC/C/15/Add.202.

UN Committee on the Rights of the Child (CRC), *Concluding Observations: India*, 23 February 2000, UN Doc. CRC/C/15/Add.115.
UN Committee on the Rights of the Child (CRC), *Concluding Observations: India*, 26 February 2004, UN Doc. CRC/C/15/Add.228.
UN Committee on the Rights of the Child (CRC), *Concluding Observations: Indonesia*, 28 February 2004, UN Doc. CRC/C/15/Add.223.
UN Committee on the Rights of the Child (CRC), *Concluding Observations: Islamic Republic of Iran*, 28 June 2000, UN Doc. CRC/C/15/Add.123.
UN Committee on the Rights of the Child (CRC), *Concluding Observations: Islamic Republic of Iran*, 31 March 2005, UN Doc. CRC/C/15/Add.254.
UN Committee on the Rights of the Child (CRC), *Concluding Observations: Israel*, 9 October 2002, UN Doc. CRC/C/15/Add.195.
UN Committee on the Rights of the Child (CRC), *Concluding Observations: Japan*, 26 February 2004, UN Doc. CRC/C/15/Add.231.
UN Committee on the Rights of the Child (CRC), *Concluding Observations: Lebanon*, 21 March 2002, UN Doc.
UN Committee on the Rights of the Child (CRC), *Concluding Observations: Lebanon*, 8 June 2006, UN Doc. CRC/C/LBN/CO/3.
UN Committee on the Rights of the Child (CRC), *Concluding Observations: Malawi*, 2 April 2002, UN Doc. CRC/C/15/Add.174.
UN Committee on the Rights of the Child (CRC), *Concluding Observations: Mexico*, 8 June 2006, UN Doc. CRC/C/MEX/CO/3.
UN Committee on the Rights of the Child (CRC), *Concluding Observations: Mozambique*, 3 April 2002, UN Doc. CRC/C/15/Add.172.
UN Committee on the Rights of the Child (CRC), *Concluding Observations: Myanmar*, 30 June 2004, UN Doc. CRC/C/15/Add.237.
UN Committee on the Rights of the Child (CRC), *Concluding Observations: Netherlands*, 26 October 1999, UN Doc. CRC/C/15/Add.114.
UN Committee on the Rights of the Child (CRC), *Concluding Observations: Netherlands*, 27 March 2009, UN Doc. CRC/C/NLD/CO/3.
UN Committee on the Rights of the Child (CRC), *Concluding Observations: Nigeria*, 30 October 1996, UN Doc. CRC/C/15/Add.61.
UN Committee on the Rights of the Child (CRC), *Concluding Observations: Nigeria*, 13 April 2005, UN Doc. CRC/C/15/Add.257.
UN Committee on the Rights of the Child (CRC), *Concluding Observations: Pakistan*, 27 October 2003, UN Doc. CRC/C/15/Add.217.
UN Committee on the Rights of the Child (CRC), *Concluding Observations: Poland*, 30 October 2002, UN Doc. CRC/C/15/Add.194.
UN Committee on the Rights of the Child (CRC), *Concluding Observations: Republic of Korea*, 18 March 2003, UN Doc. CRC/C/15/Add.197.
UN Committee on the Rights of the Child (CRC), *Concluding Observations: Republic of Moldova*, 31 October 2002, UN Doc. CRC/C/15/Add.192.

UN Committee on the Rights of the Child (CRC), *Concluding Observations: Russian Federation*, 18 February 1993, UN Doc. CRC/C/15/Add.4.

UN Committee on the Rights of the Child (CRC), *Concluding Observations: Russian Federation*, 10 November 1999, UN Doc. CRC/C/15/Add.110.

UN Committee on the Rights of the Child (CRC), *Concluding Observations: Russian Federation*, 23 November 2005, UN Doc. CRC/C/RUS/CO/3.

UN Committee on the Rights of the Child (CRC), *Concluding Observations: South Africa*, 22 February 2000, UN Doc. CRC/C/15/Add.122.

UN Committee on the Rights of the Child, *Concluding Observations: Sri Lanka*, 6 June 2003, UN Doc. CRC/C/15/Add.207.

UN Committee on the Rights of the Child (CRC), *Concluding Observations: Sudan*, 18 October 1993, UN Doc. CRC/C/15/Add.10.

UN Committee on the Rights of the Child (CRC), *Concluding Observations: The Kingdom of the Netherlands (Netherlands and Aruba)*, 26 February 2004, UN Doc. CRC/C/15/Add.227.

UN Committee on the Rights of the Child (CRC), *Concluding Observations: Trinidad and Tobago*, 17 March 2006, UN Doc. CRC/C/TTO/CO/2.

UN Committee on the Rights of the Child (CRC), *Concluding Observations: Uganda*, 21 October 1997, UN Doc. CRC/C/15/Add.80.

UN Committee on the Rights of the Child (CRC), *Concluding Observations: Uganda*, 23 November 2005, UN Doc. CRC/C/UGA/CO/2.

UN Committee on the Rights of the Child (CRC), *Concluding Observations: United Kingdom of Great Britain and Northern Ireland*, 15 January 1995, UN Doc. CRC/C/15/Add.34.

UN Committee on the Rights of the Child (CRC), *Concluding Observations: United Kingdom of Great Britain and Northern Ireland*, 9 October 2002, UN Doc. CRC/C/15/Add.188.

UN Committee on the Rights of the Child (CRC), *Concluding Observations: Uzbekistan*, 7 November 2001, UN Doc. CRC/C/15/Add.167.

UN Committee on the Rights of the Child (CRC), *Concluding observations on the consolidated second to fourth periodic reports of Bosnia and Herzegovina, adopted by the Committee at its sixty-first session (17 September – 5 October 2012)*, 29 November 2012, UN Doc. CRC/C/BIH/CO/2–4.

UN Committee on the Rights of the Child (CRC), *Concluding observations on the combined second to fourth periodic reports of Liberia, adopted by the Committee at its sixty-first session (17 September – 5 October 2012)*, 11 December 2012, UN Doc. CRC/C/LBR/CO/2–4.

UN Committee on the Rights of the Child (CRC), *Concluding observations on the combined third and fourth periodic report of Canada, adopted by the Committee at its sixty-first session (17 September – 5 October 2012)*, 6 December 2012, UN Doc. CRC/C/CAN/CO/3–4.

UN Committee on the Rights of the Child (CRC), *Consideration of reports submitted by States parties under article 44 of the Convention: Convention on the Rights of the Child: concluding observations: Algeria*, 18 July 2012, UN Doc. CRC/C/DZA/CO/3–4.

UN Committee on the Rights of the Child (CRC), *Consideration of reports submitted by States parties under article 44 of the Convention: Convention on the Rights of the Child: concluding observations: Algeria*, 12 October 2005, UN Doc. CRC/C/15/Add.269.

UN Committee on the Rights of the Child (CRC), *Consideration of reports submitted by States parties under article 44 of the Convention: Convention on the Rights of the Child: concluding observations: Bangladesh*, 26 June 2009, UN Doc. CRC/C/BGD/CO/4.

UN Committee on the Rights of the Child (CRC), *Consideration of reports submitted by States parties under article 44 of the Convention: Convention on the Rights of the Child: concluding observations: Cuba*, 20 June 2011, UN Doc. CRC/C/CUB/CO/2.

UN Committee on the Rights of the Child (CRC), *Consideration of reports submitted by States parties under article 44 of the Convention: Convention on the Rights of the Child: concluding observations: Democratic Republic of the Congo*, 10 February 2009, UN Doc. CRC/C/COD/CO/2.

UN Committee on the Rights of the Child (CRC), *Consideration of reports submitted by States parties under article 44 of the Convention: Convention on the Rights of the Child: concluding observations: Egypt*, 15 July 2011, UN Doc. CRC/C/EGY/CO/3–4.

UN Committee on the Rights of the Child (CRC), *Consideration of reports submitted by States parties under article 44 of the Convention: Convention on the Rights of the Child: concluding observations: Federal Republic of Yugoslavia (Serbia and Montenegro)*, 13 February 1996, UN Doc. CRC/C/15/Add.49.

UN Committee on the Rights of the Child (CRC), *Consideration of reports submitted by States parties under article 44 of the Convention: Convention on the Rights of the Child: concluding observations: Myanmar*, 14 March 2012, UN Doc. CRC/C/MMR/CO/3–4.

UN Committee on the Rights of the Child (CRC), *Consideration of reports submitted by States parties under article 44 of the Convention: Convention on the Rights of the Child: concluding observations: Netherlands*, 27 March 2009, UN Doc. CRC/C/NLD/CO/3.

UN Committee on the Rights of the Child (CRC), *Consideration of reports submitted by States parties under article 44 of the Convention: Convention on the Rights of the Child: concluding observations: Republic of Moldova*, 20 February 2009, UN Doc. CRC/C/MDA/CO/3.

UN Committee on the Rights of the Child (CRC), *Consideration of reports submitted by States parties under article 44 of the Convention: Convention on the Rights of the Child: concluding observations: Sudan*, 22 October 2010, UN Doc. CRC/C/SDN/CO/3–4.

UN Committee on the Rights of the Child (CRC), *Consideration of reports submitted by States parties under article 44 of the Convention: Convention on the Rights of the Child: concluding observations: Turkey*, 20 July 2012, UN Doc. CRC/C/TUR/CO/2–3.

UN Committee on the Rights of the Child (CRC), *Consideration of reports submitted by States parties under article 44 of the Convention: Convention on the Rights of the Child: concluding observations: United Kingdom of Great Britain and Northern Ireland*, 20 October 2008, UN Doc. CRC/C/GBR/CO/4.

UN Committee on the Rights of the Child (CRC), *Consideration of reports submitted by states parties under article 44 of the Convention*, 4 June 1993, UN Doc. CRC/C/3/Add.15.

General Comments

UN Committee on the Rights of the Child (CRC), *General Comment No. 3 (2003) on HIV/AIDS and the rights of the child*, 17 March 2003, UN Doc. CRC/GC/2003/3.

UN Committee on the Rights of the Child (CRC), *General Comment No. 4 (2003) on Adolescent health and development in the context of the Convention on the Rights of the Child*, 1 July 2003, UN Doc. CRC/GC/2003/4.

UN Committee on the Rights of the Child (CRC), *General Comment No. 5 (2003) on General measures of implementation of the Convention on the Rights of the Child*, 27 November 2003, UN Doc. CRC/GC/2003/5.

UN Committee on the Rights of the Child (CRC), *General Comment No. 6 (2005) on the treatment of unaccompanied and separated children outside their country of origin*, 1 September 2005, UN Doc. CRC/GC/2005/6.

UN Committee on the Rights of the Child (CRC), *General Comment No. 7 (2005): Implementing child rights in early childhood*, 20 September 2006, UN Doc. CRC/C/GC/7/Rev.1.

UN Committee on the Rights of the Child (CRC), *General Comment No. 9 (2007): The rights of children with disabilities*, 27 February 2007, UN Doc. CRC/C/GC/9.

UN Committee on the Rights of the Child (CRC), *General Comment No. 10 (2007) on Children's rights in juvenile justice*, 25 April 2007, UN Doc. CRC/C/GC/10.

UN Committee on the Rights of the Child (CRC), *General Comment No. 11 (2009): Indigenous children and their rights under the Convention*, 12 February 2009, UN Doc. CRC/C/GC/11.

UN Committee on the Rights of the Child (CRC), *General Comment No. 12 (2009) on The right of the child to be heard*, 20 July 2009, UN Doc. CRC/C/GC/12.

UN Committee on the Rights of the Child (CRC), *General Comment No. 13(2011) on Article 19: The right of the child to freedom from all forms of violence*, 17 February 2011, UN Doc. CRC/C/GC/13.

UN Committee on the Rights of the Child (CRC), *General Comment No. 15 (2013) on the right of the child to the enjoyment of the highest attainable standard of health (art. 24)*, 17 April 2013, UN Doc. CRC/C/GC/15.

UN Committee on the Rights of the Child (CRC), *General guidelines regarding the form and content of initial reports to be submitted by States Parties under article 44, paragraph 1(a), of the Convention*, 30 October 1991, UN Doc. CRC/C/5.

UN Committee on the Rights of the Child (CRC), *General Guidelines regarding the form and content of periodic reports to be submitted by states parties under article 44, paragraph 1(b), of the Convention*, 25 November 2005, UN Doc. CRC/C/58/Rev.1.

UN Committee on the Rights of the Child (CRC), *General Guidelines regarding the form and content of periodic reports to be submitted by states parties under article 44, paragraph 1(b), of the Convention*, 23 November 2010, UN Doc. CRC/C/58/Rev.2.

UN Committee on the Rights of the Child (CRC), *Initial report of the United Kingdom of Great Britain and Northern Ireland to the Committee on the Rights of the Child*, 23 March 1994, UN Doc. CRC/C/11/Add.1.

UN Committee on the Rights of the Child (CRC), 1999, UN Doc. CRC/C/87.

UN HUMAN RIGHTS COUNCIL (HRC)

UN Human Rights Council, *Joint written statement submitted by International Save the Children Alliance and World Vision International (WVI), non-governmental organizations in general consultative status, and Kindernothilfe-Help for Children in Need, SOS Kinderdorf International (SOS-KDI) and World Organisation against Torture, non-governmental organizations in special consultative status, and Plan International, Inc, a non-governmental organization on the Roster*, 26 May 2008, UN Doc. A/HRC/8/NGO/6.

UN Human Rights Council, *Open-ended Working Group on an optional protocol to the Convention on the Rights of the Child to provide a communications procedure*, 17 June 2009, UN Doc. A/HRC/RES/11/1.

UN Human Rights Council, *Open-ended Working Group on an optional protocol to the Convention on the Rights of the Child to provide a communications procedure*, 14 April 2010, UN Doc. A/HRC/RES/13/3.

UN Human Rights Council, *Proposal for a draft optional protocol prepared by the Chairperson-Rapporteur of the Open-ended Working Group on an optional protocol to the Convention on the Rights of the Child to provide a communications procedure*, 1 September 2010, UN Doc. A/HRC/WG.7/2/2.

UN Human Rights Council, *Report of the Open-ended Working Group on an optional protocol to the Convention on the Rights of the Child to provide a communications procedure*, 25 May 2011, UN Doc. A/HRC/17/36.

UN Human Rights Council, *Report of the Special Rapporteur on the Right of Everyone to the Enjoyment of the Highest Attainable Standard of Physical and Mental Health*, 17 January 2007, UN Doc. A/HRC/4/28.

UN Human Rights Council, *Report of the Special Rapporteur on the right of everyone to the enjoyment of the highest attainable standard of physical and mental health, Paul Hunt*, 31 January 2008, UN Doc. A/HRC/7/11.

UN Human Rights Council, *Revised proposal for a draft optional protocol prepared by the Chairperson-Rapporteur of the Open-ended Working Group on an optional protocol to the Convention on the Rights of the Child to provide a communications procedure*,13 January 2011, UN Doc. A/HRC/WG.7/2/4.

UN Human Rights Council, *Submission to Open-ended Working Group of the Human Rights Council, considering the possibility of elaborating an Optional Protocol to provide a communications procedure for the Convention on the Rights of the Child by Marta Santos Pais*, 14 December 2009, UN Doc. A/HRC/WG.7/1/CRP.7.

UN Human Rights Council, *Submission to Open-ended Working Group of the Human Rights Council, considering the possibility of elaborating an Optional Protocol to provide a communications procedure for the Convention on the Rights of the Child by Peter Newell*, 9 December 2009, UN Doc. A/HRC/WG.7/1/CRP.2.

OTHER SELECTED UN DOCUMENTS

- Legislative history of the Convention on the rights of the Child, Volume II, United Nations, New York and Geneva, 2007, p. 580–603.
- The UN Guiding Principles on Business and Human Rights.
- 'The World Declaration on the Protection, Survival and Development of Children', World Summit for Children, New York: 30th September 1990.
- UN Guidelines on Justice in Matters involving Child Victims and Witnessess of Crime (ECOSOC Resolution 2005/20, 22 July 2005).
- United Nations Human Development Index.
- Working Paper No. 3 of the Special-Representative of the Secretary General for Children in armed conflict: Children and justice during and in the aftermath of armed conflict, September 2011.

Working Group reports filed under:

- UN Doc. E/CN.4/1349.
- UN Doc. E/1982/12Add.1, C.
- UN Doc. E/CN.4/1983/62.
- UN Doc. E/CN.4/1984/71.
- UN Doc. E/CN.4/1985/64.
- UN Doc. E/CN.4/1987/25.
- UN Doc. E/CN.4/1988/WG.1/WP.14.
- UN Doc. E/CN.4/1989/48.
- UN Doc. E/CN.4/2003/58.
- UN Doc. E/CN.4/L.1366/Rev.1.
- UN Doc. GA/11198.
- UN Doc. HRI/GEN/1/Rev.3.
- UN Doc. HRI/GEN/2/Rev.6, 3 June 2009.
- UN Doc. HR/PUB/91/1 (Rev.1).
- UN Doc. PCNICC/2000/1/Add.1.

UNICEF

UNICEF, news report, New York, 28 December 2004.

UNICEF, report 'The State of the World's children 2010'.

UNICEF Children in an Urban World: The State of the World's Children 2012.

UNICEF, 'Progress for Children, Achieving the MDGs with equity', Number 9, September 2010.

UNICEF, 'The Progress of Nations', Annual reports.

UNICEF, Implementation Handbook for the Convention on the Rights of the Child, prepared for UNICEF by Rachel Hodgkin and Peter Newell, fully revised third edition, September 2007.

UNICEF, Defence for Children and Pharos, Research Report: 'Undocumented children and access to hospital health care', June 2010.

'A Guide to General Comment 7: Implementing Child Rights in Early Childhood', produced by Bernard van Leer Foundation and UNICEF, 2006.

UNICEF Crisis Report 'Syria's children: a lost generation?', March 2011.

CAAC Bulletin composed by UNICEF in collaboration with a wide range of other international organizations, Children Affected by Armed Conflict, Israel and the occupied Palestinian territory, 2010 Annual Review.

WHO

WHO and UNICEF, Baby-Friendly Hospital Initiative, 2009. Available at: www.who.int/nutrition/publications/infantfeeding/bfhi_trainingcourse/en/.

The WHO Health Promotion Glossary, 1998.

The world health report 2008, Primary health care – Now more than ever, Geneva, World Health Organization, 2008.

WHO 1986a Social Justice and Equity in Health: Report on a WHO Meeting, Leeds, United Kingdom, 1985.

WHO Factsheet No. 31 on the Right to health, Office of the United Nations High Commissioner for Human Rights, Geneva, June 2008.

WHO, 3rd WHO Model List of Essential Medicines for Children, March 2011.

WHO, *Everybody's Business: Strengthening Health Systems to Improve Health Outcomes*, WHO, 2007.

WHO, *International Health Regulations 2005*, (2nd ed. 2008).

WHO Office for Europe, *European Health Report 2009, Health and Health systems.*

WHO Regional Office for Europe, *European strategy for child and adolescent health and development. From resolution to action*, Copenhagen 2005. (EUR/05/5048378).

WHO Regional Office for Europe, *Millennium Development Goals in the WHO European Region: A situational analysis at the eve of the 5-year countdown*, Copenhagen: WHO 2010.

WHO Regional Office for Europe, *The European Health Report 2005, Public health action for healthier children and populations*, Copenhagen 2005.

WHO, *The world health report 2008, Primary health care – Now more than ever*, Geneva, World Health Organization, 2008.

Preamble to the Constitution of the World Health Organization, as published in World Health Organization, *Basic documents*, 45th edition, Geneva, 2006.

Preamble to the Constitution of the World Health Organization, as adopted by the International Health Conference, entered into force on 7 April 1948.

Report of a WHO Technical Consultation on Birth Spacing, Geneva, Switzerland, 13–15 June 2005.

EUROPEAN UNION

EU Doc. 12080, Recommendation 1864, on Promoting the participation by children in decisions affecting them, adopted at the 1069th meeting of the Ministers' Deputies, 4 November 2009.

EU Document 2006/C 305 E/148, Resolution of the European Parliament on improving the mental health of the population. Towards a strategy on mental health for the European Union (2006/2058(INI)). (Official Journal of 14 December 2006).

EU Document 2007/C 164/01, Council's Conclusion on the prevention of injury and the promotion of safety.

EU Document 2008/C 319/01, Resolution of the Council and the Representatives of the Governments of the Member States, meeting within the Council of 20 November 2008 on the health and well-being of young people.

EU Document 2011/C 361/4, Council conclusions of 2 December 2011 on early detection and treatment of communication disorders in children, including the use of e-Health tools and innovative solutions. (Official Journal 10 December 2011).

EU Document 2011/C 361/5, Council conclusions of 2 December 2011 on prevention, early diagnosis and treatment of chronic respiratory diseases in children. (Official Journal 10 December 2011).

EU Document Commission directive 2006/141/EC of 22 December 2006 on infant formulae and follow-on formulae and amending Directive 1999/21/EC. (Official Journal 31 December 2006).

COUNCIL OF EUROPE

European Social Charter, Conclusions of the European Committee of Social Rights.

Children's rights under the European Social Charter, Information document prepared by the secretariat of the ESC, March 2009.

Recommendation CM/Rec(2009)10 on integrated national strategies for the protection of children from violence.

Recommendation CM/Rec(2010)2 on deinstitutionalisation and community living of children with disabilities.
Recommendation Rec(2000)5 on the development of structures for citizen and patient participation in the decision-making process affecting health care.
Recommendation Rec(2006)5 on the Council of Europe Action Plan to promote the rights and full participation of people with disabilities in society: improving the quality of life of people with disabilities in Europe 2006–2015.
Recommendation Rec(2006)7 on management of patient safety and prevention of adverse events in health care.
Recommendation Rec(98)8 on children's participation in family and social life.
Recommendation of the Council of Ministers of the Council of Europe. 'Concerning the care and education of children from birth to the age of eight, REC (3) 1981.
Recommendation of the Council of Ministers of the Council of Europe. 'On child day-care', REC (8) 2002.
Recommendation of the Council of Ministers of the Council of Europe. 'On securing and promoting the health of single-parent families', REC (4) 1997.
Recommendation of the Council of Ministers of the Council of Europe. 'Safeguarding children and young people against obesity and diabetes II', (1966) 2011.
Recommendation of the Parliamentary Assembly of the Council of Europe. 'Controlling the diagnosis and treatment of hyperactive children in Europe, REC (1562) 2002.
Recommendation of the Parliamentary Assembly of the Council of Europe. 'Teenagers in distress: a social and health-based approach to youth malaise', REC (1632) 2003.
Recommendations on Communication between health care professionals children and their parents or carers.
Resolution 1804 (2011) of the Parliamentary Assembly on Safeguarding children and young people from obesity and type 2 diabetes.
OJ 2009 C41E/04, Towards an EU strategy on the rights of the child – European Parliament resolution of 16 January 2008.
Strategy 'Building a Europe for and with children' 2009–2011.
Factsheet on the right to health and the European Social Charter, Information document prepared by the secretariat of the ESC, March 2009.
International Federation of Human Rights Leagues (FIDH) v. France, Complaint No. 14/2003. (The European Committee of Social Rights).

DUTCH PARLIAMENTARY DOCUMENTS

Kamerstukken II 1989/91, 21 561, no. 6
Kamerstukken II 1991/92, 21 561, no. 11

OTHER DOCUMENTS

African Child Policy Forum, *The African Report on Child Wellbeing: Budgeting for Children*, Addis Ababa: The African Child Policy Forum 2011.

E. Anderson & Hague, *The impact of investing in children: Assessing the cross-country econometric evidence*, Working Paper 280, Overseas Development Institute, London, 2007.

Anyanwu & Erhijakpor, *Health Expenditures and Health Outcomes in Africa*, Economic Research Working Paper Series, African Development Bank, Tunis, 2007.

C. Baasch Andersen, *Reasonable Time in Article 39(1) of the CISG – Is Article 39(1) Truly a Uniform Provision?*, University of Copenhagen, 1998.

Child Rights International Network, *COMMUNICATIONS PROCEDURE: Committee on the Rights of the Child endorses campaign*, Londen: CHR News 18 June 2008.

College Zorgverzekeringen, Concept-advises on the financing of medicines for the Pompe and Fabry diseases.

Commissie-Doek, *Advies medisch-wetenschappelijk onderzoek met kinderen*, The Hague: 26 november 2009.

J.P. Costa, *Current Challenges for the European Court on Human Rights*, lecture delivered at the University of Leiden on 10 December 2011 as part of the series of Raymond and Beverly Sackler Distinguished Lectures in Human Rights at Leiden Law School.

J.A. Diaz Huertas and A.I.F. Guerreiro, Council of Europe Document No. MSN (2011) 4E.

D.P. Fidler, *Global Outbreak of Avian Influenza A (H5N1) and International Law*, ASIL Insights, January 2004.

D.P. Goldman, E.A. McGlynn, *U.S.Health care, Facts about costs, access and quality*, 2005.

K. Herr, *Pain Assessment in the Patient Unable to Self-Report, Position Statement with Clinical Practice Recommendations*, American Society for Pain Management Nursing, July 2011.

Integrated Regional Information Networks (IRIN), *Libyan Arab Jamahiriya: Aid workers call for access to the vulnerable*, 29 March 2011.

S.S. Jones, J. Caloyeras & S. Mattke, *Power to the People: The Role of Consumer-Controlled Personal Health Management Systems in the Evolution of Employer-Based Health Care Benefits.*

D. Kamin, 'Hospital rounds: How's the doctor-patient communication system?', *Vector* 2011.

U. Kilkely & M. Donnelly, *The Child's Right to be heard in the Healthcare Setting: perspectives of children, parents and health professionals*, The National Children's Strategy Research Series, October, 2006.

M.E. Klaverboer & A.E. Zijlstra, *Het belang van het kind in het vreemdelingenrecht, Kinderen uit asielzoekersgezinnen. Ontwikkeling, perspectief en juridische positie*, Rijksuniversiteit Groningen: 2008.

Langfords & Clark, *A complaints Procedure for the Convention on the Rights of the Child: Commentary on the Second Draft*, Norwegian Centre for Human Rights (University of Oslo), 7 February 2011.

Langfords & Clark, *The new kid on the block: A complaints procedure for the Convention on the Rights of the Child', Working Paper, No.1,* Socio-Economic Rights Programme, Norwegian Centre for Human Rights, University of Oslo, January 2010.

U. Müller, *Report: Children as strong as nations*, Kindernothilfe.

National Institute for Health and Clinical Excellence, 'Measuring effectiveness and cost effectiveness'.

L. Nodjadjim & K. Wyss, 'Access to health care by street children in the urban context of N'Djamena, Chad.', *International workshop paper*, Geneva, Palais des Nations – 3–6 May 2000.

A. Nolan, A.E. Yamin & B.M. Meier, Submission on the Content of a Future General Comment on the Right of the Child to the Enjoyment of the Highest Attainable Standard of Health (art. 24).

Office of the UN Secretary-General's Special Advisor on community medicine and special lessons form Haiti.

C. van Os & S. de Jong, *'The Dutch Report on 'Enhancing Vulnerable Asylum Seekers Protection' 2010*, Defence for Children International-ECPAT The Netherlands.

A.K. Sen, *Equality of What?*, Stanford University: Tanner Lectures on Human Values 1979.

D. Skinner, N. Tsheko, S. Mtero-Munyati, M. Segwabe, P. Chibatamoto, S. Mfecane, B. Chandiwana, N. Nkomo, S. Tlou, *Definition of orphaned and vulnerable children*, Cape Town: HSRC Press 2004.

R. Smith, 'The end of disease and the beginning of health', weblog for the British Medical Journal, 8 July 2008.

S.E. Smith, *In law, what is reasonable time?*, 2013.

I. Robeyn, *The Capability Approach: an interdisciplinary introduction*, Research Paper for the third international conference on the capability approach in Pavia, Italy, 9 December 2003, Amsterdam: University of Amsterdam 2003.

The NGO Physicians for Human Rights, Report 'The Bare Minimum Health Services in the Unrecognized villages in the Negev', Israel: 7 July 2009.

The NGO Physicians for Human Rights, Report on the limited access for Israeli Bedouin women, Israel: 27 April 2011.

The Partnership for Maternal, Newborn & Child Health, *A Global Review of the Key Interventions Related to Reproductive, Maternal, Newborn and Child Health (Rmnch)*, Geneva, Switzerland: PMNCH 2011.

The Royal College of Paediatrics and Child Health, *Good Medical Practice in Paediatrics and Child Health: Duties and Responsibilities of Paediatricians*, London 2002.

Working paper on Health systems in the European Union: a comparative study by the European Parliament, 1998.

Children's consent to surgery, Buckingham: Open University Press 1993, p. 154–163.

Complaints Mechanism: Summary of Final Draft Meeting.

Covenant on the Rights of the Child in the Islam of the Organisation of the Islamic Conference. Doc. OIC/9-IGGE/HRI/2004/Rep.Final.

Dutch policy document: 'Responsibility for Freedom' [Verantwoordelijkheid voor Vrijheid], April 2011.

Interpretative guide of Guiding Principles by the Office of the High Commissioner of Human Rights.

Jaarbericht Kinderrechten [Year Report Children's Rights], Voorburg/Leiden 1 May 2011.

Joint NGO Submission to the Open-ended Working Group on an Optional Protocol to the Convention on the Rights of the Child to provide a Communications Procedure, October 2010.

Joint Report on Health systems, prepared by the European Commission and the Economic Policy Committee, 2010.

KNMG-Meldcode en Stappenplan Artsen en Kindermishandeling, Utrecht, September 2008.

Lecture by W. Vanderhole at the Tobias Asser Institute in the Hague as a keynote speaker at the Research Seminar on Economic, Social and Cultural Rights: Vehicles for Social Justice?, organized by the Working Group on Economic, Social and Cultural Rights, The Netherlands School of Human Rights Research, 21 November 2012.

Lecture delivered by Professor Sloth-Nielsen on 19 November 2012 on the occasion of the inauguration of professor Ton Liefaard at the University of Leiden.

Lecture of Director UNICEF Europe, Steven Allen on the occasion of the adoption of the Guidelines on child-friendly healthcare by the Council of Europe Member States in Lissabon, September 2011.

Letter of the Minister of Health of the 21st January 2011 in reply to parliamentary questions on medicine use in children, reference GMT-U-3036517.

Making Health Care Accessible to Street Children: The 'Hospital on Wheels' Project (2000-2006), SNEHA 2008.

Notification on the increasing costs in health care as a percentage of the GDP, 20 May 2010 (Central Bureau on Statistics, The Netherlands)

Preliminary Joint NGO Submission to the Open-ended Working Group on an Optional Protocol to the convention on the Rights of the Child to provide a communications procedure, February 2011.

Report: Children's rights in the Netherlands, The third periodic report of the Dutch NGO Coalition for Children's Rights on the Implementation of the Convention on the Rights of the Child; Jantje Beton, The Foundation for Children's Welfare Stamps Netherlands, UNICEF Netherlands, Save the Children Netherlands, Plan Netherlands, National Youth Council, National Association for Child and Youth Legal Advice Centres, Defence for Children International Netherlands, Netherlands Youth Institute (advice member), July 2008.

Report in preparation to the Day of General Discussion on Human Rights on the right of the child to the enjoyment of the highest attainable standard of health, 4th of March 2013.

Report of Pharos Foundation, 'Undocumented children and access to hospital care', June 2010.

Report ZonMw 'In-depth study 'Goed Gebruik Geneesmiddelen' [Good Use of Medicines], 11 June 2010 carried out for the Ministery of Health subsequent to a preliminary report of 20 July 2009.

Submissions received to the development of CRC General Comment on the right of the child to the enjoyment of the highest attainable standard of health (art. 24).
The EACH Charter
The European Observatory on Health systems and policies
The Millennium Development Goals Report 2010, United Nations, New York, 2010.
The Patient Satisfaction Questionnaire of Rand Health.
The right to health and the European Social Charter, Information document prepared by the secretariat of the ESC, March 2009.
The Right to Health: a Resource Manual for NGOs Asher, Judith, 2004.
'The Plan of Action for Implementing the World Declaration on the Protection, Survival and Development of Children in the 1990s', World Summit for Children, New York: 30 September 1990.
'The Manual on the right to the highest attainable standard of health', The Human Rights Centre of the University of Essex and the International Federation of Health and Human Rights Organisations.
'Armoedesignalement 2010, Sociaal en Cultureel Planbureau/Centraal Bureau voor de Statistiek', Den Haag, December 2010.

NEWSPAPER ARTICLES

'Kleinste ziekenhuis van Nederland boos over sluiting geboortezorg', *Algemeen Dagblad* 9 May 2012.
S. Foley, 'GlaxoSmithKline pays $3bn for illegally marketing depression drug', *The Independent* 3 July 2012.
'The age(s) of adulthood', The Japan Times Online, 24 February 2008.

INTERNET SOURCES

www1.umn.edu
www2.ohchr.org
www.aappolicy.aappublications.org
www.actionforsickchildren.org
www.ad.nl
www.annfammed.org
www.asil.org
www.aspmn.org
www.biomedcentral.com
www.blogs.bmj.com
www.bmj.com
www.books.google.nl
www.cbs.nl

www.cfhiuk.org
www.childrenshealthcare.org
www.cisg.law.pace.edu
www.coe.int
www.content1a.omroep.nl
www.crin.org
www.daccess-dds-ny.un.org
www.dare.uva.nl
www.defenceforchildren.nl
www.definitions.uslegal.com
www.dichtbijnederland.nps.nl
www.each-for-sick-children.org
www.ec.europa.eu
www.ecpat.nl
www.ema.europa.eu
www.eur-lex.europa.eu
www.europarl.europa.eu
www.euro.who.int
www.findarticles.com
www.freud.org.uk
www.getstopic.com
www.hdr.undp.org
www.heinonline.org
www.hindawi.com
www.iasp-pain.org
www.independent.co.uk
www.indexmundi.com
www.ishr.ch
www.jopan.org
www.jus.uio.no
www.k4health.org
www.lessonsfromhaiti.org
www.lvg.org
www.medimmigrant.be
www.ncbi.nlm.nih.gov
www.nice.org.uk
www.nkfk.nl
www.nlm.nih.gov
www.nos.nl
www.oicun.org
www.paho.org
www.phr.org.il
www.rand.org

www.rijksoverheid.nl
www.rivm.nl
www.savethechildren.org.uk
www.searo.who.int
www.siaacademy.com
www.snehamumbai.org
www.soc.spbu.ru
www.shr.aaas.org
www.sum.uio.no
www.treaties.un.org
www.un.org
www.undemocracy.com
www.unicef.ca
www.unicef.org
www.vectorblog.org
www.vimeo.com
www.wcd.coe.int
www.webarchive.nationalarchives.gov.uk
www.who.int
www.whqlibdoc.who.int
www.worldatlas.com
www.worldlawdirect.com

CURRICULUM VITAE

Sarah Ida Spronk-van der Meer (Rotterdam, the Netherlands 1981) holds an LLM in international law and a MSc in health and medical anthropology. Empowering people is a central part of both her academic and program related work to enhance health, protection and well-being of children, young people and their families. In her PhD research, Spronk focuses on the right to 'the highest attainable standard of health' of the child.

Previous to her PhD research, Spronk worked for the NGO Save the Children, the International Criminal Court and a mental health institution for children and adolescents. In June 2013 Spronk completed the diplomatic training of the Ministry of Foreign Affairs of the Netherlands, where she is currently employed as a policy advisor on sexual and reproductive health and rights of children and adolescents. Topics include comprehensive sexuality education, maternal and infant mortality, protection against sexual violence, female genital mutilation and child marriages. In addition, she is involved in coaching and community projects for children to integrate sports activities, health assessments and children's rights training.

Spronk is experienced in delivering lectures, workshops and trainings on children's rights, health and empowerment to a variety of audiences. She has organized conferences and voyages for children, adolescents and (young) adults in various countries.

SUMMARY

Large numbers of children all over the world face significant health risks, such as infectious and chronic diseases, malnutrition, injuries and the consequences of natural disasters, protracted armed conflicts and poverty. Every year, 4 million babies die within the first month of their life and almost 8 million children under the age of five die from preventable diseases such as malaria, pneumonia, measles and diarrhoea. These general statistics do not reveal the underlying inequalities in health between and within countries. One of the causes of the inequalities is that, in many countries, vulnerable groups of children have no or only limited access to health services. This research aims to identify the standards in international law for realizing the right to the highest attainable standard of health of the child. The central questions that are analysed:

a. *What priorities derive from the concept of the highest attainable standard of health of the child, its definition and the interpretation of the key constituent elements on the basis of international human rights law?*
b. *How should this concept be implemented in the light of the international human rights standards?*

Chapter 1 sets out the central problem in realizing the right to health of the child. The vagueness of the concept of 'the highest attainable standard of health' makes it difficult to identify the elements of the right to health that must be prioritized for implementation in a country's health policy. Secondly, the realization of the right to the highest attainable standard of health is dependent upon the limited financial resources available. Thirdly, the realization of children's right to the highest attainable standard of health depends on both situational circumstances and individual characteristics such as the genetic predisposition and lifestyle of both the parents and the child. Unclear is therefore what elements of the right to the highest attainable standard of health fall under the responsibility of the State and what the responsibilities are of medical professionals, the parents and the child itself. Lastly, this chapter introduces the key concepts of this study, namely 'health', 'health as a right', 'primary health care' and 'vulnerable children'.

Chapter 2 identifies the priorities that follow from the right to the highest attainable standard of health of the child in the international children's right domain, namely the Convention on the Rights of the Child and the General Comments to the Convention. It identifies the key elements of article 24 CRC and its relation to other relevant articles in the Convention, namely the right to non-discrimination (art. 2 CRC), the best interests of the child (art. 3), the right to life (art.6), the right to be heard (art. 12 CRC), the role of parents (art. 5 and 18) and the right to social security (art. 26) and to an adequate standard of living (art. 27).

The right to health of the child in the CRC has a clear focus on prevention of health problems and on ensuring basic health care for all children. On the basis of articles 6 and 24 CRC, health services must be continuous, adapted to the changing circumstances in which children live and to their changing needs. Health services must be accessible to all without discrimination and age-adjusted health information must be made available to both children and their parents. Four levels of priority have been identified in the organization of health care for young children:

1. Provision of health care and information to the mother during pregnancy.
2. Obstetric health care around the birth of the child.
3. Neonatal health care for the mother and the child immediately after birth.
4. Quality health care during childhood.

Chapter 2 looks into the dilemma between protecting the health of the child and in respecting its autonomy. It establishes that in assessing children's competency for participation in health care, a distinction must be made between their competency on the one hand and the willingness of others to accept children's choices on the other. This question is relevant, because it relates to the level of responsibility that can be attributed to children for realizing their own right to health in the healthcare setting. The role of parents in ensuring their children's right to health is discussed both in terms of their primary responsibility for ensuring healthy living circumstances and in guiding their children within the health care context. Lastly, chapter 2 relates the key principles of the right to health in the CRC to the four medical ethical principles. In order to realize the right to health of the child in the daily healthcare setting, all medical professionals encountering children in their (daily) work, must be educated about children's rights in health and trained in communicating with children and families in the health care sector.

Chapter 3 analyzes how the priorities deriving from the right to health of the child as set in the Convention on the Rights of the Child and in the General Comments are interpreted by the CRC Committee in its Concluding Observations on the Country Reports for countries with different levels of development. Hereto, a selection of 35 countries was made, based on country area, population size, human development indicators and geographical spread. These Concluding Observations on the Country Reports were particularly analyzed for recommendations relating to children's right to the highest attainable standard of health. This chapter also compares the priorities as set in the Convention with the recommendations made by the CRC Committee. The most striking difference is that the recommendations made by the CRC Committee predominantly address States Parties, whereas the Convention and General Comment increasingly stress the importance of involving children, their parents and other individual stakeholders. In order to perform an accurate assessment of the progress made by the State in implementing the right to health of the child, the Committee recommends States to:

I. Establish a national plan with strategic budget lines.
II. Identify the government departments responsible for the right to health of the child.
III. Set clear, time-bound and measurable targets.
IV. Ensure disaggregated data collection and analysis.

Chapter 4 investigates the priorities for realizing the right to the highest attainable standard of health of the child as found in international health and human rights law.

The chapter identifies several factors of uncertainty, which make it difficult to identify one universal standard for the right to the highest attainable standard of health of the child. Nevertheless, several priorities are found which should be realized, including the underlying determinants of health, inclusion of all vulnerable groups of children and a specified range of health services that respond to the changing needs of mothers and children during different stages of development.

General Comment 14 to the ICESCR further establishes that the health services should be in line with the key constituent elements of the right to health: availability, accessibility, acceptability and quality. The AAAQ structure for structuring and assessing the level of realization of the general right to health offers significant insight into the way in which the highest attainable standard of health of the child can be achieved. The framework applies to both the underlying determinants of health and to the provision of medical care itself. Chapter 4 discusses the inclusion of new elements to the AAAQ structure, namely adaptability, accountability and participation. Inclusion of these elements would be responsive to the current trend to better involve patients in their own health process and it would allow for a more flexible and adaptive health system that places the best interests of the child and its family at the heart.

Chapter 5 investigates the priorities that should be met as found in European human rights law. Both from the perspective of the EU and from the Council of Europe, a clear focus is visible on the need to prevent health problems from the very beginning: before conception, during pregnancy, birth and in the earliest years of life going on in school years and through adolescence. In addition, whereas the bodies of law investigated in chapters 2, 3 and 4 predominantly focus on basic health measures, the legal frameworks in the European region focus more on the way in which the different levels of health services are organized. Also, specific subthemes relevant to the European region are identified. Chapter 5 closely looks into the Guidelines on Child-Friendly Healthcare as adopted by the Council of Europe. These guidelines establish that health care must be centered around the rights, needs and characteristics of children and their families. The elements required to meet this challenge are identified. Also, the central role of children in managing their own health status is expressly highlighted.

Chapter 6 addresses the question 'How the process of realization influences the interpretation of the highest attainable standard of health of the child and which actors are responsible in the process of implementation?' This chapter discusses the way in which the priorities found in the children's rights domain and international health and human rights law should be implemented. Whereas international human rights legislation is primarily directed towards States Parties, an increasing role is attributed to individual actors in managing their own or their children's health status. Chapter 6 makes a distinction between the obligations of States to provide for general health measures and legal remedies and the opportunities of individual actors to take responsibility for their own health and to hold States Parties accountable. This chapter looks into the value and counterarguments of legal remedies. It specifically looks into the additional value of the Optional Protocol to the Convention on the Rights of the Child to a communication procedure for children in realizing the highest attainable standard of health of the child.

The Conclusion in *Chapter 7* presents the priorities required to realize the highest attainable standard of health of the child (the capability of the child to be healthy) as found in international law. The priorities presented include a range of concrete measures that should be taken by States, parents, medical professionals and other actors, while taking into account the changing needs of children and the changing circumstances in which children live. Therefore, the measures to be taken should result in an adaptive health system that places the best interests of the child and its family at the heart. This necessarily requires the active involvement of beneficiaries, other stakeholders and the communities in which children live. This concluding chapter furthermore addresses the question how the process of realization influences the interpretation of the highest attainable standard of health of the child. This results in a definition of the highest attainable standard of health of the child that takes into account the varying capabilities of individual children and which considers children as active rights-holders, notwithstanding their age or level of development.

SAMENVATTING

Het recht op gezondheid van kinderen

Wereldwijd hebben grote groepen kinderen te maken met significante bedreigingen van hun gezondheid, zoals infectieziekten en chronische ziekten, ondervoeding, ongelukken en de gevolgen van natuurrampen, voortslepende gewapende conflicten en armoede. Elk jaar sterven 4 miljoen baby's in hun eerste levensmaand en 8 miljoen kinderen onder de 5 jaar sterven aan ziektes die voorkomen zouden kunnen worden zoals malaria, longontsteking, mazelen en diarree. Deze algemene statistieken leggen onderliggende verschillen in gezondheid tussen en binnen landen niet bloot. Eén van de redenen van deze ongelijkheid is dat kwetsbare groepen kinderen in veel landen geen of slechts beperkte toegang tot gezondheidsvoorzieningen hebben. Dit onderzoek beoogt de standaarden in het internationale recht te identificeren om het recht op het hoogst haalbare niveau van gezondheid van kinderen te bereiken.

De centrale vragen die geanalyseerd worden zijn:

a. *elke prioriteiten vloeien voort uit het concept van het recht op het hoogst haalbare niveau van gezondheid van het kind, de definitie en interpretatie van de kernelementen in het internationale recht?*

b. *Hoe zou het concept van gezondheid geïmplementeerd moeten worden op basis van deze internationaal rechtelijke standaard?*

Hoofdstuk 1 zet de centrale probleemstelling voor het realiseren van het recht op gezondheid van kinderen uiteen. De vaagheid van het concept 'het hoogst haalbare niveau van gezondheid' maakt het moeilijk om de elementen die prioriteit moeten krijgen in het gezondheidsbeleid van een land te identificeren. In de tweede plaats is de realisatie van het recht op het hoogst haalbare niveau van gezondheid afhankelijk van beperkte financiële middelen. Ten derde hangt de realisatie van het recht op het hoogst haalbare niveau van gezondheid van het kind af van omgevingsfactoren en individuele karakteristieken van het kind zoals de genetische predispositie en leefstijl van zowel de ouders als het kind. Onduidelijk is daarom welke elementen onder verantwoordelijkheid van de Staat vallen en welke de verantwoordelijkheid zijn van medische professionals, ouders en het kind zelf. Tenslotte introduceert dit hoofdstuk een aantal centrale concepten uit deze studie, te weten het concept van 'gezondheid', 'gezondheid als recht', 'basisgezondheidszorg' en 'kwetsbare kinderen'.

Hoofdstuk 2 identificeert de prioriteiten die voortvloeien uit het recht op het hoogst haalbare niveau van gezondheid van het kind in het internationaal rechtelijke kinderrechtendomein, te weten het Internationaal Verdrag voor de Rechten van het Kind en de Algemene Aanbevelingen van het Kinderrechtencomité bij dit verdrag. Het hoofdstuk identificeert de kernelementen van artikel 24 IVRK en de relatie tot andere relevante artikelen van het verdrag, te weten het recht op non-discriminatie (art. 2 IVRK), het belang van het kind (art. 3 IVRK), het recht op leven (art. 6 IVRK), het recht om gehoord te worden (art. 12 IVRK), de rol van de ouders (art. 5 en 18), het recht op sociale zekerheid (art. 26 IVRK) en het recht op een adequate levensstandaard (art. 27 IVRK). Het recht op gezondheid van het kind in het IVRK heeft een duidelijke focus op preventie van gezondheidsbescherming en op het verzekeren van basisgezondheidszorg voor alle kinderen. Op basis van de artikelen 6 en 2 4IVRK, moeten gezondheidsvoorzieningen continue zijn en aangepast aan de veranderende omstandigheden waarin kinderen leven en aan hun veranderende behoeftes. Gezondheidsvoorzieningen moeten zonder uitzondering toegankelijk zijn voor allen en leeftijdsspecifieke voorlichting moet beschikbaar zijn voor zowel kinderen als hun ouders. Bij de organisatie van gezondheidszorg voor kinderen zijn vier niveaus geïdentificeerd die prioriteit hebben:

1. Verschaffing van medische zorg en informatie aan de moeder tijdens de zwangerschap.
2. Obstetrische zorg rondom de bevalling.
3. Neonatale zorg voor de moeder en het kind direct na de geboorte.
4. Kwalitatieve gezondheidzorg tijdens de jeugd.

Hoofdstuk 2 besteedt aandacht aan het dilemma tussen bescherming van de gezondheid van het kind en respect voor zijn autonomie. Dit hoofdstuk stelt dat bij het bepalen van de competentie van kinderen voor inspraak in medische zorg, onderscheid gemaakt moet worden tussen de competentie van kinderen enerzijds en de bereidheid van anderen om de keuzes van kinderen te accepteren anderzijds. Deze vraag is relevant, omdat het verband houdt met de mate van verantwoordelijkheid die kinderen hebben om hun eigen recht op gezondheid te realiseren. De rol van ouders bij het verzekeren van het recht op gezondheid van kinderen wordt bediscussieerd in termen van hun primaire verantwoordelijkheid om een gezonde leefomgeving voor hun kind te creëren en om hun kinderen te begeleiden in de medische context. Tenslotte, legt hoofdstuk 2 het verband tussen de kernelementen van het recht op gezondheid van het kind in het IVRK en de vier medisch ethische principes. Om het recht op gezondheid van kinderen in de dagelijkse medische praktijk te realiseren, moeten alle medische professionals die kinderen in hun (dagelijkse) werk tegenkomen, onderwezen worden over kinderrechten en getraind in communicatie met kinderen en hun families in de medische context.

Hoofdstuk 3 analyseert hoe de prioriteiten die voortvloeien uit het recht op gezondheid van het kind in het IVRK en de Algemene Aanbevelingen geïnterpreteerd worden door het kinderrechtencomité in haar Concluderende Observaties van de landenrapportages voor landen met verschillende ontwikkelingsniveaus. Hiertoe is een selectie van 35 landen gemaakt, gebaseerd op landoppervlakte, bevolkingsomvang, en indicatoren van menselijke ontwikkeling, geografische spreiding. De Concluderende Observaties van de landenrapportages zijn specifiek onderzocht op aanbevelingen met betrekking tot het recht op het hoogst haalbare niveau van gezondheid van het kind. Dit hoofdstuk vergelijkt ook de prioriteiten gesteld in het IVRK met de aanbevelingen van het kinderrechtencomité in de landenrapportages. Het meest opmerkelijke verschil is dat de aanbevelingen van het kinderrechtencomité Staten adresseren, terwijl het Verdrag zelf en de Algemene Aanbevelingen ook het belang benadrukken van het betrekken van kinderen, hun ouders en andere belanghebbenden. Om een nauwkeurige beoordeling te kunnen doen van de door Staten geboekte vooruitgang bij de implementatie van het recht op gezondheid van kinderen, beveelt het kinderrechtencomité staten aan om:

I. Een nationaal plan vast te stellen met strategische budgetlijnen.
II. De verantwoordelijke overheidsorganen te identificeren.
III. Duidelijke, tijdsgebonden en meetbare doelstellingen te bepalen.
IV. Gedisaggregeerde data collectie en analyse te waarborgen.

Hoofdstuk 4 onderzoekt welke prioriteiten voor het realiseren van het recht op het hoogst haalbare niveau van gezondheid van het kind voortvloeien uit internationale mensenrechten en gezondheidsrecht. Dit hoofdstuk identificeert verschillende factoren, die het lastig maken om één universele standaard van het recht op het hoogst haalbare niveau van gezondheid van het kind vast te stellen. Desalniettemin zijn er verschillende prioriteiten gevonden die gerealiseerd zouden worden, waaronder het voorzien in onderliggende determinanten van gezondheid, inclusie van kwetsbare groepen kinderen en een aantal gezondheidsvoorzieningen die tegemoet komen aan de veranderende behoeftes van moeders en kinderen tijdens de verschillende ontwikkelingsfasen. Algemene Aanbeveling 14 bij het IVESCR stelt verder dat gezondheidsvoorzieningen in lijn moeten zijn met de vier constitutieve elementen van het recht op gezondheid: beschikbaarheid, toegankelijkheid, accepteerbaarheid en kwaliteit. Deze 'AAAQ-structuur' voor het bepalen van het niveau van realisatie van het algemene recht op gezondheid biedt inzicht in de wijze waarop ook het recht op gezondheid van kinderen gerealiseerd kan worden. Deze structuur heeft betrekking op de onderliggende determinanten van gezondheid en op de verschaffing van medische zorg zelf. Hoofdstuk 4 discussieert de inclusie van nieuwe elementen in de 'AAAQ-structuur', te weten aanpassingsvermogen, verantwoording en participatie. Inclusie van deze elementen zou aansluiten op de huidige trend om patiënten beter te betrekken bij hun eigen zorgproces en het zou een meer flexibel en adaptief gezondheidssysteem mogelijk maken, waarin het belang van het kind en diens familie centraal staan.

Hoofdstuk 5 onderzoekt de prioriteiten die gerealiseerd moeten worden zoals neergelegd in Europese mensenrechten. Zowel vanuit het perspectief van de EU als van de Raad van Europa blijkt een heldere focus op de noodzaak om gezondheidsproblemen te voorkomen vanaf het allereerste begin: voor de conceptie, tijdens de zwangerschap, geboorte en gedurende de eerste levensjaren tot in de schooltijd en de puberteit. Terwijl het juridisch kader in het kinderrechtendomein en in het internationaal gezondheidsrecht de nadruk leggen op basale gezondheidsmaatregelen, zijn de juridische kaders in de Europese regio meer gericht op de manier waarop de verschillende niveaus van gezondheidszorg georganiseerd zijn. Ook zijn een aantal specifieke subthema's geïdentificeerd die preciezer zijn uitgewerkt. Hoofdstuk 5 besteedt in het bijzonder aandacht aan de Richtlijnen voor Kindvriendelijke Gezondheidszorg zoals aangenomen door de Raad van Europa. Deze Richtlijnen bepalen dat gezondheidszorg georganiseerd moet zijn rondom de rechten, behoeftes en karakteristieken van kinderen en hun familie. De elementen die nodig zijn om dit mogelijk te maken zijn hierin uitgewerkt. Ook is de centrale rol van kinderen en hun familie in de vormgeving van hun eigen gezondheid benadrukt.

Hoofdstuk 6 beantwoordt de vraag 'Hoe beïnvloedt het proces van realisatie de interpretatie van het recht op het hoogst haalbare niveau van gezondheid van het kind en welke actoren verantwoordelijk zijn in het implementatieproces?' Dit hoofdstuk bediscussieert de manier waarop de in het internationaal juridische kader vastgestelde prioriteiten geïmplementeerd moeten worden. Terwijl internationale mensenrechtenwetgeving met name gericht is op staten, wordt een steeds grotere rol toegekend aan individuele actoren bij het vormgeven van hun eigen gezondheid of die van hun kinderen. Hoofdstuk 6 maakt een onderscheid tussen de verplichtingen van staten om algemene gezondheidsmaatregelen te nemen en rechtsmiddelen te garanderen en de mogelijkheden van individuele actoren om verantwoordelijkheid te nemen voor hun eigen gezondheid en staten verantwoordelijk te houden. Dit hoofdstuk besteedt aandacht aan de waarde en tegenargumenten voor het gebruik van juridische procedures om het recht op gezondheid af te dwingen. In het bijzonder wordt de toegevoegde waarde van het Derde Protocol bij het IVRK betreffende een klachtprocedure voor kinderen beoordeeld bij het realiseren van het recht op het hoogst haalbare niveau van gezondheid van het kind.

De conclusie in *Hoofdstuk 7* presenteert de prioriteiten die in het internationale recht gesteld zijn om het recht op het hoogst haalbare niveau van gezondheid te bereiken (het vermogen van het kind om gezond te zijn). De gepresenteerde prioriteiten bevatten een reeks concrete maatregelen die staten, ouders, medische professionals en andere actoren moeten nemen, waarbij rekening wordt gehouden met de veranderende behoeftes en levensomstandigheden van kinderen. Daartoe zouden de te treffen maatregelen moeten resulteren in een flexibel gezondheidszorgsysteem waarin het belang van het kind en diens familie centraal staan. Dit vereist de actieve betrokkenheid van de beneficianten, andere belanghebbenden en de gemeenschappen waarin kinderen leven. Dit concluderende hoofdstuk adresseert verder de vraag hoe het proces van realisatie de interpretatie van het concept van het hoogst haalbare niveau van gezondheid beïnvloedt. Dit resulteert in een definitie van het concept van het hoogst haalbare niveau van gezondheid van het kind die rekening houdt met de individuele capaciteiten van kinderen en waarbij kinderen beschouwd worden als rechthebbenden, ongeacht hun leeftijd of ontwikkelingsniveau.

www.ingramcontent.com/pod-product-compliance
Ingram Content Group UK Ltd.
Pitfield, Milton Keynes, MK11 3LW, UK
UKHW051920100926
8556IPUK00021B/1279

9 781780 682723